Contents

INTRODUCTION

You may write for your own enjoyment or for the challenge of it, but it's not until your work is published – made public – that you can truly call yourself a writer. Presumably, too, you write in the hope of making some money. If, however, you have to begin by writing for publishers who can't afford to pay you, you will still gain valuable experience, compile a clipping file, and increase your confidence for more lucrative assignments to come.

The Canadian Writer's Market is designed to serve both the aspiring and the experienced freelance writer who wants to get his or her work published but needs some guidelines and/or accurate up-to-date listings of potential markets. Use this reference tool as a guide to prepare your manuscript, acquire a literary agent, approach an editor, evaluate a contract, choose a writing class, find style guides and how-to writing books, join a writers' organization, obtain funding, or enter a writers' competition. Refer to it also to determine which publishers to pursue and what they pay for freelance work.

This new, nineteenth edition of The *Canadian Writer's Market* includes the most current information available on market opportunities in Canadian publishing. It is an industry in flux and expansion, where data change with regularity, making it imperative that this reference book maintain the standard of accuracy freelance writers have come to depend upon. Back in the 1970s, when *The Canadian Writer's Market* was first published, the country sported a mere 100 consumer magazines, about 150 trade journals, two dozen or so farm publications, and 147 book publishers. Today there are almost 2,000 Canadian magazines listed on *CARDonline* (Canadian Advertising Rates and Data) alone, and almost 300 English and French book publishers reporting to Statistics Canada. *The Canadian Writer's Market* has always kept pace.

This edition lists only English-language publishers and publications, although some publishers are bilingual. Readers looking to sell their work in the French-language market in Canada should examine *CARD* and *CARDonline* for French-language magazines and *Quill & Quire*'s biannual guide, the *Canadian Publishers Digest*, for a full listing of French-language book publishers.

As in previous editions, *The Canadian Writer's Market* puts magazines into three groups: Consumer Magazines; Literary & Scholarly Publications; and Trade, Business, Farm, & Professional Publications. To facilitate your research to find a suitable market, or to recycle an article to other buyers, these groups have been broken down further, according to subject. Consumer magazines appear in fourteen sub-groups: arts and cultural; business; city and entertainment; the environment; feminist; general interest; home and hobby; lifestyle; news, opinions, and issues; special interest; sports and outdoors; travel and tourism; women's; and youth and children's. Trade publications are divided into twenty-one sub-sections according to the professions or trades they serve. A section of prominent business journals is included in Chapter 1 in order to describe in greater detail the market they offer, but many comparable business publications retain a simplified listing in Chapter 3.

Inevitably, however, these classifications are somewhat arbitrary and have a tendency to overlap. Even the distinction between consumer and trade publications is sometimes difficult to delineate. Some "trade" periodicals – the book industry's *Quill & Quire*, for instance – have such a general popularity that they are considered consumer magazines.

Manuscripts

As a freelance writer, your manuscript is your product, and it should have a professional, uncluttered appearance. That means it ought to be as grammatically correct as you can make it and without any spelling mistakes. The more editorial work the publisher has to do on your article or book, the more expensive and time-consuming it becomes to produce; consequently, the less attractive it becomes.

A manuscript should be presented on standard 8½-by-11-inch, 20-pound, white bond paper. Your work should be computer-generated, so later it can be formatted from your electronic files. The font you select must be easily readable; italic or sans-serif typefaces should not be used as your primary font. The manuscript must be double-spaced and the margins at least one inch wide; this gives an editor space in which to write suggestions, queries, and editorial notations. The main body of text should be justified to the left-hand margins, and each page must be numbered.

The first page of your manuscript should prominently display the title of your work followed by your name. In one corner put your name again with your mailing address, phone number, and e-mail address. It is also a good idea (but not necessary) to include on this sheet a copyright notice (© Mary Smith) and the word count. To begin each chapter, start partway down the page with the chapter number and its title, if any.

A manuscript should not be bound or stapled; this impedes the editorial process. For a book-length manuscript, simply fasten it with elastic bands and support it between two sheets of cardboard, front and back, or better still, place it in a box. A magazine article can be secured with paper clips. Never send a publisher the only copy of your work.

If you are submitting your article in response to an editor's invitation or if you have signed a contract with a book publisher, it is likely you will be asked for an electronic copy of your work as well. Inquire as to what program and format is required. Microsoft Word is usually a safe bet. You may need to submit each article or chapter of a book in a separate file, but this varies from publisher to publisher.

Style

By style, most book and magazine editors mean the conventions of spelling, punctuation, and capitalization. There is, of course, no universally accepted manual for style because it varies from periodical to periodical, publishing house to publishing house, fiction to non-fiction, from genre to genre, and from discipline to discipline. Writers should remember, however, that style is an integral part of their craft, and by showing a blatant disregard for it, they can quite inadvertently prejudice an editor against their work.

Writers are expected to observe at least some of the basic house rules, and these should be obvious in what has already been published by those magazines and book-publishing houses for which they aspire to write. If they are not, the writer is always wise to find out as much as possible about what these rules are, and what stylistic traits – as idiosyncratic as many may appear to be – are preferred.

Canadian newspapers generally follow the *Canadian Press Stylebook* (which also contains some good tips on reporting), and magazines tend to develop their own standards and preferences from one authoritative source, or a compilation of several. Book publishers, however, usually adhere to well-known manuals. A selection of the best style and resource books is provided at the end of this book. Very often, a publishing house has compiled its own guide to house style, and the aspiring writer should never be afraid to ask for a copy of this.

Sending Out Queries and Submissions

It is crucial to research which magazine, newspaper, or book publisher is the best fit for your idea or manuscript. The listings in *The Canadian Writer's Market* are designed to help you determine the best publisher for your writing. In addition, read back issues of periodicals and newspapers, and study book publishers' catalogues to make sure you will not be wasting either your time or that of the editor. It's a mark of a professional to know what market in which to place your work.

Many (but not all) publishers now accept queries and submission by e-mail. When communicating electronically, resist the urge to become more informal or to take less care with your correspondence.

Of course, once you are ready to submit your writing, or even just send queries about it, you must maintain accurate records. Keep a list of dates that manuscripts or query letters were sent out, what publishers they were sent to, the date the editor responded, his or her comments, whether or not the work was sold, and, if you are fortunate, the payment particulars.

Simultaneous Submissions

There is nothing wrong with sending the same article, proposal, or book manuscript to more than one potential market at the same time. It is your work, after all, so you can do with it whatever you please. But unless you are sending off material simultaneously to magazines that are happy to buy second, third, or fourth rights (which we discuss later), you could run into problems.

The practice can sometimes be unethical. Busy magazines need at least a month to assess an idea or a manuscript properly, sometimes more. During this time, several people may be assigned the job of writing an informed critique explaining to the writer and the senior editor how the manuscript or article is effective, how it isn't, and what revisions may be necessary.

In publishing houses, this work takes considerably longer and is correspondingly more expensive. Judging a promising book proposal or an intriguing manuscript of two or three hundred pages usually means that an editor must set aside present work. If the editor is busy, an assistant or an outside reader might be engaged to do this job instead. Readers may be hired for their specialized expertise, to judge whether a writer has covered his or her chosen subject, be it fact or fiction, well and accurately. If an idea or manuscript appears tempting, the publisher may recruit market researchers to assess its sales potential. By sending the same material to several houses, the writer may automatically involve them all in the expense of assessing something only one of them would eventually be able to acquire.

Indeed, to established writers, the idea of simultaneous submissions is distasteful. Knowing how overworked editors can be, they give them reasonable time to respond – about six weeks for a magazine and three months or longer for a publishing house. If after that they have heard nothing, they fire off a reminder, then turn immediately to other productive work. The publishing business is notorious for its slowness, and, unfortunately, this is something all writers have to accept.

Postage

All publishers are under pressure to reduce costs wherever possible. Postage rates have soared in recent years, and so for any business that relies heavily on our mail system, they represent a bigger expense than ever. It should now be taken for granted that if you want your manuscript returned, you must include a self-addressed, stamped envelope (SASE) so that it will not incur any cost to the publisher. Increasingly, publishers will assume that you do not want your material back if an SASE is not included, and will simply recycle it.

Magazine and book editors stress this point again and again, and writers ignore it at their peril. If submitting to U.S. publishers, enclose international postage coupons or keep a supply of American stamps. You can order them online at http://shop.usps.com.

Rejection

Authors must learn to cope with rejection. First-timers might draw comfort from the knowledge of how many great writers could have papered their walls with publishers' rejection letters received early in their careers. Faulkner's great work *The Sound and the Fury* was rejected thirteen times before finding a publisher, as, coincidentally, was William Kennedy's Pulitzer Prize–winning *Ironweed*. On an altogether different scale, big-selling English crime writer John Creasey is said to have received no fewer than 744 rejections during his career!

Since editors usually don't have time to issue more than a standard rejection note, take heart if the rejection is sugared with qualified praise or, better still, specific constructive criticism. Chances are the editor is not simply letting you down gently but genuinely sees value in your work. Be open to suggestions, and rework your manuscript according to the advice. Take note of the editor's name and resubmit your improved work to the same person.

Copyright

Copyright means the sole right to reproduce – or allow others to reproduce – a literary or artistic work. If you own a copyright, you are solely responsible for ensuring it is not infringed, and if you use work that belongs to another, you must respect his or her copyright rights. Therefore, as a freelance writer, you must have at least a general understanding of this area of law.

Here are some of the most frequently posed questions about copyright, with general answers:

What types of work are protected by copyright law?

According to the Copyright Act, writing is protected by copyright law "if the author has used labour, skill, and ingenuity to arrange his or her ideas." It may include poetry, novels, non-fiction works, compilations of literary works, catalogues, tables, reports, translations of these works, computer programs, unpublished writing, letters, e-mail, speeches, and song lyrics. Photographs and artwork are also protected by copyright.

When does copyright protection begin?

It begins upon creation rather than on publication.

Is every piece of written work copyrighted?

No. In Canada, copyright on a work lasts for the life of the author plus fifty years. In the United States, it lasts for the life of the author plus seventy years. After that, the work falls into the public domain and may be legally copied at will.

How can I tell who the rightful owner of a copyright is?

In the first few pages of a book or magazine there is a copyright notice. Typically it will read, "Copyright Josephine Blow, 2013" or "© Joseph P. Blow & Sons, Publishers, 2013." In Canada, the use of the symbol "©" is not required to establish copyright, but it is recommended. If you hold the copyright, you may use this symbol even if you have not registered your work with the Copyright Office.

The publisher's address will usually be printed above or below the copyright notice. Even if the copyright is held in the author's name, it is generally the publisher who has the right by contract to authorize reprints of excerpts. If, however, the author has retained these rights exclusively, which may sometimes be the case, he or she can be contacted through the publisher.

If you have difficulty contacting the copyright owner, try searching the Canadian Copyrights Database at the Canadian Intellectual Property Office (www.cipo.ic.gc.ca). Sometimes copyright is held by collectives who administer the copyrights for their clients. A list of these collectives is available at www.cb-cda.gc.ca/societies-societes/index-e.html.

How does copyright infringement occur?

Usually through carelessness or ignorance. Few writers deliberately set out to steal something that doesn't belong to them. They either quote too much of someone else's work without first seeking permission to do so, or use previously written words without making a sufficient effort to rework them.

What is too much of someone else's work?

The answer to this isn't easy. It depends on several factors, principally the quantity and quality of the portion taken and whether its use will detract from the impact and/or the marketability of the original. No one minds if a writer uses a line or two from a book and indicates their source; to reproduce three or four key paragraphs without permission, however – even with an attribution – could lead to problems.

Some book publishers have established a guideline whereby permission is applied for if 100 or more words are borrowed from a single source. But, as previously stated, this is not a hard and fast rule. If the material is a key component of the original, permission may be necessary for far fewer words. Permission is required for the use of even one line of a song lyric or two lines from a short poem.

When it is determined that permission is necessary, the writer should contact the copyright holder to ask for the right to reproduce the work, quoting the extract(s) he or she wants to use in full, giving a true indication of context, details of the format (a magazine article, script, or book), size of audience or print run, the territory in which the periodical or book will be published, and the price of the publication. A neophyte writer wanting to use 100 words for publication in a small magazine probably will not be charged what a name writer would be expected to pay for a similar-sized extract in an article for one of the big players.

How can I copyright my work?

According to the Copyright Act of Canada, the act of creating the work is enough to establish copyright.

If, however, you feel there is a chance that one day the ownership of your manuscript may be in dispute or you want to be extra cautious, you may register it for a fee with the Copyright Office. If your work is registered in this way, you would be in a much stronger position if the case ever went to court. It would be up to the other party to prove that you are not the creator of your work.

You can also mail a copy of your manuscript to yourself in a registered package containing the date of creation. This will provide you with a dated receipt. Store the unopened package and its receipt in a safe place in case the manuscript's rightful ownership ever becomes a legal issue.

Does a Canadian copyright protect me worldwide?

Yes, throughout most of the world, in those countries that are signatories of the Berne Copyright Convention or the Universal Copyright Convention, which are most nations.

Can an idea be copyrighted?

No, ideas are considered part of the public domain. If, however, you worked on developing a central character and the plot of a novel, you are considered a co-author of that work even if you did not actually write it.

Can news items or real-life events be protected under copyright?

No, they are similar to ideas in that no one has exclusive rights to them; they are part of the public domain. It is the presentation of those facts, however, that is covered by copyright.

If I work for a newspaper or magazine, who owns the copyright on my work?

Usually, if you are employed by a company, it automatically owns the copyright of everything that is published by it in the course of your work. The article cannot be reproduced or re-sold in any form without permission first being obtained. Often, newspapers generously allow articles, or portions of them, to be reprinted without charge.

Can a magazine editor steal the idea contained in my story proposal and assign it to someone else to write?

Yes, because ideas are in the public domain and cannot be protected by copyright law. For this reason, it is useless to write "copyright" on your proposal. But reputable magazines and publishing houses won't take your idea. They stay in business because their editors are ethical.

What does "fair dealing" mean in regard to copyright?

The Copyright Act allows for quotes to be used without permission for purposes of criticism, review, and private, unpublished study or research. There are no limits stipulated on the number of words that can be used without permission; the courts are the only arbiter.

Should I copyright the book I have been contracted to write before sending it to the publisher?

No. All publishers will copyright your work for you, under either their name or yours, depending on the terms of the contract you have signed. They will also register it for you at the National Library in Ottawa as an original Canadian work.

Does copyright still apply when work is reproduced on the Internet?

Yes, although this can be very difficult to monitor. It is suggested that you put a copyright notice on all your work that appears on the Internet. If you use a quotation taken from a website, you will need permission if it is a significant part of the entire piece.

For specific information on copyright as it applies to periodical publishing, see Chapter 1.

Libel

Defamation is an untrue statement about a person that harms his or her reputation. A person's reputation is deemed to be his or her property, which he or she has the right to protect. It is considered to have been harmed if as a result of a statement, that person is now hated, disrespected, or held in low esteem. If the defamation is spoken, it is slander; if it is written, it is libel. Someone who defames another may be sued in civil court.

Libel does not have to be malicious or intended in order to be proven. Negligence on behalf of the author is no defence. But if a damaging statement is proven to be true, whether the subject's reputation was sullied or not, it is not libellous. In English Canada, only the living can sue for libel; in Quebec, an action can be brought by a descendant if the libel defamed him or her.

Writers should understand enough about Canadian libel law to protect both themselves and their publishers against court action. This is absolutely necessary since nearly all publishers' contracts provide for indemnification for the publisher in cases where a person maligned in a manuscript resorts to a lawsuit.

Many writers hold the mistaken belief that the use of fictitious names, or a statement saying that any resemblance between the characters in the book and living persons is purely coincidental, will automatically protect them from the possibility of a libel suit. This assumption is wrong. If the average reader associates a character described in a manuscript with an actual person, and the description reflects unfavourably on that person's reputation or integrity, there is always the danger of libel. The apparent intention to libel a person, even in fiction, could be interpreted by legal minds as a personal attack and could possibly lead to an action.

Fair and honest statements on matters of public interest, as long as they are true, are permitted. An author who comments on current affairs or writes a biography is allowed to express honest opinions or fair criticism of someone's works or accomplishments because this is usually in the public interest and serves to promote a useful purpose. Fair comment extends to criticism of books, magazines, articles, plays, and films.

In a situation where a libel suit is possible, newspapers and magazines have a distinct advantage over book publishers due to their frequency of publishing. Sometimes a timely retraction is enough to avert a court case, or at least lower damages.

Taxes

In Canada, the Income Tax Act is good to writers, allowing you to deduct legitimate work expenses from your taxable income. In return, you are trusted to show all your earnings, particularly fees that are unsupported by T4, T4A, or T5 slips from magazines and publishing houses that have printed your work.

Basically, writers come under three classifications:

- Salaried employees who supplement their incomes by earning a little extra money as occasional freelance writers.
- Part-time writers whose major income comes from another job that will almost certainly be cast aside the moment writing becomes more profitable.

• Totally self-employed, full-time writers not on any payroll who are expected to file honest returns mindful that no income taxes have been deducted at source.

Writers with other jobs need only attach to their income tax returns a statement summarizing writing income and expenses, and to show whether this extra work resulted in a profit or a loss. Any profit must be added to that taxable income earned from the other job. Losses, however, may be used to reduce it.

Writers living entirely from their craft must keep many more details: a list of all income and its sources, and receipts and vouchers to support expenses. Maintaining proper financial records not only serves as a reminder of cash that has flowed both in and out, but also helps to reduce problems that might be encountered should a tax return be audited.

Legitimate business expenses are allowable deductions from a freelance writer's gross income. Letterhead, envelopes, manuscript paper, labels, file folders, and other office supplies, including pens, pencils, erasers, and paper clips, can be deducted. The price of photocopying, copyright costs, reference books, other research materials, subscriptions to magazines and newspapers, union dues, dues in writers' organizations, bank charges (if you maintain a separate account for your writing business), the cost of administrative help, and any payment for research assistance are also deductible. Business telephone, fax, and Internet costs can be written off, as can postage and courier expenses. If you take a course related to your writing or attend up to two professional conventions per year, they are also allowable deductions.

The purchase price of a computer, printer, and other expensive office equipment can not be deducted all in one year; rather, the Canada Revenue Agency (CRA) stipulates at what rate each item can be written off. But related expenses, such as computer paper, manuals, ink cartridges, software, and equipment repairs are permitted deductions in the year they are purchased, as are the cost of other essential devices used in your work; for example, a tape recorder and tapes with which to record interviews.

An area of tax deduction often overlooked is the depreciation of office furniture and equipment. Both may be written off according to a fixed percentage determined by the income tax regulations. A computer may be depreciated by 30 to 45 per cent under the declining-balance method of depreciation. The same tax saving may be applied to printers, modems, cameras, audio recorders, filing cabinets, desks, chairs, and telephone answering machines. It is permissible to defer depreciation deductions to a future year when the business will be more profitable.

Travel is also an allowable expense, whether it is to visit a publisher or to gather research for an article, be it by bus, subway, car, or plane. The non-fiction writer may have to interview people in a different town or find other resource information there; the cost of hotels, transportation, and generally 50 per cent of the price of meals and entertainment are deductible.

Keep track of how much time you use your vehicle for business and the distance you travel, for this is a legitimate write-off, as are payments for gas, oil, insurance, lease fees, interest on a car loan, maintenance, and repairs. CRA also allows you to claim depreciation on your vehicle, if you own it.

If you are a freelance writer working in a commercial office space, you may claim its rent as an expense. If you work from an office in your home, you are permitted to write off a reasonable portion of your living space. A writer using one room as an office in a four-room apartment, for example, may claim one-quarter of the rent or mortgage interest, property taxes, home insurance, maintenance and repairs, and utilities. You can deduct 100 per cent of telephone expenses if it's a separate business line.

For more complete information on income tax and the freelance writer, obtain a copy of the Business and Professional Income tax guide, a manual published by CRA.

If you have your own business, you must also be aware of the Goods and Services Tax (GST), or Harmonized Sales Tax (HST) in Newfoundland and Labrador, Nova Scotia, New Brunswick, and Ontario. When your taxable sales of goods or services exceed $30,000 per year, you must register to file GST/HST returns. An option for some businesses with total sales under $200,000 is to use the "quick method" of calculating the amount owing as a percentage of total sales, instead of tracking the actual GST/HST paid out and collected throughout the year. A guide is available at www.ccra-adrc.gc.ca or at local CRA Tax Services offices.

Writers' Organizations

Writing is an isolating occupation, so it is good for morale as well as immensely practical to tap into one or more of the many writers' groups that exist in your community (a list of associations is provided in Chapter 10).

For professional writers with at least one published book behind them, valuable support is available from the Writers' Union of Canada, which offers members an impressive array of resources, including assistance with contracts and dealing with grievances with publishers, a manuscript evaluation service, your own web page on their website, a quarterly newsletter, and a range of practical publications free of charge. The professional guides that may be ordered from the union by non-members for a small cost are *Anthology Rates and Contracts, Income Tax Guide for Writers, Author and Editor, Author and Literary Agent, From Page to Screen, Writers' Guide to Canadian Publishers, Incorporation for Writers, Glossary of Publishing Terms, Ghost Writing, New Technologies, and Writers' Guide to Grants*. At a higher cost, their *Contracts Self-Help Package* includes a model trade-book contract and *Help Yourself to a Better Contract*. Above all, the Writers' Union of Canada gives its members the opportunity to share their concerns and experiences with fellow writers, providing a forum for collective action to support their interests.

Many of these services are also available to members of the Canadian Authors Association, which has branches across the country. Founded in Montreal in 1921, the CAA has represented the interests of Canadian writers on many fronts, from championing improved copyright protection and the Public Lending Right to helping individual writers improve their contracts with publishers. (The Public Lending Right provides published writers with income from books held in libraries by compensating them according to how often their books are borrowed. Between 2011 and 2012, 17,885 writers, translators, and illustrators received over $9.9 million.) The CAA publishes *The Canadian Writer's Guide*, a handbook for freelance writers; it administers several major literary awards (see Chapter 7); and local branches hold writing classes and workshops.

The Writers' Trust of Canada is another national non-profit service organization mandated to advance and nurture Canadian writers and writing. Since 1976, working with an ever-changing pool of corporate partners, it has done just that in a number of practical and creative ways. It sponsors several major writing awards (see Chapter 7), supports the Woodcock Fund to provide bridge funding for established writers facing financial crises, and celebrates the importance of Canadian literature through the annual Politics and the Pen gala and the Great Literary Dinner.

Specialist writers' organizations, too, offer resources and support to writers in their field. The Canadian Society of Children's Authors, Illustrators and Performers (CANSCAIP), through its newsletter, regular meetings, and other organized activities, offers practical advice, moral support, and useful contacts to writers of children's books. Members are listed on their website and in an annual directory. The Canadian Children's Book Centre also provides writers and illustrators of children's books with a range of resources and services. The centre has a comprehensive reference library of children's books, and promotes children's writers and titles through author tours, book readings, and their quarterly newsletter, *CANSCAIP News*.

For freelancers who write for magazines, newspapers, television, advertising agencies, and more, an excellent way to keep abreast of changes and developments in the industry is to join the Professional Writers Association of Canada. PWAC membership entitles you to a subscription to their informative newsletter, *PWAC Contact*, a comprehensive listing in their database; a copyright information kit; a mentoring program; and the opportunity to exchange market information and make important contacts with other writers. PWAC also sells a book called the *PWAC Guide to Roughing It in the Market*.

American Markets

The English-speaking Canadian who has begun to sell with some consistency in this country should not ignore the colossal market in the United States.

The American annual *Writer's Market* (see Chapter 11, Resources) contains thousands of listings for book publishers, consumer magazines, trade journals, and literary agents in the United

States. It also gives the names and addresses of editors, and sets out their requirements: what they expect from a manuscript in content and length, and how long it takes them to report back to a writer with a decision on whether or not they will publish. A subscription to the companion website, WritersMarket.com, provides access to additional listings and information.

Two U.S. monthly magazines are also indispensable to Canadian writers seeking new markets south of the border: *Writer's Digest* (the publisher of the *Writer's Market*), for practical-minded free-lancers, and *The Writer*, for those with more literary tastes. These journals not only keep readers informed about markets and trends, but provide both a stimulus and a constant flow of fresh ideas. In addition, Writer's Digest Books publishes an astonishing array of practical books for writers, from guides to writing genre fiction to manuals on magazine-article writing.

Remember that just as you have to research magazines or book publishers in Canada before you send out a query letter or manu-script, it is imperative that you study the American market as well. Nearly all publishers have their own special character and narrow, specific needs.

But the enormous selection of American publishers in no way diminishes the difficulty of breaking into their huge market. Ask yourself why a U.S. publisher would be interested in your story, unless it is on a theme that has broad appeal to both nations. If it is a specifically Canadian story, there must be a compelling reason why Americans should care. Some Canadian stories will, of course, have an obvious, natural tie-in with American events. A perceptive article on NAFTA from a Canadian perspective might attract the interest of a U.S. business magazine. As a Canadian writer, you will have to work hard to penetrate the American market, especially with ideas for their consumer magazines.

Most Canadians who have consistently sold their writing in the United States do so thanks to the opportunities provided by the vast collection of American trade publications. Canada is closely related to the United States through common trade channels and by having similar concerns about world politics and business. The moment American equipment and/or expertise is brought to bear on a Canadian building site, for example, there could legitimately be the makings of a story for an American trade or professional magazine. Sometimes there may also be a story in how Canada sees, or deals with, problems specific to both countries.

But there is yet another hurdle to beat. Many American trade magazines are staff-written. This means that a staff writer will travel to Canada to cover an American story rooted here, so a manuscript from a Canadian freelancer must be exceptionally strong to win a place. The odds can be beaten, though. After accepting a few manuscripts from a Canadian contributor, the editor of an American trade magazine might be willing to publish a monthly feature written by a Canadian on the Canadian viewpoint: what his or her country thinks about mutual problems and issues, and what solutions it can offer.

It is well worth trying to secure a foothold in the American market for purely economic reasons. After all, it is still extremely difficult for Canadians to make a satisfactory living by writing exclusively for magazines and publishing houses in their own country, which explains why most writers combine the crafting of poetry, novels, magazine articles, or non-fiction with other work. The situation may change, though. Writing opportunities for Canada's writers have certainly increased since this book first appeared, and let's hope the trend continues. As it does, *The Canadian Writer's Market* will be there to guide and inform you with a richer list of resources than ever.

1

CONSUMER MAGAZINES

Writing for magazines can be both lucrative and fulfilling for the freelance writer. As you will see in the list below, pay rates vary widely, from a top figure of $1 per word down to zero. It can be argued, however, that even if you receive no payment for your work, just being published is an important step in the development and growth of your career.

In order to be a valuable marketing tool, *The Canadian Writer's Market* provides thumbnail sketches for each consumer magazine to briefly explain what types of articles it publishes. This is useful because so many magazines have names that give little indication of what they really are, who reads them, and, consequently, the kinds of articles or stories they buy. No one would ever guess, for instance, that an Ottawa magazine called *Summit* is not for mountain climbers but is a forum for public-sector purchasing. Or that, far from being a farm publication, as one might first suspect, *Grain* is a spunky little literary publication that has been produced quarterly in Regina since 1973.

The term *publication* is often used throughout this book because, strictly speaking, many of its listings are not really magazines as we have come to know them. Some are tabloid newspapers, some simple, one-colour, staple-bound periodicals that feed the needs (sometimes sporadically) of a small group of loyal readers, some are online magazines. Others, however, are magazines in the traditional sense: glossy, highly professional consumer or trade journals that boast respectable circulations. The word *publication*, then, seems to safely cover all listings, both large and small.

Much more important to the freelance writer is that many of these publications provide opportunities both for established freelancers wanting to break fresh ground and for neophyte writers seeking to have their work published. Each one listed accepts outside contributions with varying frequency and for equally varying fees.

When writing for magazines, it is usual to present the idea for an article to the editor before you have completed the piece. Of course, you should do some initial research on the story so that you can decide on its focus and direction, and are able to write a compelling pitch to the magazine in your query letter. Large magazines plan their editorial content up to a year in advance. Therefore, if you have an article idea relating to a specific holiday, season, event, or anniversary, you must query the editor this far ahead.

Try to expand one article idea into several. Be alert as to how you can use the research for one story to provide the basis for other different but related pieces. For instance, background information for an article on city gardens for a general-interest consumer magazine could be utilized for a story on the gardening-centre phenomenon sold to a business journal or used for a more technical piece aimed at a trade publication.

For feature articles, editors tend to call on freelancers they have worked with before and know to be accurate and reliable. To break into this somewhat closed system, you may have to start by writing smaller pieces for a particular publication, then, after proving yourself, work your way up to the major stories. Along the way, try to establish relationships with the editors to whom you sell your work.

Researching Target Magazines

It is a waste of everyone's time to send a query letter to a gardening periodical if you are proposing to write about fly fishing. By using the list below, research what magazines publish the type of article you are proposing. Get the name of the editor or contact person. Note the frequency of publication; those magazines that publish more often require the most articles.

Read copies of the publications that are likely candidates for your story, and become familiar with their content and focus. It may be helpful to look at a magazine from the editor's point of view. His or her focus is to keep the readers resubscribing and keep them buying the advertisers' products. From this perspective, it's obvious that your article must appeal to the reader that the publication targets through its editorial and advertising focus. Use this information to either adjust the slant of your article or to determine that this is or is not a magazine to approach with your idea.

Another way to ascertain what magazines to query is to look at their mastheads and compare personnel names with the names of those who wrote each article. You may discover that a staff writer always pens the type of article or column you are intending to write. In these circumstances, it is unlikely that the editor will hire an outsider for these stories.

Find out if your target magazine has an editorial calendar or if it runs special or theme issues for which you could write a piece. The *CARD* directory and its annual supplement, *Publication Profiles*, sometimes list these. Also check a periodical's website for information about forthcoming issues.

Once you understand what a magazine requires in terms of content, you must determine what its editor wants regarding format. Check the website for guidelines or request them before you send a query letter, and follow them exactly. For example, it would be futile to offer an editor a 3,000-word article if the publication never publishes more than 2,000.

Payment Policy

Check the following listings to determine if payment for articles is due on acceptance or on publication, and always confirm this before reaching an agreement. Although you may be delighted to be published either way, you should understand the two schedules of compensation.

While payment on acceptance is much less common, it is preferable for the writer because even if the magazine decides not to publish your article or goes out of business, you will still receive the amount owing. By waiting until after the publication of your work to receive compensation, you run the risk of long delays or even the return of your work due to policy changes, a turnover of editorial staff, or a business setback.

The Query Letter

The query letter is usually the vehicle for a freelancer's initial contact with a magazine, as most editors prefer not to receive unsolicited articles. Query by phone only if the article you are proposing is time sensitive or if a magazine specifically invites telephone queries. It has been estimated that in order to sell one article, you must be prepared to send out ten queries.

No matter how ingenious your article (or idea) may be, if your query letter to an editor is not equally compelling, your work will not likely see the published page. It must be professional, well written, and convincing. As it's often the only means by which you can break into a new market, the query letter is a key factor in becoming a successful freelance writer.

Choose unadorned, business-like stationery on which you have included your name, address, telephone number, and e-mail address. Address your letter to a specific person, using Mr. or Ms. Your correspondence must be typed, using an easily read font, and single-spaced. Mail your query (or e-mail it, depending on the magazine's preference) and enclose an self-addressed, stamped envelope (SASE).

Since the query letter may be the only opportunity an editor has had to see your writing, it is crucial that the style of your letter attracts his or her attention and indicates you are a proficient journalist. Begin with an attention-grabbing intro and write in the style of your proposed article. If, for example, you want to write a humorous piece, your query must reflect that, leaving the editor in no doubt that you are up to the job.

Keep your letter to one page in length. In it you must provide a captivating, but brief, synopsis of the article you are proposing. Include your research plans and indicate what section of the magazine it would be most appropriate for. Then inform the editor why you are the person best suited to write this piece. Mention any first-hand knowledge or special interest you might have in the subject area you wish to write about. Indicate your publishing background and include the clippings most relevant to the magazine you are targeting.

Tell the editor what rights you are offering and if the article has appeared elsewhere. Provide the most accurate word count you can and the approximate delivery date. Also, mention any photos you can provide to accompany the piece (but do not send them at this time). Remember to check your spelling and grammar carefully before you send the letter.

Photographs

Photographs are another means by which you can increase the saleability of your article and earn extra money as well. By reviewing previous issues of your target publications, you will know whether they publish colour or black-and-white photos, or if they accept photos at all.

Describe in your query letter the photos you can provide. If interested, the editor will tell you the specifications the magazine requires. Before mailing off any pictures, make sure you have duplicates and print your name, address, and copyright notice on each slide or print. Captions may be typed and attached to photos individually, or several captions could be printed on a page and numbered to correspond to each image. Alternatively, your editor may prefer scanned photos and captions sent by e-mail.

Sidebars

Sidebars can be a means to help sell your article and boost your income. Also called boxes or bars, and often shaded to set them off from the rest of the text, these supplemental information bytes contain information germane to, but not intrinsically part of, the primary article. For example, if you are writing about the recording business in Canada, a sidebar might highlight the experiences of one specific record company; alternatively, a sidebar accompanying a piece about the challenges faced by XYZ Recording Company could give a broad overview of the entire industry.

Discuss the possibility of one or more sidebars with the editor; if accepted, they should earn you extra money. When preparing your manuscript, make sure sidebars are clearly marked so an editor knows they are not part of the main text.

Copyright and Contracts

Understanding how rights to published works are categorized is an important factor in making a living as a freelance writer. Before signing a contract or making a verbal agreement with a magazine or newspaper editor, you may wish to contact a lawyer specializing in this field. Nevertheless, you should still have a basic knowledge of what obligations and opportunities exist when you sell the rights to your work.

1) All rights: When you sell all rights to an article, it can be sold only once. You can, however, reuse the idea for the original work, as long as you completely rewrite and restructure the article and make it significantly different from the original by, for example, using new data, fresh quotes, a different focus, and by arriving at a contradictory conclusion.

2) First rights: First rights allow the periodical to publish your work once. After it has appeared in print, you are permitted to resell that same article as many times as you wish.

3) Second (or reprint) rights: These are the rights you are permitted to sell after your article has appeared in the publication that bought the first rights.

4) North American rights: This gives the publication the right to publish an article to be read by an audience across the continent.

5) Canadian rights: With these rights, the magazine has permission to publish a work that will be read only within the country.

6) Serial rights: This gives the publication the right to publish a work in a sister publication without having to pay extra for it.

In addition to specifying which of the above rights you are selling, the magazine or newspaper should inform you which electronic rights are included in the sale. If not, you could receive a hard lesson by discovering your work on the Internet or a commercial database without compensation.

When buying first rights, some companies now insist on acquiring second rights and electronic rights for no additional fee or for a small payment at best. Do not sign away additional rights without consulting a legal specialist; you may lose a lucrative source of income. Always aim to retain as many rights as possible. Contact the Canadian Authors Association, the Periodical Writers Association of Canada, or the Writers' Union of Canada for more information.

Online Publications

E-zines are proliferating on the Internet in part because of the lower costs of production. In addition, writers are required for online press releases, newsletters, and the larger websites. While many electronic publishers do not pay writers, their sites may provide a good starting point to get your work in print.

As with hard-copy magazines, a query letter should be your first introduction to the editor. For this format, an e-mail query is required. Resist the urge toward informality; as is the case when you write to print publications, you should correspond in a professional manner, showing the editor your best work.

The electronic medium fosters impatience in its users, so tailor the writing style of your article accordingly. Use shorter paragraphs and consider using subheads and sidebars. Long, dense articles appear daunting and tedious on a computer screen.

Arts & Cultural

Azure

460 Richmond Street W., Suite 601, Toronto, ON M5V IYI
Phone: (416) 203-9674 Fax: (416) 203-9842
E-mail: azure@azureonline.com
Website: www.azuremagazine.com
Contact: Nina Boccia, assistant editor
Circulation: 12,500
Published 8 times a year

A design review covering graphic, interior, and industrial design, architecture, landscape architecture, and contemporary art in Canada and abroad. Directed toward designers, architects, and the visually aware. Content includes reports on trade fairs, profiles of professionals, and articles on current events and issues related to design. Fees vary depending on the department and are paid on publication. Unsolicited submissions not encouraged. Guidelines available.

B.C. Musician

P.O. Box 1150, Peachland, BC V0H 1X0
Phone: (250) 762-0729 Fax: (250) 767-3337
E-mail: info@bcmusicianmag.com
Website: www.bcmusicianmag.com
Contact: Leanne V. Nash, editor
Circulation: 6,000
Published monthly

B.C. Musician Magazine is all about musicians as writers, artists, and musicmakers, and the places they play in B.C. Primary contributors are working musicians as well as the proprietors of venues where the musicians make their living. Articles 400 to 700 words.

B.C. BookWorld

3516 W. 13th Avenue, Vancouver, BC V6R 2S3
Phone: (604) 736-4011 Fax: (604) 736-4011
E-mail: bookworld@telus.net
Website: www.bcbookworld.com
Contact: David Lester, editor

Circulation: 100,000

Published quarterly

Covers books written by B.C. authors and books about B.C. Circulated by more than 700 distributors. Preferred length 500 to 750 words. Pay rates vary depending on project, but a concerted effort is made to pay higher rates than is typical for book reviews. Most writing is in-house, however, so phone or write first. This is not a trade publication or a review periodical; it's a populist, tabloid-format newspaper. Book reviews focus on providing information rather than literary critique.

BlackFlash: Photography and New Media in Art

P.O. Box 7381, Stn. Main, Saskatoon, SK S7K 4J3

Phone: (306) 374-5115

E-mail: editor@blackflash.ca

Website: www.blackflash.ca

Contact: John Shelling, managing editor

Circulation: 1,600

Published 3 times a year

Focuses on critical writing about lens-based and new-media art production. Pays $200 to $350 on publication for 1,000 to 2,500 words. Accepts proposals/outlines only. Guidelines available on website.

Border Crossings

70 Arthur Street, Suite 500, Winnipeg, MB R3B IG7

Phone: (204) 942-5778 Fax: (204) 949-0793

E-mail: info@bordercrossingsmag.com

Website: www.bordercrossingsmag.com

Contact: Meeka Walsh, editor

Circulation: 5,500

Published quarterly

An interdisciplinary arts review with an educated national and international audience, featuring articles, exhibition reviews, book reviews, artist profiles, and interviews covering the full range of the contemporary arts in Canada and beyond. Subjects include painting, drawing, photography, sculpture, performance, film. Pays a negotiated fee on publication. "Use the magazine as your guide when formulating submissions, but query first by e-mail or phone."

BOULDERPAVEMENT

E-mail: www.boulderpavement.ca
Website: www.boulderpavement.ca
Phone: (403) 762-6410 or 1-800-565-9989 Fax: (403) 762-6277
E-mail: press@banffcentre.ca
Contact: Steven Ross Smith, editor
Published 3 times a year

A multidisciplinary, multimedia, online publication of the Banff Centre Press, presenting "an array of forms including dance, music, video, sound and visual art, critique, poetry, fiction and non-fiction writing, by artists around the world." See website for issue themes and submission deadlines. "For new work or work in progress, please send a concise description no longer than 1 page, plus 1 sample up to 2 pages, and a brief bio."

Broken Pencil

P.O. Box 203, Stn. P, Toronto, ON M5S 2S7
Phone: (416) 204-1700
E-mail: editor@brokenpencil.com or fiction@brokenpencil.com
Website: www.brokenpencil.com
Contact: Lindsay Gibb, editor
Circulation: 3,000
Published quarterly

Broken Pencil is one of the few magazines in the world devoted exclusively to underground culture and the independent arts. It features reviews, articles, and rants about zines, politics, film, music, and other zaniness from an alternative perspective. Pays $30 to $300 on publication for articles and fiction. Maximum length for reports is 400 words; for rants, 700; for features, 3,000; for fiction, 3,000. "Please read the magazine before submitting. Only the knowledgeable and unconventional need apply." Guidelines available on website.

Canadian Art

215 Spadina Avenue, Suite 320, Toronto, ON M5T 2C7
Phone: (416) 368-8854, ext. 101 Fax: (416) 368-6135
E-mail: info@canadianart.ca
Contact: Richard Rhodes, editor
Circulation: 20,000

Published quarterly

Covers visual arts in Canada in a lively and opinionated way. Includes articles on painting, sculpture, film, photography, and video, with critical profiles of new artists and assessments of established art-world figures. Reviews are 400 to 500 words and features 1,500 to 3,000 words. Pays on publication $200 for reviews, $1,500 to $2,000 for features. Query first. No unsolicited submissions.

Canadian Screenwriter

366 Adelaide Street W., Suite 401, Toronto, ON M5V 1R9
Phone: (416) 979-7907 or 1-800-567-9974 Fax: (416) 979-9273
E-mail: editor@wgc.ca
Website: www.wgc.ca/magazine
Contact: David Kinahan, editor
Circulation: 4,000
Published 3 times a year

A magazine for professionals in the Canadian film and television industry. It is sent to all members of the Writers Guild of Canada as well as to film and television industry representatives, government agencies, and the media. Long features are 2,000 to 2,500 words; short features 1,200 to 1,500 words. Pays 60¢/word on acceptance. Guidelines available. "We have an editorial board that decides on the content of the magazine. Queries are welcome as well."

Canadian Theatre Review

Centre for Film and Theatre, York University, 4700 Keele Street,
    Room 317, Toronto, ON M3J 1P3
Phone: (416) 300-5317
E-mail: info@canadiantheatrereview.com
Website: www.utpjournals.com
Contact: Laura Levin, editor-in-chief
Published quarterly

Publishes playscripts, essays of interest to theatre professionals, and interviews with playwrights, actors, directors, and designers. Issues are thematic and contain at least one complete playscript, insightful articles, and informative reviews. Pay scale and guidelines available on request.

Canadian Writer's Journal

P.O. Box 1178, New Liskeard, ON POJ IPO

Phone: (705) 647-5424 or 1-800-258-5451 Fax: (705) 647-8366

E-mail: cwj@cwj.ca

Website: www.cwj.ca

Contact: Deborah Ranchuk, editor

Published annually

A perfect-bound annual compendium of information on professional, motivational, and marketing aspects of the profession of writing. Emphasis on short how-to articles for both apprentice and professional writers. Also opinion pieces, book reviews, and short poems. Preferred length 400 to 2,000 words for articles and 250 to 500 words for book reviews. Guidelines available on website. Pays on publication $7.50/page (approximately 450 words) for articles and between $2 and $5/poem, plus one complimentary copy of the issue. "Queries or complete manuscripts welcome. Writers should present specifics rather than generalities and avoid overworked subjects such as overcoming writer's block, handling rejection, etc."

CHARTattack

366 Adelaide Street E., Suite 245, Toronto, ON M5A 3X9

E-mail: hello@chartattack.com

Website: www.chartattack.com

Contact: Dan Busheikin, editor in chief

Updated daily

Online magazine covering new music for a high school/university audience, including Canadian bands, independent/alternative music, and campus radio. Pays on publication; rates vary depending on project. Guidelines available. "Generally ideas are worked through with editor(s). We rarely accept/publish completed articles as is."

Cinema Scope

465 Lytton Boulevard, Toronto, ON M5N IS5

Phone: (416) 889-5430 Fax: (416) 977-1158

E-mail: info@cinema-scope.com

Website: www.cinema-scope.com

Contact: Mark Peranson, publisher/editor

Circulation: 41,700

Published quarterly

Publishes interviews, features, and essays on film and video. *Cinema Scope* is geared to cinephiles looking for an intelligent forum on world cinema. Submissions are eagerly encouraged.

Coda

1 First Canadian Place, P.O. Box 375, Toronto, ON M5X ICI
Phone: (416) 868-1958 or 1-888-975-2999 Fax: (416) 868-1958
E-mail: editor@coda1958.com
Website: www.coda1958.com
Contact: Andrew Scott, editor
Circulation: 3,000
Published bimonthly

Specializing in jazz and improvised music for over 50 years. Publishes articles on historical subjects as well as current music. "It takes jazz very seriously." Fees negotiated and paid on publication. "The magazine requires genuine expertise in the area of jazz/improvised music under discussion."

Color

321 Railway Street, Studio 105, Vancouver, BC V6A IA4
Phone: (604) 873-6699 Fax: (604) 873-6619
E-mail: sgrison@colormagazine.ca
Website: www.colormagazine.ca
Contact: Sandro Grison, editor/publisher/creative director
Circulation: 20,000
Published quarterly

A skateboarding and contemporary art quarterly that is heavy on design, art, and graphics with beautiful photography. Distributed in Canada, the U.S., Australia, and beyond. Pays 10¢/word on publication for articles from 700 to 3,000 words. Guidelines available.

The Dance Current

15 Case Goods Lane, Studio 312, Toronto, ON M5A 3C4
Phone: (416) 588-0850 or 1-800-891-7019
E-mail: office@thedancecurrent.com
Website: www.thedancecurrent.com
Contact: Kathleen Smith, editor
Circulation: 1,150
Published 6 times a year

Provides insight into professional dance, art, and culture for artists, dance professionals, students, and the general public. Articles 500 to 1,800 words. Fees are honoraria, paid on publication, and vary depending on the project. Guidelines available.

Dance International
Scotiabank Dance Centre, 677 Davie Street, Level 6, Vancouver, BC V6B 2G6
Phone: (604) 681-1525 Fax: (604) 681-7732
E-mail: danceint@direct.ca
Website: www.danceinternational.org
Contact: Maureen Riches, managing editor
Circulation: 4,000
Published quarterly

Provides a forum for lively and critical commentary on the best in national and international dance, classical and contemporary, including features, reviews, reports, and commentaries. Preferred length 1,250 to 2,000 words. Pays on publication $100 to $150 for features, $100 for commentaries, $85 for reviews, and $125 for notebook. Both emerging and established writers and photographers welcome. Guidelines available on website.

Espace
4888 Ste-Denis, Montreal, QC H2J 2I6
Phone: (514) 844-9858 Fax: (514) 844-3661
E-mail: espace@espacesculpture.com
Website: www.espace-sculpture.com
Contact: Serge Fisette, editor
Circulation: 1,400
Published quarterly

Canada's only sculpture publication, *Espace* presents a critical tool for the understanding of contemporary sculpture. Preferred length for articles is 900 to 1,000 words. Pays $60/page on publication. Guidelines available.

Fuse Magazine
401 Richmond Street W., Suite 454, Toronto, ON M5V 3A8
Phone: (416) 340-8026 Fax: (416) 340-8026
E-mail: content@fusemagazine.org

Website: www.fusemagazine.org
Contact: Izida Zorde, editor
Circulation: 3,000
Published quarterly

Addresses all aspects of contemporary art production, both nationally and internationally. Provides thorough coverage of art and its cultural climate, with a special emphasis on issues relating to cultural differences in terms of class, race, and gender. Encourages writers to submit proposals and accepts unsolicited manuscripts. Features are 3,000 to 4,000 words; reviews about 1,000 words; columns 1,500 to 2,500 words; interviews 2,500 to 3,500 words. No fiction. Compensation is 12¢/published word on publication, 3 issues of the magazine in which your work appears, and a year's subscription. Pay for artist projects is negotiated with the editor. Guidelines on website.

Galleries West

P.O. Box 5287, Banff, AB TIL IG4
Phone: 1-866-415-3282
E-mail: editor@gallerieswest.ca
Website: www.gallerieswest.ca
Contact: Jill Sawyer, editor
Published 3 times a year

Galleries West strives to heighten awareness of the visual arts scene in Western Canada. Feature articles profile prominent artists. Query the editor with story ideas.

Maisonneuve

4413 Harvard Avenue, Montreal, QC H4A 2W9
Phone: (514) 482-5089 Fax: (514) 482-5089 (call first)
E-mail: submissions@maisonneuve.org
Website: www.maisonneuve.org
Contact: Drew Nelles, editor-in-chief
Circulation: 9,000
Published quarterly

Maisonneuve is a general-interest arts and culture publication aimed at curious-minded, media-savvy cultural consumers. Pays about 10¢/word on acceptance for articles 1,000 to 5,000 words. "Please send all submissions to submissions@maisonneuve.org." Guidelines available on website.

MastheadOnline
1606 Sedlescomb Drive, Suite 8, Mississauga, ON L4X 1M6
Phone: (905) 625-7070 Fax: (905) 625-4856
E-mail: jhayward@masthead.ca
Website: www.mastheadonline.com
Contact: Jay Hayward, editor
Circulation: 50,000 visits per month
   Offers daily online news and special feature coverage of Canada's periodical publishing industry. Fees are negotiable and paid 30 days after invoiced for articles, blog posts, etc. Guidelines available.

Montage
111 Peter Street, Suite 402, Toronto, ON M5V 2H1
Phone: (416) 482-6640 Fax: (416) 482-6639
E-mail: montage@dgc.ca
Website: www.dgc.ca
Contact: Lisa Mahal, director of communications
Circulation: 3,000
Published twice a year
   Montage is dedicated to showcasing the cutting edge creativity in Canada's vital and vibrant film and television industries. Articles 1,500 to 2,500 words. Rates vary; please inquire.

Musicworks: For Curious Ears
401 Richmond Street W., Suite 358, Toronto, ON M5V 3A8
Phone: (416) 977-3546
E-mail: editor@musicworks.ca
Website: www.musicworks.ca
Contacts: Micheline Roi, editor
Circulation: 3,000
Published 3 times a year
   Distributed with audio CDs to illustrate articles and interviews covering a broad range of contemporary classical and experimental music, as well as ethnic music and sound related to dance and visual art. Features are 1,000 to 3,500 words. Fees depend on length, complexity, and other factors. Pays on publication. Welcomes inquiries. Guidelines available.

On Site Review

1326 – 11th Avenue S.E., Calgary, AB T2G 0Z5
Phone: (403) 266-5827
E-mail: editor@onsitereview.ca
Website: www.onsitereview.ca
Contact: Stephanie White, editor
Circulation: 1,000
Published twice a year

A magazine devoted to architecture, urbanism, landscape, art, and culture. Readers include practising architects, students, and interested laypeople. Notes 100 to 150 words; letters 200 to 300 words; reports and reviews 500 words; articles 800 to 1,000 words. Themed issues. Articles accepted in English or French. Payment is an honorarium of $75 plus a complimentary 1-year subscription and 2 copies of the issue in which your work appears. "Wants sophisticated ideas in accessible language. Architectural or design training useful. Please tailor your submission to the upcoming issue's theme; themes are announced on www.onsitereview.ca/callforarticles."

On Spec

P.O. Box 4727, Edmonton, AB T6E 5G6
Phone: (403) 413-0215 Fax: (403) 413-1538
E-mail: onspec@onspec.ca
Website: www.onspec.ca
Contact: Diane Walton, managing editor
Circulation: 1,100
Published quarterly

Specializes in science fiction, fantasy, and horror. Publishes short stories and poetry from 100 to 6,000 words. Payment on acceptance: stories less than 1,000 words earn $50; stories from 1,000 to 2,999 earn $125; stories from 3,000 to 4,999 earn $175; and stories from 5,000 to 6,000 earn $200. Poetry earns $50. "We do not read e-mailed or faxed submissions, and we do not buy stories or poetry that have appeared in print or on the Internet. Non-fiction and artwork by commission only. Additional information is available on our website and/or by mailing an SASE for guidelines."

Opera Canada
366 Adelaide Street E., Suite 244, Toronto, ON M5A 3X9
Phone: (416) 363-0395 Fax: (416) 363-0396
E-mail: editorial@operacanada.ca
Contact: Wayne Gooding, editor
Circulation: 5,000
Published 5 times a year from September to June

Devoted for almost 50 years to Canadian opera. Reviews international performances, interviews Canada's best singers, and addresses opera-related cultural issues. Reviews up to 350 words; features 1,200 to 2,000 words. Accepts submissions and submission inquiries. Pays $300 to $400 on publication for features; short features $175; reviews $25. "A knowledge of opera is central for anyone wishing to write for the magazine."

POV Magazine
215 Spadina Avenue, Suite 126, Toronto, ON M5T 2C7
Phone: (416) 599-3844, ext. 4 or 1-877-467-4485
Fax: (416) 979-3936
E-mail: pov@docorg.ca
Website: www.docorg.ca
Contact: Marc Glassman, editor
Published quarterly

POV (Point of View) covers the art and business of indie docs and culture. Writers from across Canada share lively perspectives on independently produced documentary, animated, short, experimental, and feature films. Fees are 15¢/word to 25¢/word for established writers and are paid on publication for 700 to 2,000 words.

Prairie books NOW
100 Arthur Street, Suite 404, Winnipeg, MB R3B 1H3
Phone: (204) 947-2762 Fax: (204) 956-4689
E-mail: pbn@mts.net
Website: www.bookpublishers.mb.ca/pbn
Contact: Carlene Rummery, executive editor
Circulation: 55,000
Published 3 times a year

PbN is a non-scholarly tabloid focusing on books and writers across Manitoba, Saskatchewan, and Alberta. Stories 500 to 800 words. Pays $100 to $175 on publication. "Interested freelancers are asked to submit a CV and writing samples to the executive editor." Contact the executive editor for guidelines.

Prefix Photo
401 Richmond Street W., Suite 124, Toronto, ON M5V 3A8
Phone: (416) 591-0357 Fax: (416) 591-0358
E-mail: info@prefix.ca
Website: www.prefix.ca
Contact: Jayne Wilkinson, operations manager
Circulation: 2,500
Published twice a year

Prefix Photo is a magazine that features critical essays on contemporary photography, media, and digital art. The market includes photographers, artists, students, educators, and a general readership. Articles from 2,600 to 3,900 words. Pays $750/article, one-third on acceptance and two-thirds on publication. Guidelines available.

Quill & Quire
111 Queen Street E., 3rd Floor, Toronto, ON M5C 1S2
Phone: (416) 364-3333, ext. 3111 Fax: (416) 595-5415
E-mail: swoods@quillandquire.com
Website: www.quillandquire.com
Contact: Stuart Woods, editor
Circulation: 5,000
Published monthly

The news journal of the Canadian book trade for booksellers, librarians, educators, publishers, and writers. Prints news, reviews, lists of recently published and upcoming books, and profiles of authors and publishing houses. Includes the biannual digital supplement *Canadian Publishers Digest*. (Also publishes the compendious sourcebook of the publishing industry, *The Book Trade in Canada*.) Publishes short (300- to 1,200-word) and long (up to 3,000-word) news and feature stories about the business of writing, publishing, and bookselling in Canada. Author profiles are 1,800 to 3,000 words. Pays $110 for brief book reviews (350 words) and $330 for feature reviews (800 to 1,000 words). E-mail queries to editor first.

Sad Mag

2818 Main Street, Suite 534, Vancouver, BC V5T 0C1
E-mail: hello@sadmag.ca or webeditor@sadmag.ca
Website: www.sadmag.ca
Contacts: Katie Stewart, creative director and Michelle Reid, web
    editor
Circulation: 2,500–4,000
Published quarterly

Celebrates independent art and culture in "No Fun City" –
Vancouver, B.C. Publishes the work of burgeoning writers and
visual artists, primarily between the ages of 15 to 30. The Sad
Magazine Publishing Society is a non-profit organization and completely volunteer run. See website for upcoming issue themes and
contributor guidelines. "For the issues released in 2013, *Sad Mag*
will only be publishing film- and Polaroid-based photography (no
digital photography permitted)."

Vallum Magazine

P.O. Box 598, Victoria Stn., Montreal, QC H3Z 2Y6
Phone: (514) 937-8946
E-mail: info@vallummag.com (queries only); go to
    www.vallummag.com/submissions to submit work online
Website: www.vallummag.com
Contacts: Joshua Auerbach and Helen Zisimatos, editors; Drew
    McKevitt, managing editor
Circulation: 2,500
Published twice a year

Vallum publishes poems, essays, interviews, and reviews on
poetry. "Our mission is to bring together emerging voices and
established writers from Canada, the U.S., and beyond. We are
interested in original work that's fresh and edgy, something that
reflects the contemporary experience. Open to diverse styles." Pays
an honorarium. Essays, interviews, and reviews may be submitted
through the online submission form (www.vallummag.com/
submissions), but poetry must be sent by regular mail and will not
be read if submitted online. "Please send material for consideration, preferably with cover letter and SASE. No previously published texts or simultaneous submissions. Guidelines and
upcoming themes available on website. *Vallum* also conducts an

annual poetry contest. Please consult the website for entry guidelines and deadlines.

Vernissage: The Magazine of the National Gallery of Canada
P.O. Box 427, Stn. A, Ottawa, ON K1N 9N4
Phone: (613) 990-0532 Fax: (613) 990-7460
E-mail: iparisien@gallery.ca
Website: www.gallery.ca
Contact: Ivan Parisien, editor-in-chief
Circulation: 15,000
Published quarterly
    Browse rich images, eavesdrop on artists and curators, and look
behind the scenes at fascinating details of art history. Articles from
1,200 to 1,400 words. Fees are negotiated and paid on acceptance.

Visual Arts News
1113 Marginal Road, Halifax, NS B3H 4P7
Phone: (902) 423-4694 Fax: (902) 422-0881
E-mail: vanews@visualarts.ns.ca
Website: www.visualartsnews.ca
Contact: Lizzy Hill, editor
Published 3 times a year
    The only magazine dedicated to contemporary visual art in
Atlantic Canada. With a focus on Nova Scotia, we also cover national
and international art events. Features are 1,000 to 3,000 words;
exhibition reviews 500 to 750 words; artist profiles 500 to 1,500
words. Fees vary from $100 to $150/article, paid on acceptance.

Business

Aboriginal Business Quarterly
13245 – 146 Street, Edmonton, AB T5I 4S8
Phone: (780) 455-2700 Fax: (780) 455-7639
E-mail: bq@ammsa.com
Website: www.ammsa.com
Contact: Debora Steel, editor
Circulation: 27,500
Published quarterly

News and information about Aboriginal entrepreneurs, partnerships, new business initiatives, and economic issues. Articles 1,000 to 1,500 words. Pays $3.40 to $4.15/column inch on publication. Guidelines available on website.

Atlantic Business Magazine
P.O. Box 2356, Stn. C, St. John's, NL A1C 6E7
Phone: (709) 726-9300 Fax: (709) 726-3013
E-mail: dchafe@atlanticbusinessmagazine.com
Website: www.atlanticbusinessmagazine.com
Contact: Dawn Chafe, executive editor
Circulation: 35,000
Published bimonthly
Publishes stories about business activities unique to, or specifically focused on, Atlantic Canada. "We have a positive mandate to highlight the character and determination of Atlantic Canadians and the success of their economic initiatives in the global marketplace." Pays on publication 25¢/word for 1,200- to 2,500-word articles. "View recent copies online for sample of our style. Also, when pitching a story, writers new to us should reference previous published material." Guidelines available.

Backbone Magazine
1676 Wembury Road, Mississauga, ON L5J 4G3
Phone: (905) 403-0980
E-mail: pwolchak@backbonemag.com
Website: www.backbonemag.com
Contact: Peter Wolchak, editor
Circulation: 120,000
Published bimonthly
A national magazine that publishes articles on business, technology, and lifestyle. It delivers in-depth analysis and insight into the real benefits of e-commerce, online revenue strategies, and technological innovations that affect the way we live and do business. Articles from 300 to 2,000 words. Pays on publication 60¢/word. Guidelines available.

BCBusiness

4180 Lougheed Highway, 4th Floor, Burnaby, BC V5C 6A7
Phone: (604) 299-7311 Fax: (604) 299-9188
E-mail: bcb@canadawide.com
Website: www.bcbusinessonline.ca
Contacts: Tom Gierasimczuk, editor-in-chief, print; Lindsey
   Peacock, editor, online
Circulation: 26,000
Published monthly

A regional business publication covering real estate, telecommunications, personal finance, management trends and technology, and lifestyle. Directed toward business owners, managers, entrepreneurs, and professionals. Pays about 60¢/word; rates vary according to the story's complexity and the writer's experience. Full-length features run from 2,000 to 3,500 words. "No industry overviews, please. Read at least 4 back issues before querying." Query by mail or e-mail. Guidelines available on website.

Canadian Business

1 Mount Pleasant Road, 8th Floor, Toronto, ON M4Y 2Y5
Phone: (416) 764-1200 Fax: (416) 764-1255
E-mail: letters@canadianbusiness.com
Website: www.canadianbusiness.com
Contact: Emily Nastasi, editorial assistant
Published monthly in June, July, August; published bimonthly the
   rest of the year

Articles are 100 to 2,000 words. Fees are negotiated and paid on acceptance.

Canadian MoneySaver

55 King Street W., Suite 700, Kitchener, ON N2G IAI
Phone: (519) 772-7635
Contact: Peter Hodson, publisher/editor-in-chief
E-mail: moneyinfo@canadianmoneysaver.ca
Website: www.canadianmoneysaver.ca
Circulation: 42,700
Published 9 times a year

A national consumer finance magazine offering articles (800 to 2,000 words) on such current topics as personal finance, tax, investment techniques, retirement planning, consumer purchases, small business practices, and discount services. "Contributors have the opportunity to participate in national and offshore conferences, and propose other writing projects." Cannot pay but welcomes submission inquiries. Guidelines available. Also publishes online edition.

Contact Magazine

310 Front Street W., Suite 800, Toronto, ON M5V 3B5
Phone: (416) 408-2685 or 1-888-267-2772 Fax: (416) 408-2684
E-mail: editor@cpsa.com
Website: www.cpsa.com
Contact: Leslie Wu, editor
Circulation: 28,000
Published quarterly

The number-one source for sales and marketing professionals in Canada. Provides up-to-date information on what's new and important in sales and marketing. Articles 700 to 1,200 words. Some articles are unpaid; others receive approximately 70¢/word on acceptance. Guidelines available.

Corporate Knights

215 Spadina Avenue, Suite 121, Toronto, ON M5T 2C7
Phone: (416) 203-4674 Fax: (416) 979-3936
E-mail: jeremy@corporateknights.com
Website: www.corporateknights.com
Contact: Jeremy Runnalls, managing editor
Published 4 times a year

Founded in 2002, Corporate Knights Inc. is an independent Canadian-based media company that publishes the world's largest circulation magazine with an explicit focus on corporate responsibility. The mission of the company is to humanize the marketplace. Fees are negotiated and paid on publication for articles from 800 to 2,500 words. "*Corporate Knights* encourages anyone with a good idea to e-mail us one paragraph outlining the idea and why you are the one to write the article." Guidelines available on website.

Country Guide

Head office: 1666 Dublin Avenue, Winnipeg, MB R3C 3K7
Phone: (519) 674-1449 Fax: (519) 674-5229

12827 Klondyke Line, Ridgetown, ON NOP 2CO
E-mail: tom.button@fbcpublishing.com
Contact: Tom Button, editor
Website: www.country-guide.ca
Circulation: 45,000
Published monthly

Country Guide is Canada's national business magazine for farmers. Regularly contracts features on farmers who adopt innovative business ideas, plus technical articles on the application of business concepts to agriculture. Also buys profiles of agricultural companies and articles on consumer trends that represent opportunities or challenges for our readers. Pay varies by length and complexity but is based on $400 for an average story. "Please query. Pitched ideas always get read; unsolicited stories only sometimes."

The Insurance and Investment Journal

321 rue de la Commune W., Suite 100, Montreal, QC H2Y 2EI
Phone: (514) 289-9595
E-mail: donna.glasgow@insurance-journal.ca
Website: www.insurance-journal.ca
Contact: Donna Glasgow, editor-in-chief
Circulation: 20,000
Published 10 times a year

The Insurance and Investment Journal is Canada's leading news magazine for financial advisors. Covers news and developments in the life insurance, financial planning, and mutual fund industries. Articles 300 to 1,000 words. Fees are negotiated and paid on acceptance. "If you are interested in business news writing, send us an e-mail. We also have a French-language sister publication, *Le Journal de l'assurance*."

Kidscreen

366 Adelaide Street W., Suite 500, Toronto, ON M5V IR9
Phone: (416) 408-2300 Fax: (416) 408-0870
E-mail: lcastleman@brunico.com
Website: www.kidscreen.com
Contact: Lana Castleman, editor
Circulation: 11,700
Published 10 times a year

Goes to Nickelodeon, Disney, and other companies that produce entertainment for children. Contact editor with story ideas. Fees vary depending on project. Writers must have previous experience writing for this industry.

Progress
1660 Hollis Street, Penthouse, Suite 1201, Halifax, NS B3J 1V7
Phone: (902) 494-0999 or 1-877-277-3232 Fax: (902) 494-0997
E-mail: news@progressmedia.ca
Website: www.progressmedia.ca/magazine
Contact: Pamela Scott Crace, editor
Circulation: 26,500
Published 10 times a year

Progress focuses on wealth creation through profitable business growth. Its audience comprises business and community leaders in Atlantic Canada and Maine. Articles are from 750 to 3,000 words. Fees vary depending on project and are paid within 60 days of acceptance. Guidelines available.

Realscreen
366 Adelaide Street W., Suite 500, Toronto, ON M5V 1R9
Phone: (416) 408-2300 Fax: (416) 408-0870
E-mail: bwalsh@brunico.com
Website: www.realscreen.com
Contact: Barry Walsh, editor
Circulation: 7,400
Published 5 times a year

An international publication about the business of international, non-fiction film and television. Written for producers, distributors, broadcasters, and suppliers. Contact editor with story ideas. Fees vary depending on project. Writers must have previous experience writing for this industry.

ShareOwner
4 King Street W., Suite 806, Toronto, ON M5H 1B6
Phone: (416) 848-9400 Fax: (416) 595-0400
E-mail: john.bart@shareowner.com
Website: www.shareowner.com
Contact: John Bart, publisher/editor

Circulation: 10,000
Published bimonthly

A publication targeted on investment education for individual investors and investment clubs. Fees are negotiated and paid on acceptance. "Writers with personal experience owning stocks and funds are encouraged to contact the publisher."

Summit: Canada's Magazine on Public Sector Purchasing

263 Holmwood Avenue, Suite 100, Ottawa, ON K1S 2P8
Phone: (613) 688-0762 Fax: (613) 688-0767
E-mail: info@summitconnects.com or
    editor@summitconnects.com
Website: www.summitconnects.com
Contact: Anne Phillips, editor
Circulation: 20,000
Published monthly online

For public-sector purchasers at the decision-making and policy levels of hospitals, universities, school boards, and government agencies (municipal, provincial, and federal). Stories on policy matters and how-to articles. Articles 1,000 to 1,500 words. Pays on publication 75¢/published word (20% of the proposed published word count is the kill fee). "Please confirm the potential for publication before submitting your article by calling or e-mailing the contact listed. Articles must be of interest to public sector purchasers and topics may include new technology, greening issues, energy, infrastructure, policy, contracting, legal, and human resources." Guidelines available.

Up Here Business Magazine

4920 – 52nd Street, Suite 800, Yellowknife, NT X1A 3T1
Phone: (867) 766-6710, ext. 315 Fax: (867) 873-9876
E-mail: guy@uphere.ca
Website: www.upherebusiness.ca
Contacts: Guy Quenneville, editor
Circulation: 10,000
Published quarterly

"*Up Here Business* is the voice of the Yukon, the N.W.T. and Nunavut at a time when the three territories are in the news more than ever before. Our mission is to produce an intelligent, provocative monthly that does not shy away from the truth. We do so with fresh and authentic writing, photography, and illustration. We cover business in the broadest sense, including matters of public policy, social development, and environmental protection, because all contribute to the health of the business sector. Although a regional magazine, we want our voice to be heard in the south and tailor our content accordingly. We bring a Northern perspective to national and global stories and put Northern stories in the national and global contexts.

"Freelancers should be knowledgeable about Northern issues and Aboriginal issues as they pertain to the North. Freelancers should also have a basic understanding of business and how it works." Copies of the magazine are available upon request. Articles from 1,500 to 3,000 words. Fees are negotiated and the magazine pays upon publication.

City & Entertainment

Avenue (Calgary)
1900 – 11 Street S.E., Suite 100 Calgary, AB T2G 3G2
Phone: (403) 232-7706 Fax: (403) 240-9059
E-mail: klemon@redpointmedia.ca
Website: www.avenuecalgary.com
Contact: Käthe Lemon, editor
Circulation: 35,000
Published 12 times a year

A city lifestyle magazine for Calgary with well-rounded coverage of the arts, dining and wine, fashion, design, the outdoors, health, travel, and the issues and people shaping the city. Articles 1,500 to 2,500 words. Departments 500 to 1,000 words. Fees vary depending on the project and are paid on publication. "We welcome queries from new writers for stories with relevance to Calgary residents and readers who are curious about Calgary, although the magazine's local focus makes it unlikely that writers not based in the city will write for us."

Avenue (Edmonton)

10221 – 123 Street N.W., Edmonton, AB T5N IN3
Phone: (780) 451-1379 Fax: (780) 482-5417
E-mail: steven@odvodpublishing.com
Website: www.avenueedmonton.com
Contact: Steven Sandor, editor
Circulation: 35,000
Published 12 times a year

Avenue is Edmonton's premier lifestyle magazine. Each issue includes several city-relevant features (1,200 to 2,000 words), as well as the department articles (500 to 1,000 words), which fall into three categories: City (dining and arts), Life (adventure and wellness), and Style (décor, fashion, and design). Fees vary depending on the project and are paid on publication. Queries from new writers with Edmonton- and Alberta-centred stories are welcome.

Cineplex Magazine

102 Atlantic Avenue, Suite 100, Toronto, ON M6K IX9
Phone: (416) 539-8800 Fax: (416) 539-8511
E-mail: marni.weisz@cineplex.com
Contact: Marni Weisz, editor
Circulation: 650,000
Published monthly

An in-theatre magazine for Cineplex Theatres. Content focuses on movies, music, books, video games, and DVDs. Articles 600 to 1,400 words. Pays 50¢/word.

City Palate

722 – 11th Avenue S.W., Calgary, AB T2R OE4
E-mail: kathy@citypalate.ca
Website: www.citypalate.ca
Contact: Kathy Richardier, editor
Circulation: 46,000
Published bimonthly

City Palate celebrates Calgary's food culture. Highlights local people in the food industry through articles both by and about them. Also includes food and drink articles on the basis of seasonality and what's happening in the culinary universe with, as often as possible, a local focus. Welcomes editorial queries by e-mail.

The Coast: Halifax's Weekly
5567 Cunard Street, Halifax, NS B3K IC5
Phone: (902) 422-6278 Fax: (902) 425-0013
E-mail: news@thecoast or arts@thecoast.ca
Website: www.thecoast.ca
Contacts: Tim Bousquet, news editor; Sue Carter Flinn, arts editor
Circulation: 22,000

Established 1993. A free, locally owned, alternative weekly newspaper serving Metro Halifax that publishes short news stories and arts profiles as well as magazine-style features. *The Coast's* goal is to be provocative and entertaining. Pays 10¢ to 20¢/word on acceptance for 500 to 3,000 words. Rate depends on complexity of topic and is negotiated up front. Guidelines available.

East of the City
130 Commercial Avenue, Ajax, ON LIS 2H5
Phone: (905) 426-4676 Fax: (416) 426-6598
E-mail: tmckee@durhamregion.com
Contact: Tamara McKee, editor
Circulation: 25,000
Published bimonthly

Shines the spotlight on the culture in Durham Region, east of Toronto, and includes stories on home décor, gardening, health, and the personalities who call this area home. Readers are upscale, aged 35 and up, with household incomes of at least $150,000. Pay rates vary from $75 to $150, paid on publication, for articles of 800 to 1,500 words.

Fast Forward Weekly
1210 – 20th Avenue S.E., Suite 206, Calgary, AB T2G IM8
Phone: (403) 244-2235 Fax: (403) 244-1431
E-mail: charrington@ffwd.greatwest.ca
Website: www.ffwdweekly.com
Contact: Carol Harrington, editor-in-chief
Circulation: 35,000

Calgary's news and entertainment weekly. "The best way to get an article published in *Fast Forward* is to submit your ideas via mail or e-mail, along with some background information, credentials, and any writing samples you may have."

Focus

P.O. Box 5310, Victoria, BC V8R 6S4
Phone: (250) 388-7231 Fax: (250) 383-1140
E-mail: focusedit@shaw.ca
Website: www.focusonline.ca
Contact: Leslie Campbell, editor
Circulation: 35,000
Published monthly

Celebrates Victoria's creative and community spirit with diverse, intelligent editorial coverage. Publishes investigative features (2,000 to 3,000 words) and profiles (1,500 words). Please query first.

The Georgia Straight

1701 W. Broadway, Vancouver, BC V6J 1Y3
Phone: (604) 730-7000 Fax: (604) 730-7010
E-mail: contact@straight.com
Website: www.straight.com
Contact: Charlie Smith, editor
Circulation: 135,000
Published weekly

The Georgia Straight is Vancouver's premier news and entertainment weekly. Articles typically 500 to 1,500 words. Fees vary. Paid on publication.

The Grid

1 Yonge Street, 2nd Floor, Toronto, ON M5E 1E6
Phone: 416-933-3433
E-mail: grieg@thegridto.com
Website: www.thegridto.com
Contact: Greig Dymond, senior editor
Circulation: 213,000

Toronto's definitive source of alternative cultural commentary, with extensive arts and entertainment coverage, and listings. "We welcome submissions but are not responsible for unsolicited material." Fees vary and are paid on publication.

The Life and Times

11 King Street, Unit 5, Barrie, ON L4N 6B5
Phone: (705) 733-0033 Fax: 1-866-772-0893

E-mail: cb@thelifeandtimes.ca
Website: www.thelifeandtimes.ca
Contact: Catherine Beauvais, publisher/editor
Circulation: 15,000–25,000
Published monthly

Good News paper that focuses on "Recognizing People Living with Passion," past and future events, and fundraising. Nostalgia, History, and Tourism are target areas for article submissions. Readership is predominantly 45+ and female. Articles from 100 to 450 words. "Depending on the assignment, we may be able to negotiate fees. Currently, most of our contributors are businesses looking for exposure and our own staff writers." Submission inquiries welcome. Guidelines are available.

Niagara Life

3550 Schmon Parkway, Suite 1, Thorold, ON L2V 4Y6
Phone: (905) 641-1984 Fax: (905) 641-0682
E-mail: lfleming@niagaralifemag.com
Website: www.niagaralifemag.com
Contact: Liz Fleming, editor
Circulation: 45,000
Published bimonthly in Niagara, 3 times a year for Toronto-
    Burlington

A lifestyle magazine of the Niagara region, covering such topics as food, wine, art, fiction, travel, and events via issue themes of business, home and garden, health and wellness, design and décor, golf, travel and leisure, and holidays. Named "Niagara's premier magazine" by the *Buffalo News*. Articles 500 to 1,000 words. Pays on publication for Niagara-based themed features, profiles, and music, as well as book and play reviews. Fees are negotiated for submissions of copy, photography, and art. E-mail the editor.

NOW Magazine

189 Church Street, Toronto, ON M5B 1Y7
Phone: (416) 364-1300 Fax: (416) 364-1168
E-mail: news@nowtoronto.com or
    entertainment@nowtoronto.com
Website: www.nowtoronto.com

Contacts: Susan G. Cole (susanc@nowtoronto.com), senior
   entertainment editor; Ellie Kirzner, (ellie@nowtoronto.com)
   senior news editor; Joshua Errett (joshuae@nowtoronto.com),
   online editor
Circulation: 117,000
Published weekly
   NOW Magazine is a news, entertainment, and listings magazine
covering Toronto-region news, music, film, theatre, fashion, food,
and the arts. Story length from 100 to 2,000 words. Most work is
assigned. Uses very few out-of-town writers and freelancers only
occasionally in music and in news. Toronto-region news submissions with an alternative perspective have the best chance. Rates
vary. Pays on publication. All fees negotiable. Inquiries welcome.

Ottawa Magazine

43 Eccles Street, Ottawa, ON KIR 6S3
Phone: (613) 230-0333 Fax: (613) 230-4441
E-mail: sbrown@stjosephmedia.com
Website: www.ottawamagazine.com
Contact: Sarah Brown, editor
Circulation: 40,000
Published 8 times a year
   Targeted at upwardly mobile Ottawans between the ages of 25 and
50. Pays 50¢/word on acceptance for articles 800 to 3,500 words.

Scene

P.O. Box 27048, London, ON N5X 3X5
Phone: (519) 642-4780 Fax: (519) 642-0737
E-mail: bret@scenemagazine.com
Website: www.scenemagazine.com
Contact: Bret Downe, publisher/editor-in-chief
Circulation: 20,000
Published 25 times a year
   London's largest generally well-read newspaper. Founded 1988.
Articles 500 to 1,250 words. Pay starts at $40/article on accep-
tance. Guidelines available.

Toronto Life

111 Queen Street E., Suite 320, Toronto, ON M5C 1S2
Phone: (416) 364-3333 Fax: (416) 861-1169
E-mail: editorial@torontolife.com
Website: www.torontolife.com
Contact: Sarah Fulford, editor
Circulation: 86,000
Published monthly

Established 1966. A city magazine that tells readers how Toronto works, lives, and plays. Examines city politics, society, business, entertainment, sports, food and restaurants, and shopping in a unique mix of reporting and service journalism. Also publishes special-interest publications. Draws on a stable of experienced writers but also accepts outside submissions. Pays on acceptance, roughly between $300 and $6,500 for 100 to 6,000 words, depending on assignment. "Submissions should have a strong Toronto orientation. Story suggestions should be submitted in writing in the form of a one-page proposal."

TVW

4180 Lougheed Highway, 4th Floor, Burnaby, BC V5C 6A7
Phone: (604) 299-7311 Fax: (604) 299-9188
E-mail: bfurdyk@canadawide.com
Website: www.canadawide.com or tvwonline.ca
Contact: Brent Furdyk, editor
Circulation: 70,000
Published weekly

A B.C.-based television and entertainment guide. Pays 40¢/word on publication for stories of 600 to 1,600 words.

Uptown Magazine

1355 Mountain Avenue, Winnipeg, MB R2X 3B6
Phone: (204) 697-7009 Fax: (204) 953-4300
E-mail: john.kendle@uptownmag.com
Website: www.uptownmag.com
Contact: John Kendle, editor
Circulation: 20,000
Published weekly

An arts, entertainment, and news weekly for readers 15 to 50. Articles 500 to 1,000 words. Pay rates vary and are paid on publication. Contact editor regarding submissions.

Vancouver Magazine

2608 Granville Street, Suite 560, Vancouver, BC V6H 3V3
Phone: (604) 877-7732 Fax: (604) 877-4848
E-mail: mail@vancouvermagazine.com
Website: www.vancouvermagazine.com
Contact: John Burns, editor-in-chief
Circulation: 48,000
Published 10 times a year plus two annual special-interest
    magazines

The city magazine of the new Vancouver – its people, stories, and ideas – focusing on urban culture and current affairs. Articles must be Vancouver specific. Most stories are 1,500 words; no poetry or fiction. The two special-interest issues are *Eating & Drinking Guide*, which covers the best bars, restaurants, and food shops, and *Guestlife Vancouver*, which covers the best places to see, shop, sleep, eat, and explore. Query first. Read the magazine before submitting. Guidelines available.

Vue Weekly

10303 – 108 Street, Edmonton, AB T5J IL7
Phone: (780) 426-1996 Fax: (780) 426-2889
E-mail: david@vueweekly.com
Website: www.vueweekly.com
Contact: David Berry, arts/film editor
Circulation: 30,000
Published weekly

An alternative arts and entertainment weekly with a focus on Edmonton and Alberta. Pays on publication 8¢ to 12¢/word for articles of 400 to 1,500 words. "We welcome a variety of pitches, focusing on alternative news and A&E. Please check out our website to get a feel for what we do. Fiction and poetry are welcome, but we have a preference for non-fiction."

The Environment

Alternatives Journal: Canadian Environmental Ideas and Action

Faculty of Environmental Studies, University of Waterloo,
    Waterloo, ON N2L 3G1
Phone: (519) 888-4442 Fax: (519) 746-0292
E-mail: editor@alternativesjournal.ca
Website: www.alternativesjournal.ca
Contact: Nicola Ross, executive editor
Published bimonthly

A long-standing leader in environmental journalism. Articles provide a blend of practical information and analysis from across Canada and abroad. "Environment is defined in the broadest sense. Readers include environmental professionals and academics, activists, concerned citizens, and students." Feature-length articles (1,500 to 3,000 words) are peer reviewed. Also publishes reports (500 to 1,200 words) and notes (up to 500 words). Pay rates negotiable. Guidelines available on website.

Common Ground

4381 Fraser Street, Suite 204, Vancouver, BC V5V 4G4
Phone: (604) 733-2215 Fax: (604) 733-4415
E-mail: editor@commonground.ca
Contact: Joseph Roberts, publisher/senior editor
Circulation: 70,000
Published monthly

Aims to inform, inspire, and educate readers about health, wellness, ecology, personal growth, travel, professional development, and creativity. Prefers Canadian authors. Rarely accepts fiction or poetry. Pays 10¢/published word on publication for articles from 600 to 1,500 words.

Green Teacher

95 Robert Street, Toronto, ON M5S 2K5
Phone: (416) 960-1244 Fax: (416) 925-3474
E-mail: info@greenteacher.com
Website: www.greenteacher.com

Contact: Tim Grant, co-editor
Circulation: 7,000 (print); 4,500 (electronic)
Published quarterly

A magazine by and for educators that aims to provide ideas, inspiration, and classroom-ready materials to help all educators (including parents) promote environmental and global awareness among young people, preschool to college, in school and in the community. Articles 1,200 to 3,800 words. All writers are volunteers; they receive a complimentary one-year subscription. Submissions welcome. Guidelines available on website.

Nature Canada
75 Albert Street, Suite 300, Ottawa, ON KIP 5E7
Phone: (613) 562-3447, ext. 248 Fax: (613) 562-3371
E-mail: csutton@naturecanada.ca
Website: www.naturecanada.ca
Contact: Chris Sutton, manager, communications
Circulation: 20,000
Published quarterly

Mailed to supporters of Nature Canada, a non-profit conservation organization. Also, an electronic newsletter, *The Nature Nation*, is issued monthly. *Nature Canada* magazine is aimed at people interested in learning about and protecting nature. Focuses on conservation issues related to protected federal areas, endangered species, and important bird areas. Features 500 to 1,200 words. Rates vary and are paid on publication. "Stories in the print and electronic newsletters focus strongly on Nature Canada programs. General interest stories must be relevant to our programs." Guidelines available.

Feminist

Herizons
P.O. Box 128, Winnipeg, MB R3C 2GI
Phone: (204) 774-6225
E-mail: editor@herizons.ca
Website: www.herizons.ca
Contact: Penni Mitchell, editor

Circulation: 4,000
Published quarterly

A feminist periodical focusing on women's issues and the women's movement. Features 1,000 to 3,000 words. Pays 30¢/word on publication. Send query and sample of previously published work written from a feminist perspective. Guidelines available on website.

Shameless
P.O. Box 68548, 360A Bloor Street W., Toronto, ON M5A IXI
E-mail: talkingback@shamelessmag.com or
   sheila@shamelessmag.coim
Website: www.shamelessmag.com
Contact: Sheila Sampath, editorial and art director
Circulation: 3,000
Published 3 times a year

"Packed with articles about arts, culture, and current events, *Shameless* reaches out to readers who are often ignored by mainstream media: freethinkers, queer youth, trans youth, young women of colour, punk rockers, feminists, intellectuals, artists, and activists." Articles on current events, feminist issues, DIY crafts, sports, technology, food, politics, health, sexuality, advice, etc. All issues contain profiles of inspiring young women and trans youth. Features about 2,000 words; profiles 300 to 1,000 words; departments 200 to 800 words; reviews 100 words. Query first. Detailed submission guidelines on website. "We are unable to pay our writers at this point; what we can offer you is international exposure for your writing, a complimentary copy of the magazine, and our undying gratitude."

Women & Environments International Magazine
Faculty of Environmental Studies, York University, HNES
   Building, 4700 Keele Street, Room 234, Toronto, ON M3J IP3
Phone: (416) 736-2100, ext. 21055 Fax: (416) 736-5679
E-mail: weimag@yorku.ca
Website: www.weimag.com
Contact: editorial board
Published twice a year

A co-operative forum for discussion, review, and research on women's built, natural, social, and political environments for feminists, academics, and a broad base of grassroots groups. Features

1,500 to 2,500 words. Shorter pieces, book and film reviews, poetry, and artistic expressions are welcome. Contributors are not paid; writers of features receive 3 complimentary copies, while writers of shorter pieces receive 1 complimentary copy. "Clear language is essential – no academic jargon, please. We are crosscultural and international. All issues are theme related. For the next 2 years, we aim to publish issues on women, communities, health, mobility, governance, spirituality, social change, and violence." Guidelines available on website.

General Interest

Alberta Views Magazine
320 – 23 Avenue S.W., Suite 208, Calgary, AB T2S 0J2
Phone: (403) 243-5334 Fax: (403) 243-8599
E-mail: queries@albertaviews.ab.ca
Website: www.albertaviews.ab.ca
Contact: Naomi Lewis, assistant editor
Circulation: 20,000
Published 10 times a year

Publishes commentary and analysis that explores political, social, and cultural life in Alberta in order to stimulate public discussion. Articles are from 700 to 3,000 words. Pays 50¢/word on acceptance. Guidelines available on website.

Canada's History
515 Portage Avenue, Winnipeg, MB R3B 0G9
Phone: (204) 988-9300 Fax: (204) 988-9309
E-mail: editors@historysociety.ca
Website: www.thebeaver.ca
Contact: Mark Reid, editor
Circulation: 38,000
Published bimonthly

Formerly *The Beaver*. A market since 1920 for lively, well-researched, informative, expository articles on Canadian history. "We welcome popularly written features on Canadian history, particularly those based on unpublished or new material, written from a non-traditional point of view or a new interpretation of significant events or people." Interested in submissions from all parts of the country. Pays a varying rate (depending on research necessary and writer's experience) on acceptance for articles of 800 to 3,000 words. "Writers should thoroughly acquaint themselves with the magazine by reading back issues." Guidelines available on website.

Canadian Stories

P.O. Box 232, Fergus, ON N1M 2W8
Phone: (519) 823-1944
E-mail: ejanzen345@sympatico.ca
Website: www.canadianstories.net
Contact: Ed Janzen, publisher/editor
Published bimonthly

A collection of Canadian folk stories, old and recent, memories, memoirs, and historical articles. Readers are mostly middle aged and seniors. Preferred length of articles 200 to 1,200 words. Cannot pay but welcomes submission inquiries. Contributors are from across Canada and are often first-time writers. See website for examples and guidelines.

NUVO Magazine

3055 Kingsway, Vancouver, BC V5R 5J8
Phone: (604) 899-9380 or 1-877-205-6886 Fax: (604) 899-1450
E-mail: editorial@nuvomagazine.com
Website: www.nuvomagazine.com
Contact: Katie Nanton, assistant editor
Circulation: 50,000
Published quarterly

"Inspired by quality, NUVO is a lifestyle magazine for the Canadian sophisticate." Includes stories on travel, food and wine, film and TV, fashion, art, architecture, design, business, automobiles, and music. "Please pick up a copy of NUVO and visit our website before making your submission. E-mail queries only; no telephone queries are accepted." Submission guidelines available on website.

Our Canada

1100 René Levesque Boulevard W., Montreal, QC H3B 5H5
Phone: (514) 940-0751
Website: www.ourcanada.ca

Circulation: 200,000
Published bimonthly

Our Canada and its subscriber-only companion magazine, *More of Our Canada*, are published by Reader's Digest Magazines Canada. Content is composed of reader-contributed stories focused on Canadian life and experiences, primarily written in the first person. Accompanying photos accepted. Stories 200 to 1,000 words. Free 1-year gift subscription and complementary issue upon publication. Online submissions preferred. Guidelines available on website.

Reader's Digest

1100 René Levesque Boulevard W., Montreal, QC H3B 5H5
Phone: (514) 940-0751 Fax: (514) 940-7337
E-mail: editor@readersdigest.ca
Website: www.readersdigest.ca
Contact: editorial department
Circulation: 921,000
Published monthly

This mass-interest magazine is among the freelancer's most lucrative potential markets. Carries articles on everything from nature, science, and politics to drama, self-improvement, and people, prominent or otherwise. All pieces contain advice, an experience, or a philosophical message of value to the magazine's 6.4 million readers. No fiction or poetry. Commissions original articles and adaptations of Canadian subjects of between 3,500 and 5,000 words. Pays $200/anecdote. Also buys material previously published in books, magazines, or newspapers. Buys global rights and pays on acceptance for original articles, one-time or global rights for previously published "pickups." No unsolicited manuscripts. Send letter of inquiry with a 2-page outline. Guidelines available on website.

Toro

125 Blake Street, Toronto, ON M4J 3E2
Phone: (416) 850-4144 Fax: (647) 439-5521
E-mail: info@toromagazine.com or departures@toromagazine.com
Website: www.toromagazine.com
Contact: Christina Butterfield, deputy editor
Circulation: 220,000
Published online

A general interest magazine for men. Articles 150 to 6,000 words. Fees, which are paid on acceptance, are negotiated and vary depending on the project. "If a writer hasn't worked with us before or is unknown to the editors, we always suggest sending in clips along with his or her pitches." Guidelines available on website.

Up Here Magazine
4920 – 52 Street, Suite 800, Yellowknife, NT XIA 3TI
Phone: (867) 766-6720 Fax: (867) 873-9876
E-mail: aaron@uphere.ca
Website: www.uphere.ca
Contact: Aaron Spitzer, editor
Circulation: 25,000
Published 8 times a year

A lively, informative magazine about travel, wildlife, arts, culture, lifestyles, and especially the people of Canada's far northern regions. Articles 2,200 to 2,500 words (maximum 3,500 words). Fees negotiable and paid on publication. "We strongly prefer written queries that present a well-focused story and, if not samples, then suggested leads for accompanying photography. Complete manuscripts with photos are okay, but please be aware we cannot be responsible for unsolicited material. We're looking for solid reporting and research, and top-notch photos. Always tell your story through the people involved." Guidelines available.

Your Workplace
23 Queen Street, Kingston, ON K7K IAI
Phone: (613) 549-1222
E-mail: editor@yourworkplace.ca
Website: www.yourworkplace.ca
Contact: Bonita Summers, editor
Circulation: 336,000
Published 6 times a year

Provides inspiration for work and life, healthy workplaces, the work-life balance, trends, safety, and employee concerns. Articles 700 to 1,600 words. Pays 20¢/word on publication. Welcomes submission queries. Guidelines available.

Home & Hobby

BC Home & Garden

4180 Lougheed Highway, 4th Floor, Burnaby, BC V5C 6A7
Phone: (604) 299-7311 Fax: (604) 299-9188
E-mail: amair@canadawide.com
Website: www.canadawide.com or www.bcliving.ca/bc-home-and-
   garden-magazine
Contact: Amy Mair
Circulation: 35,000
Published bimonthly
   Launched in 2012 as a repositioning of *GardenWise* and
BCHome magazines. Covers "unique ideas, tips and how-to's for
your garden plus new inspiration on style, design and renovation
for your home."

The Canadian Amateur

720 Belfast Road, Suite 217, Ottawa, ON K1G 0Z5
Phone: 1-877-273-8304
E-mail: tcamag@yahoo.ca
Website: www.rac.ca
Contact: Alan Griffin, editor
Published bimonthly
   Provides radio amateurs, those interested in radio communica-
tions and electronics, and the general public with information
related to the science of telecommunications. Welcomes technical
and non-technical articles. Some articles may be published in both
English and French. Cannot pay. Guidelines on website.

Canadian Coin News

103 Lakeshore Road, Suite 202, St. Catharines, ON L2N 2T6
Phone: (905) 646-7744 Fax: (905) 646-0995
E-mail: bret@trajan.ca
Website: www.canadiancoinnews.ca
Contact: Bret Evans, managing editor
Circulation: 6,000
   Published biweekly

A tabloid magazine for Canadian collectors of coins and paper money. Query first by e-mail. Pays 2 months after publication. Fees negotiable.

Canadian Gardening
25 Sheppard Avenue W., Suite 100, Toronto, ON M2N 6S7
Phone: (416) 733-7600
Website: www.canadiangardening.com
Contact: Erin McLaughlin, editor-in-chief
Circulation: 152,000
Published 8 times a year

A magazine geared toward the avid home gardener. Carries people-oriented feature articles on home gardens, garden design, and tips and techniques on gardening in the Canadian climate. "Our rates range from $125 and up for short news items, reviews, or how-to pieces (200 to 400 words) to $350 and up for features (about 500 to 2,000 words)." Fees are paid on acceptance. "We prefer story ideas and outlines to unsolicited, finished stories." Guidelines available on website.

Canadian Homes and Cottages
2650 Meadowvale Boulevard, Unit 4, Mississauga, ON L5N 6M5
Phone: (905) 567-1440 Fax: (905) 567-1442
E-mail: editorial@homesandcottages.com
Website: www.homesandcottages.com
Contact: Steven Chester, managing editor
Circulation: 89,553
Published bimonthly

Canada's largest residential building magazine for consumers as well as building trades. Provides thought-provoking and innovative ideas and technical information to help Canadians build, renovate or landscape their homes and cottages. Articles 600 to 1,200 words. Fees vary according to complexity, but average is $300. All articles are assigned. Pays on acceptance. "We have consumer and trade editions. We write about architecture and design, but not decorating; hard landscaping, but not gardening; cottage renovation and construction, but not cottage lifestyles." Guidelines available.

Canadian Home Trends

P.O. Box 7, 20 Centre Avenue, Blumenort, MB ROA OCO
Phone: 1-866-984-0940 Fax: (204) 346-9099
E-mail: marc@canadianhometrends.ca
Contact: Marc Atiyolil, editor
Published bimonthly

"Short, informational articles relating to home décor, building and renovating, yard and garden, covering lifestyle interests, offering simple project instruction and wholesome recipes, tips on health, money management, travel and education, as well as many others."

Canadian Home Workshop

54 Saint Patrick Street, Toronto, ON M5T IVI
Phone: (416) 599-2000 Fax: (416) 599-0500
Website: www.canadianhomeworkshop.com
Contact: Douglas Thomson, editor-in-chief
Circulation: 90,000
Published 6 times a year

"Since 1977, *Canadian Home Workshop* magazine has been inspiring woodworkers and DIYers with project ideas, plans, shop tips and techniques, and practical renovation and home-maintenance information."

Canadian House & Home

511 King Street W., Suite 120, Toronto, ON M5V 2Z4
Phone: (416) 593-0204 Fax: (416) 591-1630
E-mail: jlawler@hhmedia.com
Website: www.houseandhome.com
Contacts: Alice Lawler, executive editor, and Janet Maclure, assistant to the editor
Circulation: 244,000
Published 12 times a year

Focuses on creative home decoration and design. Inspires and teaches through pictorial essays and how-to articles featuring Canadian designers, architects, and artisans. Fees vary depending on project and are paid on acceptance. "Stories are usually assigned based on acceptance of visuals. Always include colour photos with submissions. Submit story proposals only, not completed manuscripts."

Canadian Stamp News

103 Lakeshore Road, Suite 202, St. Catharines, ON L2N 2T6
Phone: (905) 646-7744 Fax: (905) 646-0995
E-mail: bret@trajan.ca
Website: www.canadianstampnews.ca
Contact: Bret Evans, managing editor
Circulation: 4,000
Published biweekly

A tabloid magazine serving Canadian philatelists and enthusiasts around the world who collect Canadian stamps. Query first by e-mail or phone. Pays 2 months after publication. Fees negotiable.

Canadian Woodworking & Home Improvement Magazine

51 Maple Avenue N., R.R. #3, Burford, ON N0E 1A0
Phone: (519) 449-2444 Fax: (519) 449-2445
E-mail: pfulcher@canadianwoodworking.com
Website: www.canadianwoodworking.com
Contact: Paul Fulcher, publisher
Circulation: 21,000
Published bimonthly

A special interest publication for the home-hobbyist woodworker and DIYer. Plans, projects, tips, tricks, and techniques. Pays $250 to $450 on publication for articles of 500 to 1,000 words.

Garden Making

111B Garrison Village Drive, Suite 204, R.R. #3, Niagara-on-the-
  Lake, ON L0S 1J0
Phone: (905) 468-2999 Fax: 1-866-857-4262
E-mail: editors@gardenmaking.com
Website: www.gardenmaking.com
Contact: Beckie Fox, editor-in-chief
Circulation: 23,000
Published quarterly

Offers avid home gardeners useful, practical, detailed articles about growing and caring for plants, and good landscaping techniques and practices. E-mail queries only; payment upon acceptance.

Home Digest
115 George Street, Unit 1524, Oakville, ON L6J OA2
Phone: (905) 844-3361
E-mail: homedigesteditor@sympatico.ca
Website: www.home-digest.com
Contact: William Roebuck, editor
Published 4 times a year

Carries articles devoted to healthy cooking, household hints, home decoration and renovation. Distributed to 700,000 mid- to upper-income homeowners in the Greater Toronto Area. Short features: 300 to 700 words; service, human interest, and humour items: 50 to 200 words. Pays 10¢/word on publication.

Homes & Living Magazine
110 – 2940 Jutland Road, Victoria, BC V8T 5K6
Phone: (250) 383-7323
E-mail: info@hlmagazine.com
Website: www.hlmagazine.com
Contact: Robert Read, publisher
Circulation: 50,000 (Vancouver edition); 35,000 (Victoria);
  20,000 (Central Vancouver Island)
Published 6 times a year

Vancouver, Victoria, and Central Vancouver Island's premier fine home and lifestyle magazine. Stories run from 500 to 800 words. Fees are about 25¢/word or $200/article, paid within 30 days of publication. "Kill fees paid at half rate if story doesn't run within 6 issues." Guidelines available.

Ontario Gardener Living
130A Cree Crescent, Winnipeg, MB R3J 3W1
Phone: (204) 940-2700 or 1-888-680-2008 Fax: (204) 940-2727
E-mail: joan.cohen@pegasuspublications.net
Website: www.localgardener.net
Contact: Joan Cohen, editor
Circulation: 18,000
Published 6 times a year

A magazine with informative, entertaining articles for passionate gardeners across Ontario. Articles 200 to 1,000 words. Pays $70 to

$350 on publication, depending on the project. "Please call or e-mail for guidelines."

Photo Life
185 St. Paul Street, Quebec City, QC G1K 3W2
Phone: 1-800-905-7468 Fax: 1-800-664-2739
E-mail: write@photolife.com
Website: www.photolife.com
Contact: Valerie Racine, editorial director
Published bimonthly

Established 1976. Delivers serious information to photographers from beginners to advanced in a readable way. Articles 600 to 1,500 words. Fees are negotiated and paid on publication. *Photo Life* offers the opportunity for photographers to have their work published. "All photography-related articles are welcome. Submission guidelines are available at our website."

Style at Home
25 Sheppard Avenue W., Suite 100, Toronto, ON M2N 6S7
Phone: (416) 733-7600
E-mail: letters@styleathome.com
Website: www.styleathome.com
Contact: Laurie Grassi, executive editor
Circulation: 235,000
Published 12 times a year

A glossy magazine featuring Canadian home-décor stories, news, products, and trends. Rates vary with project and writer, but pays up to $1/word on acceptance for stories of 300 to 700 words. "Please read several issues of *Style at Home* before presenting queries." Guidelines available.

The Upper Canadian Antique Showcase
13 Livingston Avenue, Grimsby, ON L3M 1K6
Phone: (905) 945-5757 or 1-866-333-3397 Fax: (905) 945-7982
E-mail: jherbertbond@theuppercanadian.com
Website: www.theuppercanadian.com
Contact: J. Herbert Bond, editor
Circulation: 5,000+, depending on season

Published bimonthly

Since 1963, The Upper Canadian has been the authoritative voice covering Canadian antiques, fine art, folk art, and vintage collectibles. Trusted by collectors, and valued by dealers, auctioneers, and show promoters. Articles 600 to 1,000 words. Fees vary. "We particularly appreciate writers with a passion for antiques, art, and/or collecting." Guidelines available.

Lifestyle

alive

12751 Vulcan Way, Suite 100, Richmond, BC V6V 3C8
Phone: 1-800-663-6580, ext. 610 Fax: 1-800-663-6597
E-mail: editorial@alive.com
Website: www.alive.com
Contact: Stuart Harries, editor-in-chief
Circulation: 200,000
Published monthly

A national magazine for health-conscious Canadians featuring articles on whole-foods nutrition, alternative medicine, and the environment. Articles of 800 to 3,000 words by health researchers and professionals. Pays per article on acceptance; average is 50¢/word but may vary based on writer's experience and complexity of article. "Always query. Do not send unsolicited articles or manuscripts." Guidelines available on website.

Best Health

250 Bloor Street E., Suite 502, Toronto, ON M4W 1E6
Phone: (416) 925-8941 Fax: (416) 920-6571
Website: www.besthealthmag.ca
Contact: Bonnie Munday, editor
Circulation: 100,000
Published 8 times a year

Includes information on "feeling beautiful, being healthier, eating well, and embracing life."

Canadian Family
111 Queen Street E., Suite 320, Toronto, ON M5C 1S2
Phone: (416) 364-3333
E-mail: jreynolds@canadianfamily.ca
Website: www.canadianfamily.ca
Contact: Jennifer Reynolds, editor-in-chief
Circulation: 114,800
Published 8 times a year
   Includes stories on parenting, family life, education, health, décor, fashion, beauty, and contemporary parenting issues. "We do hire freelancers but rarely accept unsolicited manuscripts. Brief pitches can be e-mailed to the editor. Tell us where you've been published before and send 1 to 2 links. If we decide to explore a pitch further, we will contact the writer at which time we will discuss guidelines, etc. Please do not send inquiries by mail. We cannot respond to every inquiry." Pays on average $1/word for articles 100 to 1,500 words. Paid on acceptance. "Please study the new, relaunched version of our magazine. We are not like the old *Canadian Family*. Writers must excel at engaging, conversational copy and not write in a pedantic or arcane style. We're fun, hip, savvy, and supportive."

Canadian Health & Lifestyle
1 Mount Pleasant Road, 7th Floor, Toronto, ON M4Y 2Y5
Phone: (416) 764-1888 Fax: (416) 764-1493
E-mail: editor@healthandlifestyle.ca
Website: www.healthandlifestyle.ca
Contact: Barbara Goodman, editor-in-chief
Circulation: 400,000
Published quarterly
   Provides information on health, wellness, beauty, fitness, and nutrition. Distributed to pharmacies, doctors' offices, and hospitals.

Canadian Living
25 Sheppard Avenue W., Suite 100, Toronto, ON M2N 6S7
Phone: (416) 733-7600 Fax: (416) 218-3636
E-mail: submissions@canadianliving.com
Contact: Susan Antonacci, editor-in-chief
Website: www.canadianliving.com

Circulation: 508,000
Published monthly

Offers service articles for Canadian women with solutions for everyday living with a focus on food, family and community, health and wellness, and style. "Suggest to us how your story could be extended or modified for use on our web site. No fiction or poetry." Length usually 750 to 2,500 words. Payment varies. Query with SASE or by e-mail.

Cottage

54 St. Patrick Street, Toronto, ON M5T IVI
Phone: (416) 599-2000 Fax: (416) 599-0800
E-mail: editor@cottagemagazine.com
Website: www.cottagemagazine.com
Contact: editor
Circulation: 12,500
Published bimonthly

A magazine for "cottagers and recreation lovers who seek stories on outdoor activities, building styles, sustainable living, cottage life, how-to information, reno tips and DIY projects. As well, *Cottage* offers profiles and visuals of unique destinations, homes and cottages across Western Canada."

Cottage Life

54 St. Patrick Street, Toronto, ON M5T IVI
Phone: (416) 599-2000 Fax: (416) 599-0800
E-mail: edit@cottagelife.com
Website: www.cottagelife.com
Contacts: Penny Caldwell, editor; Jackie Davis, assistant editor
Circulation: 70,000
Published 6 times a year

An award-winning magazine directed toward those who own and spend time at cottages on Ontario's lakes. Examines and celebrates the history, personalities, and issues of cottaging. Also provides practical advice to help readers keep their cottages, docks, and boats in working order. Pays on acceptance for articles of 150 to 3,000 words; pay rates vary depending on project. Query all ideas before submission. Guidelines available on website; consult online searchable index to see what stories have recently been published.

The Country Connection
691 Pinecrest Road, Boulter, ON KOL 1G0
Phone: (613) 332-3651
E-mail: editor@pinecone.on.ca
Website: www.pinecone.on.ca
Contact: Gus Zylstra, publisher/managing editor
Circulation: 3,000
Published 2 times a year

Ontario's magazine for history, heritage, nostalgia, nature, environment, travel and the arts – a natural choice for country folk, and those that wish they were. *The Country Connection Magazine* is dedicated to showcasing art and culture, the preservation of heritage, and the nurturing of nature-friendly lifestyles. Publishes articles of 500 to 2,000 words. Pays on publication 10¢/word for electronic submissions. "Visit our writers' guidelines on the web for detailed requirements for upcoming issues."

The Country Register of Manitoba and Saskatchewan
702 First Street, Kipling, SK SOG 2S0
Phone: (306) 736-2441 Fax: (306) 736-8389
E-mail: countryregister@sasktel.net
Website: www.countryregister.com
Contact: Marj Kearns, co-publisher
Circulation: 23,000
Published bimonthly

Publishes stories up to 300 words on crafts, gifts, hobbies, and tourism. Cannot pay but welcomes submission inquiries. Guidelines available.

CSANews
180 Lesmill Road, Toronto, ON M3B 2T5
Phone: (416) 441-7000 Fax: (416) 441-7020
E-mail: csawriteus@snowbirds.org or csastaff@snowbirds.org
Website: www.snowbirds.org
Contact: Bob Slack, editor
Circulation: 75,000
Published quarterly

The publication of the Canadian Snowbird Association. Covers seniors' travel, government lobbying, financial and retirement issues, and insurance. Articles from 600 to 1,200 words. Fees vary depending on project and are paid on publication.

Downhome
43 James Lane, St. John's, NL AIE 3H3
Phone: (709) 726-5113, ext. 235 Fax: (709) 726-2135
E-mail: editorial@downhomelife.com
Website: www.downhomelife.com
Contact: Janice Stuckless, managing editor
Circulation: 40,000
Published monthly

Downhome's mandate is to share with the world the best of everything Atlantic Canada has to offer. "From the outdoors to the arts, from the people to their values, we celebrate the downhome lifestyle of Canada's East Coast." Articles from 1,200 to 1,600 words. Fees vary depending on the project and are paid on publication. "*Downhome* is the largest paid-circulation magazine in Atlantic Canada. We prefer queries to whole manuscripts. Please read the magazine before pitching." Guidelines available.

Durham Parent
130 Commercial Avenue, Ajax, ON LIS 2H5
Phone: (905) 426-4676, ext. 221 Fax: (905) 426-6598
E-mail: tmckee@durhamregion.com
Website: www.durhamparent.com
Contact: Tamara McKee, editor
Published monthly

Durham Parent publishes information on parenting, local events, and topics of interest to parents living in Durham Region.

Elevate
365 Bloor Street E., Suite 1902, Toronto, ON M4W 3L4
Phone: (416) 869-3131 Fax: (416) 869-3008
E-mail: info@elevatemagazine.com
Website: www.elevatemagazine.com
Contact: Chantel Simmons, publisher/editor-in-chief
Circulation: 35,000
Published 6 times a year

Elevate is Canada's leading anti-aging, wellness, and enhancement magazine. Accepts queries for all sections of the publication. Pays 50¢/word. "Please send a brief query including the topic you want to write about, a sample paragraph, proposed interviewees, and proposed word count."

Fab Magazine
511 Church Street, Suite 200, Toronto, ON M4Y 2C9
Phone: (416) 925-5221 Fax: (416) 925-4817
E-mail: editor@fabmagazine.com
Website: www.fabmagazine.com
Contact: Drew Rowsome, editor
Circulation: 31,000
Published 26 times a year

Culture and lifestyle get a fierce gay spin in *Fab*, Ontario's gay scene report. Articles 180 to 1,500 words. Pays on publication.

50Plus.com
c/o Zoomer Media, 550 Queen Street E., Suite 105, Toronto, ON M5A IV2
Phone: (416) 363-7063 Fax: (416) 363-7693
E-mail: info@50plus.com
Website: www.50plus.com
Contact: Bonnie Baker Cowan, editor

The official voice of Canada's Association for the 50-Plus and a leading magazine for the over-50s. Accepts a limited number of freelance articles each year. Pays 60¢/word on acceptance for articles of 500 to 2,000 words. "Send query and writing samples. Please don't phone." Guidelines available.

Fresh Juice
25 Sheppard Ave W., Suite 100, Toronto, ON M2N 6S7
Phone: (416) 733-7600
E-mail: feedback@freshjuice.ca
Website: www.freshjuice.ca

Multi-platform publication that offers "fun, healthy and easy-to-prepare recipes; expert health, fitness and nutrition tips as well as time-savvy ways to help balance fun, family, finance and more."

Going Natural / Au naturel

P.O. Box 81128, FGPO, Ancaster, ON L9G 4XI
Phone: (905) 304-4836 Fax: (416) 410-6833
E-mail: information@fcn.ca or editor@fcn.ca
Website: www.fcn.ca/GN.html
Contact: Paul Rapoport, editor
Circulation: 2,300
Published quarterly

Features information and news for anglophone and francophone naturists (nudists) in Canada, the rest of North America, and the world. Also useful for future naturists. "Aims for an acceptance of the entire human body, of all ages and shapes, without shame or penalty (in non-erotic contexts)." Articles should not exceed 1,100 words. Fees vary depending on project and are paid on publication. "Must be comfortable with at least the concept of non-sexualized nudity and preferably the practice as well!" Guidelines available.

Good Times

2001 University Street, Suite 900, Montreal, QC H3A 2A6
Phone: (514) 499-0491 Fax: (514) 499-3078
E-mail: editor@goodtimes.ca
Website: www.goodtimes.ca
Contact: Murray Lewis, editor-in-chief
Circulation: 150,000
Published 11 times a year

Addresses the concerns of retired Canadians and those planning retirement. Topics include financial and retirement planning; health, nutrition, and fitness; lifestyles; better living and well-being; relationships; celebrity profiles; and leisure activities. Welcomes inquiries that note areas of expertise and suggestions along with writing samples. Articles 1,200 to 2,000 words. Buys first rights and pays a negotiated rate per word. E-mail queries are best.

Inuktitut Magazine

75 Albert Street, Suite 1101, Ottawa, ON KIP 5E7
Phone: (613) 238-8181 or 1-866-262-8181 (general) or (613) 277-3178 (editor) Fax: (613) 234-1991
E-mail: hendrie@itk.ca

Website: www.itk.ca
Contact: Stephen Hendrie, managing editor/director of
  communications
Circulation: 13,000
Published twice a year
  Presents the heritage of Inuit culture, language, and society.
Inuktitut is distributed in Inuit communities in Labrador, Nunavik,
Nunavut, and the Northwest Territories. Stories are published in
Inuktitut, English, and French. All articles are assigned, so query
first. Stories are generally 1,500 words or less. Pays a minimum of
50¢/word for the length of story commissioned. Guidelines available.

Island Parent Magazine
830 Pembroke Street, Suite A-10, Victoria, BC V8T 1H9
Phone: (250) 388-6905 Fax: (250) 388-6920
E-mail: editor@islandparent.ca
Website: www.islandparent.ca
Contact: Sue Fast, editor
Circulation: 20,000
Published monthly
  A resource publication for Vancouver Island families. Regular
features include a calendar of events, new parents pages, parenting
advice, book reviews, a food column, arts and entertainment,
nature education, recreation, finance, and family fun. Articles 750
to 1,500 words. Pays $35/article on publication. Guidelines avail-
able at www.islandparent.ca/contribute.html. "Most of our submissions are from Vancouver Island residents."

Kerby News
1133 – 7 Avenue S.W., Calgary, AB T2P 1B2
Phone: (403) 705-3229 Fax: (403) 705-3211
E-mail: editor@kerbycentre.com
Website: www.kerbycentre.com
Contact: Barry Whitehead, editor
Circulation: 30,000
Published monthly
  A publication targeted at those 50 years of age and over who live
in southern Alberta. Covers financial planning, seniors' events,
local and federal news, and stories on healthy eating, fitness, and

travel. Accepts submissions from older writers. Articles 500 to 800 words. Cannot pay but welcomes submission inquiries.

Lethbridge living

1518 3rd Avenue S., Lethbridge, AB T1J 0K8
Phone: (403) 381-1454 Fax: (403) 380-3922
E-mail: editor@lethbridgeliving.com
Website: www.lethbridgeliving.com
Contacts: Tim Rempel, publisher/managing editor; Jenn S.
    Rempel, publisher/managing editor
Circulation: 17,000
Published bimonthly

Features articles that focus on people and the diversity of cultures an interests in Lethbridge and the surrounding area. Pays 23¢/word on publication for articles of 500 to 3,000 words. "Writing samples are required. Preference is given to writers from our distribution area." Guidelines available.

Montreal Families

5764 Monkland Avenue, Suite 118, Montreal, QC H4A 1E9
Phone: (514) 487-8881 Fax: (514) 487-4420
E-mail: editorial@montrealfamilies.ca
Contact: Kelly Wilton, editor
Circulation: 30,000
Published monthly

A free, pickup parenting magazine. In every issue: Pediatrician Column, Book Reviews, Education Column, and Calendar of Activities. Special sections: Camps, Birthday Parties, Education, Pregnancy/Baby, and Program Guide. Fees are negotiated and paid on publication for stories of 500 to 750 words.

Natural Life

B2-125 The Queensway, Suite 52, Toronto, ON M8Y 1H6
E-mail: editor@naturallifemagazine.com
Website: www.naturallifemagazine.com
Contact: Wendy Priesnitz, editor
Circulation: 30,000
Published bimonthly

Provides information and inspiration about natural family living, including articles on natural parenting, healthy homes, organic gardening, unschooling, and renewable energy. Articles 2,000 to 3,000 words. Cannot pay but welcomes submission inquiries. "Please read the magazine first. Prefer queries by e-mail, not complete articles. Lots of back issues on website." Guidelines available on website.

North of 50°

Box 100 – 2516 Patterson Avenue, Armstrong, BC VOE IBO
Phone: (250) 546-6064 or 1-877-667-8450 Fax: (250) 546-8914
E-mail: editor@northof50.com
Website: www.northof50.com
Contact: TJ Wallis, managing editor
Circulation: 14,000
Published bimonthly

Based in the B.C. interior and "carries socially relevant and responsible, original regional content," focused on history, lifestyle, regional personalities and the arts. Welcomes unsolicited articles and queries. Pays $20 for profiles and short essays of less than 1,000 words; $50 for feature stories and photo essays of 1,000 to 1,500 words; and $100 for research-based articles and investigative reportage. All contributors receive a 1-year subscription. Guidelines on website.

Okanagan Life Magazine

1753 Dolphin Avenue, Suite 10, Kelowna, BC VIY 8A6
Phone: (250) 861-5399 or 1-888-311-1119 Fax: (250) 868-3040
E-mail: editorial@okanaganlife.com
Website: www.okanaganlife.com
Contact: Laurie Carter, senior editor
Circulation: 18,000
Published 10 times a year

A regional magazine featuring articles for on local people, issues, and lifestyle. Pays 20¢ to 25¢/published word within 30 days of publication for articles of 750 to 2,000 words. Query first by e-mail. Guidelines available on website.

ParentsCanada

65 The East Mall, Toronto, ON M8Z 5W3
Phone: (416) 537-2604, ext. 349
E-mail: janiceb@parentscanada.com
Website: www.parentscanada.com
Contact: Janice Biehn, editor
Circulation: 120,000
Published 8 times a year

Launched in 2007, *ParentsCanada* is now the general interest flagship publication of the ParentsCanada group of magazines (see below for subsidiary publications). Articles keep "the 'shoulds' to a minimum while delivering solid stories on well-being, learning, relationships, fashion, food and [children's] development." Articles 1,000 to 2,000 words. Rates vary and are paid on acceptance.

ParentsCanada Group of pre-natal & post-natal magazines: Best Wishes; Expecting; Labour and Birth Guide; Baby and Child Care Encyclopedia; and Me & Mom

65 The East Mall, Toronto, ON M8Z 5W3
Phone: (416) 537-2604, ext. 238
E-mail: amyb@parentscanada.com
Website: www.parentscanada.com
Contact: Amy Bielby, editor

ParentsCanada's Best Wishes (circulation: 140,000; est. 1948; published twice a year) is distributed through hospitals, health clinics, and doctors' offices. Articles cover topics relevant to parenting a baby from birth to 6 months of age and are written by Canadian healthcare professionals.

Expecting (circulation: 140,000) is distributed to expectant parents in doctors' offices and prenatal classes. All articles must be written by Canadian healthcare professionals and deal with topics relevant to pregnancy.

ParentsCanada's *Labour and Birth Guide* (circulation: 140,000), *Baby and Child Care Encyclopedia* (circulation: 101,000), and *Me & Mom* (circulation: 100,000) are published annually and distributed through hospitals, health clinics, and doctors' offices. *Me & Mom* is directed at parents of children aged 6 to 30 months.

Articles for all publications are 500 to 1,000 words. Rates vary and are paid on acceptance.

Real Weddings
4180 Lougheed Highway, 4th Floor, Burnaby, BC V5C 6A7
Phone: (604) 299-7311 Fax: (604) 299-9188
E-mail: kmah@canadawide.com
Website: www.realweddings.ca or www.canadawide.com
Contact: Kim Mah, editor
Circulation: 15,000
Published twice a year
   A B.C.-based bridal magazine featuring real local weddings, plus fashion, beauty, wedding planning and travel stories. Pays 35¢/word on publication for stories of 800 to 1,200 words.

Saltscapes
Suite 209, 30 Damascus Road, Bedford, NS B4A OCI
Phone: (902) 464-7258 Fax: (902) 464-5755
E-mail: jgourlay@saltscapes.com
Website: www.saltscapes.com
Contact: Jim Gourlay, editor-in-chief
Circulation: 43,000
Published 7 times a year
   Focuses on the people and places of Atlantic Canada. Feature articles 1,200 to 1,800 words. Rates vary according to project and are paid on publication. Guidelines available on website.

Senior Living
1581-H Hillside Avenue, Suite 153, Victoria, BC V8T 2CI
Phone: (250) 479-4705 Fax: (250) 479-4808
E-mail: editor@seniorlivingmag.com
Website: www.seniorlivingmag.com
Contact: Bobbie Jo Reid, editor
Circulation: 40,000
Published monthly
   The focus of these two publications is the 50-plus demographic. Features profiles of seniors and seniors' groups that are inspirational and very community oriented. Articles from 750 to 1,200 words and must be about people or groups in the published area. Pays $30 to $75 on publication. Also publishes articles on health, travel, housing, planned giving, fashion, and beauty. Guidelines available on website.

Sposa

99 Harbour Square, Suite 3111, Toronto, ON M5J 2H2
Phone: (416) 364-5899
E-mail: jobs@sposa.com
Website: www.sposa.com
Circulation: 50,000
Print edition is published twice a year; also has online edition

The world's first reality-based wedding magazine, featuring witty, provocative articles about love and marriage from a global perspective. "Wit and humour much appreciated. Bloggers welcome." Articles 800 to 1,000 words; web content may be shorter. Fees vary and are paid on acceptance. Guidelines available.

TCHAD Magazine

219 Dufferin Street, Suite 211B, Toronto, ON M6K 3T1
Phone: (905) 267-1040
E-mail: editorial@tchadmag.com
Website: www.tchadmag.com
Contact: Kim Mercer, senior writing editor
Circulation: 40,000
Published quarterly

An informative guide for those living the metropolitan lifestyle. Includes interesting articles, savvy columns, and rich photography. Pays $100 or more on acceptance for articles of 750 to 1,000 words. "Our main focus is how our male and female readers can maintain a metropolitan lifestyle and keep informed."

Today's Parent

1 Mount Pleasant Road, 8th Floor, Toronto, ON M4Y 2Y5
Phone: (416) 764-2883
E-mail: editors@todaysparent.com
Website: www.todaysparent.com
Contact: Nadine Silverthorne, managing editor
Circulation: 152,500
Published monthly

A national parenting magazine for moms and dads of children from birth to 14. "Articles tackle the complete range of parenting issues, including health, education and behaviour." Query in advance with samples of Word length and fees vary depending on the complexity of the story, usually 500 to 2,500 words and $1/word (less for personal stories). Pays on acceptance. Guidelines available.

UrbanBaby & Toddler Magazine
928 W. 20th Avenue, Vancouver, BC V5Z 1Y5
Phone: (604) 420-8760 Fax: (604) 608-9680
E-mail: info@urbanbaby.ca
Website: www.urbanbaby.ca
Contact: Emma Lee, editor
Circulation: 40,000
Published quarterly

A publication targeted at expectant parents and parents with children under 5 years. Articles from 800 to 1,400 words. Fees vary and are paid on publication. Guidelines available.

Urban Male Magazine (UMM)
131 Bank Street, Suite 300, Ottawa, ON K1P 5N7
Phone: (613) 723-6216 Fax: (613) 723-1702
E-mail: editor@umm.ca
Website: www.umm.ca
Contact: Nash Gangji, director of operations
Circulation: 100,000
Published quarterly

UMM covers any issues of interest to Canadian men, including sports, health, travel, adventure, cars, fashion, fitness, DIY, beautiful women, humour, social and political issues, and especially any ideas focusing on Canadian people, issues, or icons. Features are generally 2,000 to 3,000 words; interviews usually about 1,300 words. Accepts smaller miscellaneous pieces for the front of the magazine. Pays 20¢/word, payable 45 days after publication. "Originality in focus and style are key to catching our attention, as is a query that has had thought and care put into it. *UMM* welcomes submissions from freelancers who specialize in the topic of the article they are submitting."

Send queries to the director of operations by mail or preferably e-mail, with an outline of the proposed article and a sample paragraph. Include any relevant credentials and writing samples.

WeddingBells

111 Queen Street E., Suite 320, Toronto, ON M5C 1S2
Phone: (416) 364-3333 Fax: (416) 594-3374
E-mail: editorial@weddingbells.ca
Website: www.weddingbells.ca
Contact: Alison McGill, editor-in-chief
Circulation: 95,000
Published twice a year

Provides inspiration and planning tools for Canadian brides-to-be. "Currently all editorial is handled in-house by staff."

Wedding Essentials

50 Nashoeme Road, Suite 104, Toronto, ON M1V 5J2
Phone: (416) 498-4996 Fax: (416) 498-5997
E-mail: mail@weddingessentials.ca
Website: www.weddingessentials.ca
Contact: Brandon Jones, editorial director
Circulation: 15,000
Published twice a year

For newly engaged couples in Greater Toronto and surrounding areas who want a formal wedding and a great honeymoon. Pays 35¢/word on publication for articles from 900 to 1,500 words.

Weddings & Honeymoons; Romance Travel; Wines for Weddings; Wedding Gifts; The Newlyweds; GROOM

65 Helena Avenue, Toronto, ON M6G 2H3
Phone: (416) 653-4986 Fax: (416) 653-2291
E-mail: barwed@rogers.com
Website: www.weddingshoneymoons.com
Contact: Joyce Barslow, editor-in-chief
Website receives over 3 million hits annually
Published quarterly online

Weddings & Honeymoons (*W&H*) online publications helps brides-to-be to plan and budget their weddings: fashion and accessories, beauty, ceremonies, receptions, menus and cakes, flowers, photography, gifts, etc. *Romance Travel* features romantic places for proposals, destination weddings, honeymoons, and new travel products and services. *Wines for Weddings* features wines, spirits, food, menus, cakes, desserts, décor, and winery weddings.

Wedding Gifts features ideas for engagement and wedding gifts to and from the couple. *The Newlyweds* features information regarding homes, finance, and other practical, everyday concerns. *GROOM*, Canada's only magazine for grooms-to-be, covers engagement rings, fashion and accessories, his wedding party, grooming, and more.

Tips, trends, how-tos, and articles range from 50 to 500 words. Articles and photos are considered for credits. Pays a negotiated rate of $50 to $150. "Please e-mail submissions. Save the paper and stamps."

WellnessOptions

P.O. Box 160, Stn. D, Scarborough, ON M1R 5B5
Phone: (416) 502-9600 Fax: (416) 502-0699
E-mail: editorial@wellnessoptions.ca
Website: www.wellnessoptions.ca
Contact: Lillian Chan, editor
Circulation: 30,000
Published bimonthly

With full scientific references, *WellnessOptions* explains health conditions and treatment options from multiple disciplines and perspectives. It is an independent Canadian health magazine. Regular topics include: science and nutrition, exercise and sport wellness.

Westcoast Families

1215C – 56 Street, Box 18057, Delta, BC V4L 2M4
Phone: (604) 249-2866 Fax: (604) 676-2802
E-mail: editor@westcoastfamilies.com
Website: www.westcoastfamilies.com
Contact: Andrea Vance, managing editor
Circulation: 50,000
Published 9 times a year

A magazine geared to parents of children and teens. An information source and guide to fun for families in the Vancouver area. Articles 650 to 850 words. Rates vary according to project and are paid on publication. "All submissions must be relevant to Canadians; local content preferred. No phone calls, please." Guidelines available.

Western Living

2608 Granville Street, Suite 560, Vancouver, BC V6H 3V3

Phone: (604) 877-7732 Fax: (604) 877-4848

E-mail: wlmail@westernlivingmagazine.com

Website: www.westernlivingmagazine.com

Contact: Anicka Quin, executive editor

Circulation: 165,000

Published 10 times a year

A general interest and lifestyle magazine with a special emphasis on the home. The largest regional magazine in Canada. Regular features cover personalities and trends, regional and international travel, food and recipes, and homes and design, all with a Western Canadian focus. Article lengths and pay rates vary; contact by phone or e-mail with queries or to pitch a story.

What's UP – Canada's Family Magazine

3145 Wolfedale Road, Mississauga, ON L5C 3A9

Phone: (905) 273-8183 Fax: (905) 892-6212

E-mail: editor@whatsupfamily.ca

Website: www.whatsupfamilies.com

Contact: Erin Ruddy, editor-in-chief

Circulation: 100,000

Published bimonthly

Focuses on issues relating to families, including discipline, diet, and health. No fiction or poetry. Articles 800 to 1,800 words. Payment made on publication; fees vary depending on length. Query first; length of article will be assigned by editor. Guidelines available.

Xtra!

2 Carlton Street, Suite 1600, Toronto, ON M5B IJ3

Phone: (416) 925-6665 Fax: (416) 925-6674

E-mail: danny.glenwright@xtra.ca or editor.vancouver@xtra.ca

Website: www.xtra.ca

Contacts: Danny Glenwright, assignment editor (*Xtra!* and
    Capital Xtra!) or Robin Perelle, managing editor (*Xtra! West*)

Circulation: 45,000 (*Xtra!*), 20,000 (*Capital Xtra!*), 30,000 (*Xtra! West*)

Xtra! and *Xtra! West* are published biweekly; *Capital Xtra!* is published monthly.

Gay and lesbian periodical with news, analysis, op-ed pieces, and stories on arts and entertainment. Editions published in Toronto, Ottawa, and Vancouver. Articles 400 to 800 words. Pays about 21¢/word on publication. Queries and story pitches welcome. Guidelines available. For mailing addresses, telephone numbers, and other contact details, see website.

Zoomer Magazine

30 Jefferson Avenue, Toronto, ON M6K 1Y4
Phone: (416) 363-2277 or 1-800-363-9736 Fax: (416) 363-7693
E-mail: comment@zoomermag.com
Website: www.zoomermag.com
Contact: Suzanne Boyd, editor-in-chief
Circulation: 175,000
Published 9 times a year

Target market is Canadians aged 45-plus. "A Zoomer is a baby boomer with zip." Departments include Home, Health, Money, People, Sex, Style, Travel, Reinvention, and Entertainment.

News, Opinions, & Issues

Adbusters Magazine

1243 W. 7th Avenue, Vancouver, BC V6H 1B7
Phone: (604) 736-9401 Fax: (604) 737-6021
E-mail: editor@adbusters.org
Website: www.adbusters.org
Contact: Kalle Lasn, editor
Circulation: 120,000
Published bimonthly

Established 1989. A combative, uncompromising commentator on the politics of media control and environmental strategy. "We relish all truly political materials, whether they be scholarly probes into the decline of civilization, environmental forays into the forests, sci-fi carpet rides into cyberspace or humorous spoofs about commercial culture. More than anything, we seek compelling ideas that further the critical perspective and offer activist solutions." Pay rates vary for 100 to 1,500 words. Contact editor first if planning a lengthy submission. Guidelines available on website.

The Advocate
1529 W. 6th Avenue, Suite 103, Vancouver, BC V6J IRI
Phone: (604) 737-8274 Fax: (604) 737-8214
E-mail: charvey@maclaw.bc.ca
Website: www.the-advocate.ca
Contact: Christopher Harvey, editor
Circulation: 11,000
Published bimonthly

Published by the Vancouver Bar Association, *The Advocate* carries substantive, procedural, and other articles on legal subjects of interest to the legal profession and the judiciary, mainly in B.C. Articles are 2,000 to 10,000 words. Contributors are rarely paid.

Alberta Sweetgrass
13245 – 146th Street, Edmonton, AB T5L 4S8
Phone: (780) 455-2700 or 1-800-661-5469 Fax: (780) 455-7639
E-mail: sweetgrass@ammsa.com
Website: www.ammsa.com
Contact: Shari Narine, editor
Circulation: 8,500
Published monthly

A community newspaper highlighting Aboriginal issues, programs, people, arts, culture, and advances in Alberta. Pays $3.40 to $4.15/column inch on publication for stories of 500 to 800 words (rate depends on sources, editing, photos, etc.). Query first. Not interested in poetry or fiction. Guidelines available on website.

Anglican Journal
80 Hayden Street, Toronto, ON M4Y 3G2
Phone: (416) 924-9192, ext. 307 Fax: (416) 921-4452
E-mail: editor@national.anglican.ca
Website: www.anglicanjournal.com
Contact: Kristin Jenkins, editor
Circulation: 160,000
Published 10 times a year

Independently edited national publication (print and online) of the Anglican Church of Canada, established in 1875. Contains news and features from across Canada and abroad. Subjects include news of all denominations and faiths, and articles on a range of social and ethical issues. Stories should be of interest to a national audience. Length 600 to maximum of 1,200 words. Pays a base rate of 25¢/published word on publication. Initial inquiry strongly recommended.

bout de papier
47 Clarence Street, Suite 412, Ottawa, ON KIN 9KI
Phone: (613) 241-1391 Fax: (613) 241-5911
E-mail: boutdepapier@pafso.com
Website: www.pafso.com
Contact: Debra Hulley, managing editor
Circulation: 2,500
Published quarterly

Examines all aspects of Canadian foreign policy and life in the foreign service. Provides a unique first-hand insight into the conduct and evolution of Canadian diplomacy. Articles are published in the language of submission. Features articles, interviews, book reviews, and commentaries from 1,000 to 2,800 words. Contributors are not paid. Welcomes submission inquiries from qualified writers.

Briarpatch
2138 McIntyre Street, Regina, SK S4P 2R7
Phone: (306) 525-2949
E-mail: editor@briarpatchmagazine.com
Website: www.briarpatchmagazine.com
Contacts: Valerie Zink and Rebecca Granovsky-Larsen, co-editors
   and publishers
Circulation: 1,500
Published 6 times a year

"On the cutting edge of Canada's alternative media movement, *Briarpatch* offers readers access to under-reported news, critical perspectives on current events, and thoughtful analysis of pressing social issues. We focus on struggles to preserve our environment, to achieve equality and social justice, and to challenge systemic oppression." Carries articles of 600 to 2,500 words, and also short reviews. Pays between $50 and $150; submission inquiries are welcome.

Canadian Dimension

91 Albert Street, Suite 2E, Winnipeg, MB R3B IG5
Phone: (204) 957-1519 Fax: (204) 943-4617
E-mail: editor@canadiandimension.com
Website: www.canadiandimension.com
Contact: James Patterson, associate publisher
Circulation: 3,000
Published bimonthly

Established 1963. Publishes fact and analysis that bring Canada and the world into focus. Carries alternative information on issues concerning women, the labour movement, peace politics, Aboriginal peoples, the environment, economics, and popular culture. "*CD* is a magazine for people who want to change the world. We debate issues, share ideas, recount our victories, and evaluate our strategies for social change." Articles 600 to 2,000 words. Fees are negotiated and paid on publication. Send written query of no more than one page. Guidelines available on website.

Canadian Lawyer, Canadian Lawyer 4 Students, Canadian Lawyer InHouse

240 Edward Street, Aurora, ON L4G 3S9
Phone: (905) 841-6480 Fax: (905) 727-0017
E-mail: gail.cohen@thomsonreuters.com or
    jen.brown@thomsonreuters.com (for *Canadian Lawyer InHouse)*
Website: www.canadianlawyermag.com
Contact: Gail J. Cohen, editorial director, or Jennifer Brown,
    editor of *Canadian Lawyer InHouse*
Circulation: varies (see details below)
Publication schedule varies (see details below), however all magazines publish weekly online

Canadian Lawyer (circulation: 27,500; published in print 11 times a year) is the magazine legal practising lawyers, judges, and corporate counsel from coast to coast turn to for news, trends, and issues that shape the profession.

Canadian Lawyer 4 Students (circulation: 7,500; published in print 2 times a year) is distributed through the dean's office at 22 schools across Canada. "Topics include tips on finding summer jobs and articling positions, insider advice from the experts on résumés, interview techniques, networking, and much more."

Canadian Lawyer InHouse (circulation: 10,000; published in print 6 times a year) is distributed as a supplement to *Canadian Lawyer* and is sent to corporate counsel, presidents, CFOs, and CEOs of large organizations across Canada.

Legal Feeds is a daily online blog of Canadian legal news.

Fees vary depending on project and are paid on acceptance. Guidelines available.

Canadian Teacher Magazine

1773 El Verano Drive, Gabriola, BC VOR 1x6
Phone: (250) 247-9093 Fax: (250) 247-9083
E-mail: dmumford@canadianteachermagazine.com
Website: www.canadianteachermagazine.com
Contact: Diana Mumford, editor
Published 5 times a year

Articles on teaching, instruction, methodology, and current trends in education; reviews of books for use in school libraries or classrooms; articles on lifestyle, travel, and retirement issues relating to teachers as a demographic. Articles 1,000 to 1,500 words. Not currently paying for submissions. Guidelines available on website.

Catholic Insight

P.O. Box 625, Adelaide Stn., Toronto, ON M5C 2J8
Phone: (416) 204-9601 Fax: (416) 204-1027
E-mail: reach@catholicinsight.com
Website: www.catholicinsight.com
Contact: Alphonse de Valk, editor
Circulation: 3,500
Published 11 times a year

A journal of news and opinion on matters of religion, politics, society, and culture pertinent to Canada and the Catholic Church. "Most articles are pre-arranged for subject matter. Occasionally we accept an unsolicited freelance article." Length 740 to 1,400 words. Pays on publication from $150 to $350 for features, $130 to $170 for columns, and $75 for book reviews. Payment for interviews is negotiated.

The Columbia Journal
P.O. Box 2633, MPO, Vancouver, BC V6B 3W8
Phone: (604) 266-6552 Fax: (604) 267-3342
E-mail: editor@columbiajournal.ca
Website: www.columbiajournal.ca
Contact: Jim Lipkovits, publisher
Circulation: 20,000
Published bimonthly

The Columbia Journal is a positive, progressive alternative to the conservative corporate press in B.C. Dedicated to inform, entertain, and advocate for the people of B.C. Encourages written contributions covering public issues. Seeks comment from social activist groups, labour unions, and environmental and religious organizations. Stories should be supportive of progressive actions and policies. Covers issues related to the environment, the economy, labour, human rights, social issues, human interest, the government, and B.C. politics.

Concordia University Magazine
1455 de Maisonneuve Boulevard W., FB 520, Montreal, QC
   H3G IM8
Phone: 514-848-2424, ext. 3826 Fax: 514-848-4510
E-mail: howard.bokser@concordia.ca
Website: http://magazine.concordia.ca
Contact: Howard Bokser, editor
Circulation: 115,000
Published quarterly

The alumni magazine of Concordia University. It covers stories about Concordia alumni, the university, and education in Canada. Length 1,000 to 2,000 words. Pays $750 per feature on acceptance.

Education Canada
317 Adelaide Street W., Suite 300, Toronto, ON M5V IP9
Phone: (416) 591-6300 Fax: (416) 591-5345
E-mail: glatour@cea-ace.ca
Website: www.cea-ace.ca
Contact: Gilles Latour, business/circulation manager
Circulation: 4,000
Published 5 times a year

Canada's premier award-winning publication for informed dialogue on education. Each issue provides readers with articles of educational significance that are readable, credible, and thought-provoking. The content is varied, with features and regular articles, columns, commentary, research reviews, case studies, and letters. Cannot pay but welcomes inquiries. "Visit our website for more details." Guidelines available.

Education Forum

c/o OSSTF, 60 Mobile Drive, Toronto, ON M4A 2P3
Phone: (416) 751-8300 or 1-800-267-7867 Fax: (416) 751-3875
E-mail: allanr@osstf.on.ca
Website: www.osstf.on.ca/educationforum
Contact: Ronda Allan, editor
Circulation: 60,000
Published 3 times a year

A publication dealing with issues of education. Features range from 1,800 to 2,000 words. Cannot pay but welcomes submission inquiries.

Education Today

439 University Avenue, 18th Floor, Toronto, ON M5G 1Y8
Phone: (416) 340-2540 Fax: (416) 340-7571
E-mail: et@opsba.org
Website: www.opsba.org
Contact: Catherine Watson, editor
Circulation: 3,500
Published 3 times a year

Delivers informed commentary on Ontario's public education system. Areas covered include governance, law, and the voice of students. Articles 500 to 1,500 words. Rates vary with project and are paid on acceptance. "Interested writers should submit a query to the editor. Editorial decisions are made by the editorial board." Guidelines available.

Faith Today

M.I.P. Box 3745, Markham, ON L3R 0Y4
Phone: (905) 479-5885 Fax: (905) 479-4742
E-mail: editor@faithtoday.ca

Website: www.faithtoday.ca
Contact: Gail Reid, managing editor
Circulation: 18,000
Published bimonthly

A general-interest magazine of feature articles for Canadian evangelicals across all Protestant church traditions. Includes how-to features and profiles of Canadian individuals and ministries. Query first; does not accept unsolicited manuscripts. Features 800 to 1,750 words. Pays on acceptance 25¢/word for features, 15¢/word for essays. Guidelines available on website.

Geez Magazine

400 Edmonton Street, Winnipeg, MB R3B 2M2
Phone: (204) 942-1058
E-mail: editor@geezmagazine.org
Website: www.geezmagazine.org
Contact: Melanie Dennis Unrau, editor
Circulation: 3,000
Published quarterly

Geez offers readers a lively dose of "holy mischief in an age of fast faith." Aimed at those on the fringes of faith, this ad-free magazine explores the religious and spiritual dimension of the big issues of our day. Articles 400 to 2,000 words. Pays $25 to $150 on publication. Guidelines available online.

Humanist Perspectives

P.O. Box 3769, Stn. C, Ottawa, ON K1Y 4J8
Phone: (613) 749-9355 Fax: (613) 749-8929
E-mail: editor@humanistperspectives.org
Website: www.humanistperspectives.org
Contact: Carl Dow, editor
Circulation: 2,500
Published quarterly

Formerly *Humanist in Canada*. Explores contemporary topics from a humanistic viewpoint, reflecting the principle that human problems can be solved rationally without relying on belief in the supernatural. For non-believers with an interest in social issues. Basic payment of $25/page. Guidelines available on website. "A good opportunity for writers with alternative, divergent, or thought-provoking views."

Also features the "Voice of a Poet" in each issue. Poets are invited to send samples of their work to Henry Beissel at poetry@humanist perspectives.org. Inclusion is by invitation only.

JUST

20 Toronto Street, Suite 300, Toronto, ON M5C 2B8
Phone: (416) 869-1047, ext. 357 Fax: (416) 869-1390
E-mail: cbrennan@oba.org
Website: www.justmag.ca
Contact: Catherine Brennan, editor
Circulation: 18,000
Published six times a year

"For people with a calling." This recently launched publication of the Ontario Bar Association is distributed to lawyers, judges and law students across Ontario. Also available in a tablet edition.

Law Times

240 Edward Street, Aurora, ON L4G 3S9
Phone: (905) 841-6481 Fax: (905) 727-0017
E-mail: gdrummie@clbmedia.ca or lawtimes@clbmedia.ca
Website: www.lawtimesnews.com
Contact: Gretchen Drummie, editor
Circulation: 12,000
Published 40 times a year

Serves the Ontario legal market. Readership includes lawyers, judges, and law clerks. "If you have story ideas that would be relevant to *Law Times* readers, please feel free to send pitches to us by e-mail." Articles 800 to 1,200 words. Pays $175 to $275/article on publication. "We are always interested in pitches for news and features about or of interest to the legal community in Ontario."

Legion Magazine

86 Aird Place, Kanata, ON K2L OAI
Phone: (613) 591-0116 Fax: (613) 591-0146
E-mail: magazine@legion.ca
Website: www.legionmagazine.com
Contact: Dan Black, editor
Circulation: 274,000
Published bimonthly

A magazine for Canada's war veterans, RCMP members, forces personnel and their families, seniors, and the wider public. Carries news, views, and serious articles exploring Canada's military history, defence, veterans' affairs, health, and pensions. Offers humour and opinion columns, and also buys memoirs and nostalgia. "Average article length is between 1,500 and 2,200 words, although stories as short as 600 and as long as 3,000 words are accepted on occasion. The magazine does not accept fiction, poetry, travel writing or simultaneous transmissions." Payment ranges from $150 to $1,200. Writers whose material is reposted on the website receive 10% of the manuscript fee. "Please familiarize yourself with magazine and send an SASE with submission. Allow several months for response."

Living Light News

5306 – 89th Street, Suite 200, Edmonton, AB T6E 5P9
Phone: 1-800-932-0555, ext. 27 Fax: (780) 468-6872
E-mail: shine@livinglightnews.com
Website: www.livinglightnews.com
Contact: Jeff Caporale, editor
Circulation: 55,000 (Edmonton); 25,000 (Saskatchewan)
Published 6 times a year

A tabloid-sized evangelical newspaper with positive, contemporary, family-oriented appeal for Christians and spiritual seekers. Send query first. Features and profiles up to 1,000 words; local news stories that glorify God 650 words. Pays 10¢/word on publication for first rights, 5¢/word for reprint rights. Also pays for photos. "We are looking for writers who are evangelical Christians desiring to serve God through their writing. Our preference is on positive news that glorifies God or feature articles about well-known Christian celebrities and family-oriented subject matter." Guidelines available.

Maclean's

1 Mount Pleasant Road, 11th Floor, Toronto, ON M4Y 2Y5
Phone: (416) 764-1339 Fax: (416) 764-1332
E-mail: letters@macleans.ca
Website: www.macleans.ca
Contact: Mark Stevenson, editor
Circulation: 3,100,000
Published weekly

Canada's most widely read news magazine. Examines news events, trends, and issues from a Canadian perspective. Has correspondents in 5 Canadian cities and a network of writers around the world. Staff writers and freelancers contribute to weekly sections on politics, business, entertainment, sports, leisure, education, health, science, personal finance, justice, and technology. Pays a variable but competitive fee on publication.

National

865 Carling Avenue, Suite 500, Ottawa, ON KIS 5S8
Phone: (613) 237-2925, ext. 149 or 1-800-267-8860 Fax: (613) 237-0185
E-mail: national@cba.org or jordanf@cba.org
Website: www.cba.org/national
Contact: Jordan Furlong, editor-in-chief
Published 8 times a year

The member magazine of the Canadian Bar Association, *National* tracks trends and developments in the practice of law in Canada. Pays 75¢/word on acceptance for articles from 500 to 2,000 words.

New Internationalist

2446 Bank Street, Suite 653, Ottawa, ON KIV IA8
Phone: (613)826-1319
E-mail: nican@newint.org
Website: www.newint.org
Contact: Ian McKelvie, North American publisher
Circulation: 50,000
Published 10 times a year

An international periodical focusing on global issues such as health, environment, trade, aid, and poverty from a social justice perspective. Subscribers are aware, socially conscious, and liberal. Articles 250 to 1,500 words. Pays 35¢/word on publication.

New Socialist Webzine

719 Bloor Street W., Suite 304, Toronto, ON M6G IL5
E-mail: magazine@newsocialist.org or website@newsocialist.org
Website: www.newsocialist.org
Contact: editorial committee
Published online

A new left publication that aims to make changes by helping to build unions and support social movements. Publishes articles and interviews about developments in Canada and elsewhere, strategies for social change, and debates on the left by activists and writers. Unable to pay contributors.

Northword Magazine
P.O. Box 817, 3864 2nd Avenue, Suite 2, Smithers, BC V0J 2N0
Phone: (250) 847-4600 or 1-866-632-7688 Fax: (250) 847-4668
E-mail: joanne@northword.ca
Website: http://northword.ca
Contact: Joanne Campbell, publisher
Circulation: 10,000
Published bimonthly

Northword "aims to put in print the wide range of voices, views, and opinions of people who have a connection with the top half of B.C." First send a story query, not a finished article. Rates vary and are paid within 30 days of receiving invoice.

Our Times
P.O. Box 182, New Glasgow, NS B2H 5E2
Phone: (902) 755-6840 Fax: (902) 755-1292
E-mail: editor@ourtimes.ca
Website: www.ourtimes.ca
Contact: Lorraine Endicott, managing editor
Circulation: 3,000
Published bimonthly

Published by a not-for-profit organization to promote workers' rights, unionization, and social justice. Many articles are contributed by union activists. Query first. Features are 1,500 to 3,000 words; opinions 850 words; notes and reviews 600 to 1,000 words. Pays between $100 and $300, usually on publication; $25 for small items. Guidelines available on website. "The best way to reach the editor is by e-mail, with a story pitch."

Outlook Magazine
6184 Ash Street, Vancouver, BC V5Z 3G9
Phone: (604) 324-5101
E-mail: cjoutlook@telus.net

Website: www.vcn.bc.ca/outlook
Contact: Carl Rosenberg, editor
Published bimonthly

An independent, secular Jewish publication with a socialist-humanist perspective. Contact the editor before completing an article. Articles 1,000 to 1,500 words.

Peace Magazine

P.O. Box 248, Stn. P, Toronto, ON M5S 2S7
Phone: (416) 588-8748
E-mail: mspencer@web.net
Website: www.peacemagazine.org
Contact: Metta Spencer, editor-in-chief
Published quarterly

Welcomes submissions relating to peace, disarmament, weapons of mass destruction, conflict resolution, and political and military affairs in hot spots around the world. Articles 400 to 3,000 words. "We prefer that submissions be received by e-mail in text-only format rather than as an attachment and that suitable photographs with credits and captions be provided." Cannot pay. Guidelines available on website.

Policy Options

1470 Peel Street, Suite 200, Montreal, QC H3A 1T1
Phone: (514) 985-2461, ext. 314 Fax: (514) 985-2559
E-mail: imacdonald@irpp.org
Website: www.irpp.org/po
Contact: L. Ian MacDonald, editor
Circulation: 3,000
Published 10 times a year

A bilingual magazine published by the Institute for Research on Public Policy, a national, independent, not-for-profit think tank. Carries analyses of public policy so as to encourage wide debate on major policy issues. Articles 1,500 to 4,000 words. Contributors are unpaid, but submission inquiries by qualified writers are welcome.

Queen's Alumni Review
Office of Marketing and Communications, Stewart-Pollock Wing,
    Fleming Hall, Room 307, Queen's University, Kingston, ON
    K7L 3N6
Phone: (613) 533-6000, ext. 74125 Fax: (613) 533-6828
E-mail: review@queensu.ca
Website: www.alumnireview.queensu.ca
Contact: Ken Cuthbertson, editor
Circulation: 106,000
Published quarterly

Publishes news about and of interest to Queen's alumni, faculty, and friends of the university. Articles 250 to 2,500 words. Rates vary depending on project and are paid on acceptance. "We buy a limited amount of freelance material, but we are always in the market for well-written, timely articles. Would-be freelancers should study past issues before querying us." Guidelines available.

rabble.ca
E-mail: editor@rabble.ca
Website: www.rabble.ca
Contact: Derrick O'Keefe, editor
250,000 unique monthly visitors

Non-profit online magazine featuring "new and emerging progressive voices in Canada." Query with sample and bio first. Assigned stories range from 600 to 1,000 words. Guidelines on website.

Ryerson University Alumni
350 Victoria Street, Toronto, ON M5B 2K3
Phone: (416) 979-5000, ext. 7000 Fax: (416) 979-5166
E-mail: ryemag@ryerson.ca
Website: www.ryerson.ca/alumni/magazine
Contact: Colleen Mellor, editor
Circulation: 95,000
Published twice a year (January and June)

Published for alumni and friends of Ryerson by the Office of University Advancement. Articles 600 to 1,200 words. Pays 50¢/word on acceptance.

Saskatchewan Sage

13245 – 146 Street, Edmonton, AB T5L 4S8
Phone: (780) 455-2700 Fax: (780) 455-7639
E-mail: sage@ammsa.com
Website: www.ammsa.com
Contact: Christine Fiddler, editor
Circulation: 8,500
Published monthly

A community newspaper featuring news, arts and entertainment, reviews, and feature articles about and by Aboriginal people of Saskatchewan. No poetry or fiction. Pitch idea first. Most stories 500 to 800 words. Pays $3.40 to $4.15/column inch on publication. "Stories must be of provincial interest. Always query first, preferably by phone or e-mail." Guidelines available on website.

Teach Magazine

87 Barford Road, Toronto, ON M9W 4H8
Phone: (416) 537-2103 Fax: (416) 537-3491
E-mail: info@teachmag.com
Website: www.teachmag.com
Contact: Wili Liberman, publisher
Circulation: 22,000
Published 5 times a year (2 electronic issues, 3 printed issues)

Explores pragmatic issues and ideas for educators of grades K through 12. Articles 1,200 to 1,500 words. Fees vary and are paid on publication. "Please read the publication first, then send a query letter. E-mail is fine." Guidelines available.

This Magazine

401 Richmond Street W., Suite 396, Toronto, ON M5V 3A8
Phone: (416) 979-8400
E-mail: editor@thismagazine.ca
Website: http://this.org
Contact: Lauren McKeon, editor
Circulation: 5,000
Published bimonthly

Canada's leading alternative magazine carrying investigative features and researched commentary on culture, politics, and the arts. Features of 2,000 to 4,000 words earn $200 to $400; pay for shorter items from 500 to 1,500 words is $50 to $150. Paid on publication. "We prefer clearly focused, thoroughly researched, and sharply written investigative articles on topics the mainstream media ignore. No unsolicited poetry, fiction, or drama." Send a query letter. Guidelines available on website.

The Tyee

P.O. Box 88484, Vancouver, BC V6A 4A7
Phone: (604) 688-7483
E-mail: editor@thetyee.ca
Website: www.thetyee.ca
150,000 unique monthly visitors

Online news magazine that publishes news features, political commentary, cultural analysis, and social observation of interest to British Columbians. "We ask that news and commentary pieces be scrupulous in citing sources, that stories about life in the province be concise and conversational, and that everyone who contributes to *The Tyee* maintain a sense of humour and perspective." Generally does not pay, but occasionally will pay modest fees. Guidelines on website.

The United Church Observer

478 Huron Street, Toronto, ON M5R 2R3
Phone: (416) 960-8500, ext. 225 Fax: (416) 960-8477
E-mail: general@ucobserver.org
Website: www.ucobserver.org
Contact: David Wilson, editor
Circulation: 50,000
Published 11 times a year

Provides news of the church, the nation, and the world while maintaining an independent editorial policy. Prints serious articles on issues such as human rights, social justice, and Christian faith in action, and stories of personal courage – all with a Christian perspective. Also covers the religious dimensions of art, literature, and theatre. Articles 500 to 2,500 words. Fees are negotiated and paid on publication. Personal stories are paid at lower rates. "Should use news-feature treatment. Query first by fax or e-mail. Mostly staff written, but some freelance opportunities (also art and photography)." Guidelines available.

University Affairs

600 – 350 Albert Street, Ottawa, ON KIR IBI
Phone: (613) 563-1236, ext. 228 Fax: (613) 563-9745
E-mail: pberkowi@aucc.ca
Website: www.universityaffairs.ca
Contact: Peggy Berkowitz, editor
Circulation: 20,000
Published 10 times a year

"*University Affairs* is the most trusted news source for Canada's universities. Our award-winning magazine covers ideas and trends in higher education for readers who are among the best educated in the country. We tackle provocative topics like plagiarism and fair access to university in a balanced way. We cover news about exciting research, innovative teaching and vibrant personalities at universities across the country. Our website is filled with career advice and the most extensive job listings for Canadian academic positions." Publishes articles in both English and French. Stories from 300 to 2,000 words. Fees vary. "Please read the magazine online and the writer's guidelines before submitting a story idea."

University of Toronto Magazine

21 King's College Circle, Toronto, ON M5S 3J3
Phone: (416) 978-2102 or (416) 946-3192 Fax: (416) 978-3958
E-mail: uoft.magazine@utoronto.ca
Website: www.magazine.utoronto.ca
Contacts: Stacey Gibson, managing editor; Scott Anderson, editor
Circulation: 280,000
Published quarterly

Promotes the University of Toronto to its alumni, friends of the university, and the U. of T. community by publishing articles about alumni and campus news. U. of T. angle must be strong. Pays $1/word on acceptance for articles of 750 to 4,000 words.

The Walrus Magazine

19 Duncan Street, Suite 101, Toronto, ON M5H 3HI
Phone: (416) 971-5004 Fax: (416) 971-8768
E-mail: pitch@walrusmagazine.com (non-fiction);
    fiction@walrusmagazine.com; or poetry@walrusmagazine.com
Website: www.walrusmagazine.com

Contact: John MacFarlane, editor
Circulation: 50,000
Published 10 times a year

A general interest magazine with an international thrust. Features start at 3,000 words; columns are 1,500 to 2,500 words. Pay rates vary depending on project and are paid on publication. "Please note that we do not accept unsolicited fiction or poetry submissions." Guidelines available on website.

Western Alumni Gazette
University of Western Ontario, Westminster Hall, Suite 360,
    London, ON N6A 3K7
Phone: (519) 661-2111, ext. 88467 Fax: (519) 661-3921
E-mail: steyaert@uwo.ca
Website: www.uwo.ca or http://communications.uwo.ca/alumni/
Contact: Marcia Steyaert, editor
Circulation: 155,000
Published 3 times a year

Written for Western alumni around the world. Pays on acceptance.

Windspeaker
13245 – 146 Street, Edmonton, AB T5L 4S8
Phone: (780) 455-2700 Fax: (780) 455-7639
E-mail: windspeaker@ammsa.com
Website: www.ammsa.com
Contact: Debora Steel, editor
Circulation: 25,000
Published monthly

A national news magazine dealing with the issues and concerns of Aboriginal people in Canada from an Aboriginal perspective. Articles 800 to 1,000 words. Pays $3.40/published column inch on publication for single-source stories and $4.15/published column inch for multiple-source stories. "Remember the perspective; remember the audience." Guidelines available on website.

Special Interest

Abilities
c/o Canadian Abilities Foundation, 340 College Street, Suite 270, Toronto, ON M5T 3A9
Phone: (416) 923-1885, ext. 231 Fax: (416) 923-9829
E-mail: jennifer@abilities.ca
Website: www.abilities.ca
Contact: Jennifer Rivkin, managing editor
Circulation: 80,000
Published quarterly

Canada's lifestyle magazine for people with disabilities. Provides inspiration, information, and opportunities to people with disabilities. Articles/stories 500 to 2,000 words. "We do not publish fiction, poetry, cartoons/comics, or drama." A non-profit organization that pays honoraria to writers ranging from $50 to $325 on publication. "We are interested in new ideas, resources, or strategies that will empower our readers. Avoid telling them what they already know." Guidelines available online.

Canadian Newcomer
Phone: (416) 406-4719
E-mail: editor@cnmag.ca
Website: www.cnmag.ca
Contact: Jill Snider Lum, managing editor/associate publisher
Approximately 1,000 daily visitors
Published online

Provides free information, advice, entertainment, and encouragement to new immigrants. The magazine is published in English, and the vocabulary is kept fairly simple. The style is casual and addresses the reader. Covers employment, settlement, housing, Canadian lifestyles, health, finances, ethnic media, and education. Used as a teaching tool in many ESL schools. Seeks articles from 250 to 1,000 words. It is best to query first, although unsolicited manuscripts will be considered. Payment is negotiated, but starts at 10¢/word.

CelticLife International

133 Purcell's Cove Road, Halifax, NS B3P 1B3
E-mail: editor@celticlife.ca
Website: www.celticlife.com
Contact: Carol Moreira, editor
Circulation: 141,848
Published quarterly

CelticLife celebrates the culture of the seven Celtic Nations with profiles of modern Celts: their music, travel, recipes, heritage, history, traditions, legends, and language. "Looking for fresh material for both the magazine and the website (which publishes original material). E-mail queries preferred. For an electronic and/or print edition of the latest issue, please e-mail editor@celticlife.ca. Pays 20 cents a word for North American rights, payable 30 days after publication."

DigitalJournal.com

Phone: (416) 410-9675
E-mail: editor@digitaljournal.com
Website: www.digitaljournal.com
Contact: Chris Hogg, editor-in-chief

Founded on the Internet in 1998, *DigitalJournal.com* began as a technology news site and evolved into a daily news publication. *DigitalJournal.com* is now an alternative news network for people who want to read news, contribute to reporting, and debate and discuss news and events from around the world. Payment available for approved writers. See website for details.

The Driver

4936 Yonge Street, Suite 509, Toronto, ON M2N 6S3
Phone: (416) 398-2700 Fax: (416) 398-3272
E-mail: davidmiller@thedrivermagazine.com
Website: www.thedriver.ca
Contact: David Miller, director of operations
Circulation: 38,500
Published bimonthly

Serves drivers from 16 to 55, male and female. "Our articles are intended to inform, invigorate, and entertain." Features from 1,000 to 1,500 words; shorter pieces from 100 to 1,000 words. Pays between 10¢ to 15¢/word. Query first.

Héritage

190 Bronson Avenue, Ottawa, ON KIR 6H4
Phone: (613) 237-1066, ext. 229
E-mail: cquinn@heritagecanada.org
Website: www.heritagecanada.org
Contact: Carolyn Quinn, editor and director, communications
Circulation: 4,000
Published quarterly

The magazine for members of the Heritage Canada Foundation, a charitable, non-profit organization. Also distributed to elected officials, both federal and provincial, provincial and municipal leaders and history-related organizations. The magazine is used as the primary public relations tool of the Foundation. Covers issues and activities in the field of preservation of heritage buildings. "Articles must address preservation issues or be about historic properties that have either been rehabilitated or are endangered." Articles 1,500 to 2,000 words. Payment is negotiable. Guidelines available.

Inside Motorcycles

P.O. Box 7100, Stn. A, Toronto, ON M5W 1X7
Phone: (416) 962-7223 Fax: (416) 962-7208
E-mail: editor@insidemotorcycles.com
Website: www.insidemotorcycles.com
Contact: John Hopkins, editor
Circulation: 10,000
Published 10 times a year

Covers motorcycle racing and recreation with a Canadian perspective. Fees vary and are paid on publication.

Muse

280 Metcalfe Street, Suite 400, Ottawa, ON K2P 1R7
Phone: (613) 567-0099 Fax: (613) 233-5438
E-mail: info@museums.ca
Website: www.museums.ca
Contact: Julie Cormier-Doiron, editor
Circulation: 1,800
Published bimonthly

A source for features, news, and opinion pieces covering Canadian and international heritage institutions (museums, archives, libraries, zoos, etc.). Feature articles are 1,000 to 2,500 words; book reviews are 200 words maximum; musings are 750 words. Contributors receive copies of the issue in which their article appears. Guidelines on website.

The Navigator Magazine

P.O. Box 29126, 197 Majors Path, St. John's, NL A1A 5B5
Phone: (709) 754-7977 Fax: (709) 754-6225
E-mail: jbaker@thenavigatormagazine.com
Website: www.thenavigatormagazine.com
Contact: Jamie Baker, managing editor
Circulation: 8,600
Published monthly

The Navigator is the voice of the commercial fishing industry in Atlantic Canada. Articles from 1,000 to 1,500 words. Rates vary depending on project. Fees are negotiated in advance and paid on publication. Submission guidelines available.

Neo-opsis Science Fiction Magazine

4129 Carey Road, Victoria, BC V8Z 4G5
Phone: (250) 881-8893
E-mail: neoopsis@shaw.ca
Website: www.neo-opsis.ca
Contact: Stephanie Johanson, art director/assistant editor
Circulation: 450
Published 2 to 3 times a year

Publishes stories written from the perspective of science fiction and fantasy, with informative articles on science and nature, humorous opinion pieces, book and movie reviews, and illustrations. "It is the intention of this publication to maintain a market for the works of science fiction writers and artists, and in that process to entertain and enlighten its readership." The target market is between the ages of 26 and 50. Accepts submissions between September 1 and October 31. Preferred length of stories from 500 to 6,000 words. Pays on publication 2.5¢/word to a maximum of $125/story. Contributors receive 1 copy of the magazine if their piece is 2,000 words or less; 2 copies if it is more than 2,000 words. Guidelines available on website.

ON Nature
214 King Street W., Suite 612, Toronto, ON M5H 3S6
Phone: (416) 444-8419 Fax: (416) 444-9866
E-mail: victoriaf@ontarionature.org
Website: www.ontarionature.org
Contact: Victoria Foote, editor
Circulation: 7,500
Published quarterly

ON Nature focuses on environmental issues, conservation, and "soft" travel within Ontario. Articles 300 to 3,000 words. Rates vary depending on project and are paid on acceptance. Guidelines available.

The Scouting Life Magazine
1345 Baseline Road, Suite 100, Ottawa, ON K2C 0A7
Phone: (613) 224-5131 Fax: (613) 224-3571
E-mail: cpiccinin@scouts.ca
Website: www.scouts.ca
Circulation: 35,000
Published 4 times a year

For Scouts Canada leaders. It encourages the development of youth and leaders through program-related articles on indoor and outdoor activities including camping, computers, and crafts for ages 5 to 26. Articles are 500 to 1,500 words. Does not pay, but welcomes submission inquiries. "Those who submit material should be active Scouting members with program ideas to share." Guidelines available on website.

TRANSITION
2702 – 12th Avenue, Regina, SK S4T 1J2
Phone: (306) 525-5601 (in Regina) or 1-800-461-5483
    (Saskatchewan only) Fax: (306) 569-3788
E-mail: contactus@cmhask.com
Website: www.cmhask.com
Contact: Ted Dyck, editor
Published 2 times a year

TRANSITION publishes two kinds of works: those directly about mental health issues; and those about the individual's personal experience of those same issues. "We solicit original, unpublished articles, as well as fiction, non-fiction, poetry, book reviews, and visual art (black and white) that represent current mental health issues in our province and reflect on their impact on individuals." Maximum manuscript lengths: articles – 15 pages; all other prose – 10 pages; poetry – 10 poems or 10 pages, whichever is less; visual art – 10 pieces. Pays $25.00 per printed page ($12.50/half page); $20.00 per published visual art work; and $100.00 for cover art.

Sports & Outdoors

Athletics
3 Concorde Gate, Suite 211, Toronto, ON M3C 3N7
Phone: (416) 426-7215 Fax: (416) 426-7358
E-mail: ontrack@eol.ca
Website: www.athleticsontario.ca
Contact: John Craig, editor
Circulation: 3,500
Published 8 times a year
   Publishes in-depth stories and photographs on track and field and road running from grassroots to the Olympic level. Articles from 750 to 1,500 words. Rates vary; paid on publication.

Atlantic Boating News
162 Trider Crescent, Dartmouth, NS B3B 1R6
Phone: (902) 422-4990 Fax: (902) 422-4728
E-mail: editor@advocatemediainc.com
Website: www.atlanticboatingnews.com
Contact: Suzanne Rent, editor
Circulation: 7,000
Published bimonthly
   Geared for the Atlantic Canadian marketplace, so stories focus on all aspects of recreational boating in that region. Pay varies and is paid on publication for 600 to 800 words. Photos should accompany submissions.

BC Outdoors Magazine
1750 McLean Avenue, Unit 12, Port Coquitlam, BC V3C 1M9
Phone: 1-800-898-8811 Fax: (604) 687-1925

E-mail: mmitchell@outdoorgroupmedia.com
Website: www.bcoutdoorsmagazine.com
Contact: Mike Mitchell, editor
Circulation: 30,000
Published 7 times a year

Publishes stories about fishing/hunting in B.C. and everything that goes along with it. "We are looking for original queries from knowledgeable writers who can write factual and entertaining articles on technique, resource management, and B.C.'s world famous fishing and hunting opportunities." Carries articles from 1,500 to 2,000 words. Pays up to $500/article (with high quality photo support) on publication. "Rates are commensurate with experience and are determined by the editor." Guidelines available. "We are always looking for new writers. Please call or e-mail to query."

Camping Canada's RV Lifestyle Magazine
1121 Invicta Drive, Unit 2, Oakville, ON L6H 2R2
Phone: (905) 844-8218 Fax: (905) 844-5032
E-mail: nrosen@rvlifemag.com
Website: www.rvlifemag.com
Contact: Norm Rosen, editor
Circulation: 51,000
Published 7 times a year

Established 1971. Geared to readers who enjoy travel and camping. Readers vary from owners of towable trailers or motorhomes to young families and entry-level campers (no tenting). Half of the articles are written by freelancers. Publishes non-fiction articles on how-to, personal experience, and travel. Buys 20 to 30 manuscripts/year of 1,800 to 2,500 words. Send photos with submission. Occasionally accepts previously published submissions, if so noted. Pay varies; received on publication. Buys first North American serial rights. Byline given. Editorial lead time 3 months. Reports in 1 month on queries, 2 months on manuscripts. Sample copy free.

Canadian Biker
2220 Sooke Road, Suite 108, Victoria, BC V9B OG9
Phone: (250) 384-0333 or 1-800-667-5667 Fax: (250) 384-1832
E-mail: edit@canadianbiker.com

Website: www.canadianbiker.com
Contact: John Campbell, editorial
Circulation: 11,000
Published 10 times a year

A general motorcycle magazine with an emphasis on cruiser-type motorcycles and touring articles with a Canadian slant. Other subjects include custom and vintage motorcycles, personality profiles, event coverage, and new model reviews (including sport, sport-touring, and dual-sport motorcycles). "Although freelance material is actively sought, potential contributors are strongly urged to contact the editor before submitting if they wish to avoid disappointment." Features are 1,500 to 2,500 words; shorter stories for specific departments from 500 to 700 words. Pay rate is negotiated. "Articles paid according to quality rather than quantity and based on topic, frequency of contributions, and originality. Preference given to work sent on disk with hard copy and a minimum of two photos (captioned)." Guidelines available on website.

Canadian Horse Journal
2400 Bevan Avenue, Suite 201, Sidney, BC V8L 1W1
Phone: (250) 655-8883 or 1-800-299-3799 Fax: (250) 655-8913
E-mail: news@horsejournals.com
Website: www.horsejournals.com
Contact: Kathy Smith, publisher and editor
Circulation: 20,000
Published 11 times a year

All-breeds magazine covering horse health, training, careers with horses, lifestyle, practical tips, industry issues, and major events. Regional supplements for Pacific & Prairie and Central & Atlantic.

Canadian Hot Rods
978 Waddington Road, Nanaimo, BC V9S 4T9
Phone: (250) 753-2722 or 1-888-753-2111 Fax: (250) 753-2721
E-mail: info@canadianhotrods.com
Website: www.canadianhotrods.com
Contact: Terry Denomme, publisher and editor
Circulation: 16,000
Published six times a year

Canada's only hot rod magazine features project cars, show coverage, tech articles, and more, with "something for both the casual or diehard gearhead in every issue."

Canadian Thoroughbred

P.O. Box 670, Aurora, ON L4G 4J9
Phone: (905) 727-0107 Fax: (905) 841-1530
E-mail: info@horse-canada.com
Website: www.horse-canada.com
Contact: Lee Benson, managing editor
Published bimonthly

Focus on race horses. Accepts unsolicited material. Preferred length 750 to 2,500 words. Guidelines available.

Coast&Kayak Magazine

c/o Wild Coast Publishing, P.O. Box 24, Stn. A, Nanaimo, BC
    V9R 5K4
Phone: (250) 244-6437 or 1-866-984-6437 Fax: 1-866-654-1937
E-mail: editor@coastandkayak.com
Website: www.coastandkayak.com
Contact: John Kimantis, editor
Circulation: 20,000
Published quarterly

Formerly *Wavelength Magazine*. For paddlers, especially sea kayakers, and those interested in marine ecotourism and the marine environment, specifically on the West Coast. Articles from 1,000 to 1,500 words. Pays on publication $100 to $300, depending on length of article. "Knowledge of kayaking (or canoeing) essential. Humour and good pictures are an asset." Guidelines available on website.

Diver Magazine

241A E. 1st Street (rear), North Vancouver, BC V7L 1B4
Phone: (604) 988-0711 Fax: (604) 988-0747
E-mail: mail@divermag.com
Website: www.divermag.com
Contact: Peter Golding, editor
Circulation: 15,000
Published 8 times a year

For North American and international sport divers. Carries regular articles on travel destinations, snorkelling, and scuba and deep-water diving. Also covers marine life and underwater photography. Articles 500 to 1,000 words. Pays $2.50/column inch after publication. Check guidelines before submitting material.

Explore: Canada's Outdoor Magazine

200 W. Esplanade, Suite 500, North Vancouver, BC V7M 1A4
Phone: (604) 998-3310 Fax: (604) 998-3320
E-mail: explore@explore-mag.com
Website: www.explore-mag.com
Contact: editor
Circulation: 30,000
Published quarterly

For people who enjoy outdoor recreational activities such as backpacking, mountain biking, canoeing, kayaking, skiing, and adventure travel. Short, newsy, general interest articles for the Lowdown section are 100 to 600 words. Most features run from 2,000 to 3,000 words. Payment depends on quality and length, and ranges from $1,500 and up for features. "Excellent photographs are essential for almost every *Explore* story, and though we generally use the work of full-time pros, we occasionally rely on a writer to provide appropriate photo support." Guidelines available on website.

Get Out There Magazine

1 Aberfoyle Crescent, Suite 1200, Toronto, ON M8X 2X8
Phone: (416) 825-0854 Fax: (416) 840-4943
E-mail: info@getouttheremag.com or ron@getouttheremag.com
Website: www.getouttheremag.com
Contact: Ron Johnson, editor
Circulation: 80,000
Published bimonthly

Covers amateur sports with an outdoors focus. Articles from 500 to 750 words. Pays 40¢/word on publication. "Pitch letters and writing samples are welcome."

GolfWest

100 – 7th Avenue S., Suite 100, Cranbrook, BC VIC 2J4
Phone: (250) 426-7253 Fax: (250) 426-4125
E-mail: info@kpimedia.com
Contact: Keith Powell, publisher
Circulation: 40,000
Published annually

Covers golf destinations, course profiles, products, tips, and stories about real golfers in Western Canada. Stories 500 to 800 words. Pays $85/story, which must have a photo to accompany it. Pays when story and photo are received and approved to run.

The Hockey Reporter

91 Hemmingway Drive, Courtice, ON LIE 2C2
Phone: (905) 434-7409 Fax: (905) 434-1654
E-mail: hockeyreporter@istar.ca
Contact: Greg McDowell, managing editor
Circulation: 35,000
Published quarterly

Covers the amateur hockey scene in Ontario. Fees are negotiated and paid on publication for articles from 500 to 1,500 words.

Horse-Canada.com Magazine

P.O. Box 670, Aurora, ON L4G 4J9
Phone: (905) 727-0107 Fax: (905) 841-1530
E-mail: info@horse-canada.com
Website: www.horse-canada.com
Contact: Lee Benson, managing editor
Published bimonthly

Canada's family horse magazine for all breeds and disciplines with emphasis on equine health and care. Includes a special pull-out section for children who love horses. Accepts unsolicited material. Preferred length 750 to 2,500 words. Guidelines available.

Horse Country

P.O. Box 203, 845 Dakota Street, Suite 23, Winnipeg, MB
   R2M 5M3
Phone: (204) 256-7467 Fax: (204) 257-2467
E-mail: editor@horsecountry.ca or contact@horsecountry.ca

Website: www.horsecountry.ca
Contact: Linda Hazelwood, publisher/editor
Circulation: 8,000
Published 8 times a year

Publishes stories for all ages on Canadian prairie horse people, on all disciplines of riding, and on all breeds of horses. Accepts fiction. Fees are negotiated for commissioned work and paid on publication. Articles are from 500 to 1,000 words. Welcomes submissions from emerging writers. "Unsolicited manuscripts are accepted but not returned. Send manuscripts by e-mail. Query letters or unsolicited manuscripts should state payment rate required, or it will be assumed they are gratis. Factual training and horse health articles are particularly sought." Guidelines available on website.

Horse Sport

P.O. Box 670, Aurora, ON L4G 4J9
Phone: (905) 727-0107 Fax: (905) 841-1530
E-mail: info@horse-canada.com
Website: www.horse-canada.com
Contact: Amy Harris, editor
Published monthly

Focus on competitions. Accepts unsolicited material. Preferred length 750 to 2,500 words. Guidelines available.

Horses All

c/o Farm Business Communications, 1666 Dublin Avenue,
    Winnipeg, MB R3H OH1
Phone: (403) 200-1019 (editor) or 1-800-665-1362 (general)
    Fax: (204) 942-8463
E-mail: craig.couillard@fbcpublishing.com
Website: www.horsesall.com
Contact: Craig Couillard, editor
Circulation: 20,000
Published monthly

Horses All has featured equine news and information since 1977, focusing on people and horses, places and events. Articles 500 to 750 words. Fees vary, but average about $150/story, paid on publication. "Freelance writers must be knowledgeable horse people.

Articles must be relevant to Canadian, Western Canadian, or Albertan readers. We do not publish fiction." Guidelines available.

Impact Magazine
2007 – 2nd Street S.W., Calgary, AB T2S 1S4
Phone: (403) 228-0605 Fax: (403) 228-0627
E-mail: editor@impactmagazine.ca
Website: www.impactmagazine.ca
Contact: Chris Welner, editor
Circulation: 80,000
Published bimonthly
Western Canada's only fitness, performance, and sport magazine with editions in Calgary and Vancouver. Articles 600 to 1,000 words. Fees vary depending on the project and are paid on publication. Query by letter or e-mail before submitting. "We do not accept unsolicited articles." Guidelines available on website.

Inside Track Motorsport News
P.O. Box 7100, Stn. A, Toronto, ON M5W 1X7
Phone: (416) 962-7223 Fax: (416) 962-7208
E-mail: editor@insidetracknews.com
Website: www.insidetracknews.com
Contact: Greg MacPherson, editor
Circulation: 10,000 to 12,500
Published monthly
Aimed at Canadian motorsport racing fans. Includes race reports, features, news, and interviews. Articles 600 to 1,200 words. Fees vary and are paid on publication. "E-mail submissions preferred. Colour photos in JPG format at 300 DPI."

KANAWA: Canada's Paddling Magazine
12 Elizabeth Street, Brockville, ON K6V 7B4
Phone: (613) 342-0599
E-mail: kanawa@paddlingcanada.com
Website: www.paddlingcanada.com
Contact: Anne Baxter, managing director
Published quarterly
Canada's foremost full-colour canoeing and kayaking magazine. "Many of our contributors are individuals who share a love of

paddling and Canada's natural environment." Features 1,500 to 2,500 words; shorter articles 500 to 1,500 words. Guidelines available on website.

The New Fly Fisher Magazine

23B Northside Road, Ottawa, ON K2H 8S1
Phone: (613) 721-6113 Fax: (613) 721-8497
E-mail: editor@jencor.ca
Website: www.thenewflyfisher.com
Contact: Chris Marshall, editor
Published quarterly

An online magazine with information on Canadian fly fishing destinations, techniques, fly tying, etc. Stories must have a Canadian connection and a strong educational or informational component. Features range from 2,000 to 4,000 words, shorter pieces from 800 to 1,500 words. "Feature writers should submit many more photos than they would for a print magazine – at least 30 for a major feature." First-time writers must include a bio of 50 to 70 words. Takes most submissions on spec and responds to queries in at least 4 weeks. Pays up to $450 for major features with supporting photos and graphics, and between $100 and $200 for shorter pieces. Guidelines available on website.

Ontario Out of Doors

P.O. Box 8500, Peterborough, ON K9J 0B4
Phone: (705) 748-0076 or 1-800-361-0645 Fax: (705) 748-3415
E-mail: john.kerr@oodmag.com
Websites: www.fishontario.com and www.huntontario.com
Contact: John Kerr, editor-in-chief
Circulation: 98,500
Published 10 times a year

Ontario's leading publication for outdoors enthusiasts. Specializes in how-to, where-to, and destination pieces on all aspects of hunting and fishing. Articles 600 to 2,000 words. Pays 50¢/word on either acceptance or publication, depending on the project. Guidelines available.

Ontario Sailor Magazine

91 Hemmingway Drive, Courtice, ON L1E 2C2
Phone: (905) 434-7409 Fax: (905) 434-1654
E-mail: sails@istar.ca
Website: www.ontariosailormagazine.ca
Contact: Greg McDowell
Circulation: 10,000
Published 7 times a year

Covers the Great Lakes sailing scene in Canada and the U.S. Articles 500 to 1,500 words. Pay rates vary (start at $20/story) and are paid on publication. "Please query first. We accept freelance photos and prefer stories to be accompanied by a photo."

Outdoor Canada

25 Sheppard Avenue W., Suite 100, Toronto, ON M2N 6S7
Phone: (416) 733-7600 Fax: (416) 227-8296
E-mail: editorial@outdoorcanada.ca
Website: www.outdoorcanada.ca
Contact: Bob Sexton, associate editor
Circulation: 93,000
Published 8 times a year

Canada's only national magazine about fishing, hunting, and related conservation issues. "Our readers are passionate about this country's natural heritage, and they want to get the most out of their outdoor experiences. That's why each issue contains a solid mix of how-to articles, service pieces, entertaining features, and in-depth reporting." Articles 100 to 3,000 words. Pays on acceptance 50¢ to $1/word. Fees are established upon assignment based on complexity and length of story. "We welcome query letters from professional writers (please do not submit unsolicited manuscripts). All story ideas must be designed solely to serve the interests and needs of our readers. Contributors are therefore encouraged to first review the magazine and familiarize themselves with its tone and specific editorial departments." Guidelines available.

Outdoor Edge

202 – 9644 54th Avenue, Edmonton, AB T6E 5V1
Phone: (780) 643-3961 Fax: (780) 643-3960
E-mail: dwebb@outdoorgroupmedia.com

Website: www.westernsportsman.com
Contact: David Webb, editor
Circulation: 50,000
Published bimonthly

Publishes articles on recreational fishing, hunting, and conservation from British Columbia to Manitoba. Stories 1,600 to 2,000 words. Pays on publication. Please query. Guidelines available.

Pacific Yachting

200 W. Esplanade Street, Suite 500, North Vancouver, BC
   V7M 1A4
Phone: (604) 998-3310 Fax: (604) 998-3320
E-mail: editor@pacificyachting.com
Website: www.pacificyachting.com
Contact: Dale Miller, editor
Circulation: 60,000
Published monthly

A magazine that is all about recreational boats, boating, and the boating lifestyle. "We're looking for stories about cruising in B.C., how-to, adventure, and short 100- to 400-word news items." Length: features run up to 2,000 words and include color photos; departments run 800 to 1,000 words. "We also buy short (50- to 250-word) news items for our CURRENTS section (current events, coast guard and other government updates, trade news, people news, boat gatherings and festivals)." Pays $400 to $500 on publication for features, including photos. "Writers must be familiar with our special-interest viewpoint, language, and orientation. First-hand experience of subject is essential." Guidelines available on website.

RidersWest

100 – 7th Avenue S., Suite 100, Cranbrook, BC V1C 2J4
Phone: (250) 426-7253 Fax: (250) 426-4125
E-mail: info@kpimedia.com
Website: www.riderswestmag.com
Contact: Keith Powell, publisher
Circulation: 32,000
Published twice a year

Primarily a destinations-type magazine looking for first-person ATV travel adventure articles. Stories 500 to 800 words. Pays

$85/story, which must have a photo to accompany it. Pays when story and photo are received and approved to run.

RPM

1921 Broadway Street, Unit 1, Port Coquitlam, BC V3C 2N2
Phone: (604) 629-9669 or 1-888-500-4591 Fax: (778) 285-2449
E-mail: jordan@rpmcanada.ca
Website: www.rpmcanada.ca
Contact: Jordan Allan
Circulation: 60,000
Published bimonthly

Features car and truck reviews, new product guides, industry news, event coverage, tech features, and interviews with industry leaders.

Ski Canada

117 Indian Road, Toronto, ON M6R 2V5
Phone: (416) 538-2293
E-mail: mac@skicanadamag.com
Website: www.skicanadamag.com
Contact: Iain MacMillan, editor
Circulation: 42,000
Published 5 times a year

Publishes a balanced mix of entertainment and information for both the experienced and the intermediate skier. "Published from early autumn through winter, *SC* covers equipment, travel, instruction, competition, fashion, and general skiing- and alpine-related news and stories. Query e-mails are preferred; unsolicited manuscripts rarely fit into a determined schedule. Replies will take time. Note: yearly editorial schedules are set at least 6 months before commencement of publishing season." Articles 400 to 2,500 words. Pays (within 60 days of publication) between $100 (news) and $500 to $800 (features), depending on length, research necessary, and writer's experience.

SnoRiders

100 – 7th Avenue S., Suite 100, Cranbrook, BC V1C 2J4
Phone: (250) 426-7253 Fax: (250) 426-4125
E-mail: editor@kpimedia.com
Website: www.snoriderwest.com

Contact: Kerry Shellborn, assigning editor
Circulation: 35,000
Published 3 times a year

Primarily a destinations-type magazine looking for first-person snowmobile travel adventure articles. Stories 500 to 800 words. Pays $85/story, which must have a photo to accompany it. Pays when story and photo are received and approved to run.

Western Sportsman

9644 54th Avenue, Suite 202, Edmonton, AB T6E 5V1
Phone: (780) 643-3961 Fax: (780) 643-3960
E-mail: dwebb@outdoorgroupmedia.com
Website: www.westernsportsman.com
Contact: David Webb, editor
Circulation: 25,000
Published bimonthly

Publishes articles on recreational fishing, hunting, and conservation from west of the Rockies to Manitoba. Stories 1,600 to 2,000 words. Pays on publication. Please query. Guidelines available.

Travel & Tourism

British Columbia Magazine

1803 Douglas Street, 3rd Floor, Victoria, BC V8T 5C3
Phone: (250) 356-5860 Fax: (250) 356-5896
E-mail: editor@bcmag.ca
Website: www.bcmag.ca
Contact: Jane Nahirny, editor
Circulation: 115,000
Published monthly

Portrays a fresh view of B.C., highlighting exotic and unknown features or a new angle to a familiar place or theme. Does not publish poetry or fiction. Reviews all proposals in December and January each year, and considers spec manuscripts throughout the year (although it's best to submit before March). Especially welcomes experienced writers who can provide excellent photos. Features are usually 1,500 to 2,500 words; shorter stories from 1,000 to 1,500 words; sidebars 200 to 500 words. Pays 50¢/word on acceptance; higher rates for more complex research assignments. Guidelines on website.

DreamScapes Travel and Lifestyle Magazine

642 Simcoe Street, S.S. 1, Niagara-on-the-Lake, ON LOS IJO
Phone: (905) 468-4021 Fax: (905) 468-2382
E-mail: editor@dreamscapes.ca
Website: www.dreamscapes.ca
Contact: Donna Vieira, editor
Circulation: 124,000
Published 8 times a year

Distributed to the highest income households in 6 key markets across Canada. See website for publishing and editorial schedule. Articles from 500 to 1,200 words. Pays 30¢/word on publication; this fee covers both the printed magazine format and the online version. "Photos are required for all editorials. We do not pay for them, although we do give a photo credit." Guidelines available.

enRoute

4200 Saint-Laurent Boulevard, Suite 707, Montreal, QC H2W 2R2
Phone: (514) 844-2001 Fax: (514) 844-6001
E-mail: info@enroutemag.net or pitch@enroutemag.net
Website: www.enroutemag.com
Contacts: Ilana Weitzman, editor-in-chief; Isa Tousignant, senior
     editor
Circulation: 160,000
Published monthly

Air Canada's French-English in-flight magazine. A general travel lifestyle publication featuring trends, travel, entertainment, social stories, fashion, and food. Aimed at a high-end market. Articles 200 to 1,500 words. Pays $1 per word on acceptance. Inquire first with ideas. Always enclose tear sheets. Guidelines available on website.

Journeywoman: The Premier Travel Resource for Women

50 Prince Arthur Avenue, Toronto, ON M5R IB5
Phone: (416) 929-7654
E-mail: editor@journeywoman.com
Website: www.journeywoman.com
Contact: Evelyn Hannon, publisher/editor

An online international travel resource that publishes stories and tips focusing on the specific needs and interests of women travellers. Stories up to 900 words, with two additional sidebars and a 2- to 3-line bio. Pays a $35 honorarium for articles.

Outpost

250 Augusta Avenue, Suite 207, Toronto, ON M5T 2L7
Fax: (416) 972-6645
E-mail: editor@outpostmagazine.com
Contact: Deborah Sanborn, editor
Circulation: 25,000
Published bimonthly

Adventure-lifestyle magazine featuring destination profiles, human interest stories, environmental and cultural reportage, product reviews, and travel advice. Feature articles between 2,800 and 5,000 words. Query by letter or e-mail; no phone calls. Guidelines on website.

Prairies North

P.O. Box 520, Norquay, SK S0A 2V0
Phone: (306) 594-2455 Fax: (306) 594-2119
E-mail: lionel@prairiesnorth.com
Website: www.sasknaturally.com
Contact: Lionel Hughes, co-publisher/editor
Circulation: 22,000
Published quarterly

Stories feature the unique wildlife, people, and places of Saskatchewan, using stunning photos and fresh editorial content. Uses 5 feature articles/issue of 1,200 to 2,500 words. Pays on publication 25¢/word. Guidelines available.

RVwest

100 – 7th Avenue S., Suite 100, Cranbrook, BC V1C 2J4
Phone: (250) 426-7253 Fax: (250) 426-4125
E-mail: info@kpimedia.com
Contact: Keith Powell, publisher
Circulation: 35,000
Published bimonthly

Primarily a destinations-type magazine looking for first-person

RV travel adventure articles. Stories 500 to 800 words. Pays $85/story, which must have a photo to accompany it. Pays when story and photo are received and approved to run.

Verge Magazine
P.O. Box 147, Peterborough, ON K9J 6Y5
Phone: (705) 742-6869
E-mail: contributing@vergemagazine.ca
Website: www.vergemagazine.ca
Contact: Julia Steinecke, editor
Circulation: 12,000
Published 4 times a year

This travel magazine focuses on overseas work, study, volunteering, and adventure travel options. Pays 10¢/word on publication for articles 500 to 2,500 words. Guidelines available.

Visitors' Choice
102 E. 4th Avenue, Vancouver, BC V5T 1G2
Phone: (604) 608-5180 Fax: (604) 608-5181
E-mail: nglouberman@biv.com
Website: www.visitorschoice.com
Contact: Noa Glouberman, editor
Circulation: varies
Publication schedule varies (see below)

Visitors' Choice is a group of 20 visitor guides serving 57 communities throughout BC, with a combined 1.6 million copies distributed annually. There are 3 Vancouver English-language editions annually, as well as annual Chinese and Japanese editions. The Whistler edition is published twice a year, and all other guides are published annually. Each edition features a mix of detailed maps, dining guides, and information on attractions, shopping, and other activities.

Westworld Alberta / Westworld B.C. / Westworld Saskatchewan
4180 Lougheed Highway, 4th Floor, Burnaby, BC V5C 6A7
Phone: (604) 299-7311 Fax: (604) 299-9188
E-mail: arose@canadawide.com
Website: www.canadawide.com

Contacts: Kirsten Rodenhizer, editor (AB); Anne Rose, editor
(BC); Sheila Hansen, editor (SK)
Circulation: 1,297,000 (combined)
Published quarterly (*Westwood Alberta* published 5 times a year)

A travel (regional, national, and international), active-lifestyle, and auto-club magazine. Pays 60¢ to $1/word on publication for articles of 500 to 2,000 words. Kill fees are 50%. "Writers should review back issues for style, tone, and focus of departments and features." Guidelines available on website.

Where Calgary

1131 Kensington Road N.W., 2nd Floor, Calgary, AB T2N 3P4
Phone: (403) 299-1842 (editor) or (403) 299-1888 (general) Fax:
(403) 299-1899
E-mail: idoig@where.ca
Website: www.where.ca/calgary
Contact: Ian Doig, editor
Circulation: 50,000
Published bimonthly

News of events and attractions for visitors in Calgary and Alberta, including local dining, shopping, and fine art. Cover stories highlight things to do and see. Pays about 50¢/word on acceptance. Word count and rates vary with project. "Query first with résumé and clips. Please don't send spec manuscripts, fiction, or poetry."

Where Toronto

111 Queen Street E., Suite 320, Toronto, ON M5C 1S2
Phone: (416) 364-3333 Fax: (416) 594-3375
E-mail: editorial@where.ca or lluong@where.ca
Website: www.where.ca/toronto
Contact: Linda Luong, editor-in-chief
Circulation: 840,000
Published 10 times a year

Where Toronto is a destination magazine for affluent visitors that covers the best each month in entertainment, shopping, dining, and attractions. Articles 300 to 1,200 words. Pay rates vary depending on project and are paid on publication. "Most articles are written by the staff."

Where Vancouver
1755 W. Broadway, Suite 510, Vancouver, BC V6J 4S5
Phone: (604) 736-5586 Fax: (604) 736-3465
E-mail: sradford@where.ca
Website: www.where.ca/vancouver
Contact: Sheri Radford, editor
Circulation: 50,000
Published monthly
   A visitors' guide incorporating listings for dining, shopping, entertainment, attractions, and art. *Where Vancouver* is an intelligent magazine and city guide for the upscale traveller. Articles 750 to 850 words. Pay rates vary depending on project and are paid on acceptance. "Our need for freelance submissions is minimal. The most common mistake we see is ideas for features that would appeal to Vancouver residents but not to visitors."

Women's

Chatelaine
1 Mount Pleasant Road, 8th Floor, Toronto, ON M4Y 2Y5
Phone: (416) 764-1888 Fax: (416) 764-2891
E-mail: storyideas@chatelaine.rogers.com
Website: www.chatelaine.com
Contact: Jane Francisco, editor-in-chief
Circulation: 700,000+
Published monthly
   A high-quality, glossy magazine addressing the needs, interests, and preferences of Canadian women. Covers current issues, personalities, lifestyles, health, relationships, and politics. Features of 1,000 to 2,500 words earn $1,250 and up; 1-page columns start at $500. "For all serious articles, deep, accurate, and thorough research and rich details are required. Features on beauty, food, fashion, and home decorating are supplied by staff writers and editors only." Buys first North American serial rights in English and French (to cover possible use in French-language edition). Pays on acceptance. Query first with brief outline. Contact for writers' guidelines.

Elle Canada

25 Sheppard Avenue W., Suite 100, Toronto, ON M2N 6S7
Phone: (416) 227-8210 Fax: (416) 733-7981
E-mail: editors@ellecanada.com
Website: www.ellecanada.com
Contact: Noreen Flanagan, editor-in-chief
Circulation: 200,000
Published monthly

Features stories on women's beauty, fashion, and lifestyle. Articles 300 to 1,200 words. Pays $1/word on acceptance.

FASHION

111 Queen Street E., Suite 320, Toronto, ON M5C 1S2
Phone: (416) 364-3333
E-mail: Use editorial contact form on website
Website: www.fashionmagazine.com
Contacts: Bernadette Morra, editor-in-chief
Circulation: 150,000
Published 10 times a year

Covers national and international fashion news and trends for style-conscious readers. "Each issue of *FASHION* has a shopping section filled with everything that Canadian fashion and beauty lovers need to hit the streets. As well as delivering the best finds in Toronto, Montreal, Vancouver, Calgary, and Edmonton, we'll continue to introduce our readers to the personalities behind Canada's fashion and retail scene. We celebrate the designers, retailers and spa owners who make it all happen in Canada." Guidelines available.

Flare Magazine

1 Mount Pleasant Road, 8th Floor, Toronto, ON M4Y 2Y5
Phone: (416) 764-2450 Fax: (416) 764-2866
E-mail: editors@flare.com
Website: www.flare.com
Contact: Miranda Purves, editor-in-chief
Circulation: 160,000
Published monthly

A magazine for women aged 20 to 35, focusing on fashion, beauty, and style. Pays $1/word on acceptance for articles 600 to 1,200 words. Guidelines available.

Glow

111 Queen Street E., Suite 320, Toronto, ON M5C 1S2
Phone: (416) 364-3333 Fax: (416) 594-3374
E-mail: mwhite@glow.ca
Website: www.glow.ca
Contact: Michael White, managing editor
Circulation: 360,000
Published 8 times a year

Glow is a beauty and health magazine with a Canadian spin. Articles are 1,000 to 1,500 words. Pays $1/word on publication. "A good query letter is your best foot in the door. Be innovative and smart to get the editor's attention." Guidelines available.

The Kit

1 Yonge Street, Suite 204, Toronto, ON M5E 1E6
Phone: (416) 945-8700
E-mail: dw@thekit.ca
Website: www.thekit.ca
Contact: Doug Wallace, editor and associate publisher, content

"An informative and progressive source for beauty and fashion" that is published online, in a monthly digital magazine format, and as a weekly newspaper supplement.

More

25 Sheppard Avenue W., Suite 100, Toronto, ON M2N 6S7
E-mail: Query using website form
Website: www.more.ca
Contact: Linda Lewis, editor-in-chief
Circulation: 130,000
Published bimonthly

Celebrates women over age 40. Departments open to freelancers include More Now; Work, Money, Attitude, Relationships; Humour; Memoir; Body and Mind; Health; Travel; and Food. Send a detailed query by mail or via website form. "Word length and fees vary depending on the length and complexity of the story – usually between 1,000 and 2,500 words. Our editorial lead time is 4 to 6 months." Fees paid 30 days after acceptance. See website under "Contact us" for guidelines.

Women's Post
51 Wolseley Street, Toronto, ON M5T 1A4
Phone: (416) 645-7038 Fax: (416) 645-7046
E-mail: slambert@womenspost.ca
Website: www.womenspost.ca
Contact: Sarah Lambert, editor-in-chief
Circulation: 100,000
Published 6 times a year
   A newspaper targeting professional women between the ages of 25 and 55. Articles should be intimate, first-person narratives from 500 to 700 words. Pays approximately $75/story on publication. Guidelines available.

WORN Fashion Journal
3 MacDonnell Drive, Toronto, ON M6R 2A3
Phone: (416) 531-3145
E-mail: submissions@wornjournal.com
Website: www.wornjournal.com
Contact: editorial board
Circulation: 5,000
Published biannually
   Offers opinion and intelligent commentary on cultures, sub-cultures, histories, and personal stories of fashion. "We are VERY interested in clothing articles from a non-traditional fashion per-spective. . . . We are in no way interested in trends, what's in style, or what's Hot Right Now." Submit detailed proposal and writing sample. Magazine is volunteer-run; contributors are unpaid. Guidelines on website.

Youth & Children's

chickaDEE Magazine
10 Lower Spadina Avenue, Suite 400, Toronto, ON M5V 2Z2
Phone: (416) 340-2700, ext. 316 Fax: (416) 340-9769
E-mail: editor@owlkids.com
Website: www.owlkids.com
Contact: Mandy Ng, editor
Circulation: 100,000

Published 10 times a year

A magazine for 6- to 9-year-olds full of fun and facts, crafts, comics, and original fiction. Pays $500 on publication for 600 to 800 words on articles that introduce readers to the world around them. Prefers submission inquiries; no unsolicited manuscripts. Strongly recommends writers check back issues (available in libraries) for a sense of *chickaDEE*'s approach.

Chirp

10 Lower Spadina Avenue, Suite 400, Toronto, ON M5V 2Z2
Phone: (416) 340-2700 Fax: (416) 340-9769
E-mail: chirp@owlkids.com
Website: www.owlkids.com
Contact: Jackie Farquhar, editor
Circulation: 80,000
Published 10 times a year

The "see and do" magazine for children aged 3 to 6. Publishes puzzles, games, rhymes, stories, and songs to entertain and teach preschoolers about animals, nature, letters, numbers, and more. No unsolicited manuscripts; query first. Prefers complete articles of 300 to 450 words (fees range between $100 and $350). Short poems (25 to 40 words) are paid $50.

The Claremont Review

4980 Wesley Road, Victoria, BC V8Y 1Y9
Phone: (250) 658-5221 Fax: (250) 658-5387
E-mail: lmoran@telus.net
Website: www.theclaremontreview.ca
Contact: Linda Moran, managing editor
Circulation: 500
Published twice a year

TCR publishes youth fiction and poetry for ages 13 to 19. Pays with copies of the publication. Guidelines available.

Faze

4936 Yonge Street, Suite 2400, Toronto, ON M2N 6S3
Phone: (416) 222-3060 Fax: (416) 968-3293
E-mail: editor@fazeteen.com
Website: www.fazeteen.com

Contacts: Lorraine Zander, editor-in-chief, and Dana Marie
　　Krook, managing editor
Circulation: 105,000
Published 5 times a year

Offers Canadian teenagers a look at real life issues, entertainment, global issues, health, personal style, careers, and technology. Strives to be both entertaining and empowering. Rates vary depending on project and are paid on publication. Guidelines available.

Kayak: Canada's History Magazine for Kids

Bryce Hall, Main Floor, University of Winnipeg, 515 Portage
　　Avenue, Winnipeg, MB R3B 2E9
Phone: (204) 988-9300 Fax: (204) 988-9309
E-mail: editor@kayakmag.ca
Website: www.kayakmag.ca
Contact: Jill Foran, editor
Circulation: 6,500
Published bimonthly

Aimed at children 7 to 11 years of age, *Kayak* is a fun, engaging, sometimes irreverent but always informative voyage of discovery into Canada's past. Each issue focuses on a specific theme and encompasses games, comics, fiction, and non-fiction. Articles from 350 to 1,200 words. Very little freelance work is commissioned, and then only from Canadian writers. Does not publish freelance poetry or puzzles.

OWL

10 Lower Spadina Avenue, Suite 400, Toronto, ON M5V 2Z2
Phone: (416) 340-2700, ext. 307 Fax: (416) 340-9769
E-mail: editor@owlkids.com
Website: www.owlkids.com
Contact: Kim Cooper, editor
Circulation: 75,000
Published 10 times a year

A general interest magazine for 9- to 13-year-olds. Entertains and informs on the topics and issues that concern them. Topics include everything from sports to the environment, and pop culture to peer relationships. Pays $500 on publication for 600 to 800 words. Prefers submission inquiries; no unsolicited manuscripts.

Strongly recommends writers check back issues (available in libraries) for a sense of *OWL*'s approach.

Youthink Magazine
4180 Lougheed Highway, 4th Floor, Burnaby, BC V5C 6A7
Phone: (604) 299-7311 Fax: (604) 299-9188
E-mail: oliver@youthink.ca
Website: www.youthink.ca
Contact: Oliver Lam, acting editor
Circulation: 40,000
Published 6 times a year

   Youthink is distributed through high schools and businesses in B.C. and is written entirely by students. There is a heavy focus on entertainment, particularly music. Articles 250 to 600 words. Cannot pay but welcomes inquiries. "Only high school students are eligible to submit articles, poems, artwork, photography, etc."

ZAMOOF!
644 Spruceview Place S., Kelowna, BC V1V 2P7
Phone: (250) 762-9624 Fax: (250) 762-9654
E-mail: mail@zamoofmag.com
Website: www.zamoofmag.com
Contact: TeLeni Koochin, publisher
Circulation: 5,000
Published six times a year

   ZAMOOF! is a print publication (digital available) for kids 7 to 12 about making healthy and safe choices. Majority of content is written in-house or by youth readers, but Canadian parents, teachers, and caregivers are welcome to submit work to two categories: "Feet Up Chronicles" (narrative pieces about parenthood, 300–375 words) and "Pet Horoscopes" (about pets or animals in general, between 20 to 27 words). Pays $0.20/word. Guidelines available on website.

2

LITERARY & SCHOLARLY PUBLICATIONS

It's ironic that literary and scholarly journals, which are among the most prestigious outlets for a writer's work, can least afford to pay their contributors. Many journals rely on funding from arts councils, or from academic or professional sources, and still run at a loss. They have relatively small subscription lists, perhaps two or three unpaid or part-time staff, and attract little or no advertising support. They can rarely afford to pay their contributors much, and in many cases, modest funding and low revenues preclude payment altogether, or limit it to small honoraria or free copies.

Writers would be unwise to look to this sector of publishing as a significant source of income. Qualified writers would be just as unwise to neglect it because of this. Publishing your work in a distinguished literary or scholarly journal can add immeasurably to your reputation and may well open up other publishing opportunities. This chapter lists many of Canada's most notable journals and literary magazines. Use the information presented in each entry to help you choose the most appropriate publications to approach.

Contributors to scholarly journals are frequently graduate students, salaried academics, or professionals who draw on current areas of research. For graduate students, journal publication is often an essential element of their professional development. The successful applicant for a university teaching position, for instance, will usually have a substantial publishing history.

Before you make your submission, familiarize yourself thoroughly with the journal to which you hope to contribute. Editors take a dim view of submissions from writers who are obviously unfamiliar with their publication. Study several recent issues, or better still, subscribe. Learn what you can of the editors' approaches and points of view, and the kind of work they favour. Determine who their readers are. If they have a website, be sure to visit it.

Always request writers' guidelines or read them online, and follow these closely to ensure you meet the editors' needs. Remember to include an SASE whenever you expect a response. Refereed journals will require several copies of your submission. Scholarly articles will need to be accompanied by full documentation. Fiction, poetry, reviews, and criticism must be carefully targeted and professionally presented. The extra care and attention will pay dividends.

Acadiensis: Journal of the History of the Atlantic Region
University of New Brunswick, Campus House, Fredericton, NB
 E3B 5A3
Phone: (506) 458-7199 (editors) or (506) 453-4978 (general)
 Fax: (506) 453-5068
E-mail: acadnsis@unb.ca or acadjrnl@unb.ca
Website: www.lib.unb.ca/texts/acadiensis
Contacts: Bill Parenteau, editor, or Stephen Dutcher, managing
 editor
Circulation: 850
Published twice a year
 Includes original academic research, review articles, documents, notes, and a running bibliography compiled by librarians in the four Atlantic provinces. "Canada's most ambitious scholarly journal" – Michael Bliss, *Journal of Canadian Studies*. Articles published in English and in French. Cannot pay but welcomes submission inquiries. Guidelines available on website.

Alberta History
Historical Society of Alberta, 95 Holmwood Avenue N.W.,
 Calgary, AB T2K 2G7
Phone: (403) 289-8149 Fax: (403) 289-8144
E-mail: potaina@shaw.ca

Contact: Hugh Dempsey, editor
Circulation: 1,200
Published quarterly

Publishes articles on Alberta history from 3,000 to 5,000 words to a mostly province-wide audience. Cannot pay, but welcomes submission inquiries. Guidelines available.

The Antigonish Review

St. Francis Xavier University, P.O. Box 5000, Antigonish, NS
    B2G 2W5
Phone: (902) 867-3962 Fax: (902) 867-5563
E-mail: tar@stfx.ca
Website: www.antigonishreview.com
Contact: Bonnie McIsaac, office manager
Circulation: 1,000
Published quarterly

A creative literary review featuring poetry, fiction, reviews, and critical articles using original graphics to enliven the format. Directed at a general audience. Fiction 500 to 3,000 words; book reviews 1,000 to 2,500 words; poetry 5 to 6 pages maximum. Fiction submitted between October 1 and May 31 will be considered; fiction submitted between June 1 and September 30 will not be read. Pays on publication $50/article or essay, $50/fiction, $50/book review, $20/page to a maximum of $50 for poetry, and two copies of the publication. Guidelines available on website.

Arc Poetry Magazine

P.O. Box 81060, Ottawa, ON K1P 1B1
E-mail: arc@arcpoetry.ca
Website: www.arcpoetry.ca
Contact: Katia Grubisic, editor
Circulation: 1,300
Published 3 times a year

Publishes poetry from Canada and abroad, as well as reviews, interviews, and articles on poetry and poetry-related subjects. Unsolicited submissions of 5 poems maximum per author per reading period (September to May) may be submitted through the electronic submission manager on the website. For reviews, interviews and other prose, please query first. Pays $40/published page on publication. More information and web-exclusive content available on website.

BC Studies: The British Columbian Quarterly

University of British Columbia, 6303 N.W. Marine Drive,
    Room 2, Vancouver, BC V6T IZI
Phone: (604) 822-3727 Fax: (604) 822-0606
E-mail: info@bcstudies.com
Website: www.bcstudies.com
Contact: Leanne Coughlin, managing editor
Circulation: 600

Established in 1968, *BC Studies* is a peer-reviewed journal that explores British Columbia's cultural, economic, and political life, past and present. Each issue offers articles on a wide range of topics, in-depth reviews of current books, and a bibliography of recent publications. With a solid reputation for its authoritative and informative content, *BC Studies* is enjoyed by academics and general readers alike. Articles 7,000 to 8,000 words. Cannot pay for submissions and retains all rights to articles published. Guidelines available.

Brick

P.O. Box 609, Stn. P, Toronto, ON M5S 2Y4
Phone: (416) 593-9684
E-mail: info@brickmag.com
Website: www.brickmag.com
Contact: Laurie Graham, assistant editor and circulation manager
Circulation: 3,200
Published twice a year

Publishes literary non-fiction about books, writers, and literary pursuits. Pays on average $100 to $400 on publication for articles 250 to 3,500 words. Fees based on type of article and length. "We do not accept submissions of fiction or poetry, or non-fiction submissions sent by e-mail (hard copy only). Reading the magazine is your best guide to what we publish." Guidelines available on website.

Canadian Ethnic Studies

University of Manitoba, 301H Isbister Building, Winnipeg, MB
    R3T 2N2
Phone: (204) 474-8493 Fax: (204) 474-7653

E-mail: ces@cc.umanitoba.ca
Website: http://umanitoba.ca/publications/ces/
Contact: Natalia Aponiuk, editor
Published 3 times a year

An interdisciplinary journal devoted to the study of ethnicity, immigration, inter-group relations, and the history and cultural life of ethnic groups in Canada. Also includes book and film reviews, opinions, immigrant memoirs, translations of primary sources, an "ethnic voice" section, and an annual index. All material should address Canadian ethnicity. Charges a fee to evaluate work submitted – equivalent to an annual subscription – unless you are a member or already a subscriber. Research articles are from 20 to 30 double-spaced pages; book reviews from 750 to 850 words. Guidelines available. See website for more information.

The Canadian Historical Review
UTP Journals, 5201 Dufferin Street, Toronto, ON M3H 5T8
Phone: (416) 667-7777, ext. 7869 Fax: (416) 667-7881
E-mail: chr@utpress.utoronto.ca
Website: www.utpjournals.com/chr
Contacts: Nicole Neatby and Jeffrey L. McNairn, co-editors; Tom Pettitt, editorial assistant
Published quarterly

Publishes original research articles in all areas of Canadian history as well as research notes and book reviews. For academics and graduate students of Canadian history. Preferred length 5,000 to 10,000 words. Cannot pay but welcomes submission inquiries.

Canadian Journal of Film Studies
Concordia University, SB 419, 1455 de Maisonneuve Boulevard W., Montreal, QC H3G 1M8
Phone: (514) 398-4935 Fax: (514) 398-7247
E-mail: cjfsedit@filmstudies.ca
Website: www.filmstudies.ca
Contacts: Peter Urquhart, managing editor, and Charles Acland and Catherine Russell, editors-in-chief
Published twice a year

Distributed to members of the Film Association of Canada, to Canadian and international libraries, and to individual subscribers.

Length of articles up to 7,500 words; shorter articles for "Ciné-Documents" and "Ciné-Forum" up to 2,500 words. Contributors are not paid, but receive 5 complimentary copies of the issue in which their work appears, along with a PDF of their published article. Guidelines available on website.

Canadian Journal of History

Department of History, 9 Campus Drive, University of
   Saskatchewan, Saskatoon, SK S7N 5A5
Phone: (306) 966-5794 Fax: (306) 966-5852
E-mail: cjh@usask.ca
Website: www.usask.ca/history/cjh
Contact: Mark Meyers, editor
Published 3 times a year

Publishes general history of all countries in all periods. Articles to be based on original research with primary sources. Usually assessed by readers before publication. Detailed style guide on website.

Canadian Literature

University of British Columbia, 1866 Main Mall, Buchanan E158,
   Vancouver, BC V6T IZI
Phone: (604) 822-2780 Fax: (604) 827-4040
E-mail: can.lit@ubc.ca
Contact: Donna Chin, managing editor
Website: www.canlit.ca
Published quarterly

Devoted to studying many aspects of Canadian literature and offering a literary critique of Canadian writers. For academics, researchers, libraries, schools, and universities. Contributors are not paid. E-mail submission of articles is not accepted. Maximum length of articles 6,500 words, including notes and works cited. Must be double-spaced and submitted in triplicate with author's name removed. A few poems by Canadian writers accepted for each issue; the maximum length is 2 pages/poem. Guidelines available.

Canadian Modern Language Review

UTP Journals, 5201 Dufferin Street, Toronto, ON M3H 5T8
Phone: (416) 667-7777, ext. 7869 Fax: (416) 667-7881

E-mail: cmlr@utpress.utoronto.ca
Website: www.utpjournals.com/cmlr
Contacts: Laura Collins and Danièle Moore, co-editors; Tom
    Pettitt, editorial assistant
Circulation: 1,000
Published quarterly
    Publishes applied, linguistic, second-language theory, and peda-
gogical articles, book reviews, current advertisements, and other
material of interest to high-school and university language teachers
and academics. A balance of theory and practice. All articles are
voluntarily submitted rather than assigned and are refereed.
Preferred length 6,500 to 9,000 words. Contributors are not paid,
but submissions are welcome. Consult "Guide to Authors" in each
issue and write to editors for further information.

CNQ: Canadian Notes & Queries
P.O. Box 92, Emeryville, ON N0R 1A0
Phone: (519) 968-2206 Fax: (519) 250-5713
E-mail: info@notesandqueries.ca
Website: www.notesandqueries.ca
Contact: Daniel Wells, publisher
Published three times a year
    CNQ covers art, literature, and books in Canada.

Canadian Poetry: Studies, Documents, Reviews
Department of English, University of Western Ontario, London,
    ON N6A 3K7
Phone: (519) 661-3403 Fax: (519) 661-3776
E-mail: canadianpoetry@uwo.ca
Website: www.canadianpoetry.ca and www.canadianpoetry.org
Contact: D. M. R. Bentley, editor
Published twice a year
    A scholarly and critical refereed journal devoted to the study of
poetry from all periods and regions of Canada. Prints articles,
reviews, and documents – 500 to 5,000 words – directed toward
university and college students and teachers. No original poetry.
Cannot pay but welcomes submissions. Follow *MLA Style Manual*.
Guidelines available.

Canadian Public Administration / Administration publique du Canada

1075 Bay Street, Suite 401, Toronto, ON M5S 2BI
Phone: (416) 924-8787 Fax: (416) 924-4992
E-mail: msproule-jones@ipac.ca
Submissions: http://mc.manuscriptcentral.com/capa
Website: www.ipac.ca
Contact: Megan Sproule-Jones, managing editor
Circulation: 3,500
Published quarterly

A refereed journal, written by public administrators and academics, that examines structures, processes, and outcomes of public policy and public management related to executive, legislative, judicial, and quasi-judicial functions in municipal, provincial, and federal spheres of government. "We are a high-quality, well-established journal that is distinctive in terms of its objectives and contents." Maximum word length for articles is 7,500 words; for book reviews, 1,250 words. Contributors are unpaid. Guidelines available on website.

Canadian Social Work

383 Parkdale Avenue, Suite 402, Ottawa, ON KIY 4R4
Phone: (613) 729-6668 Fax: (613) 729-9608
E-mail: casw@casw-acts.ca
Website: www.casw-acts.ca
Contact: France Audet, administrative coordinator
Circulation: 9,000
Published once a year

Publication of the Canadian Association of Social Workers. A bilingual forum for social-work professionals through which social workers and others share their knowledge, skills, research, and information with each other and with the general public. Peer reviewed. Articles from 2,500 to 5,000 words and shorter articles 250 to 1,000. Cannot pay but welcomes submission inquiries. First preference given to CASW members. Guidelines available.

Canadian Woman Studies

210 Founders College, York University, 4700 Keele Street, North
York, ON M3J IP3

Phone: (416) 736-5356 Fax: (416) 736-5765
E-mail: cwscf@yorku.ca
Website: http://pi.library.yorku.ca/ojs/index.php/cws/
Contact: Luciana Ricciutelli, managing editor
Circulation: 5,000
Published quarterly

A bilingual, thematic journal featuring current scholarly writing and research on a wide variety of feminist topics. Welcomes creative writing, poetry, experiential articles, and essays of 750 to 3,000 words, as well as book reviews. Contributors are unpaid but receive a complimentary copy of the issue containing their work. Guidelines available.

The Capilano Review

2055 Purcell Way, North Vancouver, BC V7J 3H5
Phone: (604) 984-1712
E-mail: tcr@capilanou.ca
Website: www.thecapilanoreview.ca
Contact: Tamara Lee, managing editor
Circulation: 800
Published 3 times a year

The Capilano Review has a long history of publishing new and established Canadian writers and artists who are experimenting with or expanding the boundaries of conventional forms and contexts. Celebrating its 40th year, the magazine continues to favour the risky, the provocative, the innovative, and the dissident. "Recently we have published work by Steve McCaffery, Garry Thomas Morse, Ted Byrne, Lisa Robertson, Clint Burnham, Alan Davies, Daphne Marlatt, Christian Bök, Stephen Collis, Christos Dikeakos, Marian Penner Bancroft, Liz Magor and others." Pays $50/page to a maximum of $300 on publication. Carries stories up to 3,000 words. Guidelines and sample copies available on website. We encourage writers to read a few issues of the magazine before submitting.

Carousel

UC 274, University of Guelph, Guelph, ON N1G 2W1
E-mail: carouselbook@yahoo.ca
Website: www.carouselmagazine.ca

Contact: Mark Laliberte, managing editor
Published twice a year

A hybrid literary and arts magazine, *Carousel* is interested in representing both new and established artists, with a specific focus on positioning Canadian talent within an international context. Imposes a small fee to non-subscribers to process poetry and fiction submissions sent by e-mail. Welcomes submissions of 3 to 7 poems and fiction less than 3,000 words. Pays an honorarium on publication of $10 for 1 to 2 printed pages of fiction; $20 for 2 to 4 pages; and $25 for 5 and more pages of fiction, and $10/poem.

CHALLENGER international

Phone: (250) 991-5567
E-mail: lukivdan@hotmail.com
Website: http://challengerinternational.20m.com/index.html
Contact: Dan Lukiv, editor
Circulation: 50
Published once a year

This low-budget, high school–based literary journal publishes poetry and fiction by children through to seasoned authors. Distributed to Quesnel District high school students. Encourages young writers, especially teenagers, to submit poetry. Experimental work welcome if it makes sense. "We like poetry with vivid images and clear themes." Stories to 1,000 words. No profanity or pornography. Submissions by e-mail only. Include author details. Contributors paid in copies.

Contemporary Verse 2: The Canadian Journal of Poetry and Critical Writing

100 Arthur Street, Suite 502, Winnipeg, MB R3B 1H3
Phone: (204) 949-1365 Fax: (204) 942-5754
E-mail: cv2@mts.net
Website: www.contemporaryverse2.ca
Contact: Clarise Foster, editor
Circulation: 700
Published quarterly

Established 1975 by Dorothy Livesay, *CV2* is Canada's oldest and best read poetry quarterly. Publishes critical writing (including interviews, articles, essays, and regular features on poetry) and original verse. Poetry submissions should include no more than 4 to 6 poems; reviews should be 600 to 1000 words; interviews should be no longer than 6 to 8 double-spaced pages; articles no longer than 3 to 4 double-spaced pages; and essays no longer than 2 to 4 double-spaced pages.

For critical writing, please query first by post or e-mail (CV2_submissions@mts.net). Submission guidelines available on website. Pays $30/poem; $20 to $40 for reviews (600 to 1,000 words); $50 to $75 for interviews and articles; $40 to $75 for essays; and a complimentary copy of the issue. Please send a short bio and an SASE with your submission.

The Dalhousie Review
Dalhousie University, Halifax, NS B3H 4R2
Phone: (902) 494-2541 Fax: (902) 494-3561
E-mail: dalhousie.review@dal.ca
Website: www.dal.ca/~dalrev/
Contact: Anthony Stewart, editor
Circulation: 500
Published 3 times a year

Welcomes submissions of poetry up to 40 lines and short fiction and articles up to 5,000 words in such fields as history, literature, political science, sociology, and philosophy. Book reviews are usually commissioned but proposals will be considered; reviews are around 1,000 words. Contributors to this distinguished quarterly, first published in 1921, are given 10 off-prints and 2 complimentary copies of the issue. "Please enclose an SASE for return of your manuscript." See website for further guidelines.

Descant
P.O. Box 314, Stn. P, Toronto, ON M5S 2S8
Phone: (416) 593-2557 Fax: (416) 593-9362
E-mail: info@descant.ca
Website: www.descant.ca
Contact: Vera DeWaard, managing editor
Circulation: 1,200
Published quarterly

A literary journal publishing short fiction, poetry, essays, drama, interviews, photography, and art. Pays an honorarium of $100 to all contributors on publication. "Each manuscript submission receives a critical reading and must be approved by 3 members of our editorial board before acceptance. This process can take up to 12 months. Only unpublished material will be considered, and we request first publication rights." Guidelines available.

The Devil's Artisan

c/o The Porcupine's Quill, P.O. Box 160, 68 Main Street, Erin, ON
   NOB ITO
Phone: (519) 833-9158 Fax: (519) 833-9845
E-mail: homewood@idirect.com
Website: http://devilsartisan.ca
Contact: Don McLeod, editor
Circulation: 500
Published twice a year

The devil's artisan was a medieval term for a practitioner of the art and mystery of printing. "In publishing this journal, our desire is to maintain that early sense of curiosity about the craft of printing and bookmaking. We also present information on bibliographic and historic matters, and on communicative, sociological, and technical subjects related to printing. Each issue contains a handprinted keepsake." Pays $100 per article upon publication.

Echolocation Magazine

170 St George Street, 6th Floor, c/o Department of English,
   University of Toronto, oronto, ON M5R 2M8
E-mail: echolocation.utoronto@gmail.com
Website: http://echolocationmag.wordpress.com
Contact: editor-in-chief
Published annually

Seeks submissions of poetry, short fiction, creative non-fiction, interviews with authors and works of visual art. Maximum length for short fiction and creative non-fiction is 3,000 words. Do not send more than 10 poems per submission. Guidelines on website.

Eighteen Bridges

115 Humanities Centre, Suite 4, University of Alberta,
   Edmonton, AB T6G 2E5
E-mail: ebmag@ualberta.ca
Website: www.eighteenbridges.com
Contacts: Curtis Gillespie, editor, and Lynn Coady, senior editor
Published quarterly

Seeks in-depth stories about people, politics, culture, and ideas, grounded in the narrative tradition. Also publishes essays, fiction, and poetry. "The majority of our stories are generated through editorial commission, but we do welcome proposals." Guidelines on website.

Environments: A Journal of Interdisciplinary Studies

Geography and Environmental Studies, Wilfrid Laurier
   University, 75 University Avenue W., Waterloo, ON N2L 3C5
Phone: (519) 884-0710, ext. 2781 Fax: (519) 725-1342
E-mail: beth@environmentsjournal.ca
Website: www.environmentsjournal.ca
Contact: Beth Dempster, managing editor
Published 3 times a year

A refereed journal for scholars and practitioners. Promotes greater understanding of environmental, economic, and social change through papers (5,000 to 8,000 words) that assess the implications of change and provide information for improved decision-making. Book reviews (mostly solicited) are published and should be 500 to 800 words. Overviews of several books or publications focusing on a topic should not exceed 2,500 words. Oriented to academics, students, professionals, and concerned citizens. Does not use press releases. Cannot pay but welcomes submission inquiries. Guidelines available on website.

EVENT: The Douglas College Review

Douglas College, P.O. Box 2503, New Westminster, BC V3L 5B2
Phone: (604) 527-5293 Fax: (604) 527-5095
E-mail: event@douglascollege.ca
Website: http://eventmags.com
Contact: Ian Cockfield, managing editor
Circulation: 1,150
Published 3 times a year

Features poetry, fiction, creative non-fiction, and reviews of Canadian books. Submit up to 2 short stories of 5,000 words each or 3 to 8 poems. Pays $22/page on publication to a maximum of $500. Include a brief cover letter and an SASE with Canadian postage or an International Reply Coupon. *EVENT* is also home to Canada's longest-running non-fiction contest. Guidelines available on website.

ELQ: Exile Magazine

170 Wellington Street W., P.O. Box 308, Mount Forest, ON NOG 2LO
E-mail: exq@exilequarterly.com
Website: www.theexilewriters.com
Contact: fiction editor or poetry editor
Published quarterly

Exile draws its material – prose, poetry, drama, work in translation, and the fine arts – from English and French Canada, as well as from the U.S., Europe, Latin America, the Middle East, Asia, and all around the world. "We strongly suggest that you read two or three issues of the magazine to get an understanding of the 'flavour' of our editorial taste with regard to what we publish in our magazine. We only consider submissions that have not been placed elsewhere." Does not accept multiple submissions or e-mail submissions (send by post only). For fiction and drama, submit 10 to 20 pages; for poetry, submit up to 15 poems. Submission guidelines on website.

Existere: Journal of Arts and Literature

Vanier College, 101E, 4700 Keele Street, York University, Toronto, ON M3J IP3
E-mail: existere@yorku.ca
Website: www.yorku.ca/existere

Existere is the semi-annual arts & literature journal of York University. All genres and forms are welcome: short fiction, post-cards, poetry, short plays, reviews, criticism, essays, interviews, artworks, etc. Prose of no longer than 3,500 words to a maximum of 2 short fictions; 5 postcards; 5 poems; and/or 6 graphics will be considered from one submitter in one calendar year. Submissions must be accompanied by a brief letter, short bio, and full contact info. E-mail submissions are preferred and must be sent to existere. journal@gmail.com. Hard copy submissions must be accompanied by an SASE if return required. Small honorarium upon publication. Guidelines on website.

The Fiddlehead

Campus House, 11 Garland Court, University of New Brunswick,
    P.O. Box 4400, Fredericton, NB E3B 5A3
Phone: (506) 453-3501 Fax: (506) 453-5069
E-mail: fiddlehd@unb.ca
Website: www.thefiddlehead.ca
Contact: Kathryn Taglia, managing editor
Circulation: 1,500
Published quarterly

A highly respected literary journal, established in 1945, publishing poetry, short fiction, and some book reviews. Focuses on freshness and vitality. While retaining an interest in writers of Atlantic Canada, it is open to outstanding work from all over the English-speaking world. Stories up to 6,000 words, poetry up to 10 poems. Pays $40/published full page on publication. "Find yourself an issue and read it to get an idea of what we're about. Do not fax or e-mail submissions, and include an SASE for replies." Guidelines available.

filling Station

P.O. Box 22135, Bankers Hall, Calgary, AB T2P 4J5
E-mail: mgmt@fillingstation.ca
Website: www.fillingstation.ca
Contact: Caitlynn Cummings, managing editor
Published 3 times a year

Publishes innovative and experimental poetry, fiction, fine art, creative non-fiction, reviews, and literary journalism. Submissions received any time, preferably by e-mail. Include short bio and mailing address. Editor e-mail addresses available on website. Allow up to 4 months for reply. Successful contributors receive a 1-year subscription; subscription discount available to all submitters.

Geist Magazine

111 W. Hastings Street, Suite 210, Vancouver, BC V6B 1H4
Phone: (604) 681-9161 or 1-888-434-7834 Fax: (604) 677-6319
E-mail: geist@geist.com
Website: www.geist.com

Contact: Chelsea Novak, managing editor
Circulation: 9,000
Published quarterly

Geist is a magazine of ideas and culture made in Canada with a strong literary focus and a sense of humour. *Geist* is also the largest literary magazine in Canada. The *Geist* tone is intelligent, plain-talking, inclusive, and offbeat. Each issue reflects a convergence of fiction, non-fiction, photography, comix, reviews, little-known facts of interest, poetry, cartography, and the legendary *Geist* crossword puzzle.

Preferred length for creative non-fiction 200 to 1,000 words; for essays and short stories 2,000 to 5,000 words. Rates vary depending on project and are paid on publication. "We accept submissions online and also by snail mail. We do not accept pitches. Please read a copy of the magazine and see our website for guidelines before submitting."

Grain

P.O. Box 67, Saskatoon, SK S7K 3K1
Phone: (306) 244-2828 Fax: (306) 244-0255
E-mail: grainmag@sasktel.net
Website: www.grainmagazine.ca
Contact: Rilla Friesen, editor
Circulation: 1,200
Published quarterly

Publishes engaging, eclectic, and challenging writing and art by Canadian and international writers and artists. Published by the Saskatchewan Writers Guild since 1973, Grain has earned national and international recognition for its distinctive content. "No bias in terms of form, style, or genre; the editors welcome submissions that are diverse, idiosyncratic, intelligent, even idea- or concept-driven.

The editors want to be surprised! Submissions of creative/literary non-fiction also welcome (intellectual or theoretical, yes! Academic, no!)." Pays $50 to $225 on publication for all genres. Read back issues and submission guidelines before submitting. Guidelines available on website.

Hamilton Arts & Letters

92 Stanley Avenue, Hamilton, ON L8P 2L3
E-mail: halmagazine@gmail.com

Website: www.halmagazine.com
Contact: Paul Lisson, editor
Published biannually

Online-only magazine focused that accepts non-fiction and poetry submissions. *HA&L* "creates a sympathetic environment where a mood of engagement welcomes readers to explore the ethos of a particular place reaching out to other places."

illiterature.

130 James Street, Apartment 1, Kingston, ON K7K 1Z4
E-mail: editor@puddlesofskypress.com
Website: www.puddlesofskypress.com
Contact: Michael e. Casteels, editor

"A home for the weird." Publishes poetry, concrete/visual poetry, and short fiction. Submit by e-mail. Contributors are unpaid, but receive 2 copies of the magazine.

International Journal

45 Willcocks Street, Suite 210, Toronto, ON M5S 1C7
Phone: (416) 946-7209 or 1-800-668-2442 Fax: (416) 946-7319
E-mail: ij@opencanada.org
Website: www.internationaljournal.ca
Contact: Rima Berns-McGown, managing editor
Published quarterly

Established 1946. Recognized as Canada's preeminent scholarly publication on international relations. Writers are a mixture of scholars, practitioners, and policy-makers, Canadian and non-Canadian. Each issue has a specific theme. Length must not exceed 7,000 words. Articles assessed by at least 2 reviewers. Cannot pay contributors but welcomes submissions. Guidelines available on website.

Jeunesse: Young People, Texts, Cultures

Centre for Research in Young People's Texts and Cultures,
University of Winnipeg, 515 Portage Avenue, Winnipeg, MB R3B 2E9
E-mail: jeunesse@uwinnipeg.ca
Website: http://jeunessejournal.ca
Contact: Mavis Reimer, general editor

An interdisciplinary, refereed academic journal whose mandate is to publish research on, and to provide a forum for discussion about, cultural productions for, by, and about young people. Our scope is international; while we have a special interest in Canada, we welcome submissions concerning all areas and cultures. We are especially interested in the cultural functions and representations of "the child." This can include children's and young adult literature and media; young people's material culture, including toys; digital culture and young people; historical and contemporary constructions, functions, and roles of "the child" and adolescents; and literature, art, and films by children and young adults. We welcome articles in both English and French. Guidelines on website.

Journal of Bahá'í Studies
34 Copernicus Street, Ottawa, ON KIN 7K4
Phone: (613) 233-1903 Fax: (613) 233-3644
E-mail: editor@bahai-studies.ca
Website: www.bahai-studies.ca
Contact: Alex McGee, managing editor
Circulation: 2,000
Published twice a year
Founded in 1975. The journal of the Association for Bahá'í Studies aims to promote courses of study on the Bahá'í faith, to foster relationships with various leaders of thought and persons of capacity, to publish scholarly materials examining the Bahá'í faith, especially on the application to the concerns and needs of humanity, and to demonstrate the value of this scholarly approach in reinforcing the endeavours of the Bahá'í community to reach the diverse strata of society. Cannot pay but welcomes submissions. Guidelines available.

Journal of the Motherhood Initiative for Research and Community Involvement
140 Holland Street W., P.O. Box 13022, Bradford, ON L3Z 2Y5
Phone: (905) 775-9089
E-mail: info@motherhoodinitiative.org
Website: https://dce.yorku.ca/armsc/
Circulation: 2,500
Published twice a year

Written for scholars, researchers, artists, activists, and feminist mothers. Maximum length of articles 3,750 words. Contributors must be members of the Motherhood Initiative for Research and Community Involvement (MIRCI). Guidelines on website.

Joyland
E-mail: joylandsubmissions@gmail.com and
   joylandpoetry@gmail.com
Websites: www.joylandmagazine.com and www.joylandpoetry.com
Contact: Brian Joseph Davis, publisher

Online literary magazine that curates fiction regionally; editors work with authors with a connection to their area. Publishes short fiction, novel excerpts, and personal essays, generally between 1,200 and 8,000 words, as well as poetry. Paste work and bio into the body of an e-mail (no attachments) with a subject line indicating the city/region section. Encourages simultaneous submissions. Guidelines on website.

Lake: a journal of arts and environment
Department of Creative Studies, UBC Okanagan, 3333
   University Way, Kelowna, BC V1V 1V7
E-mail: lake.journal@ubc.ca
Website: www.lakejournal.ca
Contacts: Sharon Thesen and Nancy Holmes, editors
Published twice a year

Publishes fiction, poetry, critical essays, interviews, reviews, and visual arts related to the environment. "We are looking for invigorating, controversial and meditative works that are about our relation to the natural world." Does not accept e-mail submissions. Guidelines on website.

Lester's Army
111 W. Hastings Street, Suite 210, Vancouver, BC V6B 1J5
Phone: (604) 909-2158
E-mail: editor@lestersarmy.com
Website: www.lestersarmy.com
Contact: Leni Goggins, editor
Circulation: 1,500
Published twice a year

Lester's Army, published through the registered charity Arts in Action, strives to "bridge the gap between the young and old through storytelling and through the production of this magazine." Accepts fiction, literary non-fiction, memoir, poetry, art, and illustration. Topics covered include mortality, aging, ageism, history, identity, family, culture, and war. "Most of our contributors are under the age of 30 or over the age of 65, to fit with our mandate, however we accept submissions from people of all ages, backgrounds and levels of experience." Writers' guidelines available on website.

The Literary Review of Canada

581 Markham Street, Toronto, ON M6G 2L7
Phone: (416) 531-1483 Fax: (416) 531-1612
E-mail: editor@lrcreview.com
Website: www.reviewcanada.ca
Contact: Bronwyn Drainie, editor-in-chief
Circulation: 5,000
Published 10 times a year

A tabloid in the style of *The New York Review of Books*, carrying substantive book reviews of Canadian non-fiction and fiction, although it also publishes poetry, occasional essays, and excerpts. Provides a forum for intellectual curiosity, critical thinking, and the vigorous examination of ideas. Intriguing, incisively written, and informative, it attracts a highly educated readership. Reviews are 2,000 to 3,500 words. Prefers e-mailed proposals and outlines over those faxed or mailed, but they are also acceptable. Accepts poetry submissions by e-mail from May 1 to October 1 each year. Payment is negotiable.

The Malahat Review

University of Victoria, P.O. Box 1700, Stn. CSC, Victoria, BC
    V8W 2Y2
Phone: (250) 721-8524 Fax: (250) 472-5051
E-mail: malahat@uvic.ca
Website: www.malahatreview.ca
Contact: John Barton, editor
Circulation: 1,400
Published quarterly

Publishes Canadian and international poetry, short fiction, and creative non-fiction, as well as reviews of Canadian literary titles.

Submit 6 to 10 poems, and/or fiction or creative non-fiction of 2,000 to 6,000 words. Pays $30/page on acceptance. "Response time for poetry and creative non-fiction is 1–3 months; fiction 3–10 months. Submissions must be accompanied by either an e-mail address or an SASE with sufficient postage/IRC." Guidelines available on website.

Matrix Magazine

1400 de Maisonneuve W., Suite LB-658, Montreal, QC H3G IM8
E-mail: info@matrixmagazine.org
Website: www.matrixmagazine.org
Contact: Jon Paul Fiorentino, editor-in-chief
Published quarterly

Publishes art, essays, fiction, poetry, and photography. Looking for book reviews (250 to 350 words), especially of titles published by small presses, and short articles – opinion, point of view, and essays on art and photography. Issues are themed. "Unsolicited submissions are no longer accepted. Only submissions that respond to calls will be read." Pays $25 to $40/poem or page of prose; $15/book review.

Mosaic: A Journal for the Interdisciplinary Study of Literature

208 Tier Building, University of Manitoba, Winnipeg, MB
R3T 2N2
Phone: (204) 474-9763 Fax: (204) 474-7584
E-mail: mosaic_journal@umanitoba.ca
Website: www.umanitoba.ca/mosaic
Contact: Jackie Pantel, business manager
Circulation: 900
Published quarterly

Explores the interaction between literary study and research in other disciplines. The journal features well-established scholars, as well as emerging researchers, all of whom contribute lively discussions about literature and literary issues from all periods and genres. Invites provocative, interdisciplinary submissions (7,000 to 7,500 words) that identify and engage key issues in a variety of areas, including memory, the archive, reconsidering the documentary, post-colonial literatures, the idea of community, travel writing, the interrelations of literature and film, cryptographic imagination, architecture and text, the poetics of space, and the literary signature. Contributors are unpaid. Submission inquiries welcome. Guidelines available.

The Nashwaak Review
51 Deneen Drive, Fredericton, NB E3B 5G3
Phone: (506) 452-0614 Fax: (506) 450-9615
E-mail: tnr@stu.ca
Website: http://w3.stu.ca/stu/about/publications/nashwaak
Contacts: Stewart Donovan, editor
Circulation: 700
Published once a year

A non-profit magazine for new and established artists. Funded solely by St. Thomas University. Stories 500 to 2,000 words. "Submissions must be sent by hard copy as well as electronically as an attachment. All submissions must be accompanied by an SASE." Asks for first Canadian rights. Cannot pay but welcomes submission inquiries.

The New Quarterly: Canadian Writers & Writing
c/o St. Jerome's University, 290 University Avenue N., Waterloo,
    ON N2L 3G3
Phone: (519) 884-8111, ext. 28290 Fax: (519) 884-5759, attn:
    New Quarterly
E-mail: editor@tnq.ca for editorial queries, info@tnq.ca for
    general queries
Website: www.tnq.ca
Contact: Pamela Mulloy, editor
Circulation: 1,000

Publishes short and long fiction, poetry, literary non-fiction, interviews, and essays on writing, with a focus on "new directions in Canadian writing." Does not publish reviews. Prose can be anything from postcard fiction to novellas. "Reading us is the best way to get our measure. We don't have preconceived ideas about what we're looking for other than it must be by Canadian authors. We want something that is fresh, something that will repay a second reading, something in which the language soars." Pays $250 for fiction, $250 for essays, $40 for postcard fiction, and $40/poem, on publication. Tries to publish at least 1 or 2 new writers in each issue. "We read twice a year: spring and fall. Response within 4 months of the start of the reading period. Please see our guidelines at http://tnq.rtraction.com/submissions before submitting."

Newfoundland & Labrador Studies

Memorial University, Faculty of Arts Publications, FM 2005, St.
   John's, NL A1C 5S7
Phone: (709) 737-2144 Fax: (709) 737-4342
E-mail: nlstudies@mun.ca
Website: www.mun.ca/nls
Contact: Irene Whitfield, managing editor
Circulation: 350
Published twice a year

A refereed academic journal containing articles, reviews, and documents in English and French. Maximum length 12,000 words. Cannot pay but welcomes submission inquiries. Guidelines available.

NōD Magazine

Department of English, University of Calgary, 2500 University
   Drive N.W., Calgary, AB T2T 1N4
E-mail: nodmagazine@gmail.com
Website: http://english.ucalgary.ca/NodMagazine

A literary magazine published and edited by University of Calgary undergraduate students. Publishes prose, poetry, and art submitted by students and writers in and outside the university. "Submissions are accepted via e-mail (preferable) or snail mail. For e-mail submissions, please send your work as an attached file. Please inform us if you are an undergraduate or not when submitting to the magazine. Visual artists should be aware that their work must be easily transferable into digital format and that all work will be printed in black and white except for work chosen as cover art."

Ontario History

34 Parkview Avenue, Willowdale, ON M2N 3Y2
Phone: (416) 226-9011 Fax: (416) 226-2740
E-mail: ohs@ontariohistoricalsociety.ca
Website: www.ontariohistoricalsociety.ca

Contact: Thorold Tronrud, editor
Published twice a year

Published since 1899, *Ontario History* specializes in the history of Ontario in any period: Native to newcomer to new millennium. Articles are scholarly yet accessible to all intelligent readers. Articles should be based on original research and be from 4,500 to 8,500 words. Cannot pay but welcomes submission inquiries. Guidelines on website.

Optimum Online

263 Holmwood Avenue, Ottawa, ON KIS 2P8
Phone: (613) 688-0763 Fax: (613) 688-0767
E-mail: mcegalbreath@summitconnects.com
Website: www.optimumonline.ca
Contact: McEvoy Galbreath, managing editor
Circulation: 10,000
Published quarterly

Optimum is an online, peer-reviewed journal on Canadian public sector management issues. Its readership are public servants and academics from around the world. Articles from 2,500 to 3,500 words. Cannot pay but welcomes submission inquiries. Guidelines available on website.

Poetry Is Dead

5020 Frances Street, Burnaby, BC V5B IT3
Phone: (604) 788-2777
E-mail: editor@poetryisdead.ca
Website: www.poetryisdead.ca
Contact: Daniel Zomparelli, editor
Circulation: 1,250
Published twice a year

"Presents an edgy, humorous and not-to-be-taken-serious attitude on poetry." Contains original Canadian content and review coverage and reviews of Canadian poets and poetry books. "Please check our website for the current call for submissions. If you are wanting to write a review or essay, please query the editor first by e-mail." Does not accept submissions through e-mail; use the submission form on the website. Pays $100 for articles, and $25 per poem and per review. Provides a subscription discount for those submitting material.

Prairie Fire

100 Arthur Street, Suite 423, Winnipeg, MB R3B 1H3
Phone: (204) 943-9066 Fax: (204) 942-1555
E-mail: prfire@mts.net
Website: www.prairiefire.ca
Contact: Andris Taskans, editor
Circulation: 1,350
Published quarterly

Publishes fiction, creative non-fiction, and poetry. Submissions may be from 10 to 10,000 words. Pays on publication: for prose: 10¢/word (maximum $500); for poetry: $50 for first page, $40 for each additional page (maximum $250); for other items: $40 for first page, $30 for each additional page (maximum $125); for reviews (in our online journal, *Prairie Fire Review of Books*): 5¢/word. Guidelines and full payment schedule available. All submissions must be accompanied by an SASE or an e-mail address for reply only.

Prairie Forum

Canadian Plains Research Centre, University of Regina, Regina,
   SK S4S 0A2
Phone: (306) 585-4758 Fax: (306) 585-4699
E-mail: brian.mlazgar@uregina.ca
Website: www.cprc.uregina.ca
Contact: Howard Leeson, editor
Circulation: 300
Published twice a year

An interdisciplinary scholarly journal that publishes inter-disciplinary scholarly research on the Canadian plains region. Market largely comprises university professors. Articles 3,500 to 10,000 words. Welcomes inquiries. No fees are paid. Guidelines available.

The Prairie Journal

P.O. Box 68073, Calgary, AB T3G 3N8
E-mail: prairiejournal@yahoo.com
Website: www.prairiejournal.org
Contact: Anne Burke, editor
Circulation: 700
Published twice a year

A literary journal featuring new and established Canadian writers of poetry, short fiction, reviews, interviews, and other creative and critical writing. Articles from 1,000 to 2,000 words. Honouraria depends on grant. Query with samples before submitting reviews and interviews. No e-mail submissions accepted. "We acquire first North American rights only." Guidelines available on website. "We also publish online (poems, stories, interviews, and reviews). We welcome freelance submissions with brief bios."

PRISM international

Creative Writing Program, University of British Columbia, 1866
  Main Mall, Buchanan E462, Vancouver, BC V6T IZI
Phone: (604) 822-2514 Fax: (604) 822-3616
E- mail: prismfiction@gmail.com or prismpoetry@gmail.com
Website: www.prismmagazine.ca
Contacts: Anna Ling Kaye, fiction editor; Leah Horlick, poetry
  editor
Published quarterly

The oldest literary journal in Western Canada, *PRISM international* features innovative new fiction, poetry, drama, literary nonfiction, and translation from Canada and around the world. Maximum submission length is 25 pages, double spaced; 1 piece of fiction, non-fiction, and drama; and a maximum of 7 poems. Pays on publication $40/published page for poetry, $20/published page for prose, plus contributor copies. Do not submit more than once in a three-month period. "We are looking for striking work in all areas. Show us originality of thought and close attention to language. No genre fiction, please. Guidelines and annual contest information available on our website."

Public

303 Goldfarb Centre for Fine Arts, York University, 4700 Keele
  Street, Toronto, ON M3J IP3
E-mail: public@yorku.ca
Website: www.publicjournal.ca
Contact: Aleksandra Kaminska, managing editor
Circulation: 1,000
Published twice a year

An interdisciplinary journal with a core focus on visual art. Conceived as a hybrid intellectual and creative forum that investigates how theoretical and critical issues intersect with art and public culture. Each issue is devoted to a contemporary problem or theme and features content that combines critical writing, rich illustration throughout, and artist portfolios. Articles 1,000 to 4,500 words. Non-thematic exhibition and book reviews. Limited funds to pay for contributions, range from $25 to $150, paid upon publication. For article submissions, check website for upcoming issue calls. For reviews, e-mail a proposal and bio. Guidelines available.

Queen's Quarterly

Queen's University, 144 Barrie Street, Kingston, ON K7L 3N6
Phone: (613) 533-2667 Fax: (613) 533-6822
E-mail: queens.quarterly@queensu.ca
Website: www.queensu.ca/quarterly
Contact: Boris Castel, editor
Circulation: 3,000

A distinctive and multidisciplinary university-based review with a Canadian focus and an international outlook. First published in 1893. Features scholarly articles (2,000 to 2,500 words) of general interest on politics, history, science, the humanities, and arts and letters, plus regular music and science columns, original poetry, fiction, and extensive book reviews. Fees, which are paid on publication, are negotiated. Guidelines available.

Resources for Feminist Research

OISE, University of Toronto, 252 Bloor Street W., Toronto, ON
M5S 1V6
Phone: (416) 978-2033 Fax: (416) 926-4725
E-mail: rfrdrf@oise.utoronto.ca
Website: www.oise.utoronto.ca/rfr
Contact: Philinda Masters, editor
Circulation: 2,000
Published quarterly

A journal of feminist scholarship containing research articles, abstracts, book reviews, and bibliographies. "*RFR* is an academic journal, so we accept research articles within a feminist perspective." Preferred length 7,000 to 10,000 words. Cannot pay but welcomes submissions. Guidelines are outlined on inside back cover of journal.

Rhubarb

100 Arthur Street, Suite 606, Winnipeg, MB R3B 1H3
E-mail: submit@rhubarbmag.com or venns@mts.net
Website: www.rhubarbmag.com
Contact: Victor Enns
Circulation: 1,000
Published quarterly

Publishes new art and writing by people of Mennonite heritage for a general reading public. Poetry up to 30 lines; creative non-fiction and short fiction up to 2,500 words. *Rhubarb* also publishes humour, book reviews, and commentary. Each issue is themed. Pays a small fee on publication. Guidelines available on website.

Ricepaper Magazine

P.O. Box 74174, Hillcrest RPO, Vancouver, BC V5V 5C8
Phone: (604) 872-3464
E-mail: editor@ricepapermagazine.ca
Website: www.ricepapermagazine.ca
Contact: Ray Hsu, editor
Circulation: 2,000
Published quarterly

Focuses on Asian-Canadian art and culture. Publishes reviews, previews, interviews, profiles, essays, short fiction, poetry, visual artwork, scripts, and features on visual arts, music, dance, poetry, theatre, and culture. Notable missives (non-fiction narrative) are 200 to 1,500 words; works in progress are 400 to 3,500 words; excerpts from short stories, novels, poetry, and non-fiction are 300 to 1,500 words; short profiles are 800 to 1,000 words; reviews are 300 to 500 words; long features and stories are 2,000 to 2,500 words. Pays $50 to $200 along with an issue of the magazine. Welcomes submission inquiries; query first.

Room

P.O. Box 46160, Stn. D, Vancouver, BC V6J 5G5
E-mail: contactus@roommagazine.com
Website: www.roommagazine.com

Contact: editorial collective
Published quarterly

Solicits fine writing and art from women authors in Canada and other countries, both well-known and unknown. Features original poetry, fiction, artwork, and creative non-fiction. Submit up to 5 poems at a time rather than a single poem. Stories up to 3,500 words. Pays a small honorarium on publication, plus 2 copies of the issue and a 1-year subscription. Guidelines are available on website, but reading recent back issues will provide the best guidance.

Scrivener Creative Review

McGill University, 853 Sherbrooke Street W., Montreal, QC
  H3A 2T6
Phone: (514) 398-6588
E-mail: scrivener.creative.review@gmail.com
Website: www.scrivenerreview.com
Contacts: Klara du Plessis, coordinating editor
Circulation: 300
Published twice a year

Publishes poetry, fiction, and photography from new and established talent in Canada and abroad. Stories 200 to 9,000 words. Poetry submissions should not be longer than 15 pages and should include no more than 6 poems. Cannot pay but welcomes submissions. Guidelines available on website.

Studies in Canadian Literature/Études en littérature canadienne

Campus House, 11 Garland Court, University of New Brunswick,
  P.O. Box 4400, Fredericton, NB E3B 5A3
Phone: (506) 453-3501 Fax: (506) 453-5069
E-mail: scl@unb.ca
Website: http://journals.hil.unb.ca/index.php/SCL/index
Contact: Kathryn Taglia, managing editor
Circulation: 450
Published twice a year

A bilingual, refereed journal of literary criticism of Canadian literature. Carries scholarly articles of 6,000 to 8,000 words (including endnotes and works cited) and 4,500 to 70,000 word interviews with Canadian authors in whom there is an established academic interest. Contributors receive a complimentary 1-year subscription. The market is scholarly libraries and academics. Guidelines in journal and on website. Use *MLA Handbook* for style. Papers are blind-vetted by 2 members of an advisory board, so author's name should be separate. Electronic submissions only.

subTerrain Magazine

P.O. Box 3008, MPO, Vancouver, BC V6B 3X5
Phone: (604) 876-8710 Fax: (604) 879-2667
E-mail: subter@portal.ca
Contact: Brian Kaufman, publisher/editor-in-chief
Website: www.subterrain.ca
Published 3 times a year

Publishes first-time and established writers from across North America. Interested in progressive writing – fiction, commentary, and poetry. No unsolicited poetry. Preferred length for fiction is a maximum of 3,000 words (2,000 is better); commentary and creative non-fiction should be 4,000 words maximum. Pays on publication $25/page for prose, $25/poem. Issues are theme-driven, so identify the theme issue for which you are writing (see the website).

Taddle Creek

P.O. Box 611, Stn. P, Toronto, ON M5S 2Y4
Phone: (416) 324-9075
E-mail: editor@taddlecreekmag.com
Website: www.taddlecreekmag.com
Contact: Conan Tobias, publisher/editor-in-chief
Circulation: 1,500
Published twice a year

Publishes urban fiction and poetry by Toronto authors. Only submissions of fiction and poetry are accepted; no preferred length. Authors must currently be residing in Toronto. Pays $25/page on publication. Guidelines available on website. "Authors should not submit before reading guidelines."

The Toronto Review of Books

E-mail: jessica@torontoreviewofbooks.com
Website: www.torontoreviewofbooks.com

Contact: Jessica Duffin Wolfe, editor
Published quarterly

Online platform covering print and e-books. Also reviews "websites, art, policy, cloud formations, and everything in between." Query the editor by e-mail with your ideas and writing background, indicating whether you're interested in writing for the *TRB*'s regular issues, the Chirograph blog, or both. Publishes 1 to 3 poems in each issue. Can only pay a nominal fee.

Urban History Review

Becker Associates, 10 Morrow Avenue, Suite 202, Toronto, ON
M6R 2J1
Phone: (416) 538-1650 Fax: (416) 489-1713
E-mail: editorial@urbanhistoryreview.ca
Website: www.urbanhistoryreview.ca
Contact: Adam Becker, managing editor
Published twice a year

A bilingual interdisciplinary and refereed academic journal presenting articles covering such topics as architecture, heritage, urbanization, housing, and planning, all in an illustrated format. Regular features include in-depth articles, research notes, comprehensive book reviews, and notes and comments on conferences, urban policy, and publications. Shorter papers should be from 1,000 to 3,000 words; articles should be 6,000 to 10,000 words. Contributors are unpaid.

West Coast LINE

Simon Fraser University, 2027 East Annex, 8888 University
Drive, Burnaby, BC V5A 1S6
Phone: (778) 782-4988 Fax: (778) 782-5737
E-mail: wcl@sfu.ca
Website: www.westcoastline.ca
Contact: Michael Barnholden, managing editor
Website: www.westcoastline.ca
Published quarterly

Publishes work by contemporary writers and artists who are experimenting with or expanding the boundaries of conventional forms and contexts. Interested in work that is engaged with problems of representation, race, culture, gender, sexuality, technology, media, urban/rural spaces, nature, and language. "We advise those considering submitting work to first familiarize themselves with the journal and with the work of our recent contributors." Fiction up to 5,000 words; poetry up to 400 lines. Pays $10/page to maximum of $200 after publication. Annual reading period is from June 1 to August 31. Submissions received outside this period will be returned unread. Do not submit by e-mail. Guidelines available on website.

Windsor Review

Department of English, University of Windsor, 401 Sunset,
    Windsor, ON N9B 3P4
Phone: (519) 253-3000, ext. 2290 Fax: (519) 971-3676
E-mail: uwrevu@uwindsor.ca; mgervais@uwindsor.ca;
holbrook@uwindsor.ca
Website: http://windsorreview.wordpress.com
Contacts: Marty Gervais, managing editor; Alistair MacLeod,
    fiction editor; Susan Holbrook, poetry editor
Published twice a year

Published by the University of Windsor's Faculty of Arts and Social Sciences. Features poetry, short fiction, art, and interviews with prominent authors and artists. Fiction from 1,000 to 5,000 words. Maximum of 6 poems. Contributors receive a small payment and complimentary copies of the issue containing their work. Guidelines available on website.

3

TRADE, BUSINESS, FARM, & PROFESSIONAL PUBLICATIONS

Trade publications are a potentially lucrative sector of the writer's market that is often overlooked. Although most pay no more than $500 for a full-length article, and usually less, the writing may require considerably fewer sources than are needed for consumer magazine features. An article can often be completed in a day or two, sometimes after research and interviews conducted solely by telephone. In terms of hours spent, therefore, the pay is generally relatively good. What's more, trade editors are often keen to find competent new writers.

The secret to making money from these publications is to work frequently for as many as possible, always bearing in mind that they may want a degree of technical detail that will inform readers already well acquainted with the specific fields they serve. If you have an area of specialist knowledge, you have a significant advantage. If not, you would do well to familiarize yourself with at least one trade or business area and the publications that serve it. Most trade periodicals, however, deliberately avoid becoming too technical, and aim to appeal to a wider readership. It bears repeating that before submitting, you must familiarize yourself with the magazine thoroughly by reading back issues.

Magazines in each of the following categories carry pieces about new products and developments, unusual marketing and promotion ideas, innovative management techniques, and prominent people and events specific to the industry, trade, or profession they serve. The regional business journals are highly recommended for freelance writers with business knowledge, since they often pay top dollar for timely and well-informed contributions. Those writers who have found markets through the main business section in Chapter 1 may profitably pursue this specialty further in the business listing below.

In many cases, staff writers produce the bulk of the feature writing and call on outside experts to provide specific material. But editors will often use freelancers when there is an editorial shortfall. Some cultivate long-term relationships with regular freelancers, who produce much of their copy. Often one editor is involved in several magazines, so making yourself and your work known to him or her can lead to further commissions, especially if you show yourself to be reliable and adaptable.

This chapter offers a broadly representative selection of trade publications across a wide range of industrial and professional areas, including many well-established, dependable employment sources, and provides a solid resource for the freelance writer looking to break into a new market. However, this is perhaps the most fluid sector in publishing: periodicals come and go and reappear under a new masthead; editors move from job to job relatively often in response to industry and structural changes. Chapter 11, Resources, lists some of the larger publishers of trade magazines in Canada, who can be contacted for a list of their publications.

For a monthly updated reference source, consult Rogers's *CARD* directory or online database at your library. Check *CARD*, too, or the annual supplement *Publication Profiles* for upcoming editorial themes, media profiles, circulation figures, and other useful information.

Advertising, Marketing, & Sales

Blitz Magazine
1360 Bathurst Street, Toronto, ON M5R 3H7
Phone: 1-888-952-5478 Fax: (647) 435-0304
E-mail: editor@blitzmagazine.com
Website: www.blitzmagazine.com
Contact: Ruth Zuchter, editor
Published 4 times a year (2 e-issues, 2 print issues)

Canadian Retailer

1255 Bay Street, Suite 800, Toronto, ON M5R 2A9
Phone: (416) 922-6678 or 1-888-373-8245 Fax: (416) 922-8011
E-mail: kdavies@naylor.com
Website: www.retailcouncil.org
Contact: Kim Davies, project manager
Published bimonthly

Contact Management Magazine

137 Main Street N., Suite 302, Markham, ON L3P 1Y2
Phone: (416) 461-9647 Fax: (905) 201-6601
E-mail: ron@contactmagazine.ca
Website: www.contactmagazine.ca
Contact: Ron Glen, editor
Published quarterly

Direct Marketing

137 Main Street N., Suite 302, Markham, ON L3P 1Y2
Phone: (905) 201-6600 Fax: (905) 201-6601
E-mail: amy@dmn.ca
Website: www.dmn.ca
Contact: Amy Bostock, editor
Published monthly

Marketing

1 Mount Pleasant Road, 7th Floor, Toronto, ON M4Y 2Y5
Phone: (416) 764-2000 Fax: (416)764-3934
E-mail: lucy.collin@marketingmag.rogers.com
Website: www.marketingmag.ca
Contact: Lucy Collin, publisher
Published 18 times a year

marketingedge

25 McIntyre Place, Unit 5, Kitchener, ON N2R 1H1
Phone: (519) 575-5836 Fax: (519) 893-0849
E-mail: melanie@marketingedgemagazine.com
Website: www.marketingedgemagazine.com
Contact: Melanie Chambers, editor
Published four times a year

Marketnews
701 Evans Avenue, Suite 102, Toronto, ON M9C IA3
Phone: (416) 667-9945 Fax: (416) 667-0609
E-mail: mail@marketnews.ca
Website: www.marketnews.ca
Contact: Robert Franner, editor
Published monthly

Pool & Spa Marketing
15 Wertheim Court, Suite 710, Richmond Hill, ON L4B 3H7
Phone: (905) 771-7333, ext. 235 or 1-800-409-8688 Fax: (905)
    771-7336
E-mail: editor@kenliworth.com
Website: www.poolspamarketing.com
Contact: Blair Adams, editorial director
Published 7 times a year

Strategy
366 Adelaide Street W., Suite 500, Toronto, ON M5V IR9
Phone: (416) 408-2300 Fax: (416) 408-0870
E-mail: maddever@brunico.com
Website: www.strategyonline.ca
Contact: Mary Maddever, editorial director
Published monthly

Architecture, Building, Engineering, & Heavy Construction

Aggregates & Roadbuilding Magazine
105 Donly Drive S., Simcoe, ON N3Y 4N5
Phone: 1-888-599-2228 Fax: (519) 429-3094
E-mail: sjamieson@annexweb.com
Website: www.rocktoroad.com
Contact: Scott Jamieson, editorial director and group publisher
Published 7 times a year

Alberta Construction Magazine
816 – 55 Avenue N.E., 2nd Floor, Calgary, AB T2E 6Y4
Phone: (403) 209-3500 or 1-800-387-2446 Fax: (403) 245-8666
E-mail: cosburn@junewarren-nickles.com
Website: www.albertaconstructionmagazine.com
Contact: Chaz Osburn, editor
Published quarterly

Award Magazine
4180 Lougheed Highway, 4th Floor, Burnaby, BC V5C 6A7
Phone: (604) 299-7311 Fax: (604) 299-9188
E-mail: smiller@canadawide.com
Website: www.canadawide.com
Contact: Shannon Miller, editor
Published bimonthly

Builders' Digest (Toronto Construction Association)
70 Leek Crescent, Richmond Hill, ON L4B 1H1
Phone: (416) 499-4000 Fax: (416) 499-8752
E-mail: robertt@mediaedge.ca
Website: www.tcaconnect.com/Industry_Publications.html
Contact: Robert Thompson, publisher
Published quarterly

Building Magazine
80 Valleybrook Drive, Toronto, ON M3B 2S9
Phone: (416) 510-5134 or 1-800-268-7742 (press 1, dial 6806)
   Fax: (416) 510-5134
E-mail: peter@building.ca
Website: www.building.ca
Contact: Peter Sobchak, editor
Published bimonthly

Canadian Architect
12 Concorde Place, Suite 800, Toronto, ON M3C 4J2
Phone: (416) 510-6845 or 1-800-668-2374 Fax: (416) 442-2131
   or (416) 510-5140
E-mail: ichodikoff@canadianarchitect.com
Website: www.canadianarchitect.com

Contact: Ian Chodikoff, editor
Published monthly

Canadian Civil Engineer
4877 Sherbrooke Street W., Westmount, QC H3Z IGI
Phone: (514) 933-2634 Fax: (514) 933-3504
E-mail: info@csce.ca
Website: www.csce.ca
Contact: Louise Newman, editor
Published 5 times a year

Canadian Consulting Engineer
80 Valleybrook Drive, Toronto, ON M3B 2S9
Phone: (416) 510-5119 Fax: (416) 510-5134
E-mail: bparsons@ccemag.com
Website: www.ccemag.com
Contact: Bronwen Parsons, editor
Published 7 times a year

Contracting Canada
1697 Kelsey Court, Mississauga, ON L5L 3J8
Phone: (905) 569-2777 Fax: (905) 569-2444
E-mail: don@contractingcanada.com
Website: www.contractingcanada.com
Contact: Don Beaulieu, editorial director/publisher
Published quarterly

Contractors Magazine
124 - 2323 Boundary Road, Vancouver, BC V5M 4V8
Phone: (604) 291-9900 Fax: (604) 291-1906
E-mail: kbardker@baumpub.com
Website: http://cm.baumpub.com
Contact: Keith Barker, editor
Published bimonthly

Daily Commercial News
500 Hood Road, 4th Floor, Markham, ON L3R 9Z3
Phone: 1-800-465-6475 Fax: 1-888-396-9413
E-mail: editor@dailycommercialnews.com

Website: www.dailycommercialnews.com
Contact: Patrick McConnell, national editor

Design Engineering
80 Valleybrook Drive, Toronto, ON M3B 2S9
Phone: (416) 442-5600 ext. 3231 Fax: (416) 510-5140
E-mail:mmcleoud@design-engineering.com
Website: www.canadianmanufacturing.com
Contact: Mike McLeod, editor
Published 6 times a year

Design Product News
222 Edward Street, Aurora, ON L4G 1W6
Phone: (905) 713-4389 Fax: (905) 727-0017
E-mail: medwards@annexweb.com
Website: www.dpncanada.com
Contact: Michael Edwards, editor
Published bimonthly

Engineering Dimensions
40 Sheppard Avenue W., Suite 101, Toronto, ON M2N 6K9
Phone: (416) 224-1100 or 1-800-339-3716 Fax: (416) 224-8168
    or 1-800-268-0496
E-mail: naxworthy@peo.on.ca
Website: www.peo.on.ca
Contact: Nicole Axworthy, associate editor
Published bimonthly

Equipment Journal
5160 Explorer Drive, Unit 6, Mississauga, ON L4W 4T7
Phone: (905) 629-7500 or 1-800-667-8541 Fax: (905) 629-7988
E-mail: editor@equipmentjournal.com
Website: www.equipmentjournal.com
Contact: Nathan Medcalf, editor
Published 17 times a year

Geomatica (Canadian Institute of Geomatics)
900 Dynes Road, Suite 100 D, Ottawa, ON K2C 3L6
Phone: (613) 224-9851 Fax: (613) 224-9577

E-mail: editgeo@magma.ca
Website: www.cig-acsg.ca
Contact: Izaak de Rijcke, editor
Published quarterly

Home Builder Magazine
4819 St. Charles Boulevard, Pierrefonds, QC H9H 3C7
Phone: (514) 620-2200 Fax: (514) 620-6300
E-mail: editor@work4.ca
Website: www.homebuildercanada.com
Contact: Judy Penz Sheluk, editor
Published bimonthly

Home Improvement Retailing
245 Fairview Mall Drive, Suite 501, Toronto, ON M2J 4T1
Phone: (416) 494-1066, ext. 15 Fax: (416) 494-2536
E-mail: jhornyak@powershift.ca
Website: www.hirmagazine.com
Contact: Joe Hornyak, executive editor
Published 6 times a year

Innovation
Phone: (604) 430-8035, ext. 4866 Fax: (604) 430-8085
E-mail: mlau@apeg.bc.ca
Website: www.apeg.bc.ca
Contact: Melinda Lau, managing editor
Published bimonthly

Journal of Commerce
4299 Canada Way, Suite 101, Burnaby, BC V5G 1H3
Phone: (604) 412-2260 or 1-888-878-2121 Fax: 1-800-661-1144
E-mail: editor@journalofcommerce.com
Website: www.journalofcommerce.com
Contact: Bradley Fehr, editor
Published twice a week

Ontario Home Builder
1062 Cooke Boulevard, Burlington, ON L7T 4A8
Phone: (905) 333-9432, ext. 251 Fax: (905) 333-4001

E-mail: editor@laureloakmarketing.ca
Website: www.ohba.ca
Contact: Steve McNeill, editor
Published bimonthly

On-Site
80 Valleybrook Drive, Toronto, ON M3B 2S9
Phone: (416) 442-5600 Fax: (416) 510-5140
E-mail: clynds@on-sitemag.com
Website: www.on-sitemag.com
Contact: Corinne Lynds, editor
Published 7 times a year

The PEG
1500 Scotia One, 10060 Jasper Avenue N.W., Edmonton, AB
    T5J 4A2
Phone: (780) 426-3990 or 1-800-661-7020 Fax: (780) 426-1877
E-mail: glee@apegga.org
Website: www.apegga.org
Contact: George Lee, manager, editorial services
Published 5 times a year

Perspectives (Ontario Association of Architects)
2 Bloor Street W., Suite 2001, Toronto, ON M4W 3E2
Phone: (416) 961-1026 or 1-800-461-4828 Fax: (416) 924-4408
E-mail: gordong@oaa.on.ca
Website: www.oaa.on.ca
Contact: Gordon S. Grice, editor
Published quarterly

Wood Design & Building (Canadian Wood Council)
30 E. Beaver Creek Road, Suite 202, Richmond Hill, ON L4B 1J2
Phone: (905) 886-5040 or 1-888-232-2881 Fax: (905) 886-6615
E-mail: trogers@dvtail.com
Website: www.cwc.ca
Contacts: Theresa Rogers, executive editor
Published 4 times a year

Woodworking
520 Riverside Drive, Unit 203, Toronto, ON M6S 4B5
Phone: (416) 819-4123 Fax: (905) 727-0017
E-mail: stephan@kleisermedia.ca
Website: www.woodworkingcanada.com
Contact: Stephan Kleiser, editor
Published 7 times a year

YardStick (Western Retail Lumber Association)
100 Sutherland Avenue, Winnipeg, MB R2W 3C7
Phone: (204) 975-0454 or 1-800-665-2456 Fax: 1-800-709-5551
E-mail: lfiola@naylor.com
Contact: Caren Kelly, editor (WRLA), or Lilliane Fiola, editor
  (Naylor)
Published bimonthly

Automotive (see also Transportation & Cargo)

Auto Atlantic
51 Bethany Way, Halifax, NS B35 1H6
Phone: (902) 423-6788 or 1-866-423-3939 Fax: (902) 423-3354
E-mail: carter@autoatlantic.com
Website: www.autoatlantic.com
Contact: Carter Hammett, managing editor
Published bimonthly

Auto Recycling Canada
8980 Fraserwood Court, Unit 1, Burnaby, BC V5J 5H7
Phone: (604) 432-7987 Fax: 604-432-1713
E-mail: publish@ara.bc.ca
Website: www.collisionquarterly.ca
Contact: Kara Cunningham, editor
Published quarterly

Bodyshop
80 Valleybrook Drive, Toronto, ON M3B 2S9
Phone: 1-800-268-7742 (press 1, dial 6763) Fax: (416) 510-5140
E-mail: aross@bodyshopbiz.com

Website: www.bodyshopbiz.com
Contact: Andrew Ross, publisher
Published 6 times a year

Canadian Auto World

447 Speers Road, Suite 4, Oakville, ON L6K 3S7
Phone: (905) 842-6591 Fax: (905) 842-4432
E-mail: jhayes@formulamediagroup.com
Website: www.canadianautoworld.ca
Contact: Jackson Hayes, senior editor
Published monthly

Canadian Automotive Fleet

1001 Champlain Avenue, Suite 206, Burlington, ON L7L 5Z4
Phone: (289) 288-9994 or 1-877-870-0055 Fax: (289) 288-9996
E-mail: mario@fleetbusiness.com
Website: fleetbusiness.com
Contact: Mario Cywinski, editor
Published bimonthly

Canadian Technician

451 Attwell Drive, Toronto, ON M9W 5C4
Phone: (416) 614-5814 Fax: (416) 614-8861
E-mail: ajanssen@canadiantechnician.ca
Website: www.canadiantechnician.ca
Contact: Allan Janssen, editor
Published 10 times a year

CarCare Business

455 rue Notre Dame E, Suite 311, Montreal, QC H2Y IC9
Phone: (514) 289-0888 Fax: 514-289-5151
E-mail: sgbrown@xplornet.com
Website: www.autosphere.ca
Contact: Shirley Brown, associate publisher
Published 8 times a year

Collision Management

455 rue Notre Dame E, Suite 311, Montreal, QC H2Y IC9
Phone: (514) 289-0888 Fax: 514-289-5151

E-mail: isabelle.courteau@autosphere.ca
Website: www.autosphere.ca
Contact: Isabelle Courteau, publisher
Published quarterly

Collision Quarterly
8980 Fraserwood Court, Unit 1, Burnaby, BC V5J 5H7
Phone: (604) 432-7987 Fax: 604-432-1713
E-mail: publish@ara.bc.ca
Website: www.collisionquarterly.ca
Contact: Kara Cunningham, editor
Published quarterly

Collision Repair Magazine
645 Ossington Avenue, Toronto, ON M6G 3T6
Phone: (416) 628-8344 Fax: (905) 882-0457
E-mail: editor@collisionrepairmag.com
Website: www.collisionrepairmag.com
Contact: Mike Davey, editor
Published bimonthly

Fleetdigest
455 rue Notre Dame E., Suite 311, Montreal, QC H2Y 1C9
Phone: (514) 289-0888 Fax: 514-289-5151
E-mail: isabelle.courteau@autosphere.ca
Website: www.autosphere.ca
Contact: Isabelle Courteau, publisher
Published bimonthly

Fleet Vans & Trucks
1001 Champlain Avenue, Suite 206, Burlington, ON L7L 5Z4
Phone: (289) 288-9994 or 1-877-870-0055 Fax: (289) 288-9996
E-mail: mario@fleetbusiness.com
Website: fleetbusiness.com
Contact: Mario Cywinski, managing editor
Published 5 times a year

4WD Magazine
3310 Appaloosa Road, Suite 7, Kelowna, BC VIV 2W5
Phone: 1-866-609-2383 Fax: 1-888-541-8782
E-mail: jtansem@suncruiser.ca
Website: www.can4x4.com
Contact: Jason Tansem
Published 6 times a year

Jobber News and AutoServiceWorld.com
80 Valleybrook Drive, Toronto, ON M3B 2S9
Phone: (416) 510-6763 or 1-800-268-7742 (press 1, dial 6763)
   Fax: (416) 510-5140
E-mail: aross@jobbernews.com
Website: www.autoserviceworld.com
Contact: Andrew Ross, publisher/editor
Published monthly

Octane
508 Lawrence Avenue W., Suite 201, Toronto, ON M6A IAI
Phone: (416) 504-0504, ext. 114 Fax: (416) 256-3002
E-mail: lherzog@fulcrum.ca
Contact: Lawrence Herzog, managing editor
Published 5 times a year

SSGM (Service Station & Garage Management)
80 Valleybrook Drive, Toronto, ON M3B 2S9
Phone: (416) 510-6790 Fax: (416) 510-5140
E-mail: tom@ssgm.com
Website: www.ssgm.com
Contact: Tom Venetis, editor
Published monthly

Taxi News
38 Fairmount Crescent, Toronto, ON M4L 2H4
Phone: (416) 466-2328 Fax: (416) 466-4220
E-mail: wjmc@rogers.com
Contact: Bill McOuat, editor
Published monthly

Tire News
455 rue Notre Dame E, Suite 311, Montreal, QC H2Y IC9
Phone: (514) 289-0888 Fax: 514-289-5151
E-mail: isabelle.courteau@autosphere.ca
Website: www.autosphere.ca
Contact: Isabelle Courteau, publisher
Published bimonthly

Tow Canada
8980 Fraserwood Court, Unit 1, Burnaby, BC V5J 5H7
Phone: (604) 432-7987 Fax: 604-432-1713
E-mail: publish@ara.bc.ca
Website: www.towcanada.ca
Contact: Kara Cunningham, editor
Published 6 times a year

World of Wheels
447 Speers Road, Suite 4, Oakville, ON L6K 3S7
Phone: (905) 842-6591 Fax: (905) 842-4432
E-mail: craig.ritchie@metroland.com
Website: www.worldofwheelsmagazine.com
Contact: Craig Ritchie, editorial director
Published bimonthly

Aviation & Aerospace

Airforce
P.O. Box 2460, Stn. D, Ottawa, ON KIP 5W6
Phone: (613) 232-2303 or 1-866-351-2322 Fax: (613) 232-2156
E-mail: vjohnson@airforce.ca
Contact: Vic Johnson, editor
Published quarterly

Canadian Aviator
200 W. Esplanade, Suite 500, North Vancouver, BC V7M IA4
Phone: (250) 546-6743 Fax: (604) 998-3320
E-mail: canadianaviator@xplornet.com
Website: www.canadianaviatormagazine.com

Contact: Russ Niles, editor
Published bimonthly

COPA (Canadian Owners and Pilots Association) Flight
71 Bank Street, 7th Floor, Ottawa, ON KIP 5N2
Phone: (613) 236-4901, ext. 108 Fax: (613) 236-8648
E-mail: editorial@copanational.org
Website: www.copanational.org
Contact: Michel Hell, editor
Published monthly

Helicopters
105 Donly Drive S., Simcoe, ON N3Y 4N5
Phone: (416) 725-5637 or 1-888-599-2228 Fax: (519) 429-3094
E-mail: mnicholls@annexweb.com
Website: www.helicoptersmagazine.com
Contact: Matt Nicholls, editor
Published 5 times a year

ICAO (International Civil Aviation Organization) Journal
999 University Street, Montreal, QC H3C 5H7
Phone: (514) 954-8222 Fax: (514) 954-6376
E-mail: emacburnie@icao.int
Website: www.icao.int
Contact: Eric MacBurnie, editor
Published bimonthly

Wings
105 Donly Drive S., Simcoe, ON N3Y 4N5
Phone: (416) 725-5637 or 1-888-599-2228 Fax: (519) 429-3094
E-mail: mnicholls@annexweb.com
Website: www.wingsmagazine.com
Contact: Matt Nicholls, editor
Published bimonthly

Business, Commerce, Banking, Law, Insurance, & Pensions

Advisor's Edge
1 Mount Pleasant Road, 7th Floor, Toronto, ON M4Y 2Y5
Phone: (416)764-2000 Fax: (416) 764-3935
E-mail: melissa.chin@rci.rogers.com
Website: www.advisor.ca
Contact: Melissa Shin, managing editor

Alberta Venture
10259 – 105 Street, Edmonton, AB T5J IE3
Phone: (780) 990-0839 Fax: (780) 425-4921
E-mail: mganley@albertaventure.com
Website: www.albertaventure.com
Contact: Michael Ganley, editor
Published 12 times a year

Benefits and Pensions Monitor
245 Fairview Mall Drive, Suite 501, Toronto, ON M2J 4TI
Phone: (416) 494-1066 Fax: (416) 494-2536
E-mail: jhornyak@powershift.ca
Website: www.bpmmagazine.com
Contact: Joe Hornyak, editor
Published 8 times a year

Benefits Canada
1 Mount Pleasant Road, 7th Floor, Toronto, ON M4Y 2Y5
Phone: (416) 764-3823 Fax: (416) 764-3943
E-mail: alyssa.hodder@rci.rogers.com
Contact: Alyssa Hodder, editor
Published monthly

Biz
1074 Cooke Boulevard, Burlington, ON L7T 4A8
Phone: (905) 634-8003 Fax: (905) 634-7661
E-mail: bizeditor@townmedia.ca
Website: www.bizmagazine.ca

Contact: Ted McIntyre, editor
Published quarterly

Biz X Magazine

P.O. Box 27035, 7720 Tecumseh Road E., Windsor, ON N8T 3N5
Phone: (519) 977-2199 Fax: (519) 979-4571
E-mail: editorial@bizxmagazine.com
Website: www.bizxmagazine.com
Contact: Deborah Jones, publisher
Published 10 times a year

The Bottom Line

123 Commerce Valley Drive E., Suite 700, Markham, ON
   L3T 7W8
Phone: (905) 479-2665 or 1-800-668-6481 Fax: (905) 479-2826
E-mail: robert.kelly@lexisnexis.ca
Website: www.thebottomlinenews.ca
Contact: Robert Kelly, editor
Published 16 times a year

Business Edge

112 – 4 Avenue S.W., Suite 1260, Calgary, AB T2P 0H3
Phone: (403) 769-9359 Fax: (403) 968-7638
E-mail: news@businessedge.ca
Website: www.businessedge.ca
Contact: Megan Butler, editor
   Published 22 times a year, with 4 regional editions

Business in Calgary

101 – 6 Avenue S.W., Suite 1025, Calgary, AB T2P 3P4
Phone: (403) 264-3270 or 1-800-465-0322 Fax: (403) 264-3276
E-mail: editor@businessincalgary.com
Website: editor@businessincalgary.com
Contact: Derek Sankey, editor
Published monthly

Business in Vancouver

102 E. 4th Avenue, Vancouver, BC V5T 1G2
Phone: (604) 688-2398 Fax: (604) 688-1963

E-mail: news@biv.com
Website: www.biv.com
Contact: Tim Renshaw, managing editor
Published weekly

CA Magazine

277 Wellington Street W., Toronto, ON M5V 3H2
Phone: (416) 204-3249 Fax: (416) 204-3409
E-mail: okey.chigbo@cica.ca
Website: www.camagazine.com
Contact: Okey Chigbo, editor-in-chief
Published 10 times a year

Canadian Capital

1 Mount Pleasant Road, 7th Floor, Toronto, ON M4Y 2Y5
Phone: 416-764-3866
E-mail: m.birchallspencer@rci.rogers.com
Website: www.capitalmagazine.ca
Contact: Meredith Birchall-Spencer, managing editor
Published bimonthly

Canadian Insurance Top Broker / Canadian Insurance Risk Manager

1 Mount Pleasant Road, 7th Floor, Toronto, ON M4Y 2Y5
Phone: (416) 764-1323 Fax: (416) 764-1419
E-mail: daryl.angier@rci.rogers.com
Website: www.citopbroker.com
Contact: Daryl Angier, editor
Published monthly

Canadian Investment Review

1 Mount Pleasant Road, 7th Floor, Toronto, ON M4Y 2Y5
Phone: (416) 624-3505
E-mail: caroline.cakebread@rogers.com
Website: www.investmentreview.com
Contact: Caroline Cakebread, editor
Published online

The Canadian Manager

15 Collier Street, Lower Level, Barrie, ON L4M 1G5
Phone: (705) 725-8926 or 1-800-387-5774 Fax: (705) 725-8196
E-mail: office@cim.ca
Website: www.cim.ca
Contact: Sheila Sproule, editor
Published quarterly

Canadian Underwriter

80 Valleybrook Drive, Toronto, ON M3B 2S9
Phone: (416) 510-6796 Fax: (416) 510-6809
E-mail: david@canadianunderwriter.ca
Website: www.canadianunderwriter.ca
Contact: David Gambrill, editor
Published monthly

CGA Magazine

4200 North Fraser Way, Suite 100, Burnaby, BC V5J 5K7
Phone: 604-669-3555 Fax: 604-689-5845
E-mail: cgamagazine@cga-canada.org
Website: www.cga-canada.org
Contact: Anya Levykh, managing editor
Published bimonthly

CMA Magazine

1 Robert Speck Parkway, Suite 1400, Mississauga, ON L4Z 3M3
Phone: (905) 949-4200 or 1-800-263-7622 Fax: (905) 949-0888
E-mail: mgulens@cma-canada.org
Website: www.cmamagazine.ca
Contact: Mara Gulens, editor-in-chief
Published bimonthly

Durham Business Times

130 Commercial Avenue, Ajax, ON L1S 2H5
Phone: (905) 426-4676, ext. 24 Fax: (905) 426-6598
E-mail: businesstimes@durhamregion.com or
    tmckee@durhamregion.com
Website: www.durhambusinesstimes.com

Contact: Tamara McKee, editor
Published monthly

Financial Post Magazine
1450 Don Mills Road, Suite 300, Toronto, ON M3B 3R5
Phone: (416) 386-2828 Fax: (416) 386-2836
Website: www.financialpost.com/magazine
Contact: Terence Corcoran, editor
Circulation: 165,000
Published 9 times a year

Investment Executive
25 Sheppard Avenue W., Suite 100, Toronto, ON M2N 6S7
Phone: (416) 733-7600 Fax: (416) 218-3624
E-mail: tlemay@investmentexecutive.com
Website: www.investmentexecutive.com
Contact: Tracy Lemay, editor
Published 16 times a year

Kootenay Business Magazine
100 – 7th Avenue S., Suite 100, Cranbrook, BC V1C 2J4
Phone: (250) 426-7253 or 1-800-663-8555 Fax: (250) 426-4125
E-mail: editor@kpimedia.com
Website: www.kootenaybiz.com
Contact: Kerry Shellborn, assigning editor
Published bimonthly

The Lawyers Weekly
123 Commerce Valley Drive E., Suite 700, Markham, ON
   L3T 7W8
Phone: (905) 479-2665 or 1-800-668-6481 Fax: (905) 479-3758
Website: www.thelawyersweekly.ca
Contact: Tim Wilbur, managing editor
Published 48 times a year

Manitoba Business Magazine
294 Portage Avenue, Suite 508, Winnipeg, MB R3C 0B9
Phone: (204) 943-2940 Fax: (204) 943-2942

E-mail: ritchie.gage@shaw.ca
Website: www.maintobabusinessmagazine.com
Contact: Ritchie Gage, publisher/editor-in-chief
Published 10 times a year

Mississauga Business Times
3145 Wolfedale Road, Mississauga, ON L5C 3A9
Phone: (905) 273-8111 Fax: (905) 273-6212
E-mail: rdrennan@mississauga.net
Website: www.businesstimes.on.ca
Contact: Rick Drennan, managing editor
Published monthly

National (Canadian Bar Association)
500 – 865 Carling Avenue, Ottawa, ON KIS 5S8
Phone: (613) 237-2925 or 1-800-267-8860 Fax: (613) 237-0185
E-mail: beverleys@cba.org
Website: www.cba.org
Contact: Beverley Spencer, editor-in-chief
Published 8 times a year

Northern Ontario Business
158 Elgin Street, Sudbury, ON P3E 3N5
Phone: (705) 673-5705 or 1-800-757-2766 Fax: (705) 673-9542
E-mail:pmills@nob.on.ca
Website: www.northernontariobusiness.com
Contact: Patricia Mills, publisher
Published monthly

Northwest Business Magazine
311 Hawksbrow Mews N.W., Calgary, AB T3G 3B6
Phone: (250) 785-8833
E-mail: editornwb@gmx.com
Website: www.northwestbusiness.ca
Contact: Joei Warm, editor
Published 10 times a year

Ottawa Business Journal
P.O. Box 3814, Stn. C, Ottawa, ON KIY 4J8
Phone: (613) 238-1818
E-mail: editor@obj.ca
Contact: Peter Kovessy, editor
Published weekly

PROFIT
1 Mount Pleasant Road, 11th Floor, Toronto, ON M4Y 2Y5
Phone: (416) 764-1402 Fax: (416) 764-1404
E-mail: profit@profit.rogers.com
Website: www.profitguide.com
Contact: Ian Portsmouth, publisher/editor
Published bimonthly

Report on Business
444 Front Street W., Toronto, ON M5V 2S9
Phone: (416) 585-5000 Fax: (416) 585-3327
E-mail: echerney@globeandmail.com
Website: www.theglobeandmail.com/report-on-business
Contact: Elena Cherney, editor
Published 11 times a year

Sounding Board
999 Canada Place, Suite 400, Vancouver, BC V6C 3EI
Phone: (604) 681-2111 Fax: (604) 681-0437
E-mail: editor@boardoftrade.com
Website: wwww.boardoftrade.com
Contacts: Greg Hoekstra, editor
Published 10 times a year

Computers & Data Processing

CIO Canada
55 Town Centre Court, Suite 302, Toronto, ON MIP 4X4
Phone: (416) 290-0240 Fax: (416) 290-0238
E-mail: sschick@itworldcanada.com

Website: www.itworldcanada.com
Contact: Shane Schick, acting editor

Computer Dealer News
55 Town Centre Court, Suite 302, Toronto, ON MIP 4X4
Phone: (416) 290-0240 Fax: (416) 290-0238
E-mail: pdelnibletto@itworldcanada.com
Website: www.itworldcanada.com
Contact: Paolo Del-Nibletto, editor

ComputerWorld Canada
55 Town Centre Court, Suite 302, Toronto, ON MIP 4X4
Phone: (416) 290-0240 Fax: (416) 290-0238
E-mail: dwebb@itworldcanada.com
Website: www.itworldcanada.com
Contact: Dave Webb, editor

IT in Canada
4 Vata Court, Suite 24, Aurora, ON L4G 4B6
Phone: (905) 727-3875 Fax: (905) 727-4428
E-mail: michael.oneil@itincanada.ca
Website: www.itincanada.ca
Contact: Michael O'Neil, chief content officer

Network World Canada
55 Town Centre Court, Suite 302, Toronto, ON MIP 4X4
Phone: (416) 290-0240 Fax: (416) 290-0238
E-mail: dwebb@itworldcanada.com
Website: www.itworldcanada.com
Contact: Dave Webb, editor

Education & School Management

Professionally Speaking
101 Bloor Street W., Toronto, ON M5S OAI
Phone: (416) 961-8800 Fax: (416) 961-8822
E-mail: info@oct.ca
Website: http://professionallyspeaking.oct.ca

Contact: Philip Carter, editor
Published quarterly

Quebec Home & School News
3285 Cavendish Boulevard, Suite 560, Montreal, QC H4B 2L9
Phone: (514) 481-5619 Fax: (514) 481-5610
E-mail: info@qfhsa.org
Website: www.qfhsa.org
Published quarterly

Electronics & Electrical

Canadian Electronics
222 Edward Street, Aurora, ON L4G 1W6
Phone: (905) 727-0077 Fax: (905) 727-0017
E-mail: medwards@annexweb.com
Website: www.canadianelectronics.ca
Contact: Mike Edwards, editor
Published 4 times a year

distribution & supply
222 Edward Street, Aurora, ON L4G 1W6
Phone: (905) 727-0077 Fax: (905) 727-0017
E-mail: acapkun@clbmedia.ca
Website: www.ebmag.com
Contact: Anthony Capkun, editor
Published biannually

Electric Energy T&D
1160 Levis, Suite 100, Terrebonne, QC J6W 5S6
Phone: (450) 471-0796 or 1-888-332-3749 Fax: 1-888-243-4562
E-mail: mam@electricenergyonline.com
Website: www.electricenergyonline.com
Contact: Mike Marullo, editor-in-chief

Electrical Business
222 Edward Street, Aurora, ON L4G 1W6
Phone: (905) 727-0077 Fax: (905) 727-0017

E-mail: acapkun@clbmedia.ca
Website: www.ebmag.com
Contact: Anthony Capkun, editor
Published monthly

Electrical Line
1785 Emerson Court, North Vancouver, BC V7H 2Y6
Phone: (604) 924-3661 Fax: (604) 924-3662
E-mail: kenb@electricalline.com
Website: www.electricalline.com
Contact: Ken Buhr, publisher/editor
Published bimonthly

Electrical Source
1885 Clements Road, Unit 218, Pickering, ON L1W 3V4
Phone: (905) 686-1040 Fax: (905) 686-1078
E-mail: phil@electricityforum.com
Website: www.electrical-source.com
Contact: Phil Feltham, managing editor
Published 9 times a year

Electricity Today
1885 Clements Road, Unit 218, Pickering, ON L1W 3V4
Phone: (905) 686-1040 Fax: (905) 686-1078
E-mail: phil@electricityforum.com
Website: www.electricity-today.com
Contact: Phil Feltham, managing editor
Published 9 times a year

EP & T (Electronic Products and Technology)
80 Valleybrook Drive, Toronto, ON M3B 2S9
Phone: (416) 442-5600 Fax: (416) 510-5134
E-mail: info@ept.ca
Website: www.ept.ca
Contact: Steven Law, editor
Published 9 times a year

Here's How
701 Evans Avenue, Suite 102, Toronto, ON M9C IA3
Phone: (416) 667-9945 Fax: (416) 667-0609
E-mail: bgrierson@hereshow.ca
Website: www.hereshow.ca
Contact: Bob Grierson, publisher
Published 5 times a year

Energy, Mining, Forestry, Lumber, Pulp & Paper, & Fisheries

Aquaculture North America
4623 William Head Road, Victoria, BC V9C 3Y7
Phone: (250) 478-3973 Fax: (250) 478-3979
E-mail: peter@capamara.com
Website: www.naqua.com
Contact: Peter Chettleburgh, publisher/editor
Published bimonthly

Canadian Biomass
105 Donly Drive S., Simcoe, ON N3Y 4N5
Phone: 1-888-599-2228 Fax: (519) 429-3094
E-mail: sjamieson@annexweb.com
Website: www.canadianbiomassmagazine.ca
Contact: Scott Jamieson, editorial director
Published 6 times a year

Canadian Forest Industries
90 Morgan Road, Unit 14, Baie d'Urfe, QC H9X 3A8
Phone: (514) 457-2211 (general) or (604) 346-8416 (Bill Tice)
    Fax: (514) 457-2558
E-mail: sjamieson@forestcommunications.com or
    btice@annexweb.com
Website: www.canadianforestindustries.ca
Contacts: Scott Jamieson, editorial director, or Bill Tice, editor
Published 7 times a year

Canadian Mining Journal

80 Valleybrook Drive, Toronto, ON M3B 2S9
Phone: (416) 510-6891 or 1-800-268-7742 Fax: (416) 510-5138
E-mail: rnoble@canadianminingjournal.com
Website: www.canadianminingjournal.com
Contact: Russell Noble, editor
Published 10 times a year

Canadian Wood Products

P.O. Box 51058, Pincourt, QC J7V 9T3
Phone: 425-0025 (general) or (604) 346-8416 (Bill Tice) Fax:
    (514) 425-0068
E-mail: sjamieson@annexweb.com or btice@annexweb.com
Website: www.canadianwoodproducts.ca
Contacts: Scott Jamieson, editorial director, or Bill Tice, editor
Published 7 times a year

CIM Magazine (Canadian Institute of Mining, Metallurgy and Petroleum)

3500 de Maisonneuve Boulevard W., Suite 1250, Westmount, QC
    H3Z 3C1
Phone: (514) 939-2710 Fax: (514) 939-2714
E-mail: editor@cim.org
Website: www.cim.org
Contact: Angela Hanlyn, editor-in-chief
Published 8 times a year

energy

P.O. Box 93652, Vancouver, BC V6E 4L7
Phone: 1-800-518-8022
E-mail: editor@alternerg.com
Contact: Paul MacDonald, editor
Website: www.altenerg.com
Published bimonthly

Energy Management

222 Edward Street, Aurora, ON L4G 1W6
Phone: (905) 727-0077 Fax: (905) 727-0017
E-mail:acapkun@annexweb.com

Website: www.energy-manager.ca
Contact: Anthony Capkun, editor-in-chief
Updated daily online

Energy Processing Canada
900 – 6th Avenue S.W., Suite 500, Calgary, AB T2P 3K2
Phone: (403) 263-6881 or 1-800-526-4177 Fax: (403) 263-6886
E-mail: editor@northernstar.ab.ca
Website: www.northernstar.ab.ca
Contact: Alister Thomas, managing editor
Published bimonthly

The Forestry Chronicle
c/o The Canadian Ecology Centre, P.O. Box 430, 6905 Highway
    17 W., Mattawa, ON POH IVO
Phone: (705) 744-1715, ext. 585 Fax: (705) 744-1716
E-mail: forestrychronicle@cif-ifc.org
Website: www.cif-ifc.org
Contact: Ron Ayling, editor-in-chief, or Brian Haddon, research
    editor
Published bimonthly

ForestsWest
100 – 7th Avenue S., Suite 100, Cranbrook, BC VIC 2J4
Phone: (250) 426-7253 Fax: (250) 426-4125
E-mail: info@kpimedia.com
Contact: Keith Powell, publisher
Published twice a year

Island Fisherman Magazine
610 Azalea Place, Campbell River, BC V9W 7H2
Phone: (250) 923-0939
E-mail: ifmm@shaw.ca
Website: www.islandfishermanmagazine.com
Contact: Lance Smith, editor
Published 7 times a year

Logging & Sawmilling Journal
P.O. Box 86670, 211 E. 1st Street, North Vancouver, BC V7L 4L2
Phone: (604) 990-9970 Fax: (604) 990-9971
Website: www.forestnet.com
Contact: Paul MacDonald, editor
Published 7 times a year

Mineral Exploration
4180 Lougheed Highway, 4th Floor, Burnaby, BC V5C 6A7
Phone: (604) 299-7311 Fax: (604)-299-9188
E-mail: jbuchanan@amebc.ca
Website: www.amebc.ca
Contact: Jonathan Buchanan, editor
Published quarterly

Mining and Exploration
100 – 7th Avenue S., Suite 100, Cranbrook, BC V1C 2J4
Phone: (250) 426-7253 Fax: (250) 426-4125
E-mail: info@kpimedia.com
Contact: Keith Powell, publisher
Published 4 times a year

New Technology Magazine
816 – 55th Avenue N.E., 2nd Floor, Calgary, AB T2E 6Y4
Phone: (403) 209-3500 Fax: (403) 245-8666
E-mail: msmith@junewarren-nickles.com
Website: www.newtechmagazine.com
Contact: Maurice Smith, editor
Published 10 times a year

The Northern Miner
80 Valleybrook Drive, Toronto, ON M3B 2S9
Phone: (416) 510-6764 Fax: (416) 510-5138
E-mail: jcumming@northernminer.com
Website: www.northernminer.com
Contact: John Cumming, editor
Published weekly

Earth Resources
1300 Hollis Street, Halifax, NS B3J 1T6
Phone: (902) 422-4990 Fax: (902) 422-4728
E-mail: editor@advocatemediainc.com
Website: www.ocean-resources.com
Contact: Suzanne Rent, editor
Published bimonthly
   Canada's offshore oil and gas publication since 1981. Pay varies and is paid on publication for 600 to 800 words. Photos should accompany submissions.

Oil & Gas Inquirer
6111 – 91st Street N.W., Edmonton, AB T6E 6V6
Phone: (780) 944-9333 Fax: (780) 944-9500
E-mail: mbyfield@junewarren-nickles.com
Website: www.oilandgasinquirer.com
Contact: Mike Byfield, editor
Published monthly

Oilweek
6111 – 91st Street N.W., Edmonton, AB T6E 6V6
Phone: (780) 944-9333 Fax: (780) 944-9500
E-mail: dlunan@junewarren-nickles.com
Website: www.oilweek.com
Contact: Dale Lunan, editor
Published monthly

Propane Canada
900 – 6th Avenue S.W., Suite 500, Calgary, AB T2P 3K2
Phone: (403) 263-6881 or 1-800-526-4177 Fax: (403) 263-6886
E-mail: editor@northernstar.ab.ca
Website: www.northernstar.ab.ca
Contact: Alister Thomas, editor
Published bimonthly

The Prospector Resource Investment News
333 E. 1st Street, Suite 104, North Vancouver, BC V7L 4W9
Phone: (604) 639-5293
E-mail: editor@theprospectornews.com

Website: www.theprospectornews.com
Contact: Christian Vakenti, managing editor
Published 6 times a year

Pulp & Paper Canada
80 Valleybrook Drive, Toronto, ON M3B 2S9
Phone: (416) 510-6755 or 1-800-268-7742 Fax: (514) 510-5140
E-mail: media@pulpandpapercanada.com
Website: www.pulpandpapercanada.com
Contact: Cindy Macdonald, editor
Published 6 times a year

The Roughneck
900 – 6th Avenue S.W., Suite 500, Calgary, AB T2P 3K2
Phone: (403) 263-6881 or 1-800-526-4177 Fax: (403) 263-6886
E-mail: editor@northernstar.ab.ca
Website: www.northernstar.ab.ca
Contact: Alister Thomas, editor
Published monthly

Truck Logger BC Magazine
815 W. Hastings Street, Suite 725, Vancouver, BC V6C 1B4
Phone: (604) 684-4291 Fax: (604) 684-7134
E-mail: stice@tla.ca
Website: www.tla.ca
Contact: Sandra Tice, editor
Published quarterly

Environmental Science & Management

Environmental Science & Engineering
220 Industrial Parkway S., Unit 30, Aurora, ON L4G 3V6
Phone: (905) 727-4666, ext. 27 Fax: (905) 841-7271
E-mail: steve@esemag.com
Website: www.esemag.com
Contact: Tom Davey, senior editor
Published bimonthly

Environmental Solutions Magazine

2323 Boundary Road, Suite 124, Vancouver, BC V5M 4V8
Phone: (604) 291-9900 Fax: (604) 291-1906
E-mail: ltoop@baumpub.com
Website: http://cep.baumpub.com
Contact: Lee Toop, editor
Published 8 times a year

HazMat Management

80 Valleybrook Drive, Toronto, ON M3B 2S9
Phone: 1-800-268-7742, ex. 2580
E-mail: gcrittenden@hazmatmag.com
Website: www.hazmatmag.com
Contact: Guy Crittenden, editor
Published quarterly

Recycling Product News

2323 Boundary Road, Suite 124, Vancouver, BC V5M 4V8
Phone: (604) 291-9900 Fax: (604) 291-1906
E-mail: kbarker@baumpub.com
Website: http://rpn.baumpub.com
Contact: Keith Barker, editor
Published 8 times a year

Solid Waste & Recycling

80 Valleybrook Drive, Toronto, ON M3B 2S9
Phone: 1-800-268-7742, ex. 2580
E-mail: gcrittenden@solidwastemag.com
Website: www.solidwastemag.com
Contact: Guy Crittenden, editor
Published bimonthly

Farming

Better Farming: The Business Magazine for Ontario Agriculture

21400 Service Road, Vankleek Hill, ON K0B 1R0
Phone: (613) 678-2232 Fax: (613) 678-5993

E-mail: rirwin@betterfarming.com
Website: www.betterfarming.com
Contact: Robert Irwin, managing editor
Published 10 times a year

Canadian Cattlemen

1666 Dublin Avenue, Winnipeg, MB R3H OHI
Phone: (204) 954-1400 Fax (204) 954-1422
E-mail: gren@fbcpublishing.com
Website: www.canadiancattlemen.ca
Contact: Gren Winslow, editor
Published 13 times a year

Canadian Farm Manager

250 City Centre Avenue, Suite 300, Ottawa, ON KIR 6K7
Phone: 1-888-232-3262 Fax: 1-800-270-8301
E-mail: info@cffmc-gac.com
Website: www.farmcentre.com
Contact: Mathieu Lipari, project manager
Published bimonthly

Canadian Jersey Breeder

350 Speedvale Avenue W., Unit 9, Guelph, ON NIH 7M7
Phone: (519) 821-1020, ext. 28 Fax: (519) 821-2723
E-mail: marnie@jerseycanada.com
Website: www.jerseycanada.com
Contact: Marnie Wood, editor
Published bimonthly

Canadian Organic Grower

39 McArthur Avenue, Level 1-3, Ottawa, ON KIL 8L7
Phone: (613) 216-0741 or 1-888-375-7383 Fax: (613) 236-0743
E-mail: janet@cog.ca
Website: www.cog.ca
Contact: Janet Wallace, editor
Published quarterly

Canadian Poultry

P.O. Box 530, 105 Donly Drive S., Simcoe, ON N3Y 4N5
Phone: 1-888-599-2228, ext. 266
E-mail: knudds@annexweb.com
Website: www.canadianpoultryamg.com
Contact: Kristy Nudds, publisher
Published monthly

Country Guide

1666 Dublin Avenue, Suite 220, Winnipeg, MB R3H OHI
Phone: (204) 954-1400 Fax: (204) 954-1422
E-mail: tbutton@twinbanks.com
Website: www.country-guide.ca
Contact: Tom Button, editor
Published monthly

Country Life in B.C.

1120 E. 13th Avenue, Vancouver, BC V5T 2MI
Phone: (604) 871-0001 Fax: (604) 871-0003
E-mail: countrylifeinbc@shaw.ca
Website: www.countrylifeinbc.com
Contact: Peter Wilding, publisher/editor
Published monthly

Farm Focus

1888 Brunswick Street, Suite 609, Halifax, NS B3J 3J8
Phone: (902) 749-2525 or 1-800-717-4442, ext. 2525
E-mail: editor@atlanticfarmfocus.ca
Website: www.atlanticfarmfocus.ca
Contact: Heather Jones, editor
Published monthly

Farming for Tomorrow

2161 Scarth Street, Suite 200, Regina, SK S4P 2H8
Phone: 1-866-525-4338
E-mail: info@farmingfortomorrow.ca
Website: www.farmingfortomorrow.ca
Contacts: Tom Bradley, publisher; Bill Armstrong, editor
Published twice a year

Fruit & Vegetable Magazine

P.O. Box 530, 105 Donly Drive S., Simcoe, ON N3Y 4N5
Phone: 1-888-599-2228, ext. 269
E-mail: mland@annexweb.com
Website: www.agannex.com
Contact: Margaret Land, editor
Published 7 times a year

Germination

313 Pacific Avenue, Suite 301, Winnipeg, MB R3A OM2
Phone: (204) 453-1965 Fax: (204) 475-5247
E-mail: jmcnabb@issuesink.com
Website: www.germination.ca
Contact: Julie McNabb, editor
Published 5 times a year

Grainews

1666 Dublin Avenue, Winnipeg, MB R3H OHI
Phone: (204) 954-1400 Fax: (204) 954-1422
E-mail: leeann.minogue@fbcpublishing.com
Website: www.grainews.ca
Contact: Leeann Minogue, acting editor
Circulation: 16,000
Published 18 times a year

Grainews focuses on crop production, with useful tips and farmer experiences to help commercial grain and oilseed producers improve their profits. *Grainews* also has sections called "Cattleman's Corner," "Farm Life," and "Machinery & Shop" with tips and news on cattle production, food, and farm equipment, respectively. Pay ranges from $175 to $300 per article. A half-page article is 900 words.

The Grower

355 Elmira Road N., Unit 105, Guelph, ON NIK IS5
Phone: (416) 252-7337, ext. 202
E-mail: kdavidson@ecomente.ca
Website: www.thegrower.org
Contact: Karen Davidson, editor
Published monthly

Holstein Journal
9040 Leslie Street, Suite 301, Richmond Hill, ON L4B 3M4
Phone: (905) 886-4222 Fax: (905) 886-0037
E-mail: peter@holsteinjournal.com
Website: www.holsteinjournal.com
Contact: Peter English, publisher
Published monthly

Manitoba Co-operator
1666 Dublin Avenue, Winnipeg, MB R3H OH1
Phone: (204) 954-1400 Fax: (204) 954-1422
E-mail: laura@bfbcpublishing.com
Website: www.manitobacooperator.ca
Contact: Laura Rance, editor
Published weekly

Manure Manager
P.O. Box 530, 105 Donly Drive S., Simcoe, ON N3Y 4N5
Phone: 1-888-599-2228, ext. 269
E-mail: mland@annexweb.com
Website: www.manuremanager.com
Contact: Margaret Land, editor
Published bimonthly

The Milk Producer
6780 Campobello Road, Mississauga, ON L5N 2L8
Phone: (905) 821-8970 Fax: (905) 821-3160
E-mail: bdimmick@milk.org or slaidlaw@milk.org
Website: www.milk.org
Contacts: Bill Dimmick, editor, or Shannon Laidlaw, assistant editor
Published monthly

Niagara Farmers' Monthly
32 Main Street W., Grimsby, ON L3M 1R4
Phone: (905) 945-8392 Fax: (905) 945-3916
E-mail: editor@niagarafarmers.com
Website: www.niagarafarmers.com
Contact: Katherine Nadeau, editor
Published monthly

The Northern Horizon
901 – 100th Avenue, Dawson Creek, BC VIG IW2
Phone: (250) 782-4888 Fax: (250) 782-6300
E-mail: publisher@dcdn.ca
Contact: Dan Przybylski, publisher
Published biweekly

Ontario Farmer
P.O. Box 7400, London, ON N5Y 4X3
Phone: 1-877-358-7773, ext. 221 Fax: (519) 473-2256
E-mail: paul.mahon@sunmedia.ca
Website: www.ontariofarmer.com
Contact: Paul Mahon, publisher/editor-in-chief
Published 9 times a year

Ontario Grain Farmer
100 Stone Road W., Suite 201, Guelph, ON NIG 5L3
Phone: (519) 837-9144 Fax: (519) 767-9713
E-mail: rtelford@gfo.ca
Website: www.gfo.ca
Contact: Rachel Telford, editor
Published 10 times a year

Quebec Farmers' Advocate
555 Roland-Therrien Boulevard, Suite 255, Longueuil, QC J4H 4E7
Phone: (450) 679-0540, ext. 8536 Fax: (450) 463-5291
E-mail: qfa_advocate@upa.qc.ca
Website: www.quebecfarmers.org
Contact: Andrew McClelland, managing editor
Published 11 times a year

Rural Roots
30 – 10th Street E., Prince Albert, SK S6V OY5
Fax: (306) 764-4276
E-mail: rural.roots@paherald.sk.ca
Website: www.paherald.sk.ca
Contact: Ruth Griffiths, editor
Published weekly

Small Farm Canada
4623 William Head Road, Victoria, BC V9C 3Y7
Phone: (250) 474-3935 Fax: (250) 478-3979
E-mail: editor@smallfarmacanada.ca
Website: www.smallfarmcanada.ca
Contact: Tom Henry, editor
Published bimonthly

Today's Farmer
1147 Gainsborough Road, London, ON N6H 5L5
Phone: 1-877-358-7773 Fax: (519) 473-2256
E-mail: paul.mahon@sunmedia.ca
Website: www.todaysfarmer.ca
Contact: Paul Mahon, regional managing editor
Published biweekly

Top Crop Manager
P.O. Box 530, 105 Donly Drive S., Simcoe, ON N3Y 4N5
Phone: (519) 280-0086
E-mail: savoledo@annexweb.com
Website: www.topcropmanager.com
Contact: Sara Avoledo, Eastern editor
Published in 7 Western editions, 4 Eastern editions, and
    1 specialty edition

Western Dairy Farmer Magazine
P.O. Box 7400, London, ON N5Y 4X3
Phone: 1-877-358-7773, ext. 221 Fax: (519) 473-2256
E-mail: paul.mahon@sunmedia.ca
Website: www.ontariofarmer.com
Contact: Paul Mahon, publisher/editor-in-chief
Published bimonthly

The Western Producer
P.O. Box 2500, 2310 Millar Avenue, Saskatoon, SK S7K 2C4
Phone: (306) 665-3544 Fax: (306) 934-2401
E-mail: newsroom@producer.com
Website: www.producer.com

Contact: Terry Fries, news editor
Published weekly

Food, Drink, Hostelry, & Hotel & Restaurant Supplies

Bakers Journal

P.O. Box 530, 105 Donly Drive S., Simcoe, ON N3Y 4N5
Phone: 1-888-599-2228 Fax: (519) 429-3094
E-mail: laiken@annexweb.com
Website: www.bakersjournal.com
Contact: Laura Aiken, editor
Published 10 times a year

Bar & Beverage Business Magazine

1740 Wellington Avenue, Winnipeg, MB R3H 0E8
Phone: (204) 954-2085, ext. 208 or 1-800-337-6372 Fax: (204)
  954-2057
E-mail: fyeo@mercury.mb.ca
Website: www.barandbeverage.com
Contact: Frank Yeo, publisher and editor
Published bimonthly

Canadian Grocer

1 Mount Pleasant Road, 7th Floor, Toronto, ON M4Y 2Y5
Phone: (416) 764-1665 or 1-800-268-9119 Fax: (416) 764-1523
E-mail: rob.gerlsbeck@canadiangrocer.rogers.com or
  nancy.kwon@canadiangrocer.rogers.com
Website: www.canadiangrocer.com
Contacts: Rob Gerlsbeck, editor; Nancy Kwon, web and manag-
  ing editor
Published 10 times a year

Canadian Lodging News

2065 Dundas Street E., Suite 201, Mississauga, ON L4X 2W1
Phone: (905) 206-0150, ext. 231 or 1-800-201-8596 Fax: (905)
  206-9972
E-mail: cisherwood@can-lodgingnews.com

Website: www.can-lodgingnews.com
Contact: Colleen Isherwood, editor
Published 10 times a year

Canadian Pizza Magazine
P.O. Box 530, 105 Donly Drive S., Simcoe, ON N3Y 4N5
Phone: (416) 522-1595
E-mail: laiken@annexweb.com
Website: www.canadianpizzamag.com
Contact: Laura Aiken, editor
Published 7 times a year

Canadian Restaurant News
2065 Dundas Street E., Mississauga, ON L4X 2W1
Phone: (905) 206-0150 or 1-800-201-8596 Fax: (905) 206-9972
E-mail: sisherwood@can-restaurantnews.com
Website: www.can-restaurantnews.com
Contact: Steve Isherwood, publisher
Published online

Canadian Vending
P.O. Box 530, 105 Donly Drive S., Simcoe, ON N3Y 4N5
Phone: 1-888-599-2228 Fax: (519) 429-3094
E-mail: swallace@annexweb.com
Website: www.canadianvending.com
Contact: Stefanie Wallace, technical editor
Published bimonthly

Food in Canada
80 Valleybrook Drive, Toronto, ON M3B 2S9
Phone: (416) 442-5600, ext. 3232 Fax: (416) 510-5140
E-mail: carolyn.cooper@food.rogers.com
Website: www.foodincanada.com
Contact: Carolyn Cooper, editor
Published 9 times a year

Foodservice and Hospitality
23 Lesmill Road, Suite 101, Toronto, ON M3B 3P6
Phone: (416) 447-0888, ext. 224 Fax: (416) 447-5333

E-mail: rcaira@kostuchmedia.com
Website: www.foodserviceworld.com
Contact: Rosanna Caira, publisher/editor
Published monthly

Grocer Today
4180 Lougheed Highway, 4th Floor, Burnaby, BC V5C 6A7
Phone: (604) 299-7311 Fax: (604) 299-9188
E-mail: wthomson@canadawide.com
Website: www.hoteliermagazine.com
Contact: Wendy Thomson, editor
Published bimonthly

Hotelier
23 Lesmill Road, Suite 101, Toronto, ON M3B 3P6
Phone: (416) 447-0888 Fax: (416) 447-5333
E-mail: rcaira@foodservice.ca
Contact: Rosanna Caira, publisher/editor
Published 8 times a year

Vendor Magazine
4990 – 92 Avenue, Suite 107, Edmonton, AB T6B 2V4
Phone: (780) 415-5297 Fax: (780) 463-5280
E-mail: ads@vendormagazine.ca
Website: www.vendormagazine.ca
Contact: Ellen Schoek, editor-in-chief
Published quarterly

Western Grocer
1740 Wellington Avenue, Winnipeg, MB R3H 0E8
Phone: (204) 954-2085, ext. 208 or 1-800-337-6372 Fax: (204)
   954-2057
E-mail: fyeo@mercury.mb.ca
Website: www.westerngrocer.com
Contact: Frank Yeo, publisher and editor
Published bimonthly

Western Restaurant News
1740 Wellington Avenue, Winnipeg, MB R3H OE8
Phone: (204) 954-2085, ext. 208 or 1-800-337-6372 Fax: (204)
    954-2057
E-mail: fyeo@mercury.mb.ca
Website: www.westernrestaurantnews.com
Contact: Frank Yeo, publisher and editor
Published quarterly

Your Convenience Manager
508 Lawrence Avenue W., Suite 201, Toronto, ON M6A IAI
Phone: (416) 504-0504 Fax: (416) 256-3002
E-mail: lherzog@fulcrum.ca
Website: www.ccentral.ca
Contact: Lawrence Herzog, managing editor
Published bimonthly

Your Food Service Manager
508 Lawrence Avenue W., Suite 201, Toronto, ON M6A 1A1
Phone: (416) 504-0504 Fax: (416) 256-3002
E-mail: jauster@fulcrum.ca
Website: www.yfmonline.ca
Contact: Jane Auster
Published bimonthly

Health, Dentistry, Medicine, Pharmacy, & Nursing

Alberta Doctors' Digest
c/o Alberta Medical Association, 12230 – 106th Avenue N.W.,
    Edmonton, AB T5N 3ZI
Phone: (780) 482-2626 or 1-800-272-9680 Fax: (780) 482-5445
E-mail: amamail@albertadoctors.org
Website: www.albertadoctors.org
Contact: Dr. Dennis W. Jirsch, editor
Published bimonthly

British Columbia Medical Journal
1665 W. Broadway, Suite 115, Vancouver, BC V6J 5A4
Phone: (604) 736-5551 Fax: (604) 638-2917
E-mail: journal@bcma.bc.ca
Website: www.bcmj.org
Contact: Dr. D.R. Richardson, editor
Published 10 times a year

Canadian Chiropractor
P.O. Box 530, 105 Donly Drive S., Simcoe, ON N3Y 4N5
Phone: 1-888-599-2228, ext. 247
E-mail: mdidanieli@annexweb.com
Website: www.canadianchiropractor.ca
Contact: Maria DiDanieli, editor
Published 8 times a year

Canadian Family Physician
2630 Skymark Avenue, Mississauga, ON L4W 5A4
Phone: (905) 629-0900 or 1-800-387-6197 Fax: (905) 629-0893
E-mail: cfpmedia@cfpc.ca
Website: www.cfp.ca
Contact: Kathryn Harrington, editorial manager
Published monthly

Canadian Healthcare Manager
1 Mount Pleasant Road, 7th Floor, Toronto, ON M4Y 2Y5
Phone: (416) 764-3868 Fax: (416) 764-3931
E-mail: simon.hally@rci.rogers.com
Website: www.canadianhealthcarenetwork.ca
Contact: Simon Hally, editor
Published bimonthly

Canadian Healthcare Technology
1118 Centre Street, Suite 207, Thornhill, ON L4J 7R9
Phone: (905) 709-2330 Fax: (905) 709-2258
E-mail: jerryz@canhealth.com
Website: www.canhealth.com
Contact: Jerry Zeidenberg, publisher
Published 8 times a year

Canadian Journal of Continuing Medical Education
6500 Trans-Canada Highway, Suite 310, Pointe-Claire, QC
  H9R OA5
Phone: (514) 695-7623 (general) or (514) 695-8393, ext. 220
  (editor) Fax: (514) 695-8554
E-mail: paulb@sta.ca or cme@sta.ca
Website: www.stacommunications.com/journals/cme
Contact: Paul Brand, executive editor
Published monthly

The Canadian Journal of Hospital Pharmacy
30 Concourse Gate, Unit 3, Ottawa, ON K2E 7V7
Phone: (613) 736-9733 Fax: (613) 736-5660
E-mail: cjhpedit@cshp.ca or submit online at
  http://cjhp.msubmit.net
Website: www.cjhp-online.ca
Contact: Colleen Dranke, publications administrator
Published bimonthly

Canadian Journal of Public Health
1565 Carling Avenue, Suite 400, Ottawa, ON KIZ 8RI
Phone: (613) 725-3769 Fax: (613) 725-9826
E-mail: cjph@cpha.ca
Website: http://journal.cpha.ca
Contact: Karen Craven, assistant editor
Published bimonthly

Canadian Medical Association Journal
1867 Alta Vista Drive, Ottawa, ON KIG 5W8
Phone: 1-866-971-9171, ext. 2295 Fax: (613) 565-5471
E-mail: pubs@cmaj.ca
Submissions: http://mc.manuscriptcentral.com/cmaj
Contact: John Fletcher, editor-in-chief
Published biweekly

Canadian Nurse
50 Driveway, Ottawa, ON K2P IE2
Phone: (613) 237-2133, ext. 280 or 1-800-361-8404 Fax: (613)
  237-3520

E-mail: editor@canadian-nurse.com
Website: www.canadian-nurse.com
Contact: Lisa Brazeau, editor-in-chief
Published 9 times a year

Canadian Pharmacists Journal (CPJ)
1785 Alta Vista Drive, Ottawa, ON KIG 3Y6
Phone: (613) 523-7877 or 1-800-917-9489 Fax: (613) 523-2332
E-mail: cpj@pharmacists.ca
Website: www.cpjournal.ca
Contact: Rosemary Killeen, editor-in-chief
Published 6 times a year

Dental Practice Management
80 Valleybrook Drive, Toronto, ON M3B 2S9
Phone: (416) 510-6785 or 1-800-268-7742 Fax: (416) 510-5140
E-mail: cwilson@oralhealthjournal.com
Website: www.oralhealthjournal.com
Contact: Catherine Wilson, editorial director
Published quarterly

HEALTHbeat
9768 – 170 Street, Suite 319, Edmonton, AB T5T 5L4
Phone: 1-800-727-0782 Fax: (780) 413-9328
E-mail: jay@mccronehealthbeat.com
Website: www.mccronehealthbeat.com
Contact: Jay Sherwood, editor
Published bimonthly

Healthcare Management FORUM
c/o Canadian College of Health Service Executives, 292 Somerset
    Street W., Ottawa, ON K2P 0J6
Phone: (613) 235-7218 or 1-800-363-9056 Fax: (613) 235-5451
E-mail: editor@sympatico.ca
Website: www.healthcaremanagementforum.org
Contact: Laurie Wilson, managing editor
Published quarterly

Hospital News

Trader Corporation, 405 The West Mall, Suite 500, Etobicoke, ON
  M9C 5J5
Phone: (416) 781-5516 Fax: (416) 781-5499
E-mail: editor@hospitalnews.com
Website: www.hospitalnews.com
Contact: Kristie Jones, editor
Published monthly

Journal of the Canadian Dental Association

1815 Alta Vista Drive, Ottawa, ON KIG 3Y6
Phone: (613) 523-1770 Fax: (613) 523-7736
E-mail: jokeefe@cda-adc.ca or jcda@cda-adc.ca
Website: www.cda-adc.ca
Contact: John O'Keefe, editor-in-chief
Published 10 times a year

Long Term Care

345 Renfrew Drive, 3rd Floor, Markham, ON L3R 9S9
Phone: (905) 470-8995 Fax: (905) 470-9595
E-mail:caroline@bcsgroup.com
Website: www.oltca.com
Contact: Caroline Tapp-McDougall, editorial
Published quarterly

Ontario Dentist

4 New Street, Toronto, ON M5R IP6
Phone: (416) 355-2276 Fax: (416) 922-9005
E-mail: jkuipers@oda.ca
Website: www.youroralhealth.ca
Contact: Julia Kuipers, managing editor
Published 10 times a year

Ontario Medical Review

150 Bloor Street W., Suite 900, Toronto, ON M5S 3CI
Phone: (416) 340-2264 or 1-800-268-7215, ext. 2264 Fax: (416)
  340-2232
E-mail: omr@oma.org
Website: www.oma.org

Contact: Elizabeth Petruccelli, managing editor
Published 11 times a year

Oral Health
80 Valleybrook Drive, Toronto, ON M3B 2S9
Phone: (416) 510-6785 or 1-800-268-7742 Fax: (416) 510-5140
E-mail: cwilson@oralhealthjournal.com
Website: www.oralhealthjournal.com
Contact: Catherine Wilson, editorial director
Published monthly

Parkhurst Exchange
400 McGill Street, 3rd Floor, Montreal, QC H2Y 2G1
Phone: (514) 397-8833 Fax: (514) 397-0228
E-mail: parkex@parkpub.com
Website: www.parkhurstexchange.com
Contact: Milena Katz, managing editor
Published monthly

Pharmacy Practice
1 Mount Pleasant Road, 7th Floor, Toronto, ON M4Y 2Y5
Phone: (416) 764-3926
E-mail: tasleen.adatia@rci.rogers.com
Contact: Tasleen Adatia, managing editor
Published 8 times a year

The Standard
101 Davenport Road, Toronto, ON M5R 3P1
Phone: (416) 928-0900 or 1-800-387-5526 Fax: (416) 928-6507
E-mail: editor@cnomail.org
Website: www.cno.org
Contact: Deborah Jones, editor
Published quarterly

Senior Care Canada
12A – 4981 Highway 7 E., Suite 254, Markham, ON L3R 1N1
Phone: (905) 640-3048 Fax: (905) 640-7547
E-mail: kathryn@seniorcarecanada.com
Website: www.seniorcarecanada.com

Contact: Kathryn Lymburner, publisher and editor
Published quarterly

Industrial

Canadian Chemical News

130 Slater Street, Suite 550, Ottawa, ON KIP 6E2
Phone: (613) 232-6252 Fax: (613) 232-5862
E-mail: magazine@accn.ca
Website: www.accn.ca
Contact: Jodi Di Menna, editor
Published 10 times a year

Canadian Industrial Equipment News

80 Valleybrook Drive, Toronto, ON M3B 3S9
Phone: (416) 442-5600
E-mail: omarkovich@cienmagazine.com
Website: www.cienmagazine.com
Contact: Olga Markovich, associate publisher/editor
Published 11 times a year

Canadian Industrial Machinery

Phone: (289) 337-3290
E-mail: joet@cimindustry.com
Website: www.cimindustry.com
Contact: Joe Thompson, editor
Published monthly

Canadian Metalworking

80 Valleybrook Drive, Toronto, ON M3B 2S9
Phone: (416) 510-5148 Fax: (416) 510-5140
E-mail: janderton@canadianmetalworking.com
Website: www.canadianmetalworking.com
Contact: Jim Anderton, editor
Published 8 times a year

Canadian Occupational Safety

222 Edward Street, Aurora, ON L4G 1W6
Phone: (905) 726-5445 Fax: (905) 727-0017
E-mail: mdeguzman@annexweb.com
Website: www.cos-mag.com
Contact: Mari-Len De Guzman, editor
Published bimonthly

Canadian Packaging

80 Valleybrook Drive, Toronto, ON M3B 2S9
Phone: (416) 442-5600, ext. 3209
E-mail: gguidoni@canadianpackaging.com
Website: www.canadianpackaging.com
Contact: George Guidoni, editor
Published 11 times a year

Canadian Plastics

80 Valleybrook Drive, Toronto, ON M3B 2S9
Phone: (416) 510-5110 Fax: (416) 510-5134
E-mail: mstephen@canplastics.com
Website: www.canplastics.com
Contact: Mark Stephen, editor
Published 6 times a year

Canadian Process Equipment & Control News

588 Edward Avenue, Suite 29, Richmond Hill, ON L4C 9Y6
Phone: (905) 770-8077 Fax: (905) 770-8075
E-mail: moverment@cpecn.com
Website: www.cpecn.com
Contact: Mike Overment, editor
Published bimonthly

Hardware Merchandising

80 Valleybrook Drive, Toronto, ON M3B 2S9
Phone: (416) 442-5600, ext. 3203 Fax: (416) 510-5140
E-mail: rkoci@canadiancontractor.ca
Website: www.hardwaremagazine.ca
Contact: Robert Koci, editor
Published bimonthly

HPAC (Heating Plumbing Air Conditioning) Magazine
80 Valleybrook Drive, Toronto, ON M3B 2S9
Phone: (416) 510-5218 Fax: (416) 510-5140
E-mail: kerry.turner@hpacmag.com
Website: www.hpacmag.com
Contact: Kerry Turner, editor
Published 7 times a year

Industrial Process Products & Technology
4261 – A14 Highway 7 E., Suite 355, Markham, ON L3R 9W6
Phone: (905) 649-8966 or 1-800-572-4231 Fax: (905) 649-8967
E-mail: gscholey@ippt.ca
Website: www.ippt.ca
Contact: Glen Scholey, managing editor
Published bimonthly

Machinery & Equipment MRO
80 Valleybrook Drive, Toronto, ON M3B 2S9
Phone: (416) 510-6749 Fax: (416) 442-2214
E-mail: broebuck@mromagazine.com
Website: www.mromagazine.com
Contact: Bill Roebuck, editor
Published bimonthly

Manufacturing AUTOMATION
222 Edward Street, Aurora, ON L4G 1W6
Phone: (905) 713-4378 Fax: (905) 727-0017
E-mail editor@automationmag.com
Website: www.automationmag.com
Contact: Mary Del Ciancio, editor
Published bimonthly

Metalworking Production & Purchasing (MP&P)
240 Edward Street, Aurora, ON L4G 3S9
Phone: (905) 713-4388 Fax: (905) 727-0017
E-mail: rcoleman@annexweb.com
Website: www.metalworkingcanada.com
Contact: Robert Colman, editor
Published bimonthly

OHS Canada
80 Valleybrook Drive, Toronto, ON M3B 2S9
Phone: (416) 510-5115 Fax: (416) 510-5140
E-mail: jlian@ohsacanada.com
Website: www.ohscanada.com
Contact: Jean Lian, editor
Published 8 times a year

Ontario Industrial Magazine
1011 Upper Middle Road E., Suite 1159, Oakville, ON L6H 5Z9
Phone: (905) 446-1404 or 1-800-624-2776 Fax: (905) 446-0502
E-mail: klaverty@oim-online.com
Website: www.oim-online.com
Contact: Keith Laverty, publisher
Published monthly

Plant, Canada's Industry Newspaper
80 Valleybrook Drive, Toronto, ON M3B 2S9
Phone: (416) 442-5600 Fax: (416) 510-5140
E-mail: jterrett@plant.ca
Website: www.plant.ca
Contact: Joe Terrett, editor
Published monthly

Plant Engineering & Maintenance (PEM)
222 Edward Street, Aurora, ON L4G 1W6
Phone: (905) 726-4655 Fax: (905) 727-0017
E-mail: avoshart@annexweb.com
Website: www.pem-mag.com
Contact: André Voshart, editor
Published bimonthly

Report on Industry Magazine
282 Wellington Street, Sarnia, ON N7T 1H2
Phone: (519) 332-2255 Fax: (519) 332-6766
E-mail: jtost@roinews.com
Website: www.roimagazine.com
Contact: James Tost, publisher/editor
Published quarterly

REM (Resource Engineering and Maintenance)
222 Edward Street, Aurora, ON L4G 1W6
Phone: (905) 726-4655 Fax: (905) 727-0017
E-mail: avoshart@annexweb.com
Website: www.rem-mag.com
Contact: André Voshart, editor
Published quarterly

20/20 Magazine: Canada's Industry Association Magazine
1 Nicholas Street, Ottawa, ON KIN 7B7
Phone: (613) 238-8888, ext. 4233 Fax: (613) 563-9218
E-mail: jeff.brownlee@cme-mec.ca
Website: www.2020magazine.ca
Phone: (519) 332-2255 Fax: (519) 332-6766
Contact: Jeff Brownlee, publisher
Published bimonthly

Landscaping & Horticulture

Canadian Florist
105 Donly Drive S., Simcoe, ON N3Y 4N5
Phone: (519) 428-6471, ext. 278 Fax: (519) 429-3094
E-mail: bcowen@annexweb.com
Website: www.canadianfloristmag.com
Contact: Brandi Cowen, editor
Published 8 times a year

Canadian Garden Centre & Nursery
P.O. Box 530, 105 Donly Drive S., Simcoe, ON N3Y 4N5
Phone: 1-888-599-2228, ext. 245
E-mail: aryder@annexweb.com
Website: www.canadiangardencentre.ca
Contact: Brandi Cowen, editor
Published 5 times a year

Greenhouse Canada
105 Donly Drive S., Simcoe, ON N3Y 4N5
Phone: 1-888-599-2228, ext. 263 Fax: (519) 429-3094

E-mail: greenhouse@annexweb.com
Website: www.greenhousecanada.com
Contact: Dave Harrison, editor
Published monthly

Hortwest
5783 – 176A Street, Suite 102, Surrey, BC V3S 6S6
Phone: (604) 574-7772 Fax: (604) 574-7773
E-mail: mmanson@bclna.com
Website: www.bclna.com
Contact: Michelle Manson, editor
Published 10 times a year

Landscape Ontario
7856 Fifth Line S., R.R. #4, Milton, ON L9T 2X8
Phone: (905) 875-1805, ext. 320 or 1-800-265-5656 Fax: (905)
    875-0183
E-mail: adennis@landscapeontario.com
Contact: Allan Dennis, editor
Published monthly

Prairie Landscape Magazine
P.O. Box 85127, Calgary, AB T2A 7R7
Phone: (403) 273-6917 Fax: (403) 313-6917
E-mail: prairielandscape@shaw.ca
Contact: Jennett Jackson, publisher
Published bimonthly

Turf & Recreation
275 James Street, Delhi, ON N4B 2B2
Phone: (519) 582-8873 or 1-800-525-6825 Fax: (519) 582-8877
E-mail: turf.mike@on.aibn.com
Website: www.turfandrec.com
Contact: Mike Jiggens, editor
Published 7 times a year

Media, Music, & Communications

Broadcast Dialogue
18 Turtle Path, Lagoon City, ON L0K 1B0
Phone: (705) 484-0752
E-mail: howard@broadcastdialogue.com
Website: www.broadcastdialogue.com
Contact: Howard Christensen, publisher
Published 10 times a year

Canadian Music Trade
23 Hannover Drive, Unit 7, St. Catharines, ON L2W 1A3
Phone: (905) 641-3471 Fax: 1-888-665-1307
E-mail: aking@nor.com
Website: www.canadianmusictrade.com
Contact: Andrew King, editor
Published bimonthly

Mediacaster
80 Valleybrook Drive, Toronto, ON M3B 2S9
Phone: (416) 510-6865 Fax: (416) 510-5134
E-mail: lrickwood@mediacastermagazine.com
Website: www.mediacastermagazine.com
Contact: Lee Rickwood, editor
Published 4 times a year

News Canada
920 Yonge Street, Suite 509, Toronto, ON M4W 3C7
Phone: (416) 599-9900 or 1-888-855-NEWS Fax: (416) 599-9700
Website: www.newscanada.com
Contact: Ruth Douglas, publisher
Published monthly

Playback
366 Adelaide Street W., Suite 100, Toronto, ON M5V 1R9
Phone: (416) 408-2300 or 1-888-988-7325 Fax: (416) 408-0870
E-mail: mmaddever@brunico.com

Website: www.playbackonline.ca
Contact: Mary Maddever, publisher
Published 25 times a year

Professional Sound

23 Hannover Drive, Unit 7, St. Catharines, ON L2W IA3
Phone: (905) 641-3471 Fax: 1-888-665-1307
E-mail: aking@nor.com
Website: www.professional-sound.com
Contact: Andrew King, editor
Published bimonthly

WholeNote

720 Bathurst Street, Suite 503, Toronto, ON M5S 2R4
Phone: (416) 603-3786 Fax: (416) 603-4791
E-mail: editorial@thewholenote.com
Website: www.thewholenote.com
Contacts: David Perlman, publisher and editor-in-chief
Published 10 times a year

Miscellaneous Trade & Professional

Blue Line Magazine

12A – 4981 Highway 7E, Suite 254, Markham, ON L3R INI
Phone: (905) 640-3048 Fax: (905) 640-7547
E-mail: blueline@blueline.ca
Contact: Mark Reesor, managing editor
Published 10 times a year

Boating Business

447 Speers Road, Suite 4, Oakville, ON L6K 3S7
Phone: (905) 842-6591 Fax: (905) 842-4432
E-mail: craig.ritchie@metroland.com
Contact: Craig Ritchie, editorial director
Published bimonthly

Canadian Defence Review

132 Adrian Crescent, Markham, ON L3P 7B3
Phone: (905) 554-4586 Fax: (905) 910-0188
E-mail: editor@canadiandefencereview.com
Website: www.canadiandefencereview.com
Contact: Peter A. Kitchen, editor-in-chief
Published bimonthly

Canadian Facility Management & Design

4195 Dundas Street W., Suite 338, Toronto, ON M8X IY4
Phone: (416) 236-5856 Fax: (416) 236-5219
E-mail: cfm@sympatico.ca
Website: www.cfmd.ca
Contact: Pamela Young, editor
Published 7 times a year

Canadian Firefighter and EMS Quarterly

P.O. Box 530, 105 Donly Drive S., Simcoe, ON N3Y 4N5
Phone: (289) 259-8077 or 1-888-599-2228 Fax: (519) 429-3094
E-mail: lking@annexweb.com
Website: www.firefightingincanada.com
Contact: Laura King, editor
Published quarterly

Canadian Footwear Journal

241 Senneville Road, Senneville, QC H9X 3X5
Phone: (514) 457-8787 or 1-800-973-7463 Fax: (514) 457-5832
E-mail: bmcleish@footwearjournal.com or
    cfj@footwearjournal.com
Website: www.footwearjournal.com
Contact: Barbara McLeish, editor
Published 5 times a year

Canadian Funeral Director Magazine

178 McQuay Boulevard, Whitby, ON LIP IL5
Phone: (905) 666-8011
E-mail: scott@thefuneralmagazine.com or
    info@thefuneralmagazine.com
Website: www.canadianfuneraldirector.com

Contact: Scott Hillier, publisher/editor
Published 10 times a year

Canadian Funeral News
101 – 6th Avenue S.W., Suite 1025, Calgary, AB T2P 3P4
Phone: (403) 264-3270 or 1-800-465-0322 Fax: (403) 264-3276
E-mail: lisjoh@telus.net
Website: www.otcommunications.com/cfnindex.html
Contact: Lisa Johnston, editor
Published monthly

Canadian Government Executive
4 Vata Court, Suite 24, Aurora, ON L4G 4B6
Phone: (905) 727 4091 Fax: (905) 727-4428
E-mail: editor@netgov.ca
Website: www.canadiangovernmentexecutive.ca
Contacts: Toby Fyfe, editor-in-chief
Published 10 times a year

Canadian Hairdresser Magazine
488 Wellington Street W., Toronto, ON M5Z IE3
Phone: (416) 923-1111 Fax: (416) 968-1031
E-mail: joan@canhair.com
Website: www.canhair.com
Contact: Joan Harrison, CEO and editorial director
Published 10 times a year

Canadian HR Reporter
1 Corporate Plaza, 2075 Kennedy Road, Toronto, ON MIT 3V4
Phone: (416) 298-5196 Fax: (416) 298-5031
E-mail: todd.humber@thomsonreuters.com
Website: www.hrreporter.com
Contact: Todd Humber, managing editor
Published 22 times a year

Canadian Interiors
80 Valleybrook Drive, Toronto, ON M3B 2S9
Phone: (416) 442-6825 Fax: (416) 510-5134
E-mail: mtotzke@canadianinteriors.com

Website: www.canadianinteriors.com
Contact: Michael Totzke, editor
Published 6 times a year

Canadian Jeweller
60 Bloor Street W., Suite 1106, Toronto, ON M4W 3B8
Phone: (416) 203-7900 Fax: (416) 703-6392
E-mail: olivier@rivegauchemedia.com
Website: www.canadianjeweller.com
Contact: Olivier Felicio, publisher
Published 8 times a year

Canadian Property Management
5255 Yonge Street, Suite 1000, Toronto, ON M2N 6P4
Phone: (416) 512-8186, ext. 236 Fax: (416) 512-8344
E-mail: barbc@mediaedge.ca
Website: www.canadianpropertymanagement.ca
Contact: Barb Carss, editor-in-chief
Published 8 times a year

Canadian Rental Service
P.O. Box 530, 105 Donly Drive S., Simcoe, ON N3Y 4N5
Phone: (226) 931-0545 Fax: (519) 429-3094
E-mail: pflannery@annexweb.com
Website: www.canadianrentalservice.com
Contact: Patrick Flannery, editor
Published 9 times a year

Canadian Security
222 Edward Street, Aurora, ON L4G 1W6
Phone: (905) 727-0077 Fax: (905) 727-0017
E-mail: nsutton@annexweb.com
Website; www.canadiansecuritymagazine.cmo
Contact: Neil Sutton, editor
Published 9 times a year

The Canadian Veterinary Journal
339 Booth Street, Ottawa, ON KIR 7KI
Phone: (613) 236-1162, ext. 124 Fax: (613) 236-9681

E-mail: hbroughton@cvma-acmv.org
Submissions: http://canadianveterinarians.net/publications-
    journal-issue.aspx
Website: www.canadianveterinarians.net
Contact: Heather Broughton, managing editor
Published monthly

CM Condominium Manager
2233 Argentina Road, Suite 100, Mississauga, ON L5N 2X7
Phone: (905) 826-6890 or 1-800-265-3263 Fax: (905) 826-4873
E-mail: editor@acmo.org
Website: www.acmo.org
Contact: Diane Werbicki, executive editor
Published quarterly

Cosmetics
1 Mount Pleasant Road, 8th Floor, Toronto, ON M4Y 2Y5
Phone: (416) 764-1680
E-mail: kristen.vinakmens@cosmetics.rogers.com
Website: www.cosmeticsmag.com
Contact: Kristen Vinakmens, editor
Published bimonthly

Fire Fighting in Canada
P.O. Box 530, 105 Donly Drive S., Simcoe, ON N3Y 4N5
Phone: (289) 259-8077 or 1-888-599-2228 Fax: (519) 429-3094
E-mail: lking@annexweb.com
Website: www.firefightingincanada.com
Contact: Laura King, editor
Published 8 times a year

Fitness Business Canada
30 Mill Pond Drive, Georgetown, ON L7G 4S6
Phone: (905) 873-0850 or 1-888-920-6537 Fax: (905) 873-8611
E-mail: stephen@fitnet.ca
Website: www.fitnet.ca
Contact: Stephen Longwell, general manager
Published bimonthly

Gifts and Tablewares

80 Valleybrook Drive, Toronto, ON M3B 2S9
Phone: (416) 442-5600, ext. 3238 Fax: (416) 510-5140
E-mail: lsmith@gifts-and-tablewares.com
Website: www.giftsandtablewares.ca
Contact: Lori Smith, editor
Published 6 times a year

Glass Canada

105 Donly Drive S., Simcoe, ON N3Y 4N5
Phone: (226) 931-0545 Fax: (519) 429-3094
E-mail: pflannery@annexweb.com
Website: www.glasscanadamag.com
Contact: Patrick Flannery, editor
Published bimonthly

HomeStyle Magazine

146 Cavendish Court, Oakville, ON L6J 5S2
Phone: (905) 338-0799 Fax: (905) 338-5623
E-mail: laurie@homestylemag.ca
Website: www.homestylemag.ca
Contact: Laurie O'Halloran, publisher/editor
Published bimonthly

The Hill Times

69 Sparks Street, Ottawa, ON K1P 5A5
Phone: (613) 232-5952 Fax: (613) 232-9055
E-mail: kmalloy@hilltimes.com or news@hilltimes.com
Website: www.hilltimes.com
Contact: Kate Malloy, managing editor
Published weekly

Jewellery Business

15 Wertheim Court, Suite 710, Richmond Hill, ON L4B 3H7
Phone: (905) 771-7333 Fax: (905) 771-7336
Website: www.jewellerybusiness.com
Contact: Jacquie De Almeida, managing editor
Published bimonthly

Luggage, Leathergoods & Accessories
96 Karma Road, Markham, ON L3R 4Y3
Phone: (905) 944-0265 Fax: (416) 296-0994
E-mail: la.vidabiz@sympatico.ca or info@mediadiversified.com
Website: www.llanda.com
Contact: Vida Jurisic, editor
Published quarterly

Municipal World
42860 Sparta Line, Union, ON NOL 2LO
Phone: (519) 633-0031 Fax: (519) 633-1001
E-mail: sgardner@municipalworld.com
Website: www.municipalworld.com
Contact: Susan Gardner, executive editor
Published monthly

Optical Prism
Phone: (416) 233-2487 Fax: (416) 233-1746
E-mail: info@opticalprism.ca
Website: www.opticalprism.ca
Contact: Craig Saunders, editor
Published 9 times a year

Perspectives (Canadian Employee Relocation Council)
180 Dundas Street W., Suite 1506, Toronto, ON M5G 1Z8
Phone: (416) 593-9812 or 1-866-357-2372 Fax: (416) 593-1139
E-mail: roma@mediaedgepublishing.com
Contact: Roma Ihnatowycz, editor
Published quarterly

REM: Canada's Magazine for Real Estate Professionals
1178 – 2255B Queen Street E., Toronto, ON M4E 1G3
Phone: (416) 425-3504, ext. 3
E-mail: jim@remonline.com
Website: www.remonline.com
Contact: Jim Adair, editor
Published monthly

Salon Magazine
365 Bloor Street E., Suite 1902, Toronto, ON M4W 3L4
Phone: (416) 869-3131 Fax: (416) 869-3008
E-mail: salon@beautynet.com
Contact: Marilla Aguirre, editor-in-chief
Published 8 times a year

Security Products and Technology News
222 Edward Street, Aurora, ON L4G IW6
Phone: (905) 727-0077 Fax: (905) 727-0017
E-mail: nsutton@annexweb.com
Contact: Neil Sutton, editor
Published 10 times a year

Toys & Games
3409 Yonge Street, P.O. Box 94084, Toronto, ON M4N 3RI
Phone: (416) 487-1869 Fax: (416) 663-2353
E-mail: editor@toysandgamesmagazine.ca
Website: www.toysandgamesmagazine.ca
Contact: Lynn Winston, editor
Published bimonthly

West of the City
447 Speers Road, Suite 4, Oakville, ON L6K 3S7
Phone: (905) 845-8536 Fax: (905) 842-4432
E-mail: hcrawford@westofthecity.com
Website: www.westofthecity.com
Contact: Holly Crawford, editor
Published bimonthly

Printing & Photography

Graphic Arts Magazine
72 Main Street, Mount Albert, ON LOG IMO
Phone: 1-877-513-3999
E-mail: news@graphicartsmag.com
Website: www.graphicartsmag.ocm

Contacts: Natalia Gilewicz and Kristen Read, associate editors
Published 10 times a year

Graphic Monthly Canada
1606 Sedlescomb Drive, Unit 8, Mississauga, ON L4X 1M6
Phone: (905) 625-7070 Fax: (905) 625-4856
E-mail: ftamburri@graphicmonthly.ca
Website: www.graphicmonthly.ca
Contact: Filomena Tamburri, editor
Published bimonthly

PrintAction
610 Alden Road, Suite 100, Markham, ON L3R 9Z1
Phone: (416) 665-7333 Fax: (905) 752-1441
E-mail: jon@printaction.com
Website: www.printaction.com
Contact: Jon Robinson, editor
Published monthly

Science

Bio Business
30 E. Beaver Creek Road, Suite 202, Richmond Hill, ON L4B 1J2
Phone: (905) 886-5040 or 1-800-613-6353 Fax: (905) 886-6615
E-mail: rprice@jesmar.com
Website: www.biobusinessmag.com
Contacts: Robert Price, managing editor
Published quarterly

Biotechnology Focus
4 Vata Court, Suite 24, Aurora, ON L4G 4B6
Phone: (905) 727-3875 Fax: (905) 727-4428
E-mail: terrip@promotive.net
Website: www.bioscienceworld.ca
Contact: Terri Pavelic, publisher/editor-in-chief
Published monthly

Lab Business

30 E. Beaver Creek Road, Suite 202, Richmond Hill, ON L4B 1J2
Phone: (905) 886-5040 or 1-800-613-6353 Fax: (905) 886-6615
E-mail: rprice@jesmar.com
Website: www.labbusinessmag.com
Contact: Robert Price, managing editor
Published 5 times a year

Laboratory Product News

80 Valleybrook Drive, Toronto, ON M3B 2S9
Phone: (416) 510-6835 Fax: (416) 442-2214
E-mail: lburt@labcanada.com
Website: www.labcanada.com
Contact: Leslie Burt, publisher/editor
Published bimonthly

Physics in Canada

150 Louis Pasteur Pvt., Suite 112, McDonald Building, Ottawa,
   ON KIN 6N5
Phone: (613) 562-5614 Fax: (613) 562-5615
E-mail: cap@uottawa.ca
Website: www.cap.ca/publications/physics-canada-pic
Contact: Francine Ford, editor
Published quarterly

Transportation & Cargo

BC Shipping News

1275 W. 6th Avenue, Suite 300, Vancouver, BC V6H 1A6
Phone: (604) 893-8800 Fax: (604) 708-1920
E-mail: info@bcshippingnews.com
Website: www.bcshippingnews.com
Contact: Jane McIvor, editor
Published 10 times a year

Canadian Autodealer

85 Renfrew Drive, Markham, ON L3R 0N9
Phone: (905) 479-6370, ext. 224

E-mail: tphillips@universusmedia.com
Website: www.canadianautodealer.ca
Contact: Todd Phillips, editorial director
Published 8 times a year

Canadian Transportation & Logistics
80 Valleybrook Drive, Toronto, ON M3B 2S9
Phone: (416) 510-6881 Fax: (416) 510-5134
E-mail: lou@transportationmedia.ca
Website: www.ctl.ca
Contact: Lou Smyrlis, editorial director
Published 11 times a year

Motortruck
80 Valleybrook Drive, Toronto, ON M3B 2S9
Phone: (416) 510-6881 Fax: (416) 510-5134
E-mail: lou@transportationmedia.ca
Website: www.trucknews.com
Contact: Lou Smyrlis, editorial director
Published 11 times a year
Published bimonthly

Over the Road
18 Parkglen Drive, Ottawa, ON K2G 3G9
Phone: (613) 224-9947 or 1-800-416-8712 Fax: (613) 224-8825
E-mail: peter@otr.on.ca
Website: www.overtheroad.ca
Contact: Peter Charboneau, publisher
Published monthly

Today's Trucking
451 Attwell Drive, Toronto, ON M9W 5C4
Phone: (416) 614-5828 Fax: (416) 614-8861
E-mail: pcarter@todaystrucking.com
Website: www.todaystrucking.com
Contact: Peter Carter, editor
Published 10 times a year

Truck News / Truck West
80 Valleybrook Drive, Toronto, ON M3B 2S9
Phone: (416) 510-6881 Fax: (416) 510-5134
E-mail: lou@transportationmedia.ca
Website: www.trucknews.com
Contact: Lou Smyrlis, editorial director
Published monthly

Travel

Canadian Travel Press
310 Dupont Street, Toronto, ON M5R 1V9
Phone: (416) 968-7252 Fax: (416) 968-2377
E-mail: ebaxter@baxter.net
Website: www.travelpress.com
Contact: Edith Baxter, editor-in-chief
Published weekly

Canadian Traveller
2080 Hartley Avenue, Suite 201, Coquitlam, BC V3K 6W5
Phone: (604) 669-9990 Fax: (604) 669-9993
E-mail: janices@canadiantraveller.net
Website: www.canadiantraveller.net
Contact: Janice Strong, editor
Published monthly

GSA: The Travel Magazine for Western Canada
1945 W. 4th Avenue, Suite 201, Vancouver, BC V6J 1M7
Phone: (604) 689-2909 Fax: (604) 689-2989
E-mail: editor@gsapublishing.com
Website: www.gsapublishing.com
Contact: Vickie Sam Paget, editor
Published 24 times a year

Meetings & Incentive Travel
80 Valleybrook Drive, Toronto, ON M3B 2S9
Phone: (416) 442-5600, ext. 3254 Fax: (416) 510-5140
E-mail: ddouloff@meetingscanada.com

Website: www.meetingscanada.com
Contact: Don Douloff, managing editor
Published bimonthly

The Road Explorer
555 Burnhamthorpe Road, Suite 505, Etobicoke, ON M9C 2Y3
Phone: (416) 229-6622, ext. 223 or 1-800-665-2456 Fax: 1-800-
    709-5551
E-mail: ann@omca.com
Website: www.omca.com
Contact: Ann Fairley, managing editor
Published 3 times a year

Travel Courier
310 Dupont Street, Toronto, ON M5R 1V9
Phone: (416) 968-7252 Fax: (416) 968-2377
E-mail: baginski@baxter.net
Website: www.travelcourier.ca
Contact: Mike Baginski, editor
Published weekly

Travelweek
282 Richmond Street E., Suite 100, Toronto, ON M5A 1P4
Phone: (416) 365-1500 or 1-800-727-1429 Fax: (416) 365-1504
E-mail: travelweek@travelweek.ca
Website: www.travelweek.ca
Contact: Patrick Dineen, editor
Published weekly

4

DAILY NEWSPAPERS

Although several major daily newspapers have shuttered in recent years, there are still over a hundred English-language daily newspapers in Canada, making this a significant potential market for both experienced and less-seasoned freelance writers. Remember that many successful writing careers began in the pages of a local daily or small community newspaper.

Many of the larger city dailies pay as much as or more than the average consumer magazine for well-written, well-researched articles on important or intriguing subjects. And they settle faster: most pay at the end of the month, some even on acceptance.

Two keys to writing for newspapers are the accuracy of the story and delivering it on time. Because news loses its value as quickly as it changes, it is usually gathered hurriedly, on large and small papers, by staff reporters. Therefore, it is to your advantage to concentrate on background stories about ongoing issues or to write profiles of prominent, interesting, or unusual local citizens or institutions.

Editors look for feature articles with body and strength, as well as originality and freshness. Timing is important. Keep a calendar of dates for seasonal stories – Halloween, Thanksgiving, Christmas, Chinese New Year, Canada Day, and so on – and read behind the news for feature ideas.

The travel section of a paper typically buys the most freelance work, followed by the food section, but other categories where freelancers often contribute include hobbies, lifestyles, personal finance, business, and strong human-interest pieces, which are among the most popular in any newspaper. Most editors like to build up a resource of articles that do not have to be used immediately.

Your best preparation in tackling the newspaper market is to carefully read several issues of a specific paper. Note its editorial approach, style, story lengths, use of photographs, and the difference in content, construction, and tone between its news stories and feature articles. If you have never studied journalism, you might want to refer to *Mencher's News Reporting and Writing*, by Melvin Mencher, a professor at Columbia University's Graduate School of Journalism (see Chapter 11, Resources).

You will, of course, need more experience to sell to large, well-staffed metropolitan dailies such as *The Toronto Star* or the *Winnipeg Free Press*. But even here, the outside contributor has a chance, provided he or she has some specialized knowledge, can handle human-interest material deftly, and can write full-bodied issue stories with conviction and authority.

When approaching a newspaper, the freelancer should not use the same procedures as for magazines. Speed is a primary factor here. If you are planning to write about a breaking news event, it is permissible to telephone the editor for his or her okay. Even for less time-sensitive articles, a query letter would take too long. Instead, send the completed piece to the editor along with an SASE and a cover letter. In the letter convince the editor that he or she should buy your article, include a short outline of your experience (with tear sheets of your published work and copies of any of your letters that that paper may have published), and note the availability of photographs.

To stretch the earning potential of your newspaper article, it is acceptable to sell it to more than one paper at a time, as long as the publications serve completely different regions and not one of the papers is a national.

Don't forget to also target the magazine-style weekly supplements put out by most newspapers. Here general-interest stories usually prevail, and opportunities exist for the freelance writer. Your first approach to the editor of a supplement should either be via a query letter or else by sending in the completed article.

If you are just beginning your writing career and need to gain confidence and assemble a file of tear sheets, consider weekly community newspapers as a good starting point. With small staffs, low budgets, and no wire services to rely on, their editors are often happy to accept outside contributions, particularly feature articles that cover the local scene. And since payment is modest, there is little competition from more experienced writers. Phone the editors directly, since they have neither the time nor the resources to respond to written queries.

In addition to writing for your city paper, look for opportunities to act as a correspondent, or stringer, for one published elsewhere. The full listing of English-language Canadian daily newspapers that follows will prove useful. For suburban weeklies, check the *CARD* directory.

Alberta

Calgary Herald
Street: 215 – 16th Street S.E., Calgary, AB T2E 7P5
Mailing: P.O. Box 2400, Stn. M, Calgary, AB T2P OW8
Phone: (403) 235-7433 Fax: (403) 235-7379
E-mail: submit@theherald.canwest.com
Website: www.calgaryherald.com

Calgary Sun
2615 12th Street N.E., Calgary, AB T2E 7W9
Phone: (403) 410-1010 Fax: (403) 250-4180
E-mail: cal-news@sunmedia.ca
Website: www.calgarysun.com

Daily Herald-Tribune
10604 100 Street, Grande Prairie, AB T8V 6V4
Phone: (780) 532-1110 Fax: (780) 532-2120
Website: www.dailyheraldtribune.com
Use online form to contact the appropriate department

Edmonton Journal
10006 – 101 Street, Edmonton, AB T5J OSI
Phone: (780) 429-5100
E-mail: lchodan@edmontonjournal.com
Website: www.edmontonjournal.com

Edmonton Sun

4990 – 92 Avenue, Suite 250, Edmonton, AB T6B 3A1
Phone: (780) 468-0100 Fax: (780) 468-0139
E-mail: donna.harker@sunmedia.ca
Website: www.edmontonsun.com

Fort McMurray Today

8550 Franklin Avenue, Bag 4008, Fort McMurray, AB T9H 3G1
Phone: (780) 743-8186 Fax: (780) 715-3820
Website: www.fortmcmurraytoday.com
Use online form to contact the appropriate department

Lethbridge Herald

504 – 7th Street S., Lethbridge, AB T1J 2H1
Phone: (403) 328-4411 Fax: (403) 329-9355
E-mail: dmackinnon@lethbridgeherald.com
Website: www.lethbridgeherald.com

Medicine Hat News

3257 Dunmore Road S.E., P.O. Box 10, Medicine Hat, AB T1A 7E6
Phone: (403) 527-1101 Fax: (403) 527-1244
E-mail: ksandford@medicinehatnews.com
Website: www.medicinehatnews.com

Metro Calgary

3030 – 3 Avenue N.E., Suite 120, Calgary, AB T2A 6T7
Phone: (403) 444-0136 Fax: (403) 539-4940
E-mail: calgaryletters@metronews.ca
Website: www.metronews.ca/calgary

Metro Edmonton

10123 – 99 Street N.W., Suite 2070, Edmonton, AB T5J 3H1
Phone: (780) 702-0592 Fax: (780) 701-0356
E-mail: edmontonletters@metronews.ca
Website: www.metronews.ca/edmonton

Red Deer Advocate

2950 Bremner Avenue, Red Deer, AB T4R 1M9
Phone: (403) 343-2400 Fax: (403) 341-6560

E-mail: editorial@reddeeradvocate.com
Website: www.reddeeradvocate.com

24 Hours (Calgary)
2615 – 12 Street N.E., Calgary, AB T2E 7W9
Phone: (403) 250-4317
E-mail: jose.rodriguez@sunmedia.ca
Website: www.24hrs.ca

24 Hours (Edmonton)
4990 – 92 Avenue, Suite 250, Edmonton, AB T6B 3A1
Phone: (780) 468-0283
E-mail: steve.serviss@sunmedia.ca
Website: www.24hrs.ca

British Columbia

Abbotsford News Daily
34375 Gladys Avenue, Abbotsford, BC V2S 2H5
Phone: (604) 853-1144 Fax: (604) 852-1641
E-mail: aholota@blackpress.com
Website: www.bclocalnews.com/daily/abbotsford

Alaska Highway News
9916 – 98th Street, Fort St. John, BC V1J 3T8
Phone: (250) 785-5631 Fax: (250) 785-3522
E-mail: editor@ahnfsj.ca
Website: www.alaskahighwaynews.ca

The Alberni Valley Times
4918 Napier Street, Port Alberni, BC V9Y 3H5
Phone: (250) 723-8171 Fax: (250) 723-0586
E-mail: hthomson@avtimes.net
Website: www2.canada.com/albernivalleytimes

Campbell River Mirror
250 Dogwood Street, Suite 104, Campbell River, BC V9W 5Z5
Phone: (250) 287-9227 Fax: (250) 287-3238

E-mail: editor@campbellrivermirror.com
Website: www.campbellrivermirror.com

Cranbrook Daily Townsman
822 Cranbrook Street N., Cranbrook, BC VIC 3R9
Phone: (250) 426-5201 Fax: (250) 426-5003
E-mail: barry@dailytownsman.com
Website: www.dailytownsman.com

The Daily Courier
550 Doyle Avenue, Kelowna, BC VIY 7VI
Phone: (250) 762-4445 Fax: (250) 762-3866
E-mail: city.desk@ok.bc.ca
Website: www.kelownadailycourier.ca

The Daily News (Kamloops)
393 Seymour Street, Kamloops, BC V2C 6P6
Phone: (250) 371-6149 Fax: (250) 374-3884
E-mail: kamloopsnews@telus.net
Website: www.kamloopsnews.ca

The Dawson Creek Daily News
100 Avenue, Suite 901, Dawson Creek, BC VIG IW2
Phone: (250) 782-4888 Fax: (250) 782-6770
E-mail: news@dcdn.ca
Website: www.dawsoncreekdailynews.ca

The Kimberley Daily Bulletin
335 Spokane Street, Kimberley, BC VIA IY9
Phone: (250) 427-5333 Fax: (250) 427-5336
E-mail: bulletin@cyberlink.bc.ca
Website: www.dailybulletin.ca

Metro Vancouver
1190 Homer Street, Suite 250, Vancouver, BC V6B 2X6
Phone: (604) 602-1002 Fax: 1-866-254-6504
E-mail: vancouverletters@metronews.ca
Website: www.metronews.ca/vancouver

Vernon Morning Star
4407 – 25th Avenue, Vernon, BC V1T 1P5
Phone: (250) 545-3322 Fax: (250) 542-1510
E-mail: letters@vernonmorningstar.com
Website: www.vernonmorningstar.com

Penticton Herald
186 Nanaimo Street W., Penticton, BC V2A 1N4
Phone: (250) 492-4002 Fax: (250) 492-2403
E-mail: editor@pentictonherald.ca
Website: www.pentictonherald.ca

Prince George Citizen
P.O. Box 5700, Prince George, BC V2L 5K9
Phone: (250) 562-2441 Fax: (250) 562-7453
Website: www.princegeorgecitizen.com
Use online form to contact the appropriate department

The Province
200 Granville Street, Suite 1, Vancouver, BC V6C 3N3
Phone: (604) 605-2000 Fax: (604) 605-2759
E-mail: tabtips@theprovince.com
Website: www.theprovince.com

Times Colonist
2621 Douglas Street, Victoria, BC V8T 4M2
Phone: (250) 380-5211 Fax: (250) 380-5353
E-mail: localnews@timescolonist.com
Website: www.timescolonist.com

Trail Daily Times
1163 Cedar Avenue, Trail, BC V1R 4B8
Phone: (250) 368-8551 Fax: (250) 368-8550
E-mail: editor@trailtimes.ca
Website: www.traildailytimes.ca

24 Hours (Vancouver)
554 E. 15th Avenue, Vancouver, BC V5T 2R5
Phone: (604) 322-2340 Fax: (604) 322-3026

E-mail: van24news@sunmedia.ca
Website: www.vancouver.24hrs.ca

The Vancouver Sun
200 Granville Street, Suite 1, Vancouver, BC V6C 3N3
Phone: (604) 605-2445 or 1-866-368-5888 Fax: (604) 605-2323
E-mail: sunnewstips@vancouversun.com
Website: www.vancouversun.com

Manitoba

The Brandon Sun
501 Rosser Avenue, Brandon, MB R7A OK4
Phone: (204) 727-2451 Fax: (204) 727-0385
E-mail: opinion@brandonsun.com
Website: www.brandonsun.com

The Daily Graphic / Central Plains Herald-Leader
1941 Saskatchewan Avenue W., P.O. Box 130, Portage La Prairie,
    MB RIN 3B4
Phone: (204) 857-3427 Fax: (204) 239-1270
E-mail: news cphl.editor@sunmedia.ca
Website: www.portagedailygraphic.com

Metro Winnipeg
161 Portage Avenue E., Suite 200, Winnipeg MB R3B 2L6
Phone: (204) 943-9300 Fax: 1-888-846-0894
E-mail: winnipegletters@metronews.ca
Website: www.metronews.ca

Winnipeg Free Press
1355 Mountain Avenue, Winnipeg, MB R2X 3B6
Phone: (204) 697-7000 Fax: (204) 697-7412
E-mail: city.desk@freepress.mb.ca or
    margo.goodhand@freepress.mb.ca
Website: www.winnipegfreepress.com

Winnipeg Sun
1700 Church Avenue, Winnipeg, MB R2X 3A2
Phone: (204) 694-2022 Fax: (204) 697-0759
E-mail: mark.hamm@sunmedia.ca
Website: www.winnipegsun.com

New Brunswick

The Daily Gleaner
984 Prospect Street, P.O. Box 3370, Fredericton, NB E3B 2T8
Phone: (506) 452-6671 Fax: (506) 452-7405
Website: www.telegraphjournal.com
Use online form to contact the appropriate department

Telegraph-Journal
210 Crown Street, P.O. Box 2350, Saint John, NB E2L 3V8
Phone: (506) 632-88888Fax: (506) 639-5784
E-mail: newsroom@nbpub.com
Website: www.telegraphjournal.com
Use online form to contact the appropriate department

Times & Transcript
939 Main Street, P.O. Box 1001, Moncton, NB E1C 8P3
Phone: (506) 859-4945 Fax: (506) 859-4975
E-mail: news@timestranscript.com
Website: www.telegraphjournal.com
Use online form to contact the appropriate department

Newfoundland & Labrador

The Telegram
Box 86, 430 Topsail Road, St. John's, NL A1E 4N1
Phone: (709) 364-6300 Fax: (709) 364-3939
E-mail: telegram@thetelegram.com
Website: www.thetelegram.com

The Western Star
106 W. Street, P.O. Box 460, Corner Brook, NL A2H 6E7
Phone: (709) 634-4348 Fax: (709) 634-9824
E-mail: newsroom@thewesternstar.com
Website: www.thewesternstar.com

Nova Scotia

Amherst Daily News
147 S. Albion Street, Amherst, NS B4H 2X2
Phone: (902) 667-5102 Fax: (902) 667-0419
E-mail: dcole@amherstdaily.com
Website: www.cumberlandnewsnow.com

Cape Breton Post
255 George Street, P.O. Box 1500, Sydney, NS B1P 6K6
Phone: (902) 564-5451 Fax: (902) 562-7077
E-mail: edit@cbpost.com
Website: www.capebretonpost.com

The Chronicle-Herald
Street: 2717 Joseph Howe Drive, Halifax, NS B3L 4T9
Mailing: P.O. Box 610, Halifax, NS B3J 2T2
Phone: (902) 426-2811, ext. 1187 Fax: (902) 426-1158
E-mail: newsroom@herald.ca
Website: http://thechronicleherald.ca

Metro (Halifax)
3260 Barrington Street, Suite 102, Halifax, NS B3K 0B5
Phone: (902) 444-4444 Fax: (902) 422-5610 or (902) 422-5667
E-mail: halifaxletters@metronews.ca
Website: www.metronews.ca/halifax

The News
352 E. River Road, P.O. Box 159, New Glasgow, NS B2H 5E2
Phone: (902) 752-3000 Fax: (902) 752-1945
E-mail: news@ngnews.ca
Website: www.ngnews.ca

Truro Daily News
6 Louise Street, P.O. Box 220, Truro, NS B2N 5C3
Phone: (902) 893-9405 Fax: (902) 895-9176
E-mail: news@trurodaily.com
Website: www.trurodaily.com

Ontario

The Barrie Examiner
571 Bayfield Street N., Barrie, ON L4M 4Z9
Phone: (705) 726-6537 Fax: (705) 726-5148
Website: www.thebarrieexaminer.com
Use online form to contact the appropriate department

The Beacon Herald
789 Erie Street, Stratford, ON N4Z IAI
Phone: (519) 271-2222 Fax: (519) 271-1026
Website: www.stratfordbeaconherald.com
Use online form to contact the appropriate department

The Belleville Intelligencer
199 Front Street, Suite 535, Belleville, ON K8N 5H5
Phone: (613) 962-9171 Fax: (613) 962-9652
Website: www.intelligencer.ca
Use online form to contact the appropriate department

Brantford Expositor
195 Henry Street, Building 4, Brantford, ON N3S 5C9
Phone: (519) 756-2020 Fax: (519) 756-3285
Website: www.brantfordexpositor.ca
Use online form to contact the appropriate department

The Chatham Daily News
138 King Street W., Chatham, ON N7M 5M6
Phone: (519) 354-2000 Fax: (519) 354-3448
Website: www.chathamdailynews.ca
Use online form to contact the appropriate department

The Chronicle Journal
75 S. Cumberland Street, Thunder Bay, ON P7B IA3
Phone: (807) 343-6200 Fax: (807) 343-9409
Website: www.chroniclejournal.com
Use online form to contact the appropriate department

The Daily Observer
100 Crandall Street, Pembroke, ON K8A OBI
Phone: (613) 732-3691 Fax: (613) 732-1022
Website: www.thedailyobserver.ca
Use online form to contact the appropriate department

The Daily Press
187 Cedar Street S., Timmins, ON P4N 7GI
Phone: (705) 268-5050 Fax: (705) 268-7373
Website: www.timminspress.com
Use online form to contact the appropriate department

Fort Frances Daily Bulletin
116 First Street E., P.O. Box 339, Fort Frances, ON P9A 3M7
Phone: (807) 274-5373 Fax: (807) 274-7286
E-mail: mbehan@fortfrances.com or use online contact form
Website: www.fftimes.com

The Globe and Mail
444 Front Street W., Toronto, ON M5V 2S9
Phone: (416) 585-5000 Fax: (416) 585-5085
E-mail: newsroom@globeandmail.com
Website: www.globeandmail.com

The Guelph Mercury
14 Macdonell Street, Suite 8, Guelph, ON NIH 6P7
Phone: (519) 823-6060 Fax: (519) 822-7771
E-mail: editor@guelphmercury.com
Website: www.guelphmercury.com

The Hamilton Spectator
44 Frid Street, Hamilton, ON L8N 3G3
Phone: (905) 526-3333 Fax: (905) 526-1395

E-mail: letters@thespec.com
Website: www.thespec.com

Kenora Daily Miner and News
33 Main Street S., P.O. Box 1620, Kenora, ON P9N 3X7
Phone: (807) 468-5555 Fax: (807) 468-4318
Website: www.kenoradailyminerandnews.com
Use online form to contact the appropriate department

The Kingston Whig-Standard
6 Cataraqui Street, P.O. Box 2300, Kingston, ON K7L 4Z7
Phone: (613) 544-5000 Fax: (613) 530-4122
Website: www.thewhig.com
Use online form to contact the appropriate department

The Lindsay Post
17 William Street S., Lindsay, ON K9V 3A3
Phone: (705) 324-2113 Fax: (705) 324-0174
Website: www.thepost.ca
Use online form to contact the appropriate department

The London Free Press
369 York Street, P.O. Box 2280, London, ON N6A 4G1
Phone: (519) 667-5525 Fax: (519) 667-4528
E-mail: lfp.newsdesk@sunmedia.ca
Website: www.lfpress.com

Metro (London)
350 Talbot Street, Main Floor, London, ON N6A 2R6
Phone: (519) 434-3556
E-mail: londonletters@metronews.ca
Website: www.metronews.ca/london

Metro (Ottawa)
130 Slater Street, Suite 300, Ottawa, ON K1P 6E2
Phone: (613) 236-5058 Fax: 1-866-253-2024
E-mail: ottawaletters@metronews.ca
Website: www.metronews.ca/ottawa

Metro (Toronto)
625 Church Street, 6th Floor, Toronto, ON M4Y 2G1
Phone: (416) 486-4900 Fax: (416) 482-8097
E-mail: torontoletters@metronews.ca
Website: www.metronews.ca/toronto

National Post
1450 Don Mills Road, Suite 300, Don Mills, ON M3B 3R5
Phone: (416) 383-2300 or 1-800-267-6568 Fax: (416) 383-2305
Website: www.nationalpost.com
Use online form to contact the appropriate department

The Niagara Falls Review
4801 Valley Way, Niagara Falls, ON L2E 6T6
Phone: (905) 358-5711 Fax: (905) 356-0785
Website: www.niagarafallsreview.ca
Use online form to contact the appropriate department

North Bay Nugget
259 Worthington Street W., North Bay, ON P1B 3B5
Phone: (705) 472-3200 Fax: (705) 472-1438
Website: www.nugget.ca
Use online form to contact the appropriate department

Northern News
8 Duncan Avenue, P.O. Box 1030, Kirkland Lake, ON P2N 3L4
Phone: (705) 567-5321 Fax: (705) 567-6162
E-mail: news@northernnews.ca
Website: www.northernnews.ca

Northumberland Today
99 King St. W., Cobourg, ON K9A 2M4
Phone: (905) 372-0131 Fax: (905) 372-4966
Website: www.northumberlandtoday.com
Use online form to contact the appropriate department

The Observer
140 Front Street S., Sarnia, ON N7T 7M8
Phone: (519) 344-3641 Fax: (519) 332-2951

Website: www.theobserver.ca
Use online form to contact the appropriate department

Ottawa Citizen
1101 Baxter Road, P.O. Box 5020, Ottawa, ON K2C 3M4
Phone: (613) 829-9100 Fax: (613) 726-1198
E-mail: apotter@ottawacitizen.com
Website: www.ottawacitizen.com

Ottawa Sun
P.O. Box 9729, Stn. T, Ottawa, ON K1G 5H7
Phone: (613) 739-5112 Fax: (613) 739-8041
E-mail: ottsun.city@sunmedia.ca
Website: www.ottawasun.com

Packet & Times
425 West Street N., Suite 15, Orillia, ON L3V 7R2
Phone: (705) 325-1355 Fax: (705) 329-4033
E-mail: newsroom@orilliapacket.com
Website: www.orilliapacket.com

The Peterborough Examiner
60 Hunter Street E., P.O. Box 2890, East Peterborough, ON
    K9J 3L4
Phone: (705) 745-4641 Fax: (705) 745-3361
E-mail: newsroom@peterboroughexaminer.com
Website: www.thepeterboroughexaminer.com

The Record
160 King Street E., Kitchener, ON N2G 4E5
Phone: (519) 894-2231 Fax: (519) 894-3829
E-mail: newsroom@therecord.com
Website: http://news.therecord.com

The Recorder & Times
2479 Parkdale Avenue, Brockville, ON K6V 3H2
Phone: (613) 342-4441 Fax: (613) 342-4456
Website: www.recorder.ca
Use online form to contact the appropriate department

St. Thomas Times-Journal
16 Hincks Street, St. Thomas, ON N5R 5Z2
Phone: (519) 631-2790 Fax: (519) 631-5653
Website: www.stthomastimesjournal.com
Use online form to contact the appropriate department

The Sault Star
145 Old Garden River Road, Sault Ste. Marie, ON P6A 5M5
Phone: (705) 759-3030 Fax: (705) 759-0102
Website: www.saultstar.com
Use online form to contact the appropriate department

Sentinel-Review
16 Brock Street, Woodstock, ON N4S 3B4
Phone: (519) 537-2341 Fax: (519) 537-3049
Website: www.woodstocksentinelreview.com
Use online form to contact the appropriate department

Simcoe Reformer
50 Gilbertson Drive, Simcoe, ON N3Y 4L2
Phone: (519) 426-5710 Fax: (519) 426-9255
Website: www.simcoereformer.ca
Use online form to contact the appropriate department

The Standard
17 Queen Street, St. Catharines, ON L2R 5G5
Phone: (905) 684-7251 Fax: (905) 684-6032
Website: www.stcatharinesstandard.ca
Use online form to contact the appropriate department

Standard Freeholder
1150 Montreal Road, Cornwall, ON K6J 1E2
Phone: (613) 933-3160 Fax: (613) 933-7521
Website: www.standard-freeholder.com
Use online form to contact the appropriate department

The Sudbury Star
33 Mackenzie Street, Sudbury, ON P3B 1Y6
Phone: (705) 674-5271 Fax: (705) 674-0624

Website: www.thesudburystar.com
Use online form to contact the appropriate department

The Sun Times
290 – 9th Street E., Owen Sound, ON N4K 1N7
Phone: (519) 376-2250 Fax: (519) 372-1861
Website: www.owensoundsuntimes.com
Use online form to contact the appropriate department

t.o.night
2 Pape Avenue, Toronto, ON M4M 2V6
Phone: (647) 344-1779 Fax: (647) 436-7853
Website: www.tonightnewspaper.com
Use online contact form

The Toronto Star
1 Yonge Street, Toronto, ON M5E 1E6
Phone: (416) 869-4300 Fax: (416) 869-4328
E-mail: city@thestar.ca
Website: www.thestar.com

Toronto Sun
333 King Street E., Toronto, ON M5A 3X5
Phone: (416) 947-2222 Fax: (416) 947-1664
E-mail: torsun.citydesk@sunmedia.ca
Website: www.torontosun.com

The Tribune
228 E. Main Street, Welland, ON L3B 5P5
Phone: (905) 732-2411 Fax: (905) 732-3660
Website: www.wellandtribune.ca
Use online form to contact the appropriate department

24 Hours (Ottawa)
6 Antares Drive, Ottawa, ON K1G 5H7
Phone: (613) 739-5115 Fax: (613) 739-8043
E-mail: jackie.lawrence@sunmedia.ca
Website: www.24hrs.ca

24 Hours (Toronto)
333 King Street E., Toronto, ON M5A 3X5
Phone: (416) 350-6479 Fax: (416) 350-6524
E-mail: 24news@sunmedia.ca
Website: www.24hrs.ca

The Windsor Star
167 Ferry Street, Windsor, ON N9A 4M5
Phone: (519) 255-5743 Fax: (519) 255-5515
E-mail: letters@thestar.canwest.com
Website: www.windsorstar.com

Prince Edward Island

The Guardian
165 Prince Street, Charlottetown, PE C1A 4R7
Phone: (902) 629-6000 Fax: (902) 566-3808
E-mail: newsroom@theguardian.pe.ca
Website: www.theguardian.pe.ca

Journal Pioneer
316 Water Street, P.O. Box 2480, Summerside, PE C1N 4K5
Phone: (902) 436-2121 Fax: (902) 436-3027
E-mail: newsroom@journalpioneer.com
Website: www.journalpioneer.com

Quebec

The Gazette
1010 Ste-Catherine Street W., Suite 200, Montreal, QC H3B 5L1
Phone: (514) 987-2222 Fax: (514) 987-2399
E-mail: letters@thegazette.canwest.com
Website: www.montrealgazette.com

The Record
1195 Galt Street E., Sherbrooke, QC J1G 1Y7
Phone: (819) 569-9525 Fax: (819) 821-3179

E-mail: newsroom@sherbrookerecord.com
Website: www.sherbrookerecord.com

Saskatchewan

Leader-Post
1964 Park Street, Regina, SK S4P 3G4
Phone: (306) 781-5300 Fax: (306) 565-2588
E-mail: citydesk@leaderpost.com
Website: www.leaderpost.com

Prince Albert Daily Herald
30 – 10th Street E., Prince Albert, SK S6V 0Y5
Phone: (306) 764-4276 Fax: (306) 763-3331
E-mail: editorial@paherald.sk.ca
Website: www.paherald.sk.ca

The StarPhoenix
204 – 5th Avenue N., Saskatoon, SK S7K 2PI
Phone: (306) 657-6231 Fax: (306) 657-6437
E-mail: citydesk@sp.canwest.com
Website: www.thestarphoenix.com

Times-Herald
44 Fairford Street W., Moose Jaw, SK S6H IVI
Phone: (306) 692-6441 Fax: (306) 692-2101
E-mail: editorial@mjtimes.sk.ca
Website: www.mjtimes.sk.ca

Yukon

Whitehorse Daily Star
2149 Second Avenue, Whitehorse, YT YIA IC5
Phone: (867) 667-4481 Fax: (867) 668-7130
E-mail: editor@whitehorsestar.com
Website: www.whitehorsestar.com

5

BOOK PUBLISHERS

The first-time author should be under no illusions about the difficulties of breaking into book publishing – still less, of making a living from the often-slender proceeds, unless you are phenomenally talented or hit on that rare winning formula. Nonetheless, every year brings a new success story – another brilliant unknown author who takes the publishing world by storm. Every writer must be a realist, and an optimist.

Small presses are more likely to take an interest in an unpublished writer, and are generally more receptive to unsolicited manuscripts. They also may be more accessible, offer more personal attention to their authors, and be more willing to take a risk. Nino Ricci's prize-winning first novel, *Lives of the Saints*, was published by Cormorant Books, having been rejected by a raft of the larger players. But he had no difficulty placing his eagerly awaited second novel with McClelland & Stewart. Small presses almost always work with unagented writers. On the down side, small publishers offer small advances or none at all, their print runs tend to be low, and their distribution systems and marketing expertise cannot match those of the big houses.

Before you make any approaches to publishers, do some research. Use the following list to whittle down a selection of houses whose programs seem most compatible with your own work, then check out some of their books. Another approach is to browse through a bookstore compiling a list of publishers who are releasing books similar to yours. You can write to their publicity departments, including a large SASE, to request current catalogues, and visit their websites to learn more about their publishing programs. Familiarity with the focus of several houses can help you develop an attractive proposal, as well as target the most appropriate potential publishers.

It is important to note the difference in selling fiction and non-fiction manuscripts to book publishers. Typically a manuscript of fiction must be fully finished before you approach an editor. For non-fiction, you must have done considerable research on your topic, but usually you are required to produce only a synopsis of your story, a chapter outline, and two or three sample chapters. Remember that whether your manuscript is fiction or non-fiction, it is imperative that it begin with a strong, attention-grabbing start. If you don't capture an editor's interest in the first few minutes, he or she is likely to set aside your work and move on to the next manuscript in the pile.

The Query Letter

If you are aiming to sell your manuscript directly to a book publisher without the benefit of a literary agent, your first approach should be through a query letter. This initial correspondence is extremely important. A poorly composed letter can nix your chances of getting published before an editor has even looked at your manuscript. A compelling query letter may get your manuscript onto someone's desk for a first read.

Your letter should be typed in a plain, readable font on unadorned, business-like stationery. Include your name, address, telephone number, and e-mail address. Refer to the editor (or other contact person) by name, and address him or her as Mr. or Ms.

In a letter of no more than two pages, plus enclosures, you must convince a publishing house to at least consider investing considerable money and effort in your manuscript. Spend time to craft it in your best writing style and seize the editor's attention with a gripping intro. Remember, an editor doesn't yet have your manuscript to read; his or her judgment will be based largely upon the strength of your query.

Tell the editor the working title of your book and describe what it is about; if it is fiction, outline the characters and provide a short plot synopsis. Next, mention any special qualifications you have to write this manuscript. These might include a background in the subject covered or special access to research sources. Indicate your publishing history, who published your previous books, how many copies were sold, and if any foreign rights were bought.

Tell the editor what competing books on a similar subject are in the marketplace, and confidently assert why yours will do equally well or be more successful. Also describe what makes your manuscript different from all the others; after all, publishers want something original. Inform the editor about any research you have done to determine the markets for your book and ideas you may have for promotion.

For non-fiction queries, include a one-page synopsis of your manuscript if it could not be adequately described in your letter. Also enclose a table of contents with a brief description of what each chapter is about and an indication of the research you will undertake in writing this book. You may send one or two sample chapters or wait for a request by the editor. For a fiction query, send along a one-page synopsis and three sample chapters (including the first chapter).

If you haven't received a reply after two months, you may wish to send the editor a note attached to a copy of your original query letter. But if after three months you still haven't heard, move on to another publisher. In the case of long delays — typical in book publishing — it is permissible to send out multiple queries.

Sending the Manuscript

If you have received a positive reply from a query letter, or if you have targeted a publisher that will accept full manuscripts without an initial query, there is a certain protocol to follow when submitting your work.

Manuscripts should be prepared as indicated in the Introduction; that is, on 8½-by-11-inch bond paper, typed on a computer in a readable font and double-spaced. Of course, you should never send the only copy of your work. Manuscripts should not be stapled, but fastened with elastic bands and held between two sheets of cardboard, front and back, or better still, placed in a box.

A covering letter should accompany your work. If this is an unsolicited manuscript, include a letter similar to the query letter (above), one that sells both you and your book to the prospective publisher. When an editor has asked to see your manuscript in response to a query, enclose a covering letter reminding him or her of your previous correspondence.

It may take three months or longer for a publishing company to reply to your submission, so it is advisable to include a self-addressed stamped postcard so they can acknowledge its receipt. Be sure to also send a postage-paid envelope large enough for your manuscript so an editor can return your work if it is not accepted, otherwise you may not receive it back.

While it is perfectly permissible to send out multiple submissions, there is a general protocol that you should follow. Indicate in your covering letter that you have sent the manuscript to other publishers; you do not need to specify which publishers these are. Also state a deadline for their decision – three months is standard – before which time you must not sign a contract from one publisher without allowing the others to make counter-offers.

Contracts

Receiving a contract from a book publisher is a dream come true. While your tendency may be to sign anything that will bring your manuscript into book form, it is a very important legal document, and you must proceed with caution.

First of all, you need to seek the advice of a professional who will explain the rights, obligations, and rewards being offered by such a document. You must understand the rights you are selling and agree that the compensation is fair, or negotiate to try to improve it. You should never sign away the copyright to your work.

Royalty rates vary, but average around 10 per cent for hardcover books and in the 8-per-cent range for paperbacks. Sometimes a sliding scale is offered whereby you receive a higher rate if your book sells more than a certain number of copies. For regular sales of your book (which doesn't include book-club sales or discount sales), you should receive the royalty as a percentage of the list price of the book, not the publisher's net.

An advance is a payment against the royalties your publisher expects the book will earn. It is typically paid in either two or three installments: when the contract is signed, when the manuscript is accepted, and sometimes when the book is published. While some small presses are unable to offer their authors advances, in the industry overall advances are rising, due to the increasing aggressiveness of Canadian publishers and agents, as well as international recognition of Canadian fiction. It is rare for a first-time novelist to receive over $15,000 as an advance; for business books, an average advance would range from $5,000 to $10,000.

As print-on-demand systems and e-books gain in popularity, new contractual issues arise. When a book is out of print for a certain period of time, the rights revert to the author. But now in the United States, those rights may not revert if the book exists in electronic form. In addition, if a book appears in an electronic medium, the writer has to ensure that he or she will receive adequate compensation.

For advice on publishing contracts, contact a lawyer who specializes in the publishing field, an experienced literary agent, or the Writers' Union of Canada.

Before outlining what we cover in the rest of this chapter, perhaps it's worth clarifying what we don't. Educational publishers are not listed unless they have a significant trade-publishing arm. Today more than ever, educational publishers are commissioning their books in close collaboration with schools and colleges to meet specific curricular needs. These texts are nearly always written by specialists in the field. Very few educational publishers consider unsolicited manuscripts or proposals, and fewer still are likely to look favourably upon them unless their author has a proven track record in the area. Neither, with a few exceptions, have we included publishers that specialize in poetry. For a comprehensive listing, consult *Poetry Markets for Canadians* (8th edition), published by the League of Canadian Poets, or *Poet's Market*, an annual publication by Writer's Digest Books.

The following list of publishers comprises English-language publishing houses only. It includes the major companies, as well as most of the mid-range and many of the smaller trade publishers currently operating in Canada. Some have large general-interest lists; others are more specialized, either in their subject areas or in their regional concerns. We also include several self-publishing companies, as many authors have found that this publishing model is better suited to their goals for their books.

AB Collector Publishing

5835 Grant Street, Halifax, NS B3H 1C9
Submissions: 215 Sand Point Road, Lakeville Corner, NB
   E4B 1K5
Phone: (902) 429-5768
E-mail: darklady@nbnet.nb.ca
Website: www.abcollectorpublishing.ca
Contact: Astrid Brunner, publisher/chief editor

Publishes biography, poetry, drama, short stories, anthology, and books about ceramics, photography, art, and history. "Your significant peripheral publisher since 1990. Each book is a thing of art, a dusting of poetry, a meaning of life." Has released 21 titles since 1990. First send an inquiry, then an outline, then sample chapters with a short bio. For more information, see website.

Acorn Press

P.O. Box 22024, Charlottetown, PE C1A 1Y1
Phone: (902) 221-1061
E-mail: info@acornpresscanada.com
Website: www.acornpresscanada.com
Contact: Laurie Brinklow, publisher

Publishes books about Prince Edward Island by Prince Edward Islanders. Releases about 6 to 8 new titles a year. Accepts unsolicited manuscripts about P.E.I. only, but send inquiry first. Guidelines available.

Thomas Allen & Son Publishers

390 Steelcase Road E., Markham, ON L3R 1G2
Phone: (905) 475-9126 Fax: (416) 203-2773
E-mail: info@t-allen.com
Website: www.thomas-allen.com
Contact: Marc Côté, publisher

Publishes literary fiction and non-fiction. Non-fiction categories include history, memoirs, travel, nature, philosophy, and popular culture. No cookbooks, genre fiction, DIY, or financial books. Produces approximately 15 new titles annually. No unsolicited manuscripts; manuscript submissions must be agented or come by referral.

The Alternate Press (an imprint of Life Media)
B2-125 The Queensway, Suite 52, Toronto, ON M8Y 1H6
E-mail: alternatepress@lifemedia.ca
Website: www.lifemedia.ca/altpress
Contact: Wendy Priesnitz, editor-in-chief

Publishes adult non-fiction about ways families and individuals can live in a healthy, environmentally sound, self-reliant manner. Releases 3 new titles a year. Accepts unsolicited manuscripts, but send an inquiry first. No longer accepts proposals for print books. Guidelines available on website.

Annick Press
15 Patricia Avenue, Toronto, ON M2M 1H9
Phone: (416) 221-4802 Fax: (416) 221-8400
E-mail: annickpress@annickpress.com
Website: www.annickpress.com
Contact: Elaine Burns, office manager

Established 1975. Publishes children's literature, including picture books, teen and middle-reader fiction, and non-fiction. "We seek out works that crackle with originality and become a passageway to new ideas. Our list is designed to excite, entertain, and promote self-awareness." Publishes approximately 30 titles per year. Accepts unsolicited manuscripts. Detailed submission information on website.

Anvil Press
P.O. Box 3008, MPO, Vancouver, BC V6B 3X5
Phone: (604) 876-8710 Fax: (604) 879-2667
E-mail: info@anvilpress.com
Website: www.anvilpress.com
Contact: Brian Kaufman, publisher

An independent literary press interested in work from new and established writers. Publishes progressive, contemporary work in all genres. Releases 8 to 10 books a year. Accepts unsolicited manuscripts. No e-mail submissions; only those manuscripts with an SASE will be considered. Send synopsis with sample chapter or two. Expect a wait of 4 to 6 months for reply. "Get our guidelines online, look at our books and catalogue to get a sense of the press, and submit if you feel your work is in line with our program."

Arbeiter Ring Publishing
121 Osborne Street, Suite 201E, Winnipeg, MB R3L 1Y4
Phone: (204) 942-7058 Fax: (204) 944-9198
E-mail: info@arbeiterring.com
Website: www.arteiterring.com
Contact: Rick Wood, office manager

Publishes a combination of serious cultural work and non-fiction titles with an emphasis on progressive political analysis of social and cultural issues. Publishes 4 to 6 books a year. Send an inquiry with an outline and sample chapters first. E-mail submissions are accepted, but print submissions preferred. "Please consult our website for submission guidelines and for further information on our publishing mandate/mission."

Arsenal Pulp Press
211 E. Georgia Street, Suite 101, Vancouver, BC V6A 1Z6
Phone: (604) 687-4233 Fax: (604) 687-4283
E-mail: info@arsenalpulp.com
Website: www.arsenalpulp.com
Contact: Brian Lam, publisher

Established 1971. Genres include literary fiction and non-fiction, cultural studies, multicultural literature, gay and lesbian literature, and cookbooks. Releases between 14 and 20 titles a year. Accepts unsolicited manuscripts, but send a synopsis, an outline (for non-fiction), writing credentials, and a 50-page excerpt first. Enclose an SASE to be ensured a reply. E-mail submissions not accepted. Guidelines available on website.

Artistic Warrior
2475 Dobbin Road #22, Suite 207, West Kelowna, BC V4T 2E9
E-mail: publisher@artisticwarrior.com

Website: www.artisticwarrior.com
Contact: Darcy Nybo, publisher
   Established 2011. Publishes new and emerging Canadian authors. "We only sign authors with a tenacity for self promotion. This means sitting through boring hours at book signings, doing interviews, speaking at bookstores and using social media." Currently publishes only non-fiction of a positive or informative nature; will be expanding into "feel-good fiction" in 2013.

Baico Books
294 Albert Street, Suite 103, Ottawa, ON KIP 6E6
Phone: (613) 829-5141 Fax: (613) 829-5152
E-mail: baico@bellnet.ca
Website: www.baico.ca
Contact: Raymond Coderre, president
   Self-publishing company that offers a full complement of publishing services, including editing, production, marketing, sales, and distribution. Accepts manuscripts on a wide variety of topics. Charges a $100 administration fee plus a $1/page reading fee. See website for submission instructions.

Banff Centre Press
P.O. Box 1020, 107 Tunnel Mountain Drive, Banff, AB TIL 1H5
Phone: (403) 762-6410 or 1-800-565-9989 Fax: (403) 762-6277
E-mail: press@banffcentre.ca
Website: www.banffcentre.ca/press
Contact: Steven Ross Smith, director
   The Banff Centre Press specializes in publications on contemporary art, culture, and literature. It seeks to explore, disseminate, and garner support for the arts. Releases 4 to 6 new titles annually. Does not accept unsolicited manuscripts; submit an outline, sample chapters, and author bio first.

Baraka Books
6977 rue Lacroix, Montreal, QC H4E 2V4
Phone: 514-858-6333, ext. 226
E-mail: info@barakabooks.com
Website: www.barakabooks.com
Contact: Robin Philpot, president

Quebec-based English-language book publisher specializing in creative and political non-fiction, history and historical fiction, and fiction. Publishes 6 to 8 titles a year. First query by e-mail.

The Battered Silicon Dispatch Box

P.O. Box 50, R.R. #4, Eugenia, ON NOC IEO
Phone: (519) 924-2182 Fax: (519) 925-3482
E-mail: gav@cablerocket.com
Website: www.batteredbox.com
Contact: George A. Vanderburgh, publisher

A small press specializing in detective fiction from the golden age. "A Sherlockian publisher of first and last resort." Publishes about 40 books a year. Does not accept unsolicited manuscripts.

Bayeux Arts

119 Stratton Crescent S.W., Calgary, AB T3H IT7
E-mail: mail@bayeux.com
Website: www.bayeux.com
Contacts: Mercedes Bátiz-Benét, editor, fiction/non-
fiction/poetry, and Judd Palmer, editor, children's literature

Established 1994. "Our list is deliberately eclectic and contains books that other publishers often shy away from publishing." In addition to fiction and poetry, also publishes books on business and entrepreneurship under its Gondolier imprint. Send electronic manuscripts to the appropriate director and indicate if you are sending a simultaneous submission.

Between the Lines

401 Richmond Street W., Studio 277, Toronto, ON M5V 3A8
Phone: (416) 535-9914 or 1-800-718-7201 Fax: (416) 535-1484
E-mail: submissions@btlbooks.com
Website: http://btlbooks.com
Contact: Amanda Crocker, managing editor

Established 1977. Publishes critical, accessible non-fiction, primarily on Canadian politics and public policy, health, the environment, media, history, culture, and social issues. Accepts unsolicited manuscripts, but prefers to receive an inquiry first with an outline, sample chapters, and author bio. Accepts mailed submissions with an SASE, but prefers an e-mailed PDF.

Biblioasis

P.O. Box 92, Emeryville, ON N0R 1C0
Phone: (519) 968-2206 Fax: (519) 250 5713
E-mail: info@biblioasis.com
Website: www.biblioasis.com

Literary press "committed to publishing the best poetry, fiction and non-fiction in beautifully crafted editions."

Black Moss Press

2450 Byng Road, Windsor, ON N8W 3E8
Website: www.blackmosspress.com
Contact: Marty Gervais, editor

Seeking new poetry, fiction, and non-fiction. Publishes 2 theme anthologies each year. "Looking for new and innovative writing with an edge." Accepts unsolicited manuscripts, but send an inquiry first by mail. Submission details on website.

BookLand Press

15 Allstate Parkway, Suite 600, Markham, ON L3R 5B4
Phone: (905) 943-0950 or 1-800-535-1774
E-mail: submissions@booklandpress.com
Website: www.booklandpress.com
Contact: Robert Morgan, publisher

Independent publisher with interests in creative non-fiction, fiction, Aboriginal literature, and contemporary poetry. Strives to present books with topics that are relative to the needs of today's society. Releases about 10 books a year. Accepts unsolicited manuscripts via e-mail; submission guidelines available on website.

BookThug

260 Ryding Avenue, Toronto, ON M6N 1H5
Website: www.bookthug.ca
Contact: Hazel Millar, managing editor
E-mail: hazel@bookthug.ca

"BookThug seeks to publish innovative books of poetry, prose, and creative non-fiction that extend the tradition of experimental literature." Check website for current submission guidelines.

Borealis Press

8 Mohawk Crescent, Nepean, ON K2H 7G6
Phone: (613) 829-0150 or 1-877-696-2585 Fax: (613) 829-7783
E-mail: drt@borealispress.com
Website: www.borealispress.com

Established 1972. A general publisher, but specializes in Canadiana, including the Tecumseh Press subsidiary reserved for Canadian material. Does not consider multiple submissions or unsolicited full manuscripts. Query first, including synopsis and sample chapter or equivalent, along with SASE. Guidelines available on website.

Boulder Publications

198 Neary's Pond Road, Portugal Cove-St. Philip's, NL A1M 2Y5
Phone: (709) 895-6483 Fax: (709) 895-8041
E-mail: info@boulderpublications.ca
Website: www.boulderpublications.ca
Contact: Gavin Will, president

Publisher of Canadian fiction and non-fiction (including field guides and historical works), with an emphasis on Newfoundland and Labrador. Accepts unsolicited manuscripts but send an outline first. Contact for authors' guidelines.

BPS Books

Phone: (416) 609-2004 Fax: (416) 575-2936
Website: www.bpsbooks.com
Contact: Donald G. Bastian, publisher and editor-in-chief

Print-on-demand co-operative publishing company that offers production, marketing, and distribution services, along with expert editorial, publishing, and social media guidance. Submit manuscript through website.

Breakwater Books

P.O. Box 2188, 1 Stamp's Lane, St. John's, NL A1C 6E6
Phone: (709) 722-6680 Fax: (709) 753-0708
E-mail: info@breakwaterbooks.com
Website: www.breakwaterbooks.com
Contact: Kim Pelley, CEO

Publishes fiction, non-fiction, and educational titles, especially those related to the culture and history of Newfoundland and Labrador. Releases about 15 new titles a year. Does not accept unsolicited manuscripts or submissions by e-mail. Send an inquiry with outline and sample chapters.

Brick Books
431 Boler Road, P.O. Box 20081, London, ON N6K 4G6
Phone: (519) 657-8579
E-mail: brick.books@sympatico.ca
Website: www.brickbooks.ca
Contact: Kitty Lewis, general manager
Established 1975. Publishes Canadian poetry by Canadian authors only. Reads manuscripts January 1 through April 30 every year. Releases 7 new titles annually. Accepts unsolicited manuscripts, but first send an inquiry. Guidelines available.

Brighter Books Publishing House
4825 Fairbrook Crescent, Nanaimo, BC V9T 6M6
Phone: (250) 585-7372
Website: www.brighterbooks.com
E-mail: angela@brighterbooks.com or dean@brighterbooks.com
Contact: Angela Jungensen, chief editor, and Dean Jurgensen, editor
Established 2010. Small publisher with a focus on children's books (from picture books to young adults) and educational books. Prefers to receive submissions through website. Guidelines available.

Brindle & Glass Publishing
1105 Pandora Avenue, Suite 340, Victoria, BC V8V 3P9
Phone: (250) 360-0829 Fax: (250) 386-0829
E-mail: info@brindleandglass.com
Website: www.brindleandglass.com
Contact: Ruth Linka, publisher
A literary publisher of fiction, drama, and non-fiction. Publishes 8 new titles annually. Accepts unsolicited manuscripts, but inquire first. See website for more information.

Broadview Press

P.O. Box 1243, Peterborough, ON K9J 7H5
Phone: (705) 743-8990 Fax: (705) 743-8353
E-mail: mather@broadviewpress.com or
   slatta@broadviewpress.com
Website: www.broadviewpress.com
Contacts: Marjorie Mather, publisher and acquiring editor, English
   studies; and Stephen Latta, acquiring editor, philosophy

Established 1985. Academic press specializing in the humanities, incorporating a variety of viewpoints: liberal, conservative, libertarian, feminist, and Marxist. Subject areas include anthropology, politics, history, philosophy, sociology, English literature, and medieval studies. Most titles are relevant for undergraduate course use. Publishes about 60 new titles a year. Very rarely accepts unsolicited manuscripts. Send an inquiry with an outline. Guidelines available on website. *See* also Freehand Books, Broadview's literary imprint.

Broken Jaw Press Inc.

P.O. Box 596, Stn. A, Fredericton, NB E3B 5A6
Phone: (506) 454-5127 Fax: (506) 454-5127
E-mail: editors@brokenjaw.com
Website: www.brokenjaw.com
Contact: Joe Blades, publisher

An independent literary arts publisher of mostly Canadian-authored poetry, fiction, and creative non-fiction. Publishes some works in translation (especially from Spanish and French) with poetry often in bilingual editions. Usually publishes 3 to 8 new titles a year. Does not accept unsolicited manuscripts. Guidelines available on website.

The Brucedale Press

P.O. Box 2259, Port Elgin, ON N0H 2C0
Phone: (519) 832-6025
E-mail: brucedale@bmts.com
Website: www.bmts.com/~brucedale
Contact: Anne Duke Judd, publisher

Presents books of literary, historical, and pictorial merit focusing on the Queen's Bush and Bruce Peninsula areas of Ontario. Also publishes *The Leaf*, a twice-yearly journal with the same regional focus. Averages 3 new titles a year. Considers unsolicited manuscripts. Send an inquiry with an outline and sample chapters for fiction, the full manuscript for children's or YA books. "The reading period begins in November. Please follow guidelines carefully."

Brush Education Ltd.

1220 Kensington Road N.W., Unit 210, Calgary, AB T2N 3P5
Phone: (855) 283-0900 Fax: (855) 283-6947
E-mail: contact@brusheducation.ca
Website: www.brusheducation.ca
Contact: Laurie Fuhr, administrator

Brush Education partners with individuals, post-secondary institutions, organizations, and businesses to develop educational and training resources across a range of print and digital formats. "Using a collaborative approach, we work with our partners to create unique resources perfectly tailored to their individual requirements, whether for an individual course or an entire institution." Also provides Aboriginal resources. See website for submission guidelines.

Caitlin Press

8100 Alderwood Road, Halfmoon Bay, BC V0N 1Y1
Phone: (604) 885-9194 or 1-877-964-4953
E-mail: vici@caitlin-press.com
Website: www.caitlin-press.com
Contact: Vici Johnstone, publisher

Established 1977. A B.C. publisher specializing in trade books "concerning or by writers from the B.C. Interior and stories about and by B.C. women." Publishes 5 titles a year, including poetry, fiction, and non-fiction. Accepts unsolicited manuscripts that meet these criteria. Send outline, author bio, and sample chapters. Does not accept e-mail submissions. Guidelines available on website.

Callawind Publications

3551 St. Charles Boulevard, Suite 179, Kirkland, QC H9H 3C4
Phone: (514) 685-9109 Fax: (514) 685-7952
E-mail: info@callawind.com
Website: www.callawind.com
Contact: Marcy Claman, project manager

Provides complete publishing development (editing, design, layout, and printing) and consultation for cookbook and children's book authors. Releases 4 new titles annually. Does not accept unsolicited manuscripts. Send an inquiry.

Canadian Circumpolar Institute (CCI) Press

University of Alberta, 42 Pembina Hall, Suite 1, Edmonton, AB
   T6G 2H8
Phone: (780) 492-4512 Fax: (780) 492-1153
E-mail: ccinst@gpu.srv.ualberta.ca or
   elaine.maloney@ualberta.ca
Website: www.cci.ualberta.ca/ccipress
Contact: Elaine L. Maloney, managing editor
Publishes peer-reviewed scholarly works, educational volumes, and trade titles on northern polar and circumpolar subjects. Publishes 3 to 5 titles a year. Accepts unsolicited manuscripts, but first send an inquiry, outline, and sample chapters. Guidelines available.

Canadian Museum of Civilization Corporation –
   Publishing

100 Laurier Street, Gatineau, QC K1A 0M8
Phone: (819) 776-7000 Fax: (819) 776-8393
E-mail: publications@civilization.ca
Website: www.civilization.ca
Contact: Bill Carman, publisher
Publishes and promotes research and disseminates information on the disciplines of Canadian history, ethnography, archaeology, and folk culture. Publishes approximately 10 titles a year. Does not accept unsolicited manuscripts.

Canadian Scholars' Press Inc.

180 Bloor Street W., Suite 801, Toronto, ON M5S 2V6 (in transition, see website for current address)
Phone: (416) 929-2774 Fax: (416) 929-1926
E-mail: info@cspi.org
Websites: www.cspi.org; www.womenspress.ca
Contact: publishing manager
CSPI is a publisher of scholarly books and textbooks. The company's Women's Press imprint publishes feminist writing, both

trade and academic. Publishes 20 new books annually. First send a proposal. Guidelines available on website.

Cape Breton University Press

P.O. Box 5300, Sydney, NS BIP 6L2
Phone: (902) 563-1955 Fax: (902) 563-1177
E-mail: cbu_press@cbu.ca
Website: www.cbup.ca
Contact: Mike Hunter, editor-in-chief

Cape Breton University Press publishes works with a primary focus on Cape Breton literature and works of a broader academic nature: literary fiction including adult, poetry, and drama; and literary non-fiction, including biography, community development, history, culture, and music. Accepts unsolicited manuscripts, but first send an inquiry and outline after consulting submission guidelines on website.

Captus Press

1600 Steeles Avenue W., Units 14 & 15, Concord, ON L4K 4M2
Phone: (416) 736-5537 Fax: (416) 736-5793
E-mail: info@captus.com
Website: www.captus.com
Contact: Jason Wormald, production/acquisitions

As well as textbooks and professional books, Captus Press publishes non-fiction trade. "We assist authors in development of their books, with emphasis on those designed to enhance post-secondary education and furnish information to practising professionals." Accepts unsolicited manuscripts with an SASE. Prospective authors are asked to complete an online questionnaire to determine the feasibility of the project. Guidelines available.

Stephanie Castle Publications

8708 French Street, Suite 102, Vancouver, BC V6P 4W7
Phone: (604) 261-1695 Fax: (604) 263-9655
E-mail: stephaniecastle@shaw.ca
Website: www.stephaniecastle.ca
Contact: S.C. Heal, president

Publishes fiction and non-fiction books that have a transgender slant, seeking to "educate and explain to a general readership and, in the case of the fiction, to also entertain." Does not accept unsolicited manuscripts; send an inquiry first.

Centennial College Press
951 Carlaw Avenue, Toronto, ON M4K 3M2
Phone: (416) 289-5000, ext. 8605 Fax: (416) 289-5106
E-mail: mstanski@centennialcollege.ca
Website: www.centennialcollegepress.com
Contact: Mark Stanski, manager
"Publishes educational books and training materials for post-secondary institutions and non-academic organizations in the public and private sector." Welcomes manuscript proposals on any topic, but see website for guidelines.

Chaudiere Books
402 McLeod Street #3, Ottawa, ON K2P 1A6
Phone: (613) 239-0337
E-mail: info@chaudierebooks.com
Website: www.chaudierebooks.com
Contact: rob mclennan, publisher and senior editor
Established 2004. Publishes poetry and fiction, with preference given to Ottawa-area authors. Send full manuscripts for poetry and the first 20 pages for fiction with a paragraph-length overview; query first for non-fiction. See website for submission guidelines.

Chestnut Publishing Group
4005 Bayview Avenue, Suite 610, Toronto, ON M2M 3Z9
Phone: (416) 224-5824 Fax: (416) 224-0595
E-mail: jimwblack@gmail.com or sharkstark@sympatico.ca
Website: www.chestnutpublishing.com
Contacts: Jim Black, vice-president, editorial; Stanley Starkman,
  president
Publishes children's literature, general trade titles, education books for school and college, books for reluctant readers, and ESL materials. Accepts unsolicited manuscripts; send an outline and sample chapters first.

Clements Publishing

6021 Yonge Street, Suite 213, Toronto, ON M2M 3W2
Phone: (647) 477-2509
E-mail: info@clementspublishing.com
Website: www.clementspublishing.com

Niche publisher for the Christian college, university and seminary market in Canada. Does not publish fiction, poetry, or autobiography. E-mail completed manuscripts (not proposals) with a cover letter that includes a synopsis, description of the book's target audience, and author bio.

Coach House Books

80 bpNichol Lane, Toronto, ON M5S 3J4
Phone: (416) 979-2217 or 1-800-367-6360 Fax: (416) 977-1158
E-mail: editor@chbooks.com
Website: www.chbooks.com
Contact: Alana Wilcox, editorial director

Publishes innovative poetry, fiction, drama, and books about. Releases approximately 15 new titles annually. "Please send your complete manuscript, along with an introductory letter that describes your work and compares it to at least two current Coach House titles, explaining how your book would fit our list, and a literary CV listing your previous publications and relevant experience." Electronic submissions preferred. Guidelines available on website.

Colombo & Company

42 Dell Park Avenue, Toronto, ON M6B 2T6
Phone: (416) 782-6853 Fax: (416) 782-0285
E-mail: jrc@colombo.ca
Website: www.colombo.ca
Contact: John Robert Colombo

Publishes about 6 new titles annually. Does not accept unsolicited manuscripts. "Demonstrate that you have read at least 5 of our publications before sending an inquiry."

Commoners Publishing

631 Tubman Crescent, Ottawa, ON K1V 8L5
Phone: (613) 523-2444 Fax: 1-888-613-0329
E-mail: editor@commonerspublishing.com

Website: www.commonerspublishing.com
Contact: Glenn Cheriton, editor
    Established 1973. Publishes Canadian fiction and educational
titles with a particular specialty in books on men's culture, history,
and issues. Releases about 5 new books a year. Accepts unsolicited
manuscripts with an SASE: for fiction, full manuscripts are preferred
with author bio; for non-fiction, writers should send an outline with
sample chapter. Writer guidelines are available with an SASE.

Conundrum Press

10224 Highway #1, Wolfville, NS B4P 2R2
E-mail: conpress@ns.sympatico.ca
Website: www.conundrumpress.com
Contact: Andy Brown, publisher
    Publishes an eclectic mix of books of art, graphic novels, and
fiction. No poetry. Has been called "one of the most innovative
publishers in Canada." Released 8 new titles in 2012. Does not
accept unsolicited manuscripts.

Cordillera Books

102-8708 French Street, Vancouver, BC V6P 4W7
Phone: (604) 261-1695 Fax: (604) 263-9655
E-mail: richbook@shaw.ca
Contact: S.C. Heal, president
    Specializes in maritime history, shipping, tug and barge trans-
portation, and fishing industry books. Published 1 new title in 2011.
Does not accept unsolicited manuscripts; send an inquiry first.

Cormorant Books

390 Steelcase Road E., Markham, ON L3R IG2
Phone: (905) 475-5571 Fax: (416) 929-3596
E-mail: info@cormorantbooks.com or
    r.sarah@cormorantbooks.com (poetry)
Website: www.cormorantbooks.com
Contacts: Marc Côté, publisher, and Robyn Sarah, poetry editor
    Publishes superior literary fiction, creative non-fiction, poetry,
and children's books. Does not accept unsolicited manuscripts. See
website for poetry submission guidelines.

Coteau Books

2517 Victoria Avenue, Regina, SK S4P OT2
Phone: (306) 777-0170 Fax: (306) 522-5152
E-mail: coteau@coteaubooks.com
Website: www.coteaubooks.com
Contact: Nik L. Burton, managing editor

Established 1975. Aims to publish and present to the world market Canadian literary writing, with an emphasis on prairie and Saskatchewan writers, and to develop and publish works of juvenile fiction that demonstrate literary excellence as well as an understanding between people and the value of community. Accepts unsolicited manuscripts on the following schedule: fiction submissions between January 1 and April 30; children's literature submissions between May 1 and August 31; poetry between September 1 and December 31; non-fiction year-round. Does not accept multiple or simultaneous submissions. Guidelines on website.

Crabtree Publishing Co.

616 Welland Avenue, St. Catharines, ON L2M 5V6
Phone: (905) 682-5221 or 1-800-387-7650 Fax: 1-800-355-7166
Website: www.crabtreebooks.com

Established 1978. Publishes children's illustrated non-fiction and fiction for the educational market (K to age 8+). Topics include animals, countries, life and physical sciences, geography, and biographies. Does not accept unsolicited manuscripts.

Creative Book Publishing

P.O. Box 8660, Stn. A, St. John's, NL AIB 3T7
Phone: (709) 748-0813 Fax: (709) 579-6511
E-mail: nl.books@transcontinental.ca
Website: www.creativebookpublishing.ca
Contact: Donna Francis, editor/marketing manager

Established 1983. Publishes under 3 imprints, each having a distinctive focus. Titles released under its Creative Publishers imprint include primarily histories, biographies, pictorials, cookbooks, humour, and travel/guide books. Under its Killick Press imprint, the company publishes poetry, fiction, drama, creative non-fiction, belles lettres, essays, feminist literature, and fine art reproduction. The Tuckamore Books imprint is devoted to children's books and young-adult literature. Publishes 12 to 15 new titles a year. Send a cover letter describing the genre of the manuscript and the intended audience, an author résumé, a manuscript summary, the full manuscript, and an SASE. Guidelines on website.

Creekstone Press

7456 Driftwood Road, Smithers, BC V0J 2N7
Phone: (250) 847-3663 Fax: (250) 847-3663
E-mail: info@creekstonepress.com
Website: www.creekstonepress.com
Contact: Lynn Shervill, editor

Provides a vehicle for creative writers and artists in northern British Columbia. "Diversity of expression, accuracy, originality, craftsmanship, and regional relevance govern selection." Publishes 1 new title a year. No unsolicited manuscripts. Send an inquiry. Guidelines available.

DC Books

P.O. Box 666, St. Laurent Stn., Montreal, QC H4L 4V9
Phone: (514) 939-3990
E-mail: dcbooks@videotron.ca
Website: www.dcbooks.ca
Contact: Keith Henderson, managing editor

A literary publisher specializing in fiction, poetry, drama, and books about railroads. Published 3 books in 2012. For submissions, query first.

Deux Voiliers Publishing

E-mail: deuxvoiliers@gmail.com
Contact: Ian Shaw
Website: www.deuxvoiliers.com

Small, Ottawa-based press that operates on a collaborative basis: "Authors, editors and graphic artists pool their skills and resources to put new Canadian authors in print in a timely fashion." Publishes literary fiction, historical fiction, fantasy, travel journals, and children's literature. "Both novels and short story collections are welcome." Query by e-mail first. If work is accepted for publication, Deux Voiliers can offer assistance formatting trade paperbacks and e-books, and publishing under the Deux Voiliers label on

Amazon, Lulu, and Smashwords, at no charge. For print publication and distribution, authors bear production costs and receive revenues from online sales. Authors can also opt into the company's national distribution of trade paperbacks through Red Tuque Books. See FAQ on website for more information.

Drawn and Quarterly

P.O. Box 48056, Montreal, QC H2V 4S8
Phone: (514) 279-2221
E-mail: chris@drawnandquarterly.com
Website: www.drawnandquarterly.com
Contact: Chris Oliveros, publisher

Publishes comic books, art books, and graphic novels. Welcomes submissions to several venues: "We have a new talent forum (Drawn & Quarterly Showcase), our regular anthology (Drawn & Quarterly), and a seasonal selection of general graphic novels, comic books, and comic book series. We do not review scripts." Prefers electronic submissions (link to website or JPEGs of page samples), though photocopies are accepted (send no more than 8 pages). Does not return mailed submissions. See website for further information.

Doubleday Canada

1 Toronto Street, Suite 300, Toronto, ON M5C 2V6
Phone: (416) 364-4449 Fax: (416) 364-6863
Website: www.randomhouse.ca
Contact: acquisitions editor

Publishes quality trade fiction and non-fiction by leading and award-winning authors. Does not accept unsolicited manuscripts. An inquiry should be accompanied by an outline and sample chapters.

D&M Publishers Inc.

2323 Quebec Street, Suite 201, Vancouver, BC V5Y 2A8
Phone: (604) 254-7191 Fax: (604) 254-9099
E-mail: dm@dmpibooks.com
Website: www.dmpibooks.com
Contact: Trena White, publisher, Douglas & McIntyre and
    Greystone Books

Established 1964. Publishes general trade books under 3 imprints: Douglas & McIntyre, Greystone Books, and New Society Publishers.

Douglas & McIntyre specializes in Canadian art and culture, military and maritime history, northwest coast First Nations and Inuit studies, and literary fiction. Greystone Books specializes in natural history, ecology and the environment, popular science, health, and travel and outdoor guidebooks. New Society Publishers focuses on social justice and ecological issues, with books on food and gardening, health and wellness, energy, sustainable living, urban issues, green building, education, and parenting. Produces 50 new titles annually. Accepts unsolicited manuscripts in certain categories only; see website for detailed submission guidelines.

DreamCatcher Publishing
55 Canterbury Street, Suite 8, Saint John, NB E2L 2C6
Phone: (506) 632-4008 Fax: (506) 632-4009
E-mail: info@dreamcatcherpublishing.ca
Website: www.dreamcatcherpublishing.ca
Contact: Elizabeth Margaris, publisher
Publishes original high-quality Canadian fiction and general interest non-fiction for adults and children, with first consideration to Atlantic Canadian writers. "Especially interested in 'green' theme fiction and 'hope and inspiration' non-fiction (including autobiographies) with a humorous twist." Produces 8 to 10 new titles annually. No unsolicited manuscripts. Send an inquiry first. "Make your query letter businesslike. Include a synopsis and short bio."

Dundurn
3 Church Street, Suite 500, Toronto, ON M5E 1M2
Phone: (416) 214-5544 Fax: (416) 214-5556
E-mail: info@dundurn.com
Website: www.dundurn.com
Contact: Kirk Howard, publisher
Established 1972. Publishes history, biography, art, natural history, sports, popular non-fiction, fiction, mysteries, and juvenile fiction and non-fiction. Submission should include a synopsis, an outline of previous publishing experience, a marketing plan, a CV, 3 sample chapters (do not send complete manuscripts), and a word count for the complete manuscript. Multiple submissions accepted. Guidelines on website.

ECW Press

2120 Queen Street E., Suite 200, Toronto, ON M4E IE2
Phone: (416) 694-3348 Fax: (416) 698-9906
E-mail: info@ecwpress.com
Website: www.ecwpress.com
Contact: Jack David, publisher

Established 1974. Publishes 50–60 books a year, including fiction, pop-culture and political analysis, sports books, biography, and travel guides. Accepts unsolicited manuscripts. Submissions should include a cover letter, bio, manuscript sample (10–15 pages for poetry; 15–25 pages for fiction and non-fiction), synopsis, and an SASE if you would like your materials returned. Non-fiction submissions should also an outline and a suggested marketing plan. Guidelines available on website.

EDGE Science Fiction & Fantasy Publishing

P.O. Box 1714, Calgary, AB T2P 2L7
Phone: (403) 254-0160 Fax: (403) 254-0456
E-mail: publisher@hadespublications.com
Website: www.edgewebsite.com
Contact: Brian Hades, president and publisher

Publisher of novel-length science fiction and fantasy books, aimed at a well-read audience aged 20 and up. "We prefer novels of between 75,000 and 100,000 words, although we occasionally accept longer works. Works with new and established authors. Publishes 6 to 12 new titles annually. Accepts unsolicited manuscripts, but first send outline, sample chapters, and an SASE. Website has complete submission information. No electronic or simultaneous submissions.

Ekstasis Editions

P.O. Box 8474, MPO, Victoria, BC V8W 3SI
Phone: (250) 361-9941 Fax: (250) 385-3378
E-mail: ekstasis@islandnet.com
Website: www.ekstasiseditions.com
Contact: Richard Olafson, publisher

A literary press dedicated to publishing literary fiction, short fiction, poetry, and non-fiction titles concerned with alternative approaches to spirituality. Also publishes books for children under its Cherubim Books imprint. Averages 15 new titles annually. Accepts unsolicited manuscripts, but send query and sample chapters first. "Always send an SASE for a reply or return of materials." Guidelines available.

Engage Books
15476 Kilmore Court, Surrey, BC V3S 6N8
E-mail: alexis@engagebooks.ca
Website: www.engagebooks.ca
Contact: Alexis Roumanis, publisher
   Established 2008. Currently accepts unsolicited manuscripts for science fiction novels and short stories, humour (non-fiction), and popular science (non-fiction). Guidelines on website. Manuscripts can be submitted by mail or using website form.

Fernwood Publishing
32 Oceanvista Lane, Black Point, NS B0J 1B0
Phone: (902) 857-1388 Fax: (902) 857-1328
E-mail: editorial@fernpub.ca
Website: www.fernwoodpublishing.ca
Contact: Errol Sharpe, co-publisher
   Publishes critical non-fiction that provides in-depth analysis and challenges existing norms, focusing on the social sciences and humanities. Releases 20 to 25 new titles a year. Under its Roseway Publishing imprint, publishes literary fiction, creative non-fiction, biographies, and other literary writing concerned with social justice issues. Send a proposal first; completed manuscripts accepted only by prior arrangement. Mailed or electronic submissions accepted. Guidelines available on website.

Fifth House Publishers
195 Allstate Parkway, Markham, ON L3R 4T8
Phone: 1-800-387-9776 Fax: 1-800-260-9777
E-mail: godwit@fitzhenry.ca
Website: www.fitzhenry.ca
Contact: Stephanie Stewart, publisher
   Established 1982. Publishes general trade non-fiction, specializing in Western Canadiana, emphasizing history, biography, gardening, nature, and First Nations titles. Releases from 18 to 20 books

a year. Accepts unsolicited manuscripts, but send an inquiry with an outline and sample chapters first. "No phone calls, please." Guidelines available on website.

Firefly Books
66 Leek Crescent, Richmond Hill, ON L4B 1H1
Phone: (416) 499-8412 Fax: (416) 499-1142
E-mail: service@fireflybooks.com
Website: www.fireflybooks.com

Publishes practical how-to and illustrated books, with a special interest in gardening, cooking, astronomy, health, natural history, pictorial books, reference books (especially for children), and sports. No unsolicited manuscripts, but accepts proposals for illustrated non-fiction.

Fitzhenry & Whiteside Limited, Publishers
195 Allstate Parkway, Markham, ON L3R 4T8
Phone: (905) 477-9700 or 1-800-387-9776 Fax: 1-800-260-9777
E-mail: godwit@fitzhenry.ca
Website: www.fitzhenry.ca

Established 1966. Specializes in history, biography, poetry, sports, photographic books, reference, photography, and children's and young adult titles. Publishes 200 titles a year (including reprints). Full submission guidelines on website.

Flanker Press
P.O. Box 2522, Stn. C, St. John's, NL A1C 6K1
Phone: (709) 739-4477 or 1-866-739-4420 Fax: (709) 739-4420
E-mail: info@flankerpress.com
Website: www.flankerpress.com and www.pennywellbooks.com
Contact: Garry Cranford, president

Publishes regional non-fiction and historical fiction with a focus on Newfoundland and Labrador content. Pennywell Press imprint publishes literary fiction, short stories, poetry, drama, essay collections, young adult fiction, and children's books. Send query letter with synopsis, 3–4 sample chapters, author CV, and SASE if you would like materials returned. No e-mail submissions. Guidelines on website.

Folklore Publishing

9731 – 42 Avenue N.W., Edmonton, AB T6E 5P8
Phone: (780) 435-2376 Fax: (780) 435-0674
E-mail: fboer@folklorepublishing.com
Website: www.folklorepublishing.com
Contact: Faye Boer, publisher

Publishes popular history books and biographies of important Canadian figures and, recently, twisted history and humour books. Releases 5 to 10 new titles annually. Accepts unsolicited manuscripts, but first send an inquiry with writer's résumé, an outline, and sample chapters. Guidelines on website.

Formac Publishing Company

5502 Atlantic Street, Halifax, NS B3H 1G4
Phone: (902) 421-7022 Fax: (902) 425-0166
E-mail: jlorimer@formac.ca
Website: www.formac.ca
Contact: James Lorimer, publisher

Publishes books with a Maritime regional focus, travel guides, history books, biography, natural history, cookbooks, and children's fiction and non-fiction (series). Releases 15 new titles a year. Accepts unsolicited manuscripts, but send an outline first. Guidelines available on website.

4th Floor Press, Inc.

171 Somme Avenue S.W., Calgary, AB T2T 5J8
Phone: (403) 282-7370
E-mail: mail@4thfloorpress.com
Website: www.4thfloorpress.com
Contact: Johanna M. Bates, president and founder

Self-publishing company that provides a full range of publishing services, including ghostwriting. Accepts only hard-copy submissions. Charges a reading evaluation fee of $300 plus GST. See website for submission guidelines.

Freehand Books

815 1st Street S.W., Suite 515, Calgary, AB T2P 1N3
Phone: (403) 452-5662
E-mail: kattard@broadviewpress.com

Website: www.freehand-books.com
Contact: Kelsey Attard, managing editor
Established 2007 as an imprint of Broadview Press, specializing in fiction, poetry, and creative non-fiction by both established authors and new voices. Does not accept unsolicited manuscripts.

FriesenPress

852 Fort Street, Suite 300, Victoria, BC V8W 1H8
Phone: 1-888-378-6793
E-mail: submissions@friesenpress.com
Website: www.friesenpress.com
Self-publisher with various packages available to suit size of book's target audience: Niche Market Starter, Mass Market Essentials, and Mass Market Bestseller. Packages start at $399. Also offers authors an opportunity to get noticed by traditional publishers by providing their exclusive partners with book sales data and forwarding 5 staff nominations a year. Publishing agreement and instructions available on website.

Frog Eat Frog

Website: frogeatfrog.com
Print-on-demand publisher currently accepting book-length literary fiction and non-fiction. "Conventional or genre fiction generally isn't a fit for us, although our prime consideration is the strength of the narrative and the quality of the prose. Length is entirely open. We pay in royalties. Please visit our website to understand the print-on-demand business model before querying." Query using website form.

Frontenac House

1138 Frontenac Avenue S.W., Calgary, AB T2T 1B6
Phone: (403) 245-8588 Fax: (403) 245-2380
E-mail: connect@frontenachouse.com
Website: www.frontenachouse.com
Contact: Rose Scollard, publisher
Publishes Canadian poetry, art and photography, political satire, fiction and aviation. "Please follow the instructions on our website regarding submission dates and format."

Gaspereau Press

47 Church Avenue, Kentville, NS B4N 2M7
Phone: (902) 678-6002 Fax: (902) 678-7845
E-mail: info@gaspereau.com
Website: www.gaspereau.com
Contact: Andrew Steeves, publisher

Publishes novels, short-story collections, poetry, literary essays, creative non-fiction, history, biographies, and memoirs in quality first-edition paperbacks aimed at a Canadian readership. Released 12 new titles in 2012. Accepts unsolicited manuscripts and sample chapters. Guidelines available. "Please include a cover letter with all submissions. Samples and full manuscripts accepted. Please include a detailed synopsis of the work in full. No e-mail submissions."

General Store Publishing House

499 O'Brien Road, P.O. Box 415, Renfrew, ON K7V 4A6
Phone: (613) 432-7697 or 1-800-465-6072 Fax: (613) 432-7184
E-mail: submissions@gsph.com
Website: www.gsph.com
Contact: Tim Gordon, publisher

Established 1981. Publishes history, military, cookbooks, regional titles pertaining to the Ottawa Valley, and sports books. Releases 20 to 25 titles a year. E-mail a query letter (noting a daytime telephone number) along with a two-page outline. "Should we decide that your manuscript is something that GSPH could consider, we will have you send it (along with a cheque for $150–$200 and an SASE in order to have your manuscript returned) to one of our senior editors for evaluation. Based on the editor's comments, we will decide what type of publishing program (if any) to offer you."

Goose Lane Editions

500 Beaverbrook Court, Suite 330, Fredericton, NB E3B 5X4
Phone: (506) 450-4251 or 1-888-926-8377 Fax: (506) 459-4991
E-mail: info@gooselane.com
Website: www.gooselane.com
Contact: Susanne Alexander, publisher

Established 1954. Publishes Canadian adult literary fiction, non-fiction, and poetry. Publishes 18 to 20 print titles annually. Considers unsolicited manuscripts, but first send outline or synopsis and a 30- to 50-page sample for novels. No electronic queries or submissions. Please send a query first for poetry, story collections, and non-fiction. Guidelines on website.

Granville Island Publishing
1656 Duranleau Street, Suite 212, Vancouver, BC V6H 3S4
Phone: (604) 688-0320 or 1-877-688-0320 Fax: (604) 688-0132
E-mail: info@granvilleislandpublishing.com
Website: www.granvilleislandpublishing.com
Contact: Jo Blackmore, publisher
"We're inclined to publish books (and e-books) that make a difference. The process is financed by the author, who can approach us directly." Offers editing, proofing, custom design, marketing, and publicity services. "We recommend having a reader's report done initially." Guidelines available on website.

Great Plains Publications
345 – 955 Portage Avenue, Winnipeg, MB R3G 0P9
Phone: (204) 475-6799
E-mail: info@greatplains.mb.ca
Website: www.greatplains.mb.ca
Contacts: Gregg Shilliday, publisher, and Maurice Mierau, associate publisher
An independent publisher operating three imprints: Great Plains Publications (regional non-fiction), Enfield & Wizenty (literary fiction), and Great Plains Teen Fiction (young adult fiction). Accepts unsolicited manuscripts from authors across Canada; send an outline and sample chapter first. Guidelines available on website.

Groundwood Books
110 Spadina Avenue, Suite 801, Toronto, ON M5V 2K4
Phone: (416) 363-4343 Fax: (416) 363-1017
E-mail: genmail@groundwoodbooks.com
Website: www.groundwoodbooks.com
Contact: Kelly Joseph, editorial assistant
Publishes high-quality Canadian picture books, both fiction and non-fiction, plus a line of Spanish-language titles, Libros Tigrillo, aimed at the U.S. Latino market and the export market in Mexico and Central America. Accepts unsolicited manuscripts; send a

synopsis and sample chapters first. No e-mail submissions. Guidelines available on website.

Guernica Editions

489 Strathmore Boulevard, Toronto, ON M4C 1N8
Phone: (416) 658-9888 Fax: (416) 657-8885
E-mail: guernicaeditions@gmail.com
Website: www.guernicaeditions.com
Contact: Antonio D'Alfonso, editor

Established 1978. Specializes in fiction, non-fiction, plays, poetry, and translations. Also translates Québécois authors. Publishes about 23 new titles a year. No unsolicited manuscripts. Inquiries welcome.

Hagios Press

Box 33024, Cathedral P.O., Regina, SK S4T 7X2
Phone: (306) 522-5055
E-mail: hagiospress@accesscomm.ca
Website: www.hagiospress.com
Contacts: Donald Ward, Tina Dmytryshyn, Eric Greenway, and
    Paul Wilson, co-publishers

Established 1996. Specializes in poetry, art books, short-fiction, and literary non-fiction, "with a particular focus on books that advance a spiritual connection with the world." Published 6 books in 2012. Does not accept unsolicited manuscripts. Queries accepted by mail or e-mail. See website for submission guidelines.

Hancock House Publishers Ltd.

19313 Zero Avenue, Surrey, BC V3S 9R9
Phone: (604) 538-1114 or 1-800-938-1114 Fax: (604) 538-2262
    or 1-800-983-2262
E-mail: submissions@hancockhouse.com
Website: www.hancockhouse.com
Contact: submissions editor

Established 1970. Specializes in regional history (northern B.C., Alaska, and Pacific Northwest), biography/memoir, Native culture, nature guides, natural history, aviculture, and cryptozoology. Does not publish fiction. Publishes about 20 titles a year. Accepts unsolicited manuscripts "E-mail queries with author bio, book outline, table of contents, and sample chapters recommended. Do not send hard copy manuscripts or original photos or illustrations." Guidelines available on website.

Harbour Publishing

P.O. Box 219, Madeira Park, BC VON 2HO
Phone: (604) 883-2730 Fax: (604) 883-9451
E-mail: info@harbourpublishing.com
Website: www.harbourpublishing.com
Contact: acquisitions

Primarily focuses on regional non-fiction titles, but publishes in all genres, mainly on topics concerning the West Coast of B.C. Publishes about 20 titles a year. Accepts unsolicited manuscripts, but first send an inquiry with an outline, author bio, publication credits, and sample chapters. Guidelines available on website.

Harlequin Enterprises

225 Duncan Mill Road, 6th Floor, Don Mills, ON M3B 3K9
Phone: (416) 445-5860 Fax: (416) 448-7191
Website: www.harlequin.com
See website for contact names and e-mail addresses for each imprint

Established 1949. Each year Harlequin publishes more than 1,200 new titles in all formats (mass-market, trade, hardcover, and digital-first), including series romance (Harlequin), literary and commercial women's fiction (Harlequin MIRA and Harlequin HQN), young adult fiction (Harlequin TEEN), non-fiction (Harlequin Nonfiction), inspirational fiction (Harlequin Love Inspired), African-American fiction (Kimani Press), fantasy (Harlequin Luna), and mystery and action adventure (Gold Eagle and Worldwide Library imprints). Accepts query letters. Tip sheets available. Check website for writers' guidelines. New authors are contracted only on full manuscript.

HarperCollins Publishers

2 Bloor Street E., 20th Floor, Toronto, ON M4W 1A8
Phone: (416) 975-9334 Fax: (416) 975-9884
Website: www.harpercollins.ca
Contact: editorial department

Publishes a wide range of fiction, non-fiction, business, reference, cookbooks, young-adult, and children's books. Produces over 80 new titles each year. No unsolicited manuscripts or proposals. The company also operates an online writing community, authonomy™ (www.authonomy.com), which invites unpublished and self-published authors to post their manuscripts for visitors to read online.

The Frederick Harris Music Co.

5865 McLaughlin Road, Unit 1, Mississauga, ON L5R IB8
Phone: (905) 501-1595 Fax: (905) 501-0929
E-mail: fhmc@frederickharrismusic.com
Website: www.frederickharrismusic.com

Established 1904. A not-for-profit publisher of music education materials, particularly curriculum material for the Royal
Conservatory of Music. Interested in manuscripts in 6 main categories: piano, violin, guitar, voice, theory, and musicianship. Send a
sample chapter and table of contents. Guidelines available.

Hedgerow Press

P.O. Box 2471, Sidney, BC V8L 3Y3
Phone: (250) 656-9320 Fax: (250) 656-9320
E-mail: hedgep@telus.net
Website: www.hedgerowpress.com
Contact: Joan Coldwell, publisher

Publishes high quality paperbacks of literary and visual beauty,
limiting annual production so as to give greater attention to each
book. Preference given to Canadian authors and artists. Does not
publish novels, academic works, or illustrated children's books. No
longer accepts unsolicited manuscripts.

Heritage House Publishing Co. Ltd.

1105 Pandora Avenue, Suite 340, Victoria, BC V8V 3P9
Phone: (250) 360-0829 Fax: (250) 386-0829
E-mail: editorial@heritagehouse.ca
Website: www.heritagehouse.ca
Contact: senior editor

Publishes Canadian non-fiction with a focus on subjects of interest to western Canada, including history, biography, contemporary
issues, and pictorials. Also publishes quick-read non-fiction in the
Amazing Stories series. Publishes 20–30 new titles each year.
Accepts unsolicited manuscripts if they conform to submission
guidelines on website.

House of Anansi Press

110 Spadina Avenue, Suite 801, Toronto, ON M5V 2K4
Phone: (416) 363-4343 Fax: (416) 363-1017
Website: www.houseofanansi.com
Contact: editorial department

Publishes literary fiction, non-fiction, and poetry. Releases approximately 20 titles a year, 4 of which are poetry. Accepts unsolicited manuscripts, but first send an outline and sample chapters. Does not accept electronic submissions. "We regret that we are unable to respond to queries regarding our submission guidelines. For complete guidelines, please visit our website."

Iguana Books

155 Dalhousie Street, Suite 701, Toronto, ON M5B 2P7
Phone: (416) 214-0760 Fax: (416): 214-0235
E-mail: info@iguanabooks.com
Contact: Greg Ioannou, publisher
Website: www.iguanabooks.com

Established 2011. Online self-publishing platform with a focus on e-books. "Iguana publishes every book that meets our quality standards – but we publish *only* the books that meet our standards." Pays authors an 85% royalty rate. See website for submission information.

Inanna Publications

210 Founders College, York University, 4700 Keele Street,
    Toronto, ON M3J 1P3
Phone: (416) 736-5356 Fax: (416) 736-5765
E-mail: inanna.publications@inanna.ca
Website: www.inanna.ca
Contact: Luciana Ricciutelli, editor-in-chief

Founded 1978. Publishes literary fiction, poetry, and creative non-fiction by and about women. "Our priorities are to publish literary books, in particularly by fresh, new Canadian voices, that are intellectually rigorous, speak to women's hearts, and tell truths about the lives of the broad diversity of Canadian women – smart books for people who want to read and think about real women's lives." See website for submission guidelines.

Insomniac Press

520 Princess Avenue, London, ON N6B 2B8

Phone: (416) 619-5912 Fax: (647) 722-4989

E-mail: mike@insomniacpress.com

Website: www.insomniacpress.com

Contact: Mike O'Connor, publisher

Established 1992. Publishes fiction, non-fiction in a wide variety of areas, and poetry. Releases about 20 new titles annually. Accepts unsolicited manuscripts, but first send sample chapters by mail only. Guidelines available on website. "Please visit our website for an idea of the books we have published recently."

Invisible Publishing

2578 Maynard Street, Halifax, NS B3K 3V5

E-mail: submissions@invisiblepublishing.com

Website: www.invisiblepublishing.com

Independent publisher committed to working exclusively with emerging and under-published authors. Accepts literary fiction and creative non-fiction submissions. "All narrative works with contemporary themes will be considered, however, we are not generally interested in poetry, genre fiction or YA projects." Query first (e-mail queries are encouraged); do not send full manuscripts. See website for submission guidelines.

ISER Books, Faculty of Arts Publications (Institute of Social and Economic Research)

Memorial University of Newfoundland, St. John's, NL A1C 5S7

Phone: (709) 864-3453 Fax: (709) 864-4342

E-mail: iser-books@mun.ca

Website: www.arts.mun.ca/iserbooks

Contact: Lawrence Felt, academic editor

Publishes research relevant to Newfoundland and Labrador, and the North Atlantic Rim, especially research pertaining to social and economic development in Newfoundland and Labrador. Specializes in anthropology, sociology, folklore, women's studies, geography, history, and economics. Periodic collections on Native peoples and the nation-state, social-science advocacy, and the fishing crisis. Publishes 3 or 4 titles each year. Does not accept unsolicited manuscripts. Send an inquiry with an outline and sample chapters. Guidelines available on website.

Island Studies Press

Institute of Island Studies, University of Prince Edward Island,
    550 University Avenue, Charlottetown, PE CIA 4P3
Phone: (902) 566-0386 Fax: (902) 566-0756
E-mail: iis@upei.ca
Website: www.upei.ca/iis/isp
Contact: Irene Novaczek, director

Releases 1 to 2 new titles a year. Accepts unsolicited manuscripts about P.E.I. and other islands, mostly with a scholarly focus, but send inquiry first.

Kegedonce Press

872 – 16th Street W., RR #7, Owen Sound, ON N4K 6V5
Phone: (519) 371-1434 Fax: (519) 371-5011
E-mail: info@kegedonce.com
Website: www.kegedonce.com
Contact: R. K. Abram, publishing manager

Committed to the development, promotion, and publication of the work of indigenous writers. Releases 2 new titles on average per year. Accepts unsolicited manuscripts, but first send an inquiry and sample chapters. "Prior publishing credits (magazines, etc.) are required for serious consideration. Aboriginal/indigenous authors only." Guidelines available on website.

The Key Publishing House

1075 Bay Street, Suite A102/230, Toronto, ON M5S 2B2
Phone: (416) 935-1790 Fax: (416) 935-1790
E-mail: info@thekeypublish.com
Website: www.thekeypublish.com

Publishes both academic and non-academic books on topics related to (but not limited to) the humanities, social science, and physical science. Welcomes manuscript proposals by e-mail that include a cover letter, synopsis, table of contents, sample chapters, and author CV. See editorial guidelines on website.

Kids Can Press

25 Dockside Drive, Toronto, ON M5A 0B5
Phone: (416) 479-7000 Fax: (416) 960-5437
E-mail: info@kidscan.com
Website: www.kidscanpress.com
Contact: acquisitions editor

Established 1973. Publishes quality books for children of all ages, including picture books, poetry, non-fiction, fiction, and activity books. Released 46 new titles in 2012. Accepts unsolicited manuscripts. Send outline and sample chapters only for longer fiction. "Please familiarize yourself with our list before sending a manuscript – our website provides a good sense of the entire publishing program." Submission guidelines available on website.

Alfred A. Knopf Canada

1 Toronto Street, Suite 300, Toronto, ON M5C 2V6
Phone: (416) 364-4449 Fax: (416) 364-6863
Website: www.randomhouse.ca
Contact: acquiring editor

"Knopf Canada publishes exceptional literary fiction and nonfiction from Canada and around the world." Releases approximately 40 new titles a year. Does not accept unsolicited manuscripts.

Leaf Press

P.O. Box 416, Lantzville, BC V0R 2H0
E-mail: ursulavaira@leafpress.ca
Website: www.leafpress.ca

Established 2001. "Publishing poetry only," including trade poetry, chapbooks, anthologies, and weekly online poems. Published 4 books in 2011. See website for submission guidelines.

Linda Leith Publishing

P.O. Box 322, Victoria Stn., Westmount, QC H3Z 2V8
E-mail: linda@lindaleith.com
Website: www.lindaleith.com
Contact: Linda Leith, publisher

Established 2011. Literary press specializing in singles (15,000 to 18,000 words), literary fiction, and political satire, in the tradition of underground pamphlets and samizdat publishing. Query by e-mail, including a 2- to 3-paragraph description of the proposed book as well as a sample chapter and biographical information on the author.

Lobster Press

1620 Sherbrooke Street W., Suites C & D, Montreal, QC H3H 1C9
Phone: (514) 904-1100 Fax: (514) 904-1101
E-mail: editorial@lobsterpress.com
Website: www.lobsterpress.com
Contact: Cameron McKeich, acting managing editor

Publishes high quality books – fiction and non-fiction – for children, tweens, and teens. Does not accept unsolicited manuscripts. Send an e-mail inquiry with outline and sample chapters first. Guidelines available on website.

Lone Pine Publishing

2311 – 96 Street, Edmonton, AB T6E 1W9
Phone: (780) 450-6223 or 1-800-875-7108 Fax: (780) 450-1857
E-mail: info@lonepinepublishing.com
Website: www.lonepinepublishing.com
Contact: editorial director

Established 1980. Specializes in regional books on natural history, outdoor recreation, gardening, and popular history. Offices in Edmonton and Washington State. Publishes about 35 new titles each year. Accepts unsolicited manuscripts, but first send an inquiry by mail (after familiarizing yourself with Lone Pine's current titles). Guidelines available on website.

James Lorimer & Company

317 Adelaide Street W., Suite 1002, Toronto, ON M5V 1P9
Phone: (416) 362-4762 Fax: (416) 362-3939
E-mail: jlorimer@lorimer.ca
Website: www.lorimer.ca
Contact: James Lorimer, publisher

Seeking manuscripts on the following Canadian topics that fit into our current series: biography, history, cookbooks (with a Canadian or regional focus), education, public issues, and children's fiction. Publishes about 30 new titles a year. Does not accept unsolicited manuscripts. Send an inquiry with an outline and sample chapters. Submission guidelines available on website.

Mansfield Press

25 Mansfield Avenue, Toronto, ON M6J 2A9
Phone: (416) 532-2086
E-mail: info@mansfieldpress.net
Website: www.mansfieldpress.net
Contact: Denis De Klerck, publisher

Small press with a mandate of nurturing new voices. Publishes fiction, literary non-fiction, and poetry. Accepts multiple submissions. For poetry, submit the full manuscript; for prose, send an outline and sample chapters. Include a list of publishing credits: "Except in very rare circumstances, it is unlikely that Mansfield will accept a manuscript from someone who has no publishing history." Guidelines on website.

McClelland & Stewart Ltd.

1 Toronto Street, Suite 300, Toronto, ON M5C 2V6
Phone: (416) 364-4449 Fax: (416) 364-6863
E-mail: editorial@mcclelland.com
Website: www.mcclelland.com
Contact: editorial department

Established 1906. Publishes fine fiction by authors such as Margaret Atwood, Alistair MacLeod, Rohinton Mistry, Alice Munro, Madeleine Thien, and Trevor Cole; a wide selection of non-fiction books on biography, history, natural history, politics, Native issues, religion, and sports; and poetry by writers such as Lorna Crozier and Don McKay. No unsolicited manuscripts; send a query for fiction, an outline for non-fiction.

McGill-Queen's University Press

Montreal office: 1010 Sherbrooke W., Suite 1720, Montreal, QC
   H3A 2R7
Phone: (514) 398-3750 Fax: (514) 398-4333
E-mail: mqup@mcgill.ca
Website: http://mqup.mcgill.ca
Contact: Philip Cercone, executive director and senior editor

Kingston office: Queen's University, Kingston, ON K7L 3N6
Phone: (613) 533-2155 Fax: (613) 533-6822
E-mail: mqup@queensu.ca

Established 1969. A non-profit joint venture of McGill and Queen's Universities. Its mission is to serve the Canadian and international scholarly communities as a vehicle for the publication of scholarly works of the highest quality. Publishes scholarly books on northern and Native studies, history, political science, Canadian literature, anthropology, sociology, biography, art history, philosophy, and religion. Does not publish works of fiction. Averages 130 new titles a year, a third of which are destined for the trade market. Submit a proposal before sending a manuscript. Guidelines available on website.

McKellar & Martin Publishing Group
5256 Prince Edward Street, Vancouver, BC V5W 2X5
Phone: (778) 833-1499 or (604) 240-7606
E-mail: tonya@mckellarmartin.com
Website: www.mckellarmartin.com
Contact: Tonya Martin, co-publisher and editor-in-chief

Established 2010. Publishes "books for kids who love to read . . . *and* for those who don't." Holds a biannual open call for submissions; see website for dates.

The Mercury Press
P.O. Box 672, Stn. P, Toronto, ON M5S 2Y4
Phone: (416) 531-4338 Fax: (416) 531-0765
E-mail: contact@themercurypress.ca
Website: www.themercurypress.ca

Publishes poetry, fiction, murder mysteries, and culturally significant non-fiction. Does not consider e-mail submissions. Refer to submission guidelines on website.

MOD Publishing
4 Fairview Boulevard, Toronto, ON M4K IL9
Phone: (416) 466-9275 Fax: (416) 466-7493
E-mail: jean.weihs@rogers.com
Website: www.modpublishing.com
Contact: Jean Weihs, joint owner

Publishes resource materials and study guides for teachers and students. Does not accept unsolicited manuscripts.

Moose Enterprise Book and Theatre Play Publishing
684 Walls Road, Sault Ste. Marie, ON P6A 5K6
Phone: (705) 779-3331 Fax: (705) 779-3331
E-mail: mooseenterprises@on.aibn.com
Website: www.moosehidebooks.com
Contact: Richard Mousseau, publisher/editor
  "We assist new and up-and-coming writers, those needing help developing their work. We accept submissions from unpublished and published authors." Imprint is Moose Hide Books. Releases around 5 titles a year. Accepts unsolicited manuscripts, but first send a query. "We accept only works of moral content. Be original." Guidelines available.

Mosaic Press
1252 Speers Road, Units 1 & 2, Oakville, ON L6L 5N9
Phone: (905) 825-2130 Fax: (905) 825-2130
E-mail: info@mosaic-press.com
Website: www.mosaic-press.com
Contact: Keith Daniel, managing director
  Focuses on literature, including fiction, short fiction, and poetry; the arts, including theatre, art, architecture, and music; social studies; and international studies. Publishes 20 new titles annually. Accepts unsolicited manuscripts, but send sample chapters, résumé, and outline/prospectus first.

New Star Books
3477 Commercial Drive, Suite 107, Vancouver, BC V5N 4E8
Phone: (604) 738-9429 Fax: (604) 738-9332
E-mail: info@newstarbooks.com
Website: www.newstarbooks.com
Contact: Rolf Maurer, publisher
  Publishes progressive books on social issues, politics, British Columbia, and the West, along with literary novels and short fiction. Does not accept unsolicited poetry. For non-fiction, send either the full manuscript with a query letter or an outline and sample chapters with a query letter. For fiction, send the full man-

uscript with a query letter. No fax submissions, and no telephone queries. Guidelines available on website.

New World Publishing

P.O. Box 36075, Halifax, NS B3J 3S9
Phone: (902) 576-2055 or 1-877-211-3334
E-mail: editor@newworldpublishing.com
Website: www.newworldpublishing.com

Established 1995. Publishes in the following genres: health and wellness, self-esteem and safety; historical and art publications (Atlantic region only); historical memoirs. Typically puts out 4 books a year, with 1 or 2 of these on a national basis. Send queries by e-mail. See website for guidelines.

NeWest Press

8540 – 109th Street, Suite 201, Edmonton, AB T6G 1E6
Phone: (780) 432-9427 Fax: (780) 433-3179
E-mail: info@newestpress.com
Website: www.newestpress.com
Contact: Paul Matwychuk, general manager

A literary publisher that focuses on Western Canadian authors of fiction, poetry, drama, literary criticism, and regional non-fiction. Releases approximately 10 new books a year. Accepts unsolicited manuscripts. "Manuscripts are reviewed by an editorial board, and it can take up to 9 months to receive a response." Guidelines available on website.

Nightwood Editions

P.O. Box 1779, Gibsons, BC V0N 1V0
Phone: (604) 886-8668
E-mail: info@nightwoodeditions.com
Website: www.nightwoodeditions.com
Contacts: Silas White, managing editor

Has provided more than 40 years of Canadian literature. Does not accept unsolicited manuscripts, however, "if your work is unfamiliar to us feel free to e-mail a bio, a synopsis of your manuscript (if applicable) and a 15-page sample of your work. When we are soliciting manuscripts, we'll contact you if we want to see more."

Nimbus Publishing

3731 Mackintosh Street, Halifax, NS B3K 5A5
Phone: (902) 455-4286 Fax: (902) 455-5440
E-mail: editorial@nimbus.ca
Website: www.nimbus.ca
Contact: Patrick Murphy, managing editor

Established 1978. The largest trade publisher in Atlantic Canada. Publishes and distributes books on all aspects of Atlantic Canada. Non-fiction topics include natural history, political and social issues, and history. Also publishes guidebooks, cookbooks, books of photography, and children's literature; and under the Vagrant Press imprint, fiction. Does not publish poetry or genre fiction. Releases about 32 new titles each year. Proposals should include an outline with sample chapters. Do not send original materials. Further guidelines available on website.

Novalis

10 Lower Spadina Avenue, Suite 400, Toronto, ON M5V 2Z2
Phone: (416) 363-3303, ext. 250 Fax: (416) 363-9409
E-mail: joseph.sinasac@novalis.ca
Website: www.novalis.ca
Contact: Joseph Sinasac, publishing director (English)

Established 1936. Publishes resources that help people explore the dynamics of their faith, to pray, and to foster their spiritual growth. Founded by a Roman Catholic yet dedicated to ecumenical and interfaith dialogue and understanding. Releases about 30 new books each year in English and a similar number in French. Also publishes a number of periodicals, including *Living with Christ* and *Celebrate!* Accepts unsolicited manuscripts, but first send an inquiry with sample chapters and author résumé. Guidelines available on website.

Now Or Never Publishing

1003 Pacific Street, Suite 1101, Vancouver, BC V6E 4P2
E-mail: chris@nonpublishing.com
Website: www.nonpublishing.com
Contact: Chris Needham, publisher

Literary publisher interested in contemporary Canadian fiction and poetry. Accepts e-mail submissions only. Send the complete manuscript. See website for guidelines.

Oberon Press

145 Spruce Street, Suite 205, Ottawa, ON KIR 6PI
Phone: (613) 238-3275 Fax: (613) 238-3275
E-mail: oberon@sympatico.ca
Website: www.oberonpress.ca
Contact: Nicholas Macklem, publisher
   Established 1966. Publishes Canadian literary fiction, poetry, and non-fiction (biographies, memoirs, literary criticism, and essays). No genre fiction. Averages 8 new books a year. Accepts unsolicited manuscripts, but first send outline and sample chapters. Multiple submissions not considered. All manuscripts must be accompanied by an SASE.

Oolichan Books

P.O. Box 2278, Fernie, BC VOR IMO
Phone: (250) 423-6113
E-mail: info@oolichan.com
Website: www.oolichan.com
Contact: Randal Macnair, publisher
   Since 1974 Oolichan has published quality Canadian literary fiction, poetry, and literary non-fiction. Also publishes selected children's and young adult books. No genre fiction. Releases 10 new titles a year. Considers unsolicited submissions, but send initial letter of inquiry and sample. "Please check our website for submission guidelines before submitting."

Orca Book Publishers

P.O. Box 5626, Stn. B, Victoria, BC V8R 6S4
Phone: 1-800-210-5277 Fax: 1-877-408-1551
E-mail: orca@orcabook.com
Website: www.orcabook.com
Contacts: Bob Tyrrell or Sarah Harvey for teen fiction; Bob Tyrell
   for Rapid Reads (short novels and non-fiction books for
   adults); Andrew Wooldridge for Orca Soundings; Melanie Jeffs
   for Orca Currents; Christi Howes for Orca Sports, early
   readers and picture books
   Established 1984. Publishes award-winning books for young readers by Canadian authors, including picture books, first readers, and juvenile and teen fiction. Only occasionally publishes

non-fiction. Releases approximately 60 new titles a year. Unsolicited manuscripts accepted for picture books (send an SASE); for
novels, send query, outline, and sample chapters (send an SASE).
See submission guidelines on website. No submissions via e-mail.

Owlkids Books
10 Lower Spadina Avenue, Suite 400, Toronto, ON M5V 2Z2
Phone: (416) 340-2700 Fax: (416) 340-9769
E-mail: owlkids@owlkids.com
Website: www.owlkids.com
Contact: submissions editor

Publishes high-quality innovative information books, art and
activity books, graphic novels and picture books for children.
Emphasis on science, nature, animals, history, and art activities.
Averages 15 to 20 new titles a year. Accepts unsolicited manuscripts,
but first send query and outline for longer non-fiction works; full
manuscript for picture books. Before submitting, spend some time
familiarizing yourself with Owlkids books at the library or on our
website. An SASE is required for response. Guidelines available.

Oxford University Press Canada
8 Sampson Mews, Suite 204, Don Mills, ON M3C OH5
Phone: (416) 441-2941 Fax: (416) 444-0427
E-mail: editorial.hed.ca@oup.com
Website: www.oupcanada.com
Contact: Katherine Skene, executive acquisitions editor

Established in Canada in 1904. The Canadian trade publishing
program is small and focuses mainly on history and reference. It
includes only books intended for a general audience, and everything on this list either has a Canadian subject or examines a topic
from a distinctly Canadian point of view. No novels, short stories by
one author, how-to or self-help books, cookbooks, coffee-table
books, books of poetry, or books for children or young adults.
Accepts unsolicited manuscripts, but first send a query with a brief
synopsis. Guidelines available on website.

Palimpsest Press
5 King Street, Kingsville, ON N9Y 1H9
E-mail: info@palimpsestpress.ca

Website: www.palimpsestpress.ca
Contact: Dawn Kresan, publisher
  Established in 2000. Publishes both trade and limited edition poetry and literary non-fiction that deals with poetics, the writing life, and cultural criticism. "We look for poetry that displays technical mastery, precise language, and an authentic voice." Releases 5–6 books a year. Open submissions only accepted and read between January 1 to March 31 of each year. Accepts multiple submissions. Submission guidelines available on website.

Pedlar Press
See website for current mailing address and phone number
E-mail: feralgrl@interlog.com
Website: www.pedlarpress.com
Contact: Beth Follett, publisher/editor
  Publishes Canadian fiction, poetry, and art books. Sees its role as an innovator; produces beautiful books. Released 7 new titles in 2011. Accepts unsolicited manuscripts, but first send an inquiry, outline, and sample chapters. Guidelines available. "Canada's most important small-press publisher from a literary standpoint." – George Fetherling.

Pemmican Publications Inc.
150 Henry Avenue, Winnipeg, MB R3B OJ7
Phone: (204) 589-6346 Fax: (204) 589-2063
E-mail: pemmican@pemmican.mb.ca
Website: www.pemmicanpublications.ca
Contact: Randal McIlroy, managing editor
  Established 1980 by the Manitoba Métis Federation as a creative and vocational venue for the Métis people of Manitoba. Publishes adult fiction and non-fiction, with an emphasis on social history and biography reflecting Métis experience, and children's and YA titles. Accepts unsolicited manuscripts, but first send author bio and synopsis. E-mail and fax submissions will not be accepted. Guidelines available on website.

Penguin Group (Canada)
90 Eglinton Avenue E., Suite 700, Toronto, ON M4P 2Y3
Phone: (416) 925-2249 Fax: (416) 925-0068

E-mail: info@ca.penguingroup.com
Website: www.penguin.ca

Established in Canada in 1974. Mainstream publisher that features fiction, fantasy fiction, non-fiction, and young-adult titles for 8- to 12-year-olds. Notable authors include Margaret MacMillan, Michael Ignatieff, John Ralston Saul, Stuart McLean, Mark Kingwell, Guy Gavriel Kay, Jack Whyte, Adrienne Clarkson, and Joan Clark. No unsolicited manuscripts.

Penumbra Press
P.O. Box 20011, Newcastle, ON LIB IM3
Phone and Fax: (905) 446-0380
E-mail: john@penumbrapress.ca
Website: www.penumbrapress.com
Contact: John Flood, president

Publishes northern and First Nations literature and art; children's books; poetry; memoirs. Imprint includes Archives of Canadian Arts, Culture, and Heritage. Releases about 6 new titles a year. Occasionally accepts unsolicited manuscripts, but prefers enquiries with outline, sample chapter, intended market, and brief bio.

Playwrights Canada Press
269 Richmond Street W., Suite 202, Toronto, ON M5V IXI
Phone: (416) 703-0013
E-mail: submissions@playwrightscanada.com
Website: www.playwrightscanada.com
Contact: Annie Gibson, publisher

Established 1984. Publishes professionally produced plays, theatre history, and criticism. Accepts unsolicited manuscripts. Guidelines available on website.

The Porcupine's Quill
68 Main Street, Erin, ON NOB ITO
Phone: (519) 833-9158 Fax: (519) 833-9845
E-mail: pql@sentex.net
Website: www.porcupinesquill.ca
Contact: Tim Inkster, publisher

Established 1974. Specializes in Canadian literary fiction. Published 10 new titles in 2012. Does not accept unsolicited manuscripts.

Portage & Main Press

318 McDermot Avenue, Suite 100, Winnipeg, MB R3A 0A2
Phone: (204) 987-3500 or 1-800-667-9673 Fax: 1-866-734-8477
E-mail: books@pandmpress.com
Website: www.portageandmainpress.com
Contact: Catherine Gerbasi, director

A publisher of educational resources for teachers of grades K to 8 in all subjects. Publishes about 20 new titles a year. Does not accept unsolicited manuscripts. Send a query. Guidelines available on website.

Pottersfield Press

83 Leslie Road, East Lawrencetown, NS B2Z 1P8
Website: www.pottersfieldpress.com
Contact: Lesley Choyce, editor

Established 1979. Publishes general non-fiction, novels, and books of interest to Atlantic Canada. Particularly interested in biography proposals. Averages 6 new titles a year. Accepts proposals and/or full manuscripts. No phone calls, please.

Prairie House Books

P.O. Box 84007, Market Mall, Calgary, AB T3A 5C4
Phone: (403) 202-5438 Fax: (403) 202-5437
E-mail: phbooks@telusplanet.net
Website: http://english-idioms.net/wm
Contact: Wayne Magnuson, publisher/editor

A self-publishing company providing services from editing to proofreading to shipping of printed, bound books. Publishes 2 books annually. Does not accept unsolicited manuscripts. First send an e-mail inquiry. "A book worth reading bares the soul of its author." – Ken Lewis.

Productive Publications

7-B Pleasant Boulevard, Suite 1210, Toronto, ON M4T 1K2
Phone: (416) 483-0634 Fax: (416) 322-7434
E-mail: productivepublications@rogers.com
Website: www.productivepublications.ca
Contact: Iain Williamson, publisher

Publishes softcover books on small business, entrepreneurship, business management, health and wellness, computer software, and the Internet – especially non-fiction books to help people succeed during a recession. Accepts unsolicited manuscripts, but send an inquiry first. "We are looking for books of 100 to 200 pages that are well written by people who know their subject well."

Purich Publishing

P.O. Box 23032, Market Mall P.O., Saskatoon, SK S7J 5H3
Phone: (306) 373-5311 Fax: (306) 373-5315
E-mail: purich@sasktel.net
Website: www.purichpublishing.com
Contacts: Don Purch; Karen Bolstad

Specializes in books on Aboriginal and social justice issues, law, and Western history for the academic and reference market. Publishes 3–4 titles a year. Accepts unsolicited manuscripts, but first send a query and outline. Guidelines available.

Quattro Books

89 Pinewood Avenue, Toronto, ON M6C 2V2
Phone: 647-748-7484
E-mail: info@quattrobooks.ca
Website: www.quattrobooks.ca

Established 2006. "We are interested in publishing meaningful literature regardless of its linguistic, cultural, or national background and, in the process, contributing to a community that reflects the multiplicity and excitement of literary production in Canada." Has three lines: Quattro Poetry, Quattro Fiction, and Quattro International. Accepts only unsolicited novella submissions (of 20,000 and 40,000 words), between September 1 and March 1; outside of these dates, submissions accepted only for the Ken Klonsky Novella Contest. See website for guidelines.

Random House Canada

1 Toronto Street, Suite 300, Toronto, ON M5C 2V6
Phone: (416) 364-4449 Fax: (416) 364-6863
Website: www.randomhouse.ca

A general trade publisher of quality fiction and non-fiction, primarily general interest, literary, and culinary titles. Only accepts manuscripts submitted by an agent.

Red Deer Press
195 Allstate Parkway, Markham, ON L3T 4T8
Phone: (905) 477-9700 Fax: (905) 477-9179
E-mail: rdp@reddeerpress.com
Website: www.reddeerpress.com
Contacts: Richard Dionne, publisher; Peter Carver, children's and
  YA editor
Established 1975. Publishes literary fiction and non-fiction for
adults and children, illustrated children's books, young-adult and
teen fiction, poetry, and drama. Produced 18 books in 2011.
Accepts children's and YA unsolicited manuscripts. Send a synopsis
and 3 sample chapters first. For adult material, accepts e-mail
queries only. Canadian authors only. "Children's list is usually
booked 2 to 3 years in advance. Reports in 4 to 6 months."

Rocky Mountain Books
406 – 13 Avenue N.E., Calgary, AB T2E IC2
Phone: (403) 249-9490 Fax: (403) 249-2968
E-mail: don@rmbooks.com
Website: www.rmbooks.com
Contact: Don Gorman, publisher
Established 1976. Specializes in outdoor recreational guides to
the Canadian Rockies and Western Canada, and books on mountain culture, mountaineering, mountain people, and local history in
mountain areas. Does not accept unsolicited manuscripts or hard-
copy proposals. Send a query letter with an outline and sample
chapter. Submission guidelines available on website.

Ronsdale Press
3350 W. 21st Avenue, Vancouver, BC V6S IG7
Phone: (604) 738-4688 or 1-855-738-4688 Fax: (604) 731-4548
E-mail: ronsdale@shaw.ca
Website: www.ronsdalepress.com
Contact: Ronald B. Hatch, director
Established 1988. A literary press specializing in fiction, poetry,
biography, regional literature, and books of ideas. Also publishes
children's literature, but not picture books. Interested in quality
and experimental literature. Releases 12 to 14 books each year.
Accepts unsolicited manuscripts. "We expect our authors to read

widely in contemporary and past literature. Poets must have some publishing credits. With children's literature, we are interested in Canadian historical fiction." Guidelines available on website.

Royal BC Museum Publishing

675 Belleville Street, Victoria, BC V8W 9W2
Phone: (250) 387-2478 Fax: (250) 387-0102
E-mail: gtruscott@royalbcmuseum.bc.ca
Website: www.royalbcmuseum.bc.ca/Publications
Contact: Gerry Truscott, publisher

Established 1891. Publishes scholarly and popular non-fiction concerning the human history and natural history of British Columbia, and about the collections and activities of the provincial museum and archives. Produces about 4 new titles a year. No unsolicited manuscripts. Send an inquiry. Guidelines available.

Scholastic Canada Ltd.

175 Hillmount Road, Markham, ON L6C 1Z7
Phone: (905) 887-7323 Fax: (905) 887-3643
Website: www.scholastic.ca
Contact: editor

Publishes books for children and young people up to age 14 with a focus on Canadian authors and illustrators. No unsolicited manuscripts at the present time. For up-to-date information on the submissions policy, phone (905) 887-7323, ext. 4308, or visit the website.

Scrivener Press

465 Loach's Road, Sudbury, ON P3E 2R2
Phone: (705) 522-5126 Fax: (705) 522-5126
E-mail: laurence@yourscrivenerpress.com
Website: www.scrivenerpress.com
Contact: Laurence Steven, publisher and editor

Established 1995. Regional publisher of poetry, short stories, and novels. Brings out 4–6 titles a year. "While we will consider full manuscripts, we much prefer receiving book proposals. We do not consider faxed or e-mailed submissions. We wish to be informed if your work is being submitted elsewhere simultaneously." See website for submission guidelines.

Second Story Press

20 Maud Street, Suite 401, Toronto, ON M5V 2M5
Phone: (416) 537-7850 Fax: (416) 537-0588
E-mail: info@secondstorypress.ca
Website: www.secondstorypress.ca
Contact: Margie Wolfe, publisher

An award-winning publisher of progressive books for children and adults. At the core of the list are books with anti-sexist, anti-racist, socially conscious themes, mostly by women. Released 13 titles in 2012. Accepts unsolicited manuscripts. "Please ensure that your manuscript is a good fit for our list by perusing our website and reviewing our titles and submission guidelines prior to contact."

Self-Counsel Press

1481 Charlotte Road, North Vancouver, BC V7J 1H1
Phone: (604) 986-3366 Fax: (604) 986-3947
E-mail: editor@self-counsel.com
Website: www.self-counsel.com
Contact: Richard Day, publisher

Established 1971. Publishes non-fiction (digital first, then print) in 3 categories: legal series for lay readers, business series for small-business operators, and how to start and run a specific type of business. Also publishes how-to books on topics such as buying a house and understanding accounting. Produces at least 24 new titles each year. Accepts unsolicited manuscripts, but first send an outline, sample chapter, a résumé of your credentials, and the reasons this book is needed. "We seek fact-rich books written by experts in their field. Most manuscripts accepted are 50,000 to 70,000 words; also publishes digital "shorts" of 12,000 to 20,000 words. We publish for the Canadian and U.S. markets, as well as titles for global sales." Guidelines available on website.

Seraphim Editions

54 Bay Street, Woodstock, ON N4S 3K9
Phone: (519) 290-5509 Fax: (519) 290-5509
E-mail: info@seraphimeditions.com
Website: www.seraphimeditions.com
Contact: Maureen Whyte, publisher

Founded 1995. Publishes fiction, non-fiction, and poetry. For submission queries, contact publisher by e-mail.

J. Gordon Shillingford Publishing

P.O. Box 86, RPO Corydon Avenue, Winnipeg, MB R3M 3S3
Phone: (204) 779-6967 Fax: (204) 779-6970
E-mail: jgshill@allstream.net
Website: www.jgshillingford.com
Contact: Gordon Shillingford, president

Publishes Canadian drama (under its Scirocco Drama imprint), poetry (under its Muses' Company imprint), and non-fiction (social history, biography, Native issues, and politics, under its J. Gordon Shillingford / Watson & Dwyer imprint). Produces about 14 new titles a year. No unsolicited manuscripts. Send an inquiry. "We do not publish fiction or children's books."

Shoreline Press

23 Ste-Anne, Ste-Anne-de-Bellevue, QC H9X ILI
Phone: (514) 457-5733 Fax: (514) 457-5733
E-mail: info@shorelinepress.ca
Website: www.shorelinepress.ca
Contact: Judy Isherwood, editor

Aims to give first-time authors a chance in the marketplace, but it must be quality work. Publishes non-fiction (biographies, history, and social and church stories) and some poetry. No unsolicited manuscripts. Send a query with an outline and sample chapters. Author guidelines available.

Signature Editions

P.O. Box 206, RPO Corydon, Winnipeg, MB R3M 3S7
Phone: (204) 779-7803 Fax: (204) 779-6970
E-mail: signature@allstream.net
Website: www.signature-editions.com
Contact: Karen Haughian, publisher

Publishes literary works by Canadians in the genres of fiction, non-fiction, poetry, and drama. Releases 6 to 7 new titles a year. Accepts unsolicited manuscripts or a sample with a covering letter, a synopsis, and a CV specifying previous published works. Include an SASE for a reply. Does not usually publish novice writers. Guidelines available on website.

Simply Read Books

5525 W. Boulevard, Suite 501, Vancouver, BC V6M 3W6
E-mail: go@simplyreadbooks.com
Website: www.simplyreadbooks.com

Specializes in high-quality picture books and fiction. Currently accepting manuscripts in the following genres: picture books, early chapter books, and early readers. "We will only reply if your manuscript is accepted, and don't return manuscripts."

Snare Books

E-mail: info.snarebooks@gmail.com
Website: snarebooks.wordpress.com
Contact: Jon Paul Fiorentino, publisher

Founded 2006. "Our mandate is to publish emerging and innovative writers who work in the experimental Canadian literary tradition. We plan to focus primarily on poetry, as well as publishing the occasional experimental novel or short story collection."

Talonbooks

P.O. Box 2076, Vancouver, BC V6B 3S3
Phone: (604) 444-4889 or 1-888-445-4176 Fax: (604) 444-4119
E-mail: info@talonbooks.com
Website: www.talonbooks.com
Contact: Kevin Williams, publisher

Established 1967. Invites submissions of drama, criticism, history, cultural studies, and literary fiction. Accepts unsolicited manuscripts, but send an inquiry first. "We consider for publication only playscripts that have been professionally produced. We do not accept poetry manuscripts or publish historical, romance, adventure, science fiction, children's literature, or cookbooks." Guidelines available.

Theytus Books

Lot 45, Green Mountain Road, R.R. #2, Site 50, Comp. 8,
    Penticton, BC V2A 6J7
Phone: (250) 493-7181 Fax: (250) 493-5302

E-mail: info@theytus.com
Website: www.theytus.com

An Aboriginal-owned and -run publishing house that publishes Aboriginal authors only. *Theytus* is a Salishan word that means "preserving for the sake of handing down." "We strive to produce appropriate reading material and information about Aboriginal peoples through the promotion of Aboriginal authors." Publishes literary fiction, non-fiction in social history and policy as it relates to Aboriginal issues, Aboriginal critical literary pieces, non-fiction (creative and humorous), and children's and YA titles. Send synopsis with sample chapters by mail only; no e-mail or fax submissions. Guidelines available on website.

Thistledown Press
118 – 20th Street W., Saskatoon, SK S7M 0W6
Phone: (306) 244-1722 Fax: (306) 244-1762
E-mail: tdpress@thistledownpress.com
Website: www.thistledownpress.com
Contact: Jackie Forrie, publishing and production manager

Established 1975. Aims to publish Canadian literature of the highest quality, representing the wealth of the nation's culture and heritage. Specializes in Canadian fiction, poetry, and young adult fiction. Publishes about 14 new titles a year. The New Leaf Editions series is devoted to books of 64 pages by previously unpublished writers from Saskatchewan. Does not accept unsolicited manuscripts. Query first. Guidelines available on website.

Three O'Clock Press
180 Bloor Street W., Suite 801, Toronto, ON M5S 2V6
Phone: (416) 929-2964 Fax: (416) 929-1926
E-mail: info@threeoclockpress.com
Website: www.threeoclockpress.com
Contact: publisher

Established 2010. Small literary press, comprising the Sumach Press and Women's Press Literary imprints, devoted to groundbreaking women's writing that is feminist, queer positive, inclusive, and anti-oppressive in nature. Accepts submissions of feminist stories for young adults, Canadian music and culture (specifically subcultures), fiction, creative non-fiction, graphic novels, and queer literature. Guidelines available on website.

Tightrope Books
17 Greyton Crescent, Toronto, ON M6E 2GI
Phone: (416) 787-4202 Fax: (416) 787-4202
E-mail: info@tightropebooks.com
Website: www.tightropebooks.com
Contact: Halli Villegas, publisher

Established in 2005. "We are known for our innovative, progressive list." Publishes poetry, fiction, and some non-fiction. 8 to 10 titles a year. Check website to determine if unsolicited submissions are currently being accepted.

Timeless Books
P.O. Box 9, Walker's Landing Road, Kootenay, BC VOB IXO
Phone: (250) 227-9224 Fax: (250) 227-9494
E-mail: contact@timeless.org
Website: www.timeless.org
Contact: Clea McDougall, editor

Since 1978, Timeless Books has been offering readers in-depth and inspired books on yoga. "As an independent Canadian micropress, we aim to publish intelligent material instilled with care and quality, while embodying ethical and environmental business practices. All of our titles are printed on 100% PCW recycled paper, and are carbon neutral."

TouchWood Editions
1105 Pandora Avenue, Suite 340, Victoria, BC V8V 3P9
Phone: (250) 360-0829 Fax: (250) 386-0829
E-mail: info@touchwoodeditions.com
Website: www.touchwoodeditions.com
Contact: Ruth Linka, publisher

Publishes a variety of fiction and non-fiction, with a focus on crime fiction, cookbooks, and food and wine books. Also publishes historical fiction and regional biography, history, and guidebooks. Accepts unsolicited manuscripts, see website for more information.

Tradewind Books

1807 Maritime Mews, Suite 202, Vancouver, BC V6H 3W7
Phone: (604) 662-4405 Fax: (604) 730-0454
Website: www.tradewindbooks.com
Contact: Michael Katz, publisher

Publishes high-quality literature for children and young adults. Released 6 new titles in 2012. Accepts unsolicited manuscripts, but send a sample chapter first. "We ask that writers read at least 3 of our titles before submitting a manuscript."

TSAR Books

P.O. Box 6996, Stn. A, Toronto, ON M5W 1X7
Phone: (416) 483-7191 Fax: (416) 486-0706
E-mail: inquiries@tsarbooks.com
Website: www.tsarbooks.com
Contact: Nurjehan Aziz, publisher

Established 2008. "Our focus is on works that can loosely be termed 'multicultural' and particularly those that pertain to Asia and Africa." Publishes 6 to 8 titles of fiction, poetry, and non-fiction (literary criticism, history) each year. Query first by e-mail.

Tundra Books

1 Toronto Street, Suite 300, Toronto, ON M5C 2V6
Phone: (416) 364-4449 Fax: (416) 364-6863
E-mail: tundra@mcclelland.com
Website: www.tundrabooks.com
Contact: Tara Walker, editorial director

Established 1967. Specializes in children's publishing: picture books, YA non-fiction, YA fiction, and historical fiction. Releases 35 to 40 new titles a year. Accepts unsolicited manuscripts. "Please visit our website."

Turnstone Press

100 Arthur Street, Suite 206, Winnipeg, MB R3B 1H3
Phone: (204) 947-1555 Fax: (204) 942-1555
E-mail: info@turnstonepress.com
Website: www.turnstonepress.com
Contact: Jamis Paulson, associate publisher

Established 1976. A literary press publishing fiction, poetry, non-fiction, and literary criticism. Through its imprint Ravenstone, it publishes non-formula genre fiction. Releases 10 new titles a year. Accepts unsolicited manuscripts. Send sample chapters first. Guidelines available on website.

UBC Press
2029 West Mall, Vancouver, BC V6T 1Z2
Phone: (604) 822-5959 Fax: (604) 822-6083
E-mail: frontdesk@ubcpress.ca
Website: www.ubcpress.ca
Contact: Melissa Pitts, director
Established 1971. Publishes non-fiction for scholarly, educational, and general audiences in the social sciences and natural sciences. Subject areas include history, political science, Native studies, Asian studies, law and society, natural resources, planning, and health and sexuality studies. Releases approximately 60 new titles each year. No unsolicited manuscripts. Send an inquiry first. Guidelines available online. "Check the website for a complete description of the press's publications and procedures."

Ulysses Travel Guides
4176 Ste-Denis Street, Montreal, QC H2W 2M5
Phone: (514) 843-9447 Fax: (514) 843-9448
E-mail: text@ulysses.ca
Website: www.ulyssesguides.com
Contact: Daniel Desjardins, president
Publishes travel guides and outdoor activity guides for Canadians. Releases 2 new titles a year. Accepts unsolicited manuscripts, but first send an outline and sample chapters. Guidelines available.

United Church Publishing House
3250 Bloor Street W., Suite 300, Toronto, ON M8X 2Y4
Phone: (416) 231-5931 Fax: (416) 231-3103
E-mail: bookpub@united-church.ca
Website: www.united-church.ca/sales/ucph
Contact: Rebekah Chevalier, senior editor
Established in 1829 as Ryerson Press. Aims to meet the spiritual needs of both its church members and others. Committed to

publishing books that help people engage in Christian ministry, attracting readers, regardless of denomination or faith, to consider the spiritual aspects of their lives. Not accepting unsolicited manuscripts.

University of Alberta Press
Ring House 2, University of Alberta, Edmonton, AB T6G 2E1
Phone: (780) 492-3662 Fax: (780) 492-0719
E-mail: petem@ualberta.ca
Website: www.uap.ualberta.ca
Contacts: Peter Midgley, senior editor (acquisitions) or Linda
   Cameron, director
   Established 1969. The UAP publishes in the areas of biography, history, literature, natural history, regional interest, travel narratives, and reference books. Special series include Wayfarer, a literary travel series; Mountain Cairns, a series on the history and culture of the Canadian Rocky Mountains; and the Robert Kroetsch series, a Canadian literature series. Publishes 25 to 28 new titles a year. Accepts unsolicited scholarly manuscripts, but does not accept unsolicited poetry or fiction. First send a query with an outline and/or sample chapters. Guidelines available on request and on website.

University of Calgary Press
2500 University Drive N.W., Calgary, AB T2N 1N4
Phone: (403) 220-7578 Fax: (403) 282-0085
E-mail: livingsd@ucalgary.ca
Website: www.uofcpress.com
Contact: Donna Livingstone, director
   Established in 1981, the University of Calgary Press disseminates academic research in the form of peer-reviewed books and journals that make a difference and push the scholarly argument forward. Primary focus is on Western Canada including history, women's studies, art and architecture, Aboriginal studies, parks and heritage sites, and food studies; energy, ecology and the environment; northern studies; African studies; and Canadian military and strategic Studies. Accepts unsolicited complete manuscripts. Author guidelines available on website.

University of Manitoba Press

301 St. John's College, Winnipeg, MB R3T 2M5
Phone: (204) 474-9495 Fax: (204) 474-7566
E-mail: carr@cc.umanitoba.ca
Website: www.umanitoba.ca/uofmpress
Contact: David Carr, director

Established 1967. Publishes non-fiction for trade and academic markets in Native and Canadian history, Native studies, and Canadian literary studies. Averages 5 to 8 new titles each year. Accepts either an electronic proposal or a paper manuscript, along with an author bio and assessment of the market. Manuscripts under consideration are peer reviewed. Complete guidelines available on website.

University of Ottawa Press / Presses de l'Université d'Ottawa

542 King Edward Avenue, Ottawa, ON KIN 6N5
Phone: (613) 562-5246 Fax: (613) 562-5247
E-mail: puo-uop@uottawa.ca
Website: www.press.uottawa.ca
Contact: use general e-mail and phone number

The University of Ottawa Press is Canada's oldest French language university press and the only bilingual university press in North America. UOP publishes in both official languages and is committed to bilingualism and multiculturalism. The publishing program reflects and promotes critical thinking, first-class research, intellectual integrity, ethical judgment, social responsibility, and innovation. It publishes academic non-fiction in anthropology, sociology, political science, psychology, criminology, media studies, economics, education, language and culture, law, history, literature, translation studies, philosophy, public administration, health sciences, and religious studies. Only accepts unsolicited manuscripts with complete proposals. Author guidelines available on website.

University of Toronto Press

10 St. Mary Street, Suite 700, Toronto, ON M4Y 2W8
Phone: (416) 978-2239 Fax: (416) 978-4738

E-mail: publishing@utpress.utoronto.ca (UTP) or
 requests@utphighereducation.com (UTP Higher Education)
Website: www.utppublishing.com

Established 1901. A large university press publishing scholarly and general works, and many academic journals. Editorial program includes classical, medieval, Renaissance, and Victorian studies, modern languages, English and Canadian literature, literary theory and criticism, women's studies, social sciences, Native studies, philosophy, law, religion, music, education, modern history, geography, and political science. In May 2008, University of Toronto Press acquired the Broadview Press publishing lists in anthropology, history, politics, and sociology, as well as the Garamond imprint. Broadview's editors in these areas, as well as the sales, marketing, production and management teams, formed a new division known as UTP Higher Education, which publishes books with potential for course adoption and in subject areas that complement those of the Scholarly Publishing Division.

Both divisions accept unsolicited manuscripts, but prefer prior inquiry with outline, partial bibliography, sample chapters, and a CV. Use *Chicago* or *MLA* for style, though internal consistency is most important.

Véhicule Press
P.O. Box 125, Place du Parc Stn., Montreal, QC H2X 4A3
Phone: (514) 844-6073 Fax: (514) 844-7543
E-mail: vp@vehiculepress.com
Website: www.vehiculepress.com
Contact: Vicki Marcok, general manager

Established 1973. Publishes literature in the context of social history – fiction, poetry, and non-fiction, as well as guidebooks. Authors are mostly Canadian. Releases approximately 15 new titles annually. Accepts unsolicited manuscripts, but send sample chapters first. "Send an SASE with submissions or we do not respond." Guidelines available.

Whitecap Books
351 Lynn Avenue, North Vancouver, BC V7J 2C4
Phone: (604) 980-9852 Fax: (604) 980-8197

E-mail: whitecap@whitecap.ca
Website: www.whitecap.ca
Contact: editor

Established 1977. Publishes books on cookery, wine and spirits, and gardening books. Authors include well-known chefs, celebrity gardeners, and renowned experts. Also publishes scenic colour books on U.S. and Canadian topics, most often initiated in-house. Releases 40 to 45 books a year. Accepts unsolicited manuscripts; please send an outline and sample chapters first. Submission guidelines available on website. No electronic submissions; no phone or e-mail queries.

Wilfrid Laurier University Press

75 University Avenue W., Waterloo, ON N2L 3C5
Phone: (519) 884-0710, ext. 6124 Fax: (519) 725-1399
E-mail: press@wlu.ca
Website: www.press.wlu.ca
Contact: Lisa M. Quinn, acquisitions editor

Established 1974. Publishes scholarly books (and academic journals) in the humanities and social sciences, and literary non-fiction. Subject areas include film, literature, literary criticism, literature in translation, cultural studies, Native studies, religious studies, Canadian studies, life writing, philosophy, history, and women's studies. Produces 20 to 30 new books a year. Accepts unsolicited manuscripts, but first send CV, outline, and sample chapter. Guidelines available on website.

Wolsak and Wynn

69 Hughson Street N., Suite 102, Hamilton, ON L8R 1G5
Phone: (905) 972-9885
E-mail: info@wolsakandwynn.ca
Website: www.wolsakandwynn.ca
Contact: Noelle Allen, publisher

A small literary press specializing in poetry and non-fiction. Published 9 new titles in 2011. Accepts unsolicited manuscripts; send an inquiry first. "Poetry submissions are accepted only during the first quarter of the year." Guidelines available.

The Workhorsery

132 Heward Avenue, Toronto, ON M4M 2T7

E-mail: read@theworkhorsery.ca

Website: www.theworkhorsery.ca

Publishes novel-length fiction (70,000+ words). "We are looking for the stuff that falls off the map, fiction that's not quite sure where it belongs but totally knocks our socks off." See website for submission guidelines. "We love unpublished authors!"

YYZBOOKS

401 Richmond Street W., Suite 140, Toronto, ON M5V 3A8

Phone: (416) 598-4546 Fax: (416) 598-2282

E-mail: publish@yyzartistsoutlet.org

Website: www.yyzbooks.com

Dedicated to publishing critical writing on art and culture. Seeks collections of provocative writing and artists' projects.

6

LITERARY AGENTS

Acquiring a literary agent can sometimes be more challenging than finding a publisher. So why bother? Why pay a percentage of your hard-earned royalties to someone who didn't share those long hours writing at your computer, agonizing over every word, tormented with insecurity and overwork?

If you focus your writing on periodicals, you probably will not require an agent, but if your aspiration is to have a book published, an agent is someone you should seriously consider. Canadian book publishers are increasingly reluctant to deal with unagented manuscripts, or if they do accept them, it is often without the same serious scrutiny that is given to work submitted by an agent. Publishers respect the professionalism of agents, and realize that if an agent considers a manuscript to be worth their while, it must be a saleable commodity.

Good agents have extensive contacts in the publishing industry, affording them valuable insight as to which publishers and editors to approach with your project. They are experienced in negotiating the most favourable contracts for their clients, obtaining the best royalty rate and highest advance, and typically do business with the larger publishers, those who have the most money to spend. Agents will attempt to retain as many rights to their clients' work as possible, then pursue the sale of subsidiary rights, which may include foreign and film rights. They will follow up on contracts to ensure that all obligations are fulfilled, examining royalty statements and collecting all monies due. An agent's expertise is in the business side of publishing, an area in which most writers have neither the time nor inclination to become proficient.

In addition, agents can provide writers with professional career guidance and be an invaluable sounding-board for ideas, since they are acutely familiar with the marketplace. They will critique your work so that changes can be made before a publisher has the opportunity to turn it down.

Finding an agent to represent you can be a difficult task, especially if you are an unpublished author. Typically, agencies work overtime to represent the clients they already have and are often reluctant to invest their time and money in an unproven entity. That is why some of them charge a reading fee. A referral from an interested publisher or from one of their clients could help pique some interest, but getting your foot in an agent's door is not an easy process.

Although this chapter lists most of the active literary agencies in Canada, you will notice that many of them will not accept unsolicited manuscripts. In such cases, a query letter will be your first entry into an agent's office. Resist the urge to send out a mass mailing to every agent in the country. First, examine their subject interests and specialties, as indicated below, noting only the agencies that represent the type of work you are writing, then target those. Contacting agencies that do not handle your area of interest is a waste of everyone's time.

A query letter to an agent should contain a brief outline of the work you want him or her to sell and a description of your writing experience. If you have previously had a book in print, a prospective agent will want to know who published it, as well as how many copies and which foreign rights were sold. In other words, a busy agency must be convinced that your work has earning power. If you have no publishing history, your query letter needs to persuade an agent that your project will appeal to a lucrative market. Enclose an SASE for his or her reply.

Before agreeing to be represented by an agency, you should check its track record and ask for a client list. You may wish to obtain specialized legal advice before signing a contract with it or, alternatively, contact the Writers' Union of Canada or your regional branch of the Canadian Authors Association to assist you with any questions you may have.

Agents in Canada usually charge 15 per cent of the value of all rights sold, which may increase to 20 per cent for foreign sales. Some agencies also tack on fees for reading, evaluation, and editorial services, as well as charging the author for such office costs as photocopying, postage, couriers, and long-distance telephone expenses. Be certain that all such obligations are disclosed and agreed to before you become that agency's client, and insist on an accounting of fees and expenses, as well as an upper limit to such charges.

Acacia House Publishing Services Ltd.

62 Chestnut Avenue, Brantford, ON N3T 4C2
Phone: (519) 752-0978 Fax: (519) 752-8349
E-mail: bhanna.acacia@rogers.com
Contact: Bill Hanna

Subject interests: Fiction with international potential. No horror or occult. For non-fiction, no self-help or fitness. Special non-fiction interests: history, philosophy, and military subjects, and business books.

Comments: Accepts unsolicited queries only, with writing sample (up to 50 double-spaced pages). Reads unpublished writers. Does not charge evaluation, editorial, or other handling fees. All queries and submissions must be accompanied by an SASE.

Aurora Artists

19 Wroxeter Avenue, Toronto, ON M4K 1J5
Phone: (416) 463-4634 Fax: (416) 463-4889
E-mail: aurora.artists@sympatico.ca
Contact: Janine Cheeseman

Subject interests: Primarily a film and television literary agency with crossover management of rights for publication, etc.

Comments: Accepts unsolicited queries only. Does not read unpublished writers.

Author Author Literary Agency

P.O. Box 42522, Columbia Square, 1005 Columbia Street, Suite
   130, New Westminster, BC V3M 6H5
Phone: (604) 777-7766
E-mail: joan@authorauthorliteraryagency.com

Website: www.authorauthorliteraryagency.com

Contact: Joan Rickard, president

Subject interests: Book-length adult/juvenile fiction and non-fiction. "Sorry, no poetry or screenplays."

Comments: Welcomes unpublished writers. No evaluation fees for authors book-published in the same genre as current endeavours (excluding electronic, print-on-demand, and self-published books). Otherwise, there is an entry evaluation fee of $125 per proposal (certified cheques or bank money orders; international bank money order if outside Canada). Evaluation fees are deducted from the agency's commission when properties are sold to publishers. Please submit hard copy only (no fax or disk submissions). Reports in about 8 weeks from receipt of submissions. Also provides editing and ghostwriting services. See website for complete details of services, policies, and submission guidelines.

Johanna M. Bates Literary Consultants Inc.

171 Somme Avenue S.W., Calgary, AB T2T 5J8

Phone: (403) 282-7370

E-mail: query@batesliterary.com

Website: www.batesliterary.com

Contact: Johanna M. Bates

Subject interests: Literary fiction, children's books, and thriller/suspense novels.

Comments: Accepts queries from unpublished writers. No unsolicited manuscripts. An evaluation fee is charged: $125 for the first 10 pages, $2 per page thereafter, plus GST.

Marilyn Biderman Literary Agency

Toronto, ON

Phone: (416) 603-8585

E-mail: marilyn@mblm.ca

Subject interests: literary, book-club fiction; commercial fiction, memoir, narrative and expert non-fiction. "No poetry, picture books, screenplays, sci-fi or non-crossover YA."

Comments: Query by e-mail with a summary of the subject matter and thesis for non-fiction, or a detailed description or synopsis for fiction. Include biographical information.

Rick Broadhead & Associates: Literary and Media Agents

47 St. Clair Avenue W., Suite 501, Toronto, ON M4V 3A5
Phone: (416) 929-0516 Fax: (416) 927-8732
E-mail: submissions@rbaliterary.com
Website: www.rbaliterary.com
Contact: Rick Broadhead, president and CEO

Subject interests: Non-fiction books only, especially history, politics, current affairs, investigative journalism, food narratives, business, sports/hockey, self-help, health and medicine, parenting, science, true crime, memoir, military history, and quirky/offbeat reference.

Comments: E-mail queries are welcome: please include a brief description of the book you are writing and an overview of your background and credentials. If there is interest in your project, you will be contacted and asked for a proposal. Represents non-fiction projects only. Please do not pitch novels, film scripts, or children's books.

The Bukowski Agency

14 Prince Arthur Avenue, Suite 202, Toronto, ON M5R 1A9
Phone: (416) 928-6728 Fax: (416) 963-9978
E-mail: assistant@thebukowskiagency.com
Website: www.thebukowskiagency.com
Contact: Denise Bukowski

Subject interests: General adult trade books. Prefers literary fiction and non-fiction. No genre fiction (science fiction, romance, westerns); no children's books; no scriptwriters or playwrights. Specializes in projects with international potential and suitability for other media.

Comments: No unsolicited manuscripts or unpublished writers. Does not charge evaluation or other handling fees. Query first, by mail only, with writing samples and credentials. "What future projects do you have planned? Before making an investment in a little-known writer, I need to be convinced that you are not only talented but ambitious and driven as a writer." No phone or e-mail queries, please.

The Cooke Agency

Toronto office: 278 Bloor Street E., Suite 305, Toronto, ON M4W 3M4

Vancouver office: P.O. Box 76003, Coal Harbour, Vancouver, BC
 V6E 4T2
Phone: (416) 406-3390 Fax: (416) 406-3389
E-mail: agents@cookeagency.ca
Website: www.cookeagency.ca
Contact: Elizabeth Griffin
 Subject interests: Commercial and literary fiction, narrative non-
fiction, middle-grade and YA fiction.
 Comments: No evaluation or other handling fees are charged.
Visit our website for submission guidelines and more information
about the agency.

The Core Group Talent Agency Inc.
140 Wolfrey Avenue, Toronto, ON M4K IL3
Phone: (416) 466-4929
E-mail: coreliterary@gmail.com
Website: www.coreliteraryinc.com
Contact: Charles Northcote
 Subject interests: Writing for film, theatre, and television. Deals
primarily with scripts and producing and publishing them. Does
not handle novels, short stories, poetry, etc.
 Comments: Referrals preferred. Accepts e-mail queries from
unproduced writers. No unsolicited material. No evaluation fee.

Credentials
55 Livingston Road, PH 2, Toronto, ON MIE IK9
Phone: (416) 926-1507 Fax: (416) 926-0372
E-mail: credent@rogers.com
Contact: Lynn Kinney
 Subject interests: Published or unpublished material suitable for
film and television.
 Comments: No unsolicited manuscripts; send a query letter first
with a 2- to 3-page synopsis. No evaluation fee.

Arnold Gosewich, Literary Agent and Consultant
40 Oaklands Avenue, Suite 207, Toronto, ON M4V 2E5
Phone: (416) 925-7836
E-mail: jackee@sympatico.ca

Website: www.arnoldgbooks.com
Contact: Arnold Gosewich
   Subject interests: Non-fiction, commercial fiction, young adult novels.
   Comments: No unsolicited manuscripts; send a query first. Reads unpublished writers. No evaluation fee.

Great North Artists Management, Inc.

350 Dupont Street, Toronto, ON M5R 1V9
Phone: (416) 925-2051 Fax: (416) 925-3904
E-mail: gnaminc@gnaminc.com
Contacts: Ralph Zimmerman, Rena Zimmerman, and Emma
   Fedderson
   Subject interests: Film and television properties.
   Comments: No evaluation or other handling fees. Queries by mail or e-mail only. No unsolicited manuscripts. Prefer referral from industry professional.

Great Titles Inc.

18 Greenfield Drive, Etobicoke, ON M9B 1G9
Phone: (416) 231-6686 Fax: (416) 231-7913
E-mail: atsallas@allstream.net
Contact: Tina Tsallas
   Subject interests: Women's fiction and mainstream fiction with strong characters. Also interested in mysteries that have a little edge to them. Children's material must be for the YA market only. Non-fiction must have broad audience appeal.
   Comments: Accepts queries from unpublished and published writers. Submit query with first 3 chapters and a detailed synopsis (or complete manuscript with detailed synopsis). "Know the market for which you are writing." No reading fee. No submissions by e-mail. Always send an SASE.

Green Light Artist Management, Inc.

1240 Bay Street, Suite 804, Toronto, ON M5R 2A7
Phone: (416) 920-5110 Fax: (416) 920-4113
E-mail: info@glam.on.ca
Website: www.glam.on.ca
Contact: Lara Bryant

Subject interests: Film and television writers only in the areas of animation, comedy, and drama.

Comments: Does not accept unsolicited queries or manuscripts. Will not consider unpublished writers. No reading fee. Does not represent novelists or poets.

Helen Heller Agency

216 Heath Street W., Suite 4, Toronto, ON M5P 1N7
Phone: (416) 489-0396
E-mail: info@helenhelleragency.com
Website: www.helenhelleragency.com
Contact: Helen Heller

Subject interests: Commercial adult fiction, crime/mystery, literary fiction, non-fiction, YA.

Comments: Does not handle screenplays or illustrated children's books. Query using website form. "No unscheduled walk-ins, please."

Kensington Literary Representation

34 St. Andrew Street, Toronto, ON M5T 1K6
Phone: (416) 979-0187
E-mail: kensingtonlit@rogers.com
Contact: Michael Petrasek, president

Subject interests: Plays, fiction, non-fiction.

Robert Lecker Agency, Inc.

4055 Melrose Avenue, Montreal, QC H4A 2S5
Phone: (514) 830-4818 Fax: (514) 483-1644
E-mail: leckerlink@aol.com
Website: www.leckeragency.com
Contact: Robert Lecker

Subject interests: Non-fiction sports, food, travel, popular science, and academic books with trade potential.

Comments: Accepts queries from unpublished writers. No unsolicited manuscripts. No evaluation or handling fee.

Lucas Talent Inc.

1238 Homer Street, Suite 6, Vancouver, BC V6B 1Y5
Phone: (604) 685-0345 Fax: (604) 685-0341

E-mail: doreen.holmes@lucastalent.com or
    anna.archer@lucastalent.com
Website: www.lucastalent.com
Contacts: Doreen Holmes and Anna Archer
    Subject interests: Writing for film and television only.
    Comments: Accepts inquiries from western Canadian writers only. No unsolicited manuscripts. Occasionally considers unpublished writers. No evaluation or other handling fees are charged.

Anne McDermid and Associates Ltd.
64 Bloem Avenue, Toronto, ON M6E ISI
Phone: (416) 324-8845 Fax: (416) 324-8870
E-mail: info@mcdermidagency.com
Website: www.mcdermidagency.com
Contacts: Anne McDermid, Martha Webb, or Chris Bucci
    Subject interests: Literary and commercial fiction and narrative non-fiction, children's and young adult literature. No self-help or how-to.
    Comments: Accepts mailed queries with synopsis, CV, and a short sample, but no unsolicited manuscripts. No telephone or e-mail queries, please. Check website for details. Also offer digital consultancy service for authors through dropCapLiterary (see www.dropcapliterary.com).

Mensour Agency Ltd.
41 Springfield Road, Ottawa, ON KIM IC8
Phone: (613) 241-1677 Fax: (613) 241-4360
E-mail: info@mensour.ca or kate@mensour.ca
Website: www.mensour.ca
Contact: Catherine Mensour
    Subject interests: Theatre, animation, television, and film.
    Comments: Does not accept unsolicited queries or manuscripts, but will sometimes read unpublished writers. No evaluation or other handling fees are charged.

Pamela Paul Agency Inc.
12 Westrose Avenue, Toronto, ON M8X 2AI
Phone: (416) 410-5395 Fax: (416) 410-4949

E-mail: agency@interlog.com
Contact: James Gordon
   Subject interests: Literary fiction, children's fiction, film, theatre, television, and radio.
   Comments: Will review new writers' material only with a referral. No e-mail queries or submissions will be accepted.

Bella Pomer Agency Inc.
355 St. Clair Avenue W., Suite 801, Toronto, ON M5P 1N5
Phone: (416) 920-4949
E-mail: belpom@sympatico.ca
Website: www.bellapomeragency.com
Contact: Bella Pomer
   Comments: "Not taking on new clients. List is closed."

P.S. Literary Agency
520 Kerr Street, Unit 20033, Oakville, ON L6K 3C7
Phone: (416) 907-8325
E-mail: query@psliterary.com
Website: www.psliterary.com
Contacts: Curtis Russell and Carly Watters
   Subject interests: commercial mainstream fiction, women's fiction, mysteries and thrillers, romance, literary, world literature, young adult, middle-grade, and picture books. Non-fiction: memoir, history, politics, current affairs, business, health, wellness, pop science, and pop psychology.
   Comments: Accepts queries from unpublished and published writers. Accepts queries via e-mail only. Limit query letter to 1 page. Do not send attachments. No reading fee. Does not represent poetry or screenplays.

The Rights Factory
P.O. Box 499, Stn. C, Toronto, ON M6J 3P6
Phone: (416) 966-5367
Website: www.therightsfactory.com
Contacts: Sam Hiyate, president; Kelvin Kong, rights manager;
   Ali McDonald, children's agent; Haskell Nussbaum, associate
   agent; Drea Cohane, associate agent

Subject interests: literary fiction, memoir, historical fiction and non-fiction (science, history, lifestyle, narrative, humour, pop culture), commercial fiction (mystery/crime, thrillers, sci-fi/fantasy, women's /romance), young adult, and middle grade fiction.

Comments: Query using website form. Accepts queries from unpublished and published writers. Submit query with first 3 chapters and a detailed synopsis or complete manuscript with detailed synopsis. No reading fee. No submissions by e-mail. For printed submissions, always send an SASE.

The Saint Agency
18 Gloucester Lane, Suite 200, Toronto, ON M4Y IL5
Phone: (416) 944-8200 Fax: (416) 944-3700
E-mail: linda@thesaintagency.com
Website: www.thesaintagency.com
Contact: Linda Saint

Subject interests: film, television series, and television writers.

Comments: "Please call or write to enquire before sending scripts." Accepts inquiries, but no unsolicited scripts. Reads unpublished writers. No evaluation fee.

Saunders Associates
337 Kenilworth Avenue, Toronto, ON M4L 2S9
Phone: 905-717-8313
E-mail: saundersassoc@web.ca
Contact: Peter Saunders

Subject interests: academic monographs, textbooks, edited collections, serious non-fiction. Specializes in works in the social sciences and humanities, including gender, media, labour, environmental, and development studies.

Comments: No evaluation fee. Charge on a fee-for-service basis; does not take share of royalties.

Seventh Avenue Literary Agency
2052 – 124th Street, Surrey, BC V4A 9K3
Phone and Fax: (604) 538-7252
E-mail: info@seventhavenuelit.com
Website: www.seventhavenuelit.com
Contact: Robert Mackwood

Subject interests: Primarily non-fiction in the following areas: business, popular culture, technology/science, travel, house and home, sports, food, and memoir.

Comments: Accepts unsolicited queries; see website for submission guidelines. No unsolicited manuscripts. Will occasionally read work from unpublished writers if the subject area is of interest. No evaluation fee. "Our client list includes writers from Canada, the U.S., the U.K., and other parts of the world. We have been successful selling translation rights through an expanding team of sub-agents."

Beverley Slopen Literary Agency

131 Bloor Street W., Suite 711, Toronto, ON M5S 1S3
Phone: (416) 964-9598
E-mail: beverley@slopenagency.ca
Website: www.slopenagency.ca
Contact: Beverley Slopen

Subject interests: Narrative or serious non-fiction and literary and commercial fiction.

Comments: No unsolicited manuscripts. Only occasionally reads unpublished writers if referred. Does not charge evaluation/handling fees.

P. Stathonikos Agency

264 Springbluff Avenue S.W., Calgary, AB T3H 5B7
Phone: (403) 245-2087
E-mail: pastath@shaw.ca

Subject interests: Juvenile, young adult, and Canadiana. No academic material, science fiction, or plays.

Comments: Accepts queries and unsolicited manuscripts from unpublished writers. Charges a handling fee of $100.

Carolyn Swayze Literary Agency Ltd.

P.O. Box 39588, RPO, White Rock, Surrey, BC V4A 0A9
Phone: (604) 538-3478
E-mail: carolyn@swayzeagency.com or
    reception@swayzeagency.com
Website: www.swayzeagency.com
Contacts: Carolyn Swayze, principal agent; Kris Rothstein, associate agent

Subject interests: Literary fiction, teen and middle-grade fiction and non-fiction, memoir, limited commercial fiction, military history, humour, strong, well-written narrative non-fiction, science, and social history.

Comments: Accepts queries and unsolicited manuscripts of non-fiction works. For fiction, send first 10 pages. Reads work by unpublished writers. No evaluation or handling fees. "No science fiction, romance, fantasy, children's picture books or screenplays, please."

Transatlantic Literary Agency, Inc.
2 Bloor Street E., Suite 3500, Toronto, ON M4W 1A8
Phone: (416) 488-9214
E-mail: info@tla1.com
Website: www.tla1.com
Contact: Lynn Bennett

Subject interests: literary fiction and non-fiction, young adult and children's fiction.

Comments: Accepts queries but no unsolicited manuscripts. Usually not interested in unpublished writers. Also has offices in the United States and has more than 20 sub-agents worldwide. The company currently represents 200 authors and illustrators across Canada and around the world. Review the website for further guidelines and submission information.

Westwood Creative Artists
94 Harbord Street, Toronto, ON M5S 1G6
Phone: (416) 964-3302 Fax: (416) 975-9209
E-mail: wca_office@wcaltd.com
Website: www.wcaltd.com

Subject interests: Literary fiction and non-fiction, YA, and some children's books. No poetry or screenplays.

Comments: Will consider unpublished writers. Please query before sending an unsolicited manuscript. No evaluation or handling fees. "We do not accept e-mail queries or submissions."

Woolf & Lapin
777 rue de Bellechasse, Suite 203, Montreal, QC H2S 1X7
Phone: (514) 726-2440 Fax: (514) 271-6291
E-mail: sdubreuil@woolflapin.com

Website: www.woolflapin.com

Contact: Stephan Dubreuil

Subject interests: English and French adult and children's fiction, historical and graphic novels, biography, and screenplays of all genres.

Comments: Send queries by e-mail only. No unsolicited manuscripts. Will consider unpublished writers. No evaluation or handling fees. "Your query letter should include a brief synopsis. We represent talent for the book publishing, motion picture, television, and new media industries."

7

WRITING AWARDS
& COMPETITIONS

This chapter surveys a broad range of the literary prizes and competitions open to Canadian writers. Most of the prizes and competitions may be applied for directly. Among a number of high-profile exceptions are the Charles Taylor Prize, conferred each year for an exemplary work of non-fiction, and the Journey Prize, sponsored by the Writers' Trust of Canada and McClelland & Stewart, for the best short fiction from Canada's literary journals. In some cases, the judges prefer to receive submissions from publishers, but usually, as long as the application criteria are met, individual applications are also accepted.

Please note that application deadlines and details are subject to change, and that the following entries do not include full eligibility criteria or entry conditions. Many awards, for instance, require the provision of several copies of the work so that it can be circulated among the nominating jury. Applicants should always obtain full guidelines before making a submission.

Canadian writers are also eligible for a range of overseas awards, and you'll find many of these listed in standard international reference books such as *Literary Market Place*. New Canadian awards are usually advertised in *Quill & Quire* and in some literary journals.

Acorn-Plantos Award
Jeff Seffinga, 36 Sunset Avenue, Hamilton, ON L8R 1V6
Phone: (905) 521-9196

E-mail: jeffseff@allstream.net
Deadline: June 30

A $500 prize and the People's Poet medal is awarded annually to a poet based on the best volume in the People's Poetry tradition published during the previous calendar year. Entry fee $25. May be entered by the poet or the publisher. Authors must be Canadian citizens or landed immigrants. No posthumous awards.

Acrostic Story Contest

The Brucedale Press, P.O. Box 2259, Port Elgin, ON N0H 2C0
Phone: (519) 832-6025
E-mail: brucedale@bmts.com
Website: www.bmts.com/~brucedale
Deadline: January 31

Alphabetically arranged, 26 sentences must tell a complete story. The opening phrase is set by the contest administrators and changes each year. Following sentences must begin with words in the sequence of the English alphabet. Any subject or theme is acceptable, and the stories should be original and unpublished. First prize 25% of entry fees, second prize 15% of entry fees, third prize 10% of entry fees. There may be up to 3 honourable mentions. Winning stories will be published in *The Leaf*. Entry fee $5/story. Annual.

The Multiple Sclerosis John Alexander Media Awards

Marketing and Communications Department, Multiple Sclerosis Society of Canada, 175 Bloor Street E., Suite 700, North Tower, Toronto, ON M4W 3R8
Phone: (416) 922-6065
E-mail: info@mssociety.ca
Website: www.mssociety.ca/en/awards.htm
Deadline: January 31

A $500 award is given annually to the author of the best English or French newspaper or magazine article (and another $500 to the creator of the best television or radio broadcast) about some aspect of multiple sclerosis.

The Antigonish Review Writing Contests

P.O. Box 5000, St. Francis Xavier University, Antigonish, NS B2G 2W5

Phone: (902) 867-3962
E-mail: tar@stfx.ca
Website: www.antigonishreview.com

Sheldon Currie Fiction Prize
Deadline: May 31

A first prize of $600, second prize of $400, and third prize of $200 are awarded for the best stories on any subject. Prizes also include publication in *The Antigonish Review*. Total entry not to exceed 20 pages (double-spaced). Entry fee $25 ($35 if outside North America), which includes a 1-year subscription. Send only original, unpublished material. Annual.

Great Blue Heron Poetry Contest
Deadline: June 30

A first prize of $600, second prize of $400, and third prize of $200 are awarded to the best poems on any subject matter. Prizes also include publication in *The Antigonish Review*. Total entry not to exceed 4 pages (maximum 150 lines), which may include 1 long poem or several shorter ones. Entry fee $25 ($35 if outside North America), which includes a 1-year subscription. Send only original, unpublished material. Annual.

Arc Poetry Contests and Prizes
P.O. Box 81060, Ottawa, ON KIP IBI
E-mail: arc@arcpoetry.ca
Website: www.arcpoetry.ca

Arc Poem of the Year Contest
Deadline: June 30

Grand prize of $5000 is awarded to the best poem. Entry fee is $23 for up to 2 unpublished poems (maximum 100 lines each), plus $5 per additional poem. Entry fee includes a 1-year subscription to *Arc*. Annual. Full guidelines on website.

Diana Brebner Prize
Deadline: October 1

A $500 award for National Capital Region poets who have not been published in book form. Length of poem not to exceed 30 lines. Entry fee $14 for up to 2 poems, which includes a 1-year sub-scription to *Arc*. Annual.

Confederation Poets Prize

Honouring Archibald Lampman, William Wilfred Campbell, and Duncan Campbell-Scott. A prize of $250 is awarded for the best poem published in Arc in the previous calendar year. All poems published in *Arc* are automatically entered. Annual.

Critic's Desk Award

Honours excellence in reviewing books of poetry. A prize of $250 is given annually for a feature review and a prize of $100 for a brief review that has been published in *Arc* in the previous calendar year. Reviews are automatically entered for this award.

Archibald Lampman Award

Deadline: March 31

Named in honour of the 19th-century Confederation poet Archibald Lampman, this $1,500 award recognizes an outstanding book of English-language poetry by an author living in the Ottawa area. Books must have been published between January and December of the previous year and have no fewer than 48 pages.

Ascent Aspirations Magazine Anthology Contests

David Fraser, Ascent Aspirations Publishing, 1560 Arbutus Drive, Nanoose Bay, BC V9P 9C8

Phone: (250) 468-7313

E-mail: ascentaspirations@shaw.ca

Website: www.ascentaspirations.ca

Ascent Aspirations publishes anthologies comprising the best sub-missions to their contests. The anthology consists of poetry and flash fiction: first prize for poetry and fiction $100, second prize $50, third prize $25, and each prize winner receives 1 copy of the anthology. In addition, 6 honourable mentions receive $10 each and 1 copy of the anthology. The anthology is approximately 120 to 130 pages with a colour cover featuring original artwork.

Poems and flash fiction may have been published elsewhere. Maximum length for poems is 60 lines. Entry fees $5 for 1 poem or $10 for 3 poems. Maximum length for flash fiction is 800 words. Entry fee $10/story. See website for submissions details and deadlines.

Atlantic Journalism Awards

Bill Skerret, coordinator, 1723 Holis Street, Halifax, NS B3J 1V9
Phone: (902) 425-2727
E-mail: office@ajas.ca
Website: www.ajas.ca
Deadline: end of January

Framed certificates are awarded to the winners in 23 categories. Only print and broadcast journalists working in the Atlantic region are eligible. Entry fee $50. Annual.

Atlantic Poetry Prize. *See* Writers' Federation of Nova Scotia Awards.

Atlantic Writing Competition for Unpublished Manuscripts. *See* Writers' Federation of Nova Scotia Awards.

Prix Aurora Awards

Clint Budd, chair
Phone: (604) 886-0723
E-mail: info@prixaurorawards.ca
Website: www.prixaurorawards.ca
Deadline: dates vary (check website)

A handcrafted trophy by Alberta artist Frank Johnson is awarded for the best work in 3 categories of writing in English. Annual.

Best Long-Form Work in English

Awarded for the best science-fiction or fantasy novel or fiction collection by a Canadian writer released in Canada in the previous calendar year.

Best Short-Form Work in English

Awarded for the best science-fiction or fantasy novella, novelette, short story, or poem by a Canadian writer released in Canada in the previous calendar year.

Best Work in English – Other
Awarded for the best piece of science-fiction or fantasy writing by a Canadian not encompassed by the previous 2 categories; for example, critical writing, media presentations, anthologies, magazines, or translation into English.

The Alfred G. Bailey Prize. *See* **Writers' Federation of New Brunswick Literary Competition.**

Marilyn Baillie Picture Book Award. *See* **Canadian Children's Book Centre Awards.**

Bancroft Award. *See* **the Royal Society of Canada Awards.**

Banff Mountain Book Competition
P.O. Box 1020, 107 Tunnel Mountain Drive, Banff, AB TIL IH5
Phone: (403) 762-6347 Fax: (403) 762-6277
E-mail: banffmountainbooks@banffcentre.ca
Website: www.banffmountainfestivals.ca
Deadline: June 30
Over $5,000 will be awarded to books in the following categories: mountain and wilderness literature, mountain guide, mountain image, and adventure travel. Presented in conjunction with the Banff Mountain Book Festival. Annual.

B.C. Book Prizes
West Coast Book Prize Society, 207 W. Hastings Street, Suite 901, Vancouver, BC V6B IH7
Phone: (604) 687-2405 Fax: (604) 687-2435
E-mail: info@bcbookprizes.ca
Website: www.bcbookprizes.ca
Deadline: December 1 (exception: Lieutenant Governor's Award for Literary Excellence)

Bill Duthie Booksellers' Choice Award
A $2,000 prize is awarded annually to the originating publisher and author of the best book in terms of public appeal, initiative, design, production, and content. The publisher must have its head office in B.C. or the Yukon, and the creative control in terms of

editing, design, and production must have been within B.C. or the Yukon. The membership of the B.C. Booksellers' Association determines the winner by ballot.

Sheila A. Egoff Children's Literature Prize

A $2,000 prize is awarded annually to the author of the best novel for juveniles and young adults, and the best non-fiction book for children (including biography) that have not been highly illustrated. The author must be a B.C. or Yukon resident or have lived in B.C. or the Yukon for 3 of the past 5 years. The book may have been published anywhere.

Hubert Evans Non-Fiction Prize

A $2,000 prize is awarded annually to the author of the best original non-fiction literary work (philosophy, belles lettres, biography, history, etc.). Quality of research and writing, insight, and originality are major considerations in the judging of this prize. The author must be a B.C. or Yukon resident or have lived in B.C. or the Yukon for 3 of the past 5 years. The book may have been published anywhere.

Roderick Haig-Brown Regional Prize

A $2,000 prize is awarded annually to the author of the book that contributes most to the enjoyment and understanding of B.C. The book may deal with any aspect of the province (people, history, geography, oceanography, etc.) and must be original. Reprints, revised editions, guide books, and how-to books are not considered. The book may have been published anywhere, and the author may reside outside B.C.

Christie Harris Illustrated Children's Literature Prize

An annual $2,000 prize is shared by the author and illustrator of the best children's picture book, picture storybook, or illustrated non-fiction book. The author and/or illustrator must be a B.C. or Yukon resident or have lived in B.C. or the Yukon for 3 of the past 5 years. The book may have been published anywhere.

Lieutenant Governor's Award for Literary Excellence

A $5,000 prize is awarded annually to honour late-career authors for their entire body of work. Established in 2003 by the

Honourable Iona Campagnolo to recognize British Columbia writers who have contributed to the development of literary excellence in the province.

Dorothy Livesay Poetry Prize

A $2,000 prize is awarded annually to the author of the best work of poetry. The author must be a B.C. or Yukon resident or have lived in B.C. or the Yukon for 3 of the past 5 years. No anthologies or "best of" collections. The book may have been published anywhere.

Ethel Wilson Fiction Prize

A $2,000 prize is awarded annually to the author of the best work of fiction. The author must be a B.C. or Yukon resident or have lived in B.C. or the Yukon for 3 of the past 5 years. No anthologies.

The B.C. Lieutenant-Governor's Medal for Historical Writing

Bill Morrison, chair of the BCHF Book Competition, B.C.
   Historical Federation
E-mail: writing@bchistory.ca
Website: http://bchistory.ca/awards/book/index.html
Deadline: December 31. Entries are accepted beginning October 1.

Awarded to the writer whose book contributes most significantly to the recorded history of British Columbia. Any new book presenting any facet of B.C. history is eligible. Judges look for appropriate illustrations, careful proofreading, and an adequate index, table of contents, and bibliography. The prizes are $1,000, $500, and $250, plus an invitation to the awards banquet. Books must be submitted in their year of publication. Annual.

The Pierre Berton Award

Canada's History, Bryce Hall, Main Floor, 515 Portage Ave,
   Winnipeg, MB R3B 2E9
Phone: 1-866-952-3444 Fax: (204) 988-9309
E-mail: prixbertonawards@canadashistory.ca
Website: www.canadashistory.ca
Deadline: April 27

Celebrates those who have brought Canadian history to a wider audience. Canada's National History Society established this award in 1994 for distinguished achievement in presenting Canadian history in an informative and engaging manner. Canadian writer and popular historian Pierre Berton was the first recipient and agreed to lend his name to future awards. The award continues to honour those who, like the award's namesake, have introduced Canadian characters and events of the past to the national and international public. Eligible nominees are individuals or organizations that have helped popularize Canadian history with the written word through such means as publications, film, radio, television, theatre, or the web. The recipient(s) will receive a medal and a $5,000 cash prize. Annual.

Bill Duthie Booksellers' Choice Award. *See* **B.C. Book Prizes.**

Geoffrey Bilson Award for Historical Fiction for Young People. *See* **Canadian Children's Book Centre Awards.**

Earle Birney Prize for Poetry. *See* **PRISM international Writing Prizes.**

BMO Winterset Award
Reg Winsor, Executive Director, Newfoundland and Labrador Arts
    Council, 1 Springdale Street, P.O. Box 98, St. John's, NL A1C 5H5
Phone: (709) 726-2212 or 1-866-726-2212 Fax: (709) 726-0619
E-mail: rwinsor@nlac.ca
Website: www.nlac.ca/awards/winterset.htm
Deadline: December 31
    The Winterset Award is awarded to an outstanding literary work in any writing genre (fiction, non-fiction, poetry, published drama), regardless of the subject matter. The overriding consideration will be excellence in writing by Newfoundlanders and Labradorians as determined by the jury. Sponsored by the BMO Financial Group and the Sandra Fraser Gwyn Foundation, and administered by the Newfoundland and Labrador Arts Council. One prize of $10,000 and 2 prizes of $2,500 will be awarded. Annual.
    Published literary works, written either by a native-born Newfoundlander and Labradorian or by a resident of the province (residency is defined as having lived in Newfoundland and Labrador

for 12 months at the time of submission of the work) are eligible for consideration. Works must have been published in the calendar year for which the award is being considered. Both emerging and established writers will be considered. Submissions must be made by the publisher.

CAA Carol Bolt Award for Drama. *See* **Canadian Authors Association Literary Awards.**

Joseph Brant Award. *See* **Ontario Historical Society Awards for Authors.**

Diana Brebner Prize. *See* **Arc Poetry Contests and Prizes.**

Ann Connor Brimer Award for Children's Literature. *See* **Writers' Federation of Nova Scotia Awards.**

John Bullen Prize. *See* **Canadian Historical Association Awards.**

Burnaby Writers' Society Competition

Eileen Kernaghan, Burnaby Writers' Society, 6584 Deer Lake Avenue, Burnaby, BC V5G 3T7
Phone: (604) 522-1811
E-mail: info@bws.bc.ca
Website: www.bws.bc.ca
Deadline: May 31

Annual cash prizes of $200, $100, and $50 are given to the top 3 entries in the competition. Categories and themes change from year to year. Open to B.C. residents only. Entry fee $5. Write for guidelines.

Canada-Japan Literary Awards

Luiza Pereira, program officer, Endowments and Prizes, Canada Council for the Arts, P.O. Box 1047, 350 Albert Street, Ottawa, ON KIP 5V8
Phone: (613) 566-4414, ext. 4086 or 1-800-263-5588 Fax: (613) 566-4430
E-mail: luiza.pereira@canadacouncil.ca
Website: www.canadacouncil.ca

Two cash prizes of $10,000 are usually awarded every 2 years for outstanding books of fiction, non-fiction, drama, or poetry about Japan or on Japanese themes by Canadian authors or for translations of Japanese books into French or English. Only publishers of eligible books may nominate titles for this award.

Canadian Authors Association Literary Awards
P.O. Box 581, Stn. Main, Orillia, ON L3V 6K5
Phone: (705) 653-0323 or 1-866-216-6222
E-mail: admin@canauthors.org
Website: www.canauthors.org/awards

CAA Emerging Writer Award
Deadline: March 31

A prize of $500, a silver medal, 1-year membership in the Canadian Authors Association, and travel to and from the CAA conference is awarded for the Canadian or landed immigrant under age 30 deemed to show the most promise in the field of literary creation. No entry fee. Annual.

CAA Lela Common Award for Canadian History
Deadline: December 15

A prize of $2,500 for the best work of historical non-fiction on a Canadian topic written in English by a Canadian author. Entry fee $35. Annual.

CAA Award for Fiction
Deadline: December 15

A prize of $2,500 and a sterling-silver medal is awarded in recognition of the year's outstanding full-length novel by a Canadian writer. Entries should manifest "literary excellence without sacrifice of popular appeal." Nominations from the author, publisher, an individual, or group are eligible. Entry fee $35. Annual.

CAA Poetry Award
Deadline: December 15

A prize of $1,000 and a sterling-silver medal is awarded in recognition of the year's outstanding book of poetry by a Canadian writer. Entries should manifest "literary excellence without sacrifice of popular appeal." Nominations from author, publisher, individual, or group are eligible. Entry fee $35. Annual.

Canadian Booksellers Association Libris Awards

Emily Sinkins, general manager, 1255 Bay Street, Suite 902,
    Toronto, ON M5R 2A9
Phone: (416) 467-7883 or toll-free 1-866-788-0790 Fax: (416)
    467-7886
E-mail: enquiries@cbabook.org
Website: www.cbabook.org

Author of the Year Award
Deadline: June 1

A trophy is awarded to the Canadian author of an outstanding literary work that contributes to Canadian culture and combines readability with strong sales. A call for nominations is sent to members of the book community. The shortlist comprises the 3 candidates with the most nominations.

Children's Picture Book Of The Year
Deadline: June 1

For a Canadian picture book from the previous year whose imaginative storyline and creative visuals engaged, entertained, and delighted young children while generating customer attention and strong sales. A call for nominations is sent to members of the book community. The shortlist comprises the 3 candidates with the most nominations.

Fiction Book of the Year Award
Deadline: June 1

A trophy is awarded for a Canadian work of fiction that had an outstanding impact on the Canadian bookselling industry, created wide media attention, brought people into bookstores, and had strong sales. A call for nominations is sent to members of the book community. The shortlist comprises the 3 candidates with the most nominations.

Non-Fiction Book of the Year Award
Deadline: June 1

A trophy is awarded for a Canadian work of non-fiction that had an outstanding impact on the Canadian bookselling industry, created wide media attention, brought people into bookstores, and had strong sales. A call for nominations is sent to members of the book community. The shortlist comprises the 3 candidates with the most nominations.

Young Readers' Book of the Year
Deadline: June 1

For an outstanding Canadian literary work for young readers in the previous year that combines readability with strong sales – a book that captivated its intended reading audience with skillful, inventive, and gripping storytelling. A call for nominations is sent to members of the book community. The shortlist comprises the 3 candidates with the most nominations.

Canadian Children's Book Centre Awards

Meghan Howe, 40 Orchard View Boulevard, Suite 217, Toronto,
ON M4R IB9
Phone: (416) 975-0010 Fax: (416) 975-8970
E-mail: info@bookcentre.ca
Website: www.bookcentre.ca

Marilyn Baillie Picture Book Award
Deadline: early December

A $20,000 prize is awarded to an outstanding picture book in which the author and the illustrator achieve artistic and literary unity. Should be aimed at children ages 3 to 8. To be eligible, it must be an original work in English, written and illustrated by Canadian citizens or landed immigrants, and first published in Canada. Genres include fiction, non-fiction, and poetry. Annual. The winner is chosen by a jury appointed by the CCBC.

Geoffrey Bilson Award for Historical Fiction for Young People
Deadline: early December

An annual prize of $5,000 is awarded to the author of an outstanding work of historical fiction for young people. The author must be a Canadian citizen or a landed immigrant. The winner is chosen by a jury appointed by the CCBC. Annual.

John Spray Mystery Award
Deadline: early December

The prize honours excellence in the mystery book genre. The prize is awarded annually with a cash prize of $5,000. The book must be an original work in English, intended for readers 8 to 16, and written by a Canadian citizen or landed immigrant. A mystery book can be a thriller, a crime novel or a whodunit. The winner is chosen by a jury appointed by the CCBC. Annual.

Monica Hughes Award for Science Fiction and Fantasy
Deadline: early December

Established in 2011, this award honours excellence in science fiction and fantasy writing for children and adolescents. The prize is awarded annually with a cash prize of $5,000. The author must be a Canadian citizen or a landed immigrant. The winner is chosen by a jury appointed by the CCBC. Annual.

Norma Fleck Award for a Canadian Children's Non-Fiction Book
Deadline: early December

A $10,000 prize is awarded to the author of the best children's non-fiction book. The text must be of exceptional quality and present the subject matter in a way that both informs and excites interest.

Visuals, also of exceptional quality, should clarify, extend, and complement the text. Only books written and illustrated by Canadian citizens or landed immigrants will be considered. Annual. The winner is chosen by a jury appointed by the CCBC.

TD Canadian Children's Literature Award
Deadline: early December

Two grand prizes of $25,000 each are awarded for the most distinguished book written in English and for the most distinguished book written in French. In addition, there is a total of $20,000 for honour book winners, with a maximum of 4 books on the honour list in each language category. All books in any genre written by a Canadian citizen or a landed immigrant for children ages 1 through

12 will be eligible. In the case of a picture book, both the author and illustrator must be Canadian citizens/landed immigrants and the cash prize will be equally divided between them. Only books first published in Canada will be considered. Annual. The winner is chosen by 2 juries chosen by the CCBC.

Canadian Ethnic Media Association Awards

Mr. Dat Nguyen, 24 Tarlton Road, Toronto, ON M5P 2M4
Phone: (416) 764-3081 Fax: (416) 764-3245
E-mail: datnguyen@webnewsprinting.com
Website: www.canadianethnicmedia.com
Deadline: March 31

Annual prizes of a plaque and free tickets to the awards event are presented to the best working journalists in ethnic print, radio, television, and Internet, or to mainstream journalists writing on subjects concerning Canada's diversity. Awards are given for the best news or feature story and for the best editorial or opinion piece in 4 categories: print, radio, television, and Internet magazine. Annual.

Canadian Farm Writer's Federation Annual Writers Award

Christina Franc, Awards Administrator, Quanglo, P.O. Box 250,
  Ormstown, QC J0S 1K0
Phone: 1-877-782-6456, ext. 706
E-mail: office@cfwf.ca
Website: www.cfwf.ca
Deadline: early summer (check website for details)

Annual award for stories from general periodicals, news releases, technical features, press features, editorials, columns, and daily, weekly, and monthly press reports. Writing must be about production agriculture. For each category: first prize $300, second $200, and third $100. Entry fee is $20 for members, $30 for non-members. Winners announced at annual CFWF conference in early fall.

Canadian Historical Association Awards and Prizes

Michel Duquet, 130 Albert Street, Suite 501, Ottawa, ON
  K1P 5G4
Phone: (613) 233-7885 Fax: (613) 567-3110
E-mail: cha-shc@cha-shc.ca
Website: www.cha-shc.ca

John Bullen Prize
Deadline: December 31
A prize of $500 is awarded for the best doctoral historical dissertation written by a Canadian citizen or landed immigrant.

The Clio Awards
Deadline: December 31
Annual awards given for meritorious publications or for exceptional contributions by individuals or organizations to regional history.

The Wallace K. Ferguson Prize
Deadline: December 31
A $1,000 prize is awarded annually to a Canadian citizen or landed immigrant who has published an outstanding scholarly book in a field of history other than Canadian history.

The Eugene A. Forsey Prize
Deadline: June 1
Prizes are awarded annually for the best undergraduate essay, or the equivalent, and the best graduate thesis completed in the past 3 years on Canadian labour and working-class history.

Sir John A. Macdonald Prize
Deadline: December 31
A prize of $1,000 is awarded in recognition of the non-fiction work of Canadian history judged to have made the most significant contribution to an understanding of Canada's past. Annual.

The Hilda Neatby Prize in Women's History
Deadline: February 1
Awarded for an academic article (one in English and the other in French), published in a Canadian journal or book during the previous year, deemed to have made an original and scholarly contribution to the field of women's history and gender history as it relates to women. Annual.

The Journal of the Canadian Historical Association Prize
Awarded annually to the best article published in the printed version of the journal.

The Online Journal of the Canadian Historical Association Prize
Awarded annually to the best article submitted to the online version of the journal.

Prize for Best Article on the History of Sexuality in Canada
Canadian Committee on the History of Sexuality, c/o Steven
Maynard, Department of History, Queen's University,
Kingston, ON K7L 3N6
Deadline: February 1
An award designed to recognize excellence in, and encourage the growth of, scholarly work in the history of sexuality in Canada. The winning article will be one that makes an original contribution in this field. Articles must be previously published and written in either English or French. Awarded every 2 years.

Canadian Library Association Book Awards
Valerie Delrue, CLA Membership Services, 328 Frank Street,
Ottawa, ON K2P 0X8
Phone: (613) 232-9625, ext. 301 Fax: (613) 563-9895
E-mail: info@cla.ca
Website: www.cla.ca
Deadline for all awards: December 31 annually

Book of the Year for Children Award
Presented to the author of an outstanding book suitable for children up to the age of 12 published in Canada during the previous calendar year. Any creative work (fiction, poetry, anthologies, etc.) will be deemed eligible. Author must be a Canadian citizen or permanent resident. Nominations invited from CLA members and publishers. Check website for full submission guidelines.

Amelia Frances Howard-Gibbon Illustrator's Award
Presented to an outstanding illustrator of a children's book suitable for children up to the age of 12 published in Canada during

the previous calendar year. To be eligible for this award, an illustrator must be a Canadian citizen or a permanent resident of Canada, and the illustrations of the book must be worthy of the text. Check website for full submission guidelines.

Young Adult Canadian Book Award

This award recognizes the author of an outstanding English-language book written in the preceding calendar year that appeals to young adults between the ages of 13 and 18. The book must be a work of fiction published in Canada, and the author a Canadian citizen or landed immigrant. Check website for full submission guidelines.

Canadian Political Science Association Prizes

260 Dalhousie Street, Suite 204, Ottawa, ON K1N 7E4
Phone: (613) 562-1202 Fax: (613) 241-0019
E-mail: cpsa-acsp@cpsa-acsp.ca
Website: www.cpsa-acsp.ca

C. B. Macpherson Prize
Deadline: December

A commemorative plaque is presented to the author of the best book published in English or French in the field of political theory. No textbooks, edited texts, collections of essays, or multiple-authored works will be considered. Books must have been published in the previous 2 years. The author must be a Canadian citizen or permanent resident. Biannual.

CPSA Prize in Comparative Politics
Deadline: December

A commemorative plaque is awarded to the best book published, in English or in French, in the field of comparative politics. Books must have been published in the previous 2 years. The author must be a Canadian citizen or permanent resident. Biannual.

CPSA Prize in International Relations
Deadline: December

A commemorative plaque is awarded to the best book published, in English or in French, in the field of international relations. Books must have been published in the previous 2 years. The author must be a Canadian citizen or permanent resident. Biannual.

Donald Smiley Prize
Deadline: December
A commemorative plaque will be given to the author of the best book, published in English or French, in a field relating to the study of government and politics in Canada. Books must have been published in the previous year. The author must be a Canadian citizen or permanent resident. Biannual.

Canadian Writer's Journal Short Fiction Contest
P.O. Box 1178, New Liskeard, ON P0J 1P0
Phone: (705) 647-5424 or toll-free 1-800-258-5451 Fax: (705) 647-8366
E-mail: cwj@cwj.ca
Website: www.cwj.ca
Deadline: April 30
The writers of the best short fiction receive awards of $150, $100, and $50, and publication in *Canadian Writer's Journal* and in a chapbook entitled *Choice Works*. Entries must be original, unpublished stories in any genre to a maximum length of 2,500 words. Entrants must be Canadian citizens or permanent residents. Entry fee $10/story.

Bliss Carman Poetry Award. *See* **Prairie Fire Writing Contests.**

Canada Writes / CBC Literary Awards
c/o CBC Radio, P.O. Box 6000, Montreal, QC H3C 3A8
E-mail: canadawrites@cbc.ca
Website: www.cbc.ca/canadawrites

CBC Short Story Prize / Deadline: November 1
CBC Creative Nonfiction Prize / Deadline: February 1
CBC Poetry Prize / Deadline: May 1
The CBC Literary Prizes are the flagship competitions of Canada Writes. Formerly the CBC Literary Awards, the CBC Literary Prizes (presented in partnership with Canada Council for the Arts,

enRoute magazine, and the Banff Centre) are now made up of 3 separate competitions that take place throughout the year.

The CBC Literary Prizes recognize the best in original, unpublished writing by Canadians. Canada Council for the Arts awards the first-place winner of each prize $6,000 and each of the 4 finalists $1,000. The first-prize winner will be published in *enRoute* magazine and online on Canada Writes as well as broadcast on CBC Radio. They will also be awarded a 2-week residency at The Banff Centre's Leighton Artists' Colony.

Chocolate Lily Book Awards
Harmina Jansen, 8898 – 156 Street, Surrey, BC V3R 4K8
E-mail: ahjansen@shaw.ca
Website: www.chocolatelilyawards.com
Deadline: January 31

Through an annual non-profit literacy program, grade school students in British Columbia read books nominated for the Chocolate Lily Book Awards – the best fiction by B.C. children's authors and illustrators – and vote for their favourite. In June each year, an award is presented for the novel and picture book that receive the most student votes.

Nominated books are selected by a panel of teachers, librarians, and authors. There are 2 categories: best picture book (for kindergarten to grade 3) and best chapter book/novel (for grades 4 to 8). Authors must reside part- or full-time in British Columbia and the books must have been published in the previous year.

The City of Calgary W. O. Mitchell Book Prize. *See* Writers Guild of Alberta Awards.

The City of Edmonton Book Prize. *See* Writers Guild of Alberta Awards.

City of Toronto Book Awards
Toronto Protocol, City Clerk's Office, 2nd Floor, West Tower, City Hall, Toronto, ON M5H 2N2
Phone: (416) 392-8191
E-mail: protocol@toronto.ca
Website: www.toronto.ca/book_awards

Deadline: end of March

Each year prize money totaling $15,000 is apportioned in recognition of works of literary merit in all genres that are evocative of Toronto. Fiction and non-fiction published in English for adults and/or children are eligible. Each shortlisted author receives $1,000, the balance going to the winner. No residency requirements. Reprints, textbooks, and manuscripts are not eligible.

City of Vancouver Book Award

Marnie Rice, Cultural Services Department, City of Vancouver,
    111 W. Hastings Street, Suite 501, Vancouver, BC V6B 1H4
Phone: (604) 871-6634 Fax: (604) 871-6005
E-mail: marnie.rice@vancouver.ca
Website: http://vancouver.ca/commsvcs/cultural/gasp/awards/book/
Deadline: mid-May

An annual $2,000 cash prize is awarded in October to recognize books for their excellence and their contribution to an appreciation and understanding of Vancouver, its history, and the achievements of its residents. Entered books must be primarily set in or about Vancouver (though the author's place of residence is not restricted), and the book may have been written/published anywhere in the world. Books may be fiction, non-fiction, poetry, or drama, written for children or adults, and may deal with any aspect of the city, including its history, geography, current affairs, or the arts. See website for guidelines.

City of Victoria Book Prizes

Mary Virtue, president, Victoria Book Prize Society, 78 Linden
    Avenue, Victoria, BC V8V 4C8
Phone: (250) 386-5933
E-mail: info@victoriabookprizes.ca
Website: www.victoriabookprizes.ca

Bolen Books Children's Book Prize
Deadline: May 29

A $5,000 prize is awarded to the author/illustrator of the best book published in the area of books for youth. The author or illustrator must have been a resident in Greater Victoria for the previous

2 years and must be either a Canadian citizen or permanent resident. Self-published books will not be considered. Annual.

Butler Book Prize
Deadline: May 29

This $5,000 prize is awarded to a local author for the best book published in the preceding year in the categories of poetry, non-fiction, and fiction. Writers must have been residents in Greater Victoria for the previous 2 years and must be either a Canadian citizen or permanent resident. Bibliographies, cookbooks, travel guides, exhibition catalogues, instruction manuals, self-help books, scholarly books, textbooks, reference books, chapbooks, and self-published books are ineligible. Annual.

The Claremont Review Annual Writing Contests
4980 Wesley Road, Victoria, BC V8Y 1Y9
Phone: (250) 658-5221 Fax: (250) 658-5387
Website: www.theclaremontreview.ca

Fiction Contest
Deadline: March 15

First prize $500, second prize $300, and third prize $200 for the best work of fiction by a writer aged 13 to 19. Winning entries will be published in *The Claremont Review* and on the abebooks.com website. Entry fee $18 for 1 category and $20 for both. Each entrant receives a 1-year subscription to *The Claremont Review*.

Poetry Contest
Deadline: March 15

First prize $500, second prize $300, and third prize $200 for the best poem by a writer aged 13 to 19. Entry fee $18 for 1 category and $20 for both. Each entrant receives a 1-year subscription to *The Claremont Review*.

The Clio Awards. *See* Canadian Historical Association Awards.

Matt Cohen Award: In Celebration of a Writing Life. *See* the Writers' Trust of Canada Awards.

Shaughnessy Cohen Prize for Political Writing. *See* the Writers' Trust of Canada Awards.

The Winston Collins/Descant Prize for Best Canadian Poem

Mark Laliberte, Managing Editor, Descant, P.O. Box 314, Stn. P, Toronto, ON M5S 2S8

Phone: (416) 593-2557 Fax: (416) 593-9362

E-mail: info@descant.ca

Website: www.descant.ca/contest.html

Deadline: October (check website for exact date)

Awarded in memory of Winston Collins, writer and enthusiastic teacher of literature at the universities of Cincinnati, Princeton, and Toronto. The prize perpetuates his remarkable talent for encouraging self-expression through writing. First prize is $1,000 plus payment for publication in *Descant*. Two honourable mentions will receive $250 plus payment for publication in *Descant*. Applicants must be Canadian citizens or landed immigrants. Maximum length of poems is 100 lines. Previously published material is not accepted. Entry fee $30, which includes a 1-year subscription to *Descant*. Annual.

CAA Lela Common Award for Canadian History. *See* Canadian Authors Association Literary Awards.

Confederation Poets Prize. *See* Arc Poetry Contests and Prizes.

Contemporary Verse 2 Literary Contests

Clarise Foster, 100 Arthur Street, Suite 207, Winnipeg, MB R3B 1H3

Phone: (204) 949-1365 Fax: (204) 942-5754

E-mail: cv2@mts.net

Website: www.contemporaryverse2.ca

CV2 sponsors the 2-Day Poem Contest in the spring. Awards are $300 for first prize, $150 for second, and $75 for third. Each winner also receives a 1-year subscription to the magazine, and the first- and second-prize winners are published as part of the award. Guidelines and themes are available on the website.

Show Me the Book
Deadline: April 30

Biannual national poetry competition created by *Contemporary Verse 2* and The Muses' Company (the poetry imprint of J. Gordon Shillingford Publishing). Grand prize is a book publication contract with The Muses' Company, a feature interview, a poetry selection published in *Contemporary Verse 2*, a cash prize of $400, and a silver medallion. Second prize is $300, a feature interview, and a selection of poetry published in *Contemporary Verse 2*. Third prize is $200 and a selection of poetry published in *Contemporary Verse 2*. In addition, all winners will receive paid publication. Entry fee is $24 and includes a subscription to *Contemporary Verse 2*.

Donald Grant Creighton Award. *See* **Ontario Historical Society Awards for Authors.**

Critic's Desk Award. *See* **Arc Poetry Contests and Prizes.**

Sheldon Currie Fiction Prize. *See* **the Antigonish Review Writing Contests.**

Dafoe Book Prize
James Fergusson, Honorary Secretary, J. W. Dafoe Foundation, 359 University College, University of Manitoba, Winnipeg, MB R3T 2M8
Phone: (204) 474-6606 Fax: (204) 474-7645
E-mail: ferguss@cc.umanitoba.ca
Deadline: early December

A $10,000 prize is awarded annually for distinguished writing by a Canadian or resident of Canada that contributes to the understanding of Canada, Canadians, and/or Canada's place in the world. Books published in the previous calendar year are eligible.

Dartmouth Book Awards
Heather MacKenzie, Halifax Public Libraries, 60 Alderney Drive, Dartmouth, NS B2Y 4P8

Phone: (902) 490-5991 Fax: (902) 490-5889
E-mail: mackenh@halifaxpubliclibraries.ca
Website: www.halifax.ca/bookawards
Deadline: December 4

Two prizes of $1,500 each are awarded to honour the adult fiction and non-fiction books that have contributed most to the enjoyment and understanding of the cultural heritage of Nova Scotia. The winning titles best celebrate the spirit of Nova Scotia and its people. Open to any Canadian citizen or landed immigrant. Submission fee $10. The awards are presented at the Atlantic Writing Awards ceremony in the spring of each year. Annual.

The Margaret and John Savage First Book Award
Deadline: December 4

A prize of $1,500 is awarded annually to the best first published book (adult fiction or non-fiction) by an Atlantic Canadian author. Author must be resident in Atlantic Canada at the time of nomination; children's books are not eligible.

The Donner Prize
Prize Manager, The Donner Prize, 400 Logan Avenue, Toronto,
   ON M4N 2N9
Phone: (416) 368-8253
E-mail: sherry@mdgassociates.com
Website: www.donnerbookprize.com
Deadline: November 30

An annual award of $50,000 is awarded for the best public policy book by a Canadian, with prizes of $7,500 each to the other finalists. The jury is looking for provocative, readable, and inspiring books on public policy by a Canadian that cover a broad spectrum of issues, including health care, social issues, educational reform, public finance, environment, regulatory and legal reform, urban affairs, youth issues, and social policy. The author must be Canadian, and the publisher of the book must be either Canadian or American.

Sheila A. Egoff Children's Literature Prize. *See* **B.C. Book Prizes.**

Arthur Ellis Awards

Melodie Campbell, general manager, Crime Writers of Canada,
  240 Westwood Road, Suite 4C, Guelph, ON N1H 7W9
Phone: (905)582-0967
E-mail: info@crimewriterscanada.com
Website: www.crimewriterscanada.com
Deadline: December 15

Established 1984 and named after the *nom de travail* of Canada's official hangman. Prizes are awarded annually for works published for the first time in the preceding year in the following crime genre categories: best crime novel, best crime non-fiction, best first crime novel, best crime short story, best juvenile crime book, and best crime book in French. Cash prizes awarded depending on availability. Open to Canadian writers, including Canadians living abroad. Setting and imprint immaterial. Rules posted on website in early September. Check website for entry fees.

Unhanged Arthur Award: Arthur Ellis Award for Best Unpublished
  First Crime Novel

Open to any writer resident in Canada or a Canadian living abroad who has never had a novel published commercially. Winner receives a cash prize plus the opportunity of having the manuscript published.

Norma Epstein Award for Creative Writing: National
Literary Contest for University Students

Khamla Sengthavy, University College, 15 King's College Circle,
  Room A102, Toronto, ON M5S 3H7
Phone: (416) 978-8083 Fax: (416) 971-2806
E-mail: uc.programs@utoronto.ca
Website: www.utoronto.ca/ucwriting/epsteinnational.html
Deadline: May 1

Open to any student regularly enrolled in an undergraduate or graduate degree course at a Canadian university. A prize of $2,000 is available every other year for substantial work in each of these categories: fiction, drama, and verse.

Hubert Evans Non-Fiction Prize. *See* B.C. Book Prizes.

Event Creative Non-Fiction Contest
P.O. Box 2503, New Westminster, BC V3L 5B2
Phone: (604) 527-5293 Fax: (604) 527-5095
E-mail: event@douglascollege.ca
Website: www.eventmags.com
Deadline: mid-April (see website for exact date)

EVENT magazine's annual contest invites good writing that explores the creative non-fiction forms of personal narrative, essay, biography, documentary, and life and travel writing. $1,500 in prizes. Judges reserve the right to award either 2 prizes valued at $750 or 3 at $500. Winners will also be published in *EVENT*. Accepts previously unpublished submissions up to 5,000 words. Entry fee $34.95/submission, which includes a 1-year subscription to *EVENT*.

The Wallace K. Ferguson Prize. *See* **Canadian Historical Association Awards.**

The Fiddlehead Contests
Kathryn Taglia, managing editor, *The Fiddlehead*, Campus House, 11 Garland Court, University of New Brunswick, Fredericton, NB E3B 5A3
Phone: (506) 453-3501 Fax: (506) 453-5069
E-mail: fiddlehd@unb.ca
Website: www.thefiddlehead.ca/FHcontest.html
Deadline: December 1

Fiction Prize for Best Story
A prize of $2,000 is awarded, plus publication, for first place, and $250 each for 2 honourable mentions. Submissions to be no more than 6,000 words. No previously published stories are accepted. Entry fee $30, which includes a 1-year subscription to *The Fiddlehead*. Annual.

Ralph Gustafson Prize for Best Poem
A prize of $2,000 is awarded, plus publication, for first place, and $250 each for 2 honourable mentions. Submissions to be no more than 3 poems, a maximum of 100 lines/poem. No previously published poems are accepted. Entry fee $30, which includes a 1-year subscription to *The Fiddlehead*. Annual.

Finding the Right Words Flash Fiction Contest
Betty Dobson, 163 Main Avenue, Halifax, NS B3M 1B3
Phone: (902) 444-1615 Fax: (902) 444-1691
E-mail: contests@inkspotter.com
Website: http://inkspotter.com/contests.htm
Deadline: July 21
    A first prize of $60 and second prize of $30, plus publication in *InkSpotter News*, is awarded for fiction of 500 words or less on a new theme each year (check website). Entry fee $2. Annual.

The Sheree Fitch Prize. *See* **Writers' Federation of New Brunswick Literary Competition.**

The Norma Fleck Award for a Canadian Children's Non-Fiction Book. *See* **Canadian Children's Book Centre Awards.**

The Eugene A. Forsey Prize. *See* **the Canadian Historical Association Awards.**

Yves Fortier Earth Science Journalism Award. *See* **Science in Society Journalism Awards.**

Freefall's Fiction and Poetry Contests
Lynn C. Fraser, managing editor, *Freefall*, 922 – 9th Avenue S.E.,
    Calgary, AB T2G 0S4
Phone: (403) 590-7835
E-mail: freefallmagazine@yahoo.ca
Website: www.freefallmagazine.ca
Deadline: December 31
    Prizes of $300 for first place, $150 for second place, and $75 for third place are awarded for the fiction and poetry categories. Open to anyone. Maximum length for fiction is 3,000 words. May submit up to 5 poems, not to exceed 6 pages each. Entry fee for members of the Alexandra Writers' Centre Society is $10; non-members $21; additional entries $5. Annual. Entries can be submitted online.

Fresh Fish Award for Emerging Writers. *See* **Writers' Alliance of Newfoundland and Labrador Literary Awards.**

Mavis Gallant Prize for Non-Fiction. *See* **Quebec Writers' Federation Book Awards.**

The Lionel Gelber Prize

Prize manager, Munk Centre for International Studies, University
   of Toronto, 1 Devonshire Place, Toronto, ON M5S 3K7
Phone: (416) 946-8901 Fax: (416) 946-8915
E-mail: gelberprize.munk@utoronto.ca
Website: www.utoronto.ca/mcis/gelber
Deadline: October 31

A $15,000 prize is awarded to the best non-fiction book on inter-national affairs written in English or translated into English. Each submission should deal with significant issues in foreign relations. Priority is given to books that provide information to the general audience through new perspectives and analysis. Biographies, auto-biographies, and historical works are appropriate. Presented by the Lionel Gelber Foundation in partnership with the Munk Centre for International Studies at the University of Toronto and the Washington-based *Foreign Policy Magazine*. Annual.

The Giller Prize. *See* the Scotiabank Giller Prize.

John Glassco Translation Prize

Glassco Prize Committee, LTAC, LB, 601 Concordia University,
   1455 de Maisonneuve Boulevard W., Montréal QC H3G 1M8
Phone: (514) 848-2424 x8702
E-mail: info@attlc-ltac.org
Website: www.attlc-ltac.org/glasscoe.htm
Deadline for publication of entry: June 30

A $1,000 prize is awarded by the Literary Translators' Associa-tion of Canada for a translator's first book-length literary transla-tion into English or French published in Canada during the previous year. Eligible genres include fiction, non-fiction, drama, poetry, and children's literature. Entrants must be Canadian citi-zens or landed immigrants. Annual.

Danuta Gleed Literary Award. *See* **the Writers' Union of Canada Awards and Competitions.**

Government of Newfoundland and Labrador Arts and Letters Awards

P.O. Box 1854, St. John's, NL A1C 5P9
Phone: (709) 729-5253
Website: www.gov.nl.ca/artsandletters
Deadline: mid-February

Percy Janes First Novel Award

One prize of $1,500 is awarded for the best unpublished manuscript of at least 30,000 words. Entrants must be unpublished novelists who reside in Newfoundland and Labrador. One entry permitted per person.

Literary Arts Section Awards – Junior Division

Four prizes of $250 are awarded every year for ages 12 to 14 in 2 categories: poetry and prose. Six prizes of $250 are also awarded for ages 15 to 18 in the same categories. Entrants must be residents of Newfoundland and Labrador.

Literary Arts Section Awards – Senior Division

Prizes of $1,000 are awarded every year in recognition of outstanding original work in each of the following categories: 6 awards for poetry, 5 awards for short fiction (maximum 5,000 words), 3 awards for non-fiction prose (maximum 5,000 words), and 2 awards for dramatic script. Entrants must be residents of Newfoundland and Labrador. The awards are open to amateurs and professionals.

Governor General's Literary Awards

Diane Miljours, Writing and Publishing Section, Canada Council for the Arts, P.O. Box 1047, 350 Albert Street, Ottawa, ON K1P 5V8
Phone: (613) 566-4414, ext. 5573, or 1-800-263-5588 Fax: (613) 566-4410
E-mail: diane.miljours@canadacouncil.ca
Website: www.canadacouncil.ca
Deadlines: March 15, June 1, and August 7

Seven annual awards of $25,000 are conferred in recognition of the best books of the year in English and in French in the following categories: fiction, literary non-fiction, poetry, drama, children's literature (text), children's literature (illustration), and translation (from French to English and from English to French). In addition, the publishers of the winning titles receive a $3,000 grant for the promotion of the prize-winning books. Non-winning finalists each receive $1,000. Books must be first-edition trade books and be written, translated, or illustrated by Canadian citizens or permanent residents. For translations, the original work must also be written by a Canadian. Administered by the Canada Council for the Arts. Write for eligibility criteria and registration forms or consult the website.

John H. Gray Award for Short Nonfiction. *See* **Writers Guild of Alberta Literary Awards.**

Great Blue Heron Poetry Contest. *See* **the Antigonish Review Writing Contests.**

The Great Canadian Literary Hunt. *See* **This Magazine Great Canadian Literary Hunt.**

Dave Greber Freelance Writers Award
Shirley Dunn, award developer, 606 52 Avenue S.W., Calgary, AB
   T2V 0B4
Phone: 1-877-271-3283
E-mail: info@greberwritingaward.com
Website: www.greberwritingaward.com
Deadline: June (see website for exact date)
   Presented to a Canadian freelance writer who has a contract for publication of a non-fiction magazine article or book. "Projects that delve into issues associated with social justice, whether in the Canadian context or globally, are strongly encouraged." One $5,000 book award and one $2,000 magazine award are presented annually.

The Griffin Poetry Prize
Ruth Smith, manager, The Griffin Trust for Excellence in Poetry,
   363 Parkridge Crescent, Oakville, ON L6M 1A8
Phone: (905) 618-0420
E-mail: info@griffinpoetryprize.com
Website: www.griffinpoetryprize.com
Deadline: December 31

Two prizes of $65,000 are awarded annually in the categories of international and Canadian poetry. In each category, the prize will be for the best collection of poetry written in or translated into English published during the preceding year. Entries must be worldwide first editions and may only be submitted by publishers.

Ralph Gustafson Prize for Best Poem. *See* **the Fiddlehead Contests.**

Hackmatack Children's Choice Book Award
Kate Watson, P.O. Box 34055, Scotia Square RPO, Halifax, NS
  B3J 3S1
Phone: (902) 424-3774 Fax: (902) 424-0613
E-mail: hackmatack@hackmatack.ca
Website: www.hackmatack.ca
Deadline: October 1
A plaque is awarded annually for the best book in each of 3 categories – English fiction, English non-fiction, and French – written by a Canadian author for readers in grades 4 to 6. Books are chosen for their literary, cultural, and enjoyment factors, with an emphasis on Atlantic-authored materials. Children in reading groups vote for the nominees, who tour the region, giving readings to hundreds of children.

Roderick Haig-Brown Regional Prize. *See* **B.C. Book Prizes.**

Christie Harris Illustrated Children's Literature Prize. *See* **B.C. Book Prizes.**

Hibernating with Words. *See* **Pandora's Collective Poetry Contests.**

Hidden Brook Press Poetry Awards
109 Bayshore Road, R.R. #4, Brighton, ON K0K 1H0
Phone: (613) 475-2368
E-mail: writers@hiddenbrookpress.com
Website: www.hiddenbrookpress.com

The Open Window Poetry Anthology Contest
Deadline: November 1

Ten cash prizes from $10 to $100 plus 10 honourable mentions are awarded annually. Submit 5 poems, previously unpublished, of any style, theme, or length. Up to 300 poems will be published. Entry fee of $15 includes purchase of the resulting book.

Seeds International Poetry Chapbook Anthology Contest
Deadlines: April 1 and October 1

Cash prizes and honourable mentions are awarded twice a year. Submit 3 poems of any style, theme, or length. Up to 300 poems will be published. Entry fee of $12 includes purchase of the resulting book.

The John Hirsch Award for Most Promising Manitoba Writer. *See* **Manitoba Writing and Publishing Awards.**

K. M. Hunter Artists Awards
Awards Office, Ontario Arts Council, 151 Bloor Street W., 5th
   Floor, Toronto, ON M5S 1T6
Phone: (416) 969-7422 or 1-800-387-0058, ext. 7422 Fax: (416)
   961-7796
E-mail: mwarren@arts.on.ca
Website: www.arts.on.ca

Five awards of $8,000 each are given in the disciplines of visual arts, dance, literature, theatre, film and video, and music. Recipients are chosen from a selection of grant applications recommended by the Ontario Arts Council juries; in the case of writers, the shortlist comes from the OAC's Works in Progress program. Annual.

Innis-Gérin Medal. See the Royal Society of Canada Awards.

International 3-Day Novel Contest
P.O. Box 2106, Station Terminal, Vancouver, BC V6B 3T5
E-mail: info@3daynovel.com
Website: www.3daynovel.com
Deadline: Friday before Labour Day

Writers must pre-register, then write a novel over the 3-day Labour Day weekend. Research and brief outlines are permitted before the contest. The winner is published by 3-Day Books (with distribution by Arsenal Pulp Press). Cash and other prizes are offered to the runner-up and shortlist. Entry fee $50. Annual.

IODE Violet Downey Book Award. *See* **The National Chapter of Canada IODE Violet Downey Book Award.**

Alexander Kennedy Isbister Award for Non-Fiction. *See* **Manitoba Writing and Publishing Awards.**

Percy Janes First Novel Award. *See* **Government of Newfoundland and Labrador Arts and Letters Awards.**

Kisses and Popsicles Spring Poetry Contest. *See* **Pandora's Collective Poetry Contests.**

A. M. Klein Prize for Poetry. *See* **Quebec Writers' Federation Book Awards.**

The Kobzar Literary Award
Ukrainian Canadian Foundation of Taras Shevchenko, 952 Main
    Street, Suite 202, Winnipeg, MB R2W 3P4
Phone: (204) 944-9128 or 1-866-524-5314 Fax: (204) 944-9135
E-mail: lesia@shevchenkofoundation.ca
Website: www.shevchenkofoundation.ca
Deadline: March 15
    A $25,000 award ($20,000 to the author, $5,000 to the publisher) to recognize an outstanding contribution to Canadian literature with a Ukrainian-Canadian theme. Accepts literary non-fiction, fiction, children's literature, poetry, and drama in English, French, or Ukrainian. Awarded every 2 years.

Gerald Lampert Memorial Award. *See* **League of Canadian Poets Awards.**

Herb Lampert Student Writing Award. *See* **Science in Society Journalism Awards.**

Archibald Lampman Award. *See* **Arc Poetry Contests and Prizes.**

Fred Landon Award. *See* **Ontario Historical Society Awards for Authors.**

Lydia Langstaff Memorial Prize
Diane Walton, managing editor, *On Spec* Magazine, P.O. Box
    4727, Edmonton, AB T6E 5G8
Phone: (780) 413-0215 Fax: (780) 413-1538
E-mail: onspec@onspec.ca
Website: www.onspec.ca
Deadline: January 31
A prize of $100 and a certificate are awarded to an emerging Canadian writer under the age of 30 whose work has been published in *On Spec* during the preceding calendar year. The winner is selected by the editors of the magazine.

Margaret Laurence Award for Fiction. *See* **Manitoba Writing and Publishing Awards.**

Lawrence House Short Story Competition
Lawrence House Centre for the Arts, 127 Christina Street S.,
    Sarnia, ON N7T 2M8
Phone: (519) 337-0507 Fax: (519) 337-0482
E-mail: lawrencehousesarnia@gmail.com
Website: www.lawrencehouse.ca
Deadline: September 30
A first prize of $250, second prize of $150, and third prize of $100 are awarded for the best short story. Stories must be unpublished, 2,500 words or less, and in English. Entry fee $20. Open to all Canadian citizens and landed immigrants. Annual.

Stephen Leacock Memorial Medal for Humour
Judith Rapson, chair, Awards Committee, Stephen Leacock
    Association, 4223 Line 12 N., R.R. #2, Coldwater, ON L0K 1E0
Phone: (705) 835-3218
E-mail: judith.rapson@gmail.com

Website: www.leacock.ca
Deadline: November 30

A sterling-silver medal and a cash award of $15,000 is awarded for the year's best book of humour written by a Canadian citizen in prose, verse, or as drama. Four finalists receive $1,500. Send 10 copies of the book, a $150 entry fee, plus author bio and photo. Full submission guidelines on website. Annual.

League of Canadian Poets Awards
192 Spadina Avenue, Suite 312, Toronto, ON M5T 2C2
Phone: (416) 504-1657 Fax: (416) 504-0096
E-mail: readings@poets.ca
Websites: www.poets.ca or www.youngpoets.ca

Gerald Lampert Memorial Award
Deadline: November 1

This $1,000 annual award recognizes the best first book of poetry published by a Canadian in the preceding year. Entry fee $25.

Pat Lowther Memorial Award
Deadline: November 1

A $1,000 annual prize for the best book of poetry by a Canadian woman published in the preceding year. Entry fee $25.

Jessamy Stursberg Poetry Contest for Canadian Youth
Deadline: January 15

The contest's categories consist of junior and senior age groups. Winning poets in each group are awarded a cash prize of $350 (first place), $300 (second place), and $200 (third place). The winning and shortlisted poems will be featured in the April issue of the LCP e-zine, *Re:verse*. No entry fee.

Lieutenant Governor's Award for Literary Excellence. *See* B.C. Book Prizes.

The Lieutenant-Governor's Awards for High Achievement in the Arts: English-Language Literary Arts
Akoulina Connell, executive director, New Brunswick Arts Board, 61 Carleton Street, Fredericton, NB E3B 3T2

Phone: (506) 444-4444 or 1-866-460-2787 (toll-free in NB) Fax:
(506) 444-5543
E-mail: rbryar@artsnb.ca
Website: www.artsnb.ca
Deadline: June 15

Designed to recognize the outstanding contribution of certain
individuals to the English-Language Literary Arts of New
Brunswick, this award includes a certificate of honour and a cash
prize of $20,000 to be presented by the Lieutenant-Governor
during an annual ceremony. Past recipients (including winners of
the previous version of this award, the Alden Nowlan Award for
Excellence) must wait 5 years since their award before being eligible for this new award program. Nominees must have been born in
New Brunswick or have lived there for at least 5 years. A nomina-
tion form can be downloaded from the website. Although the award
is presented annually, it alternates between English-language and
French-language entries.

The Dorothy Livesay Poetry Prize. *See* **B.C. Book Prizes.**

Pat Lowther Memorial Award. *See* **League of Canadian
Poets Awards.**

Lush Triumphant Literary Awards
subTerrain Magazine, P.O. Box 3008, MPO, Vancouver, BC V6B 3X5
Phone: (604) 876-8710 Fax: (604) 879-2667
E-mail: subter@portal.ca
Website: www.subterrain.ca
Deadline: May 15

The winning entries in 3 categories – fiction, poetry, and creative
non-fiction – will receive a $750 cash prize and be published in the
following year's spring issue of *subTerrain*. The first runner-up in
each category will receive a $250 cash prize and be published in a
future issue of the magazine. Fee is $25/entry. Entrants may submit
as many entries in as many categories as they wish. All work must
be previously unpublished material and not currently under consideration in any other contest or competition. All entrants will
receive a complimentary 1-year subscription to *subTerrain*. Annual.

Sir John A. Macdonald Prize. *See* **Canadian Historical Association Awards.**

Grant MacEwan Literary Arts Award

Alberta Foundation for the Arts Literary Awards, 10708 – 105
    Avenue, Edmonton, AB T5H OAI
Phone: (780) 427-9968 Fax: (780) 422-9132
Website: www.affta.ab.ca
Deadline: May 1 (check website to see if nominations are being
    accepted in the current year)

This award program recognizes an individual Albertan who has made an outstanding contribution to artistic excellence in the literary arts over a significant period of time. The $50,000 award is selected biennially.

C. B. Macpherson Prize. *See* **Canadian Political Science Association Prizes.**

The Malahat Review Prizes

John Barton, The Malahat Review, University of Victoria, P.O.
    Box 1700, Stn. CSC, Victoria, BC V8W 2Y2
Phone: (250) 721-8524
E-mail: malahat@uvic.ca
Website: www.malahatreview.ca

Long Poem Prize
Deadline: February 1

Two prizes of $1,000 are awarded biennially for the best original, unpublished long poems or cycles of poems of no more than 20 pages. Entry fee of $35 covers a subscription to *The Malahat Review*.

Novella Prize
Deadline: February 1

A prize of $1,500 is awarded biennially for the best original, unpublished prose work no longer than 20,000 words. Entry fee of $35 covers a subscription to *The Malahat Review*.

Far Horizons Contest
Deadline: May 1

For writers who have yet to be published in book format. A prize of $1,000 is awarded annually, with alternating genres of short fiction (odd years) and poetry (even years). Entry fee of $25 covers a subscription to *The Malahat Review*.

Constance Rooke Creative Nonfiction Contest
Deadline: August 1

A prize of $1,000 is awarded annually. Entry fee of $35 covers a subscription to *The Malahat Review*.

Open Season Awards
Deadline: November 1

A prize of $1,000 awarded to 3 categories (poetry, short fiction, and creative non-fiction) annually as a "spring showcase" of literary excellence. Up to 3 poems per entry with a maximum length of 100 lines per poem, and short fiction and creative non-may be no longer than 2,500. Entry fee of $35 covers a subscription to *The Malahat Review*.

Manitoba Book Awards

The Manitoba Book Awards are co-facilitated by the Manitoba Writers' Guild (www.mbwriter.mb.ca) and the Association for Manitoba Book Publishers (www.bookpublishers.mb.ca). See www.bookpublishers.mb.ca/mba for submission instructions, forms, and deadlines.

Aqua Books Lansdowne Prize for Poetry

A prize of $1,000 is presented to the Manitoba writer whose book is judged the best book of poetry written in either English or French. Entry fee $25. Annual.

Alexander Kennedy Isbister Award for Non-Fiction

A cash prize of $3,500 is presented to the Manitoba writer whose book is judged the best book of adult non-fiction (excluding encyclopedias, textbooks, and dictionaries) written in English during the previous year. Entry fee $25. Annual.

John Hirsch Award for Most Promising Manitoba Writer
A cash prize of $2,500, donated by the estate of the late John Hirsch, co-founder of the Manitoba Theatre Centre, is awarded annually to the most promising Manitoba writer. Authors of poetry, fiction, creative non-fiction, and drama are eligible.

Margaret Laurence Award for Fiction
An annual cash prize of $3,500 is presented to the Manitoba writer whose book, published during the previous year, is judged the best book of adult fiction written in English. Entry fee $25.

McNally Robinson Book for Young People Awards
Two annual cash prizes of $2,500, donated by McNally Robinson Booksellers, are awarded for the best young person's books written by a Manitoba author, one in the category of young adult and the other for children. Books of fiction, poetry, non-fiction, and drama are eligible. Entry fee $25.

McNally Robinson Book of the Year Award
An annual cash prize of $5,000, donated by McNally Robinson Booksellers, is awarded for an outstanding book in any genre (except YA or children's books) written by a Manitoba resident. The title must be non-academic and written in English. Books of fiction, poetry, creative non-fiction, non-fiction, and drama are eligible. Entry fee $25.

Mary Scorer Award for Best Book by a Manitoba Publisher
Presented annually for the best book published by a Manitoba publisher written for the trade, educational, academic, or scholarly market. The author receives a cash prize of $1,000, donated by Friesens Corporation. Books are judged on innovation of content, quality of editing and writing, and excellence in design and illustrations. Promotional activity and market acceptance will be considered. Entry fee $25.

Carol Shields Winnipeg Book Award
A juried annual prize of $5,000 honouring books that evoke the special character of Winnipeg, or contribute to the appreciation or

understanding of the city. All genres are eligible and entries may be written in English or French. Entry fee $25.

Michael Van Rooy Award for Genre Fiction
One prize of $1,500 is awarded biennially to the author of the best book of genre fiction written in English.

Eileen McTavish Sykes Award for Best First Book
Presented annually to the author whose first professionally published book is judged the best written. The author receives a cash prize of $1,500, donated by Manitoba children's author Eileen McTavish Sykes through the Winnipeg Foundation. Each entry must be a non-academic title written in English. Books of fiction, poetry, non-fiction, children's and young adult literature, and drama will be considered. Entry fee $25/title.

McAuslan First Book Award. *See* **Quebec Writers' Federation Book Awards.**

McNally Robinson Book for Young People Awards. *See* **Manitoba Book Awards.**

McNally Robinson Book of the Year Award. *See* **Manitoba Book Awards.**

Margaret McWilliams Award Program
Manitoba Historical Society, 61 Carlton Street, Winnipeg, MB
   R3C IN7
Phone: (204) 947-0559
E-mail: info@mhs.mb.ca
Website: www.mhs.mb.ca
Deadline: mid-December (see website for exact date)
The Margaret McWilliams Awards, among the oldest book awards in Canada, are presented annually to books that focus on the history of Manitoba. Awards are offered in several categories, including scholarly history, popular history, and local history. Visit website for a complete listing of categories and entry forms. Awards are not necessarily presented in every category each year. $25 entry fee per submission.

Vicky Metcalf Award for Children's Literature. *See* **the Writers' Trust of Canada Awards.**

CAA Award for Fiction. *See* **Canadian Authors Association Literary Awards.**

National Business Book Awards

Mary Ann Freedman, Freedman & Associates Inc., 121
    Richmond Street W., Suite 605, Toronto, ON M5H 2KI
Phone: (416) 868-1500
E-mail: mafreedman@freedmanandassociates.com
Website: www.nbbaward.com
Deadline: end of November

An annual award of $20,000 recognizes excellence in business writing for books published in Canada during the previous year. PricewaterhouseCoopers LLP and the BMO Financial Group are co-sponsors of this award. The media sponsor is the *Globe and Mail.*

The National Chapter of Canada IODE Violet Downey Book Award

40 Orchard View Boulevard, Suite 254, Toronto, ON M4R 1B9
Phone: (416) 487-4416 Fax: (416) 487-4417
E-mail: iodecanada@bellnet.ca
Website: www.iode.ca
Deadline: December 31

Award of $3,000 for the author of the best English-language book in any category, suitable for children ages 13 and under. The author must be Canadian and the book must have been published in Canada during the previous year. Books are submitted by the publisher. Annual.

National Magazine Awards

425 Adelaide Street W., Suite 700, Toronto, ON M5V 3CI
Phone: (416) 422-1358 Fax: (416) 504-0437
E-mail: staff@magazine-awards.com
Website: www.magazine-awards.com
Deadline: early January (see website for exact date)

There are a total of 40 awards categories, 23 of which are for written work. Category definitions are on the website. Most entries are $85 each and must be entered online and followed by tear sheets couriered to the office.

In order to ensure that the contest truly acknowledges the best work in the Canadian magazine industry, the National Magazine Awards Foundation offers a co-financing plan to help smaller magazines participate. Details on the website.

Canadian staff or freelance contributors are eligible. Magazine publishers, editors, or freelancers may submit. Gold awards, Best New Writer, and Best Student Writer awards are $1,000 and a certificate; silver awards are $500 and a certificate. Editors are encouraged to make submissions on behalf of new writers. Annual.

The Hilda Neatby Prize in Women's History. *See* **Canadian Historical Association Awards.**

Hilary Weston Writers' Trust Non-Fiction Prize. *See* **the Writers' Trust of Canada Awards.**

Newfoundland and Labrador Book Awards. *See* **Writers' Alliance of Newfoundland and Labrador Literary Awards.**

The bpNichol Chapbook Award
Attn: Philip McKenna, 316 Dupont Street, Toronto, ON M5R IV9
Phone: (416) 964-7919 Fax: (416) 964-6941
E-mail: info@pcwf.ca
Website: www.pcwf.ca/bp-nichol-chap-book-award
Deadline: March 30

A prize of $2,000 is offered each year for the best poetry chapbook published in English in Canada. Entry made by publisher or author. The chapbook should be between 10 and 48 pages long. Send 3 copies (not returnable) and a short C.V. Organized by the Phoenix Community Works Foundation.

Dayne Oglivie Prize. *See* **the Writers' Trust of Canada Awards.**

Ontario Historical Society Awards for Authors
34 Parkview Avenue, Willowdale, ON M2N 3Y2
Phone: (416) 226-9011 Fax: (416) 226-2740

E-mail: ohs@ontariohistoricalsociety.ca
Website: www.ontariohistoricalsociety.ca
Deadlines: end of October

An annual program that honours individuals who have contributed significantly to the preservation and promotion of Ontario's heritage. All award recipients receive recognition in publicity and a framed certificate accompanied by a copy of the citation acknowledging their contribution. Self-nominations are accepted. A book may be nominated in 1 award category only.

Joseph Brant Award

Honours the best book on multicultural history in Ontario. Must have been published within the past 3 years. Entry fee $10/title with 3 copies of each book.

Donald Grant Creighton Award

Honours the best book of biography or autobiography highlighting life in Ontario, past or present, published within the past 3 years. Entry fee $10/title with 3 copies of each book.

Fred Landon Award

Honours the best book on regional history in Ontario. Must have been published within the past 3 years. Entry fee $10/title with 3 copies of each book.

Huguenot Society of Canada Award

Honours the best or substantial article published in Ontario which has brought public awareness to the principles of freedom of conscience and freedom of thought. Must have been published within the past 3 years. Entry fee $10/title with 3 copies of each book.

Alison Prentice Award

Honours the best book on women's history. Must have been published within the past 3 years. Entry fee $10/title with 3 copies of each book.

Riddell Award

Honours the best article on Ontario's history. Must have been published within the award year.

The Open Window Poetry Anthology Contest. *See* **Hidden Brook Press Poetry Awards.**

Ottawa Book Awards

Faith Seltzer, City of Ottawa (01-49), Cultural Services Division,
   110 Laurier Avenue W., Ottawa, ON KIP IJI
Phone: (613) 580-2424, ext. 27412 Fax: (613) 580-2632
E-mail: faith.seltzer@ottawa.ca
Website: www.ottawabookawards.ca
Deadline: early January (check website for exact date)

A $7,500 award is presented each year to the author of a book of literary merit in each of 4 categories: English fiction, English non-fiction, French fiction, and French non-fiction. All shortlisted authors will receive a $1,000 prize. The author must reside in the city of Ottawa.

Pandora's Collective Poetry Contests

P.O. Box 29118, Delamont P.O., 1950 W. Broadway, Vancouver,
   BC V6J 5C2
Phone: (604) 321-4039
E-mail: blnish_pandoras@yahoo.ca
Website: www.pandorascollective.com

Pandora's Collective offers 3 "blind submission" contests each year. Submissions must be in triplicate (please divide poems into 3 piles for 3 separate judges – only 1 cover letter needed), typed, with no name or address appearing on the same page as the poem. A cover letter must be included showing age category, name, address, telephone number and/or e-mail address, as well as the title of the poem/poems for clarification and the dollar amount included. Please do not use staples.

Guidelines for each contest: Accepts poems on any theme and up to 40 lines. No previously published poems. Awards for adults: first prize $100 and publication, second prize $50 and publication, third prize is publication. Awards for teens (ages 14–19): first prize $70 and publication, second prize $35 and publication, third prize is publication. Awards for children (13 and under): first prize $40 and publication, second prize $20 and publication, third prize is publication. Entry fees $5/poem for adults; $4/poem for teens; $3/poem for children.

Hibernating with Words
Deadline: January 15

Kisses and Popsicles Spring Poetry Contest
Deadline: May 15

The Summer Dream Poetry Contest
Deadline: September 15

Paragraphe Hugh MacLennan Prize for Fiction. *See*
Quebec Writers' Federation Book Awards.

Lorne Pierce Medal. *See* **the Royal Society of Canada**
Awards.

Prairie Fire Writing Contests
100 Arthur Street, Suite 423, Winnipeg, MB R3B IH3
Phone: (204) 943-9066
E-mail: prfire@mts.net
Website: www.prairiefire.ca
Deadline: November 30
    Offers 3 writing contests, each with a first prize of $1,250, second
prize of $500, and third prize of $250, plus publication in *Prairie
Fire*. Each submission must be unpublished. Entry fee $32/category,
which includes a 1-year subscription to *Prairie Fire*. Annual.

The Banff Centre Bliss Carman Poetry Award
    First prize is in part donated by the Banff Centre for the Arts,
which will also award a jeweller-cast replica of Carman's silver-
and-turquoise ring to the first-prize winner. Submit 1 to 3 poems,
with a maximum of 150 lines/poem.

Short Fiction Contest
    Submit a maximum of 10,000 words; 1 story/submission.

Creative Non-Fiction Contest
    Submit a maximum of 5,000 words; 1 story/submission.

The E. J. Pratt Medal and Prize in Poetry

E. J. Pratt Poetry Competition, Enrolment Services, 172 St.
   George Street, University of Toronto, Toronto, ON M5R OA3
Phone: (416) 978-2190 Fax: (416) 978-7022
Website: www.adm.utoronto.ca/adm-
   awards/html/awards/notices/pratt_e_j.htm
Deadline: late March/early April (check website for exact date)

The E. J. Pratt Medal is awarded as a stimulus to poetic composition in the belief that good poetry is the best assurance of a
vital language and a healthy culture. The competition is open to
any student proceeding toward a first or a postgraduate degree at
the University of Toronto. Entries should be approximately 100
lines long. No previously published compositions will be considered, except for work in campus student publications. The award
will be offered annually; however, if the selection committee determines that no submission is of sufficient excellence, the award will
not be given.

Alison Prentice Award. *See* **Ontario Historical Society
   Awards for Authors.**

PRISM international Writing Prizes

Creative Writing Program, University of British Columbia,
   Buchanan E462, 1866 Main Mall, Vancouver, BC V6T 1Z1
Phone: (604) 822-2514 Fax: (604) 822-3616
E-mail: prismcontest@gmail.com
Website: www.prismmagazine.ca/contests

Earle Birney Prize for Poetry
Deadline: not applicable

One award of $500 will be won by a poet whose work has
appeared in *PRISM international* during the previous year. Poets
need not apply; their work is automatically considered upon publication. Awarded annually.

PRISM international Literary Non-Fiction Contest
Deadline: November 30

A $1,500 first prize is awarded annually to the author of an out-
standing piece of literary non-fiction (up to 25 double-spaced

pages). The winning entry will be published in *PRISM international's* Non-Fiction Contest Issue, will earn an additional payment of $20/page for publication, and receive a 1-year subscription. Works of translation are eligible. Entry fee $25 for 1 story, plus $7 for each additional piece. Anyone who has taken a UBC creative writing course within the previous 2 years is ineligible to enter the contest.

PRISM international Annual Short Fiction Contest
Deadline: January 29

A $2,000 prize is awarded for the best original, unpublished short story (up to 25 double-spaced pages). The winner also receives publication payment in PRISM *international's* Fiction Contest Issue. Three runner-up prizes of $200 are also conferred. Works of translation are eligible. Entry fee $25 for 1 story, plus $7 for each additional story. All entries receive a 1-year subscription to *PRISM international.* Anyone who has taken a UBC creative writing course within the previous 2 years is ineligible to enter the contest.

PRISM international Annual Poetry Contest
Deadline: January 29

A $1,000 prize is awarded for the best original, unpublished poem (5 poems, up to 25 pages). $300 and $200 for runners-up. The winner receives publication payment for inclusion in *PRISM international's* Poetry and Fiction Contest issue. Works of translation are eligible. Entry fee $25 for 5 poems, plus $7 for each additional entry. All entries receive a 1-year subscription to PRISM international. Anyone who has taken a UBC creative writing course within the previous 2 years is ineligible to enter the contest.

Quebec Writers' Federation Book Awards

Quebec Writers' Federation Awards, 1200 Atwater Avenue, Westmount, QC H3Z IX4
Phone: (514) 933-0878 Fax: (514) 933-0878
E-mail: info@qwf.org
Website: www.qwf.org/awards
Deadlines: May 31 (for books published between October 1 and May 15) and August 1 (for books published between May 16 and September 30)

All entry fees $20. Criteria and entry forms available on website. Books may be submitted by publishers or authors.

Mavis Gallant Prize for Non-Fiction

An annual cash prize of $2,000 is awarded for the best book of literary non-fiction written in English by a writer who has lived in Quebec for at least 3 of the past 5 years.

A. M. Klein Prize for Poetry

An annual cash prize of $2,000 is awarded for the best book of poetry written in English by a writer who has lived in Quebec for at least 3 of the past 5 years.

McAuslan First Book Award

An annual cash prize of $2,000 is awarded for the best first book written in English by a writer who has lived in Quebec for at least 3 of the past 5 years.

Paragraphe Hugh MacLennan Prize for Fiction

An annual cash prize of $2,000 is awarded for the best book of fiction written in English by a writer who has lived in Quebec for at least 3 of the past 5 years.

QWF Prize for Children's and Young Adult Literature

An annual cash prize of $2,000 is awarded for the best book of children's or young adult literature (fiction, non-fiction, or poetry) written in English by a writer who has lived in Quebec for at least 3 of the past 5 years.

QWF Translation Prize

An annual cash prize of $2,000 is awarded for the best translation. The prize alternates on an annual basis between a book translated from English to French and a book translated from French to English, with a 2-year eligibility span for each. The 2 subcategories have different eligibility criteria.

Thomas Head Raddall Atlantic Fiction Award. *See* **Writers' Federation of Nova Scotia Awards.**

Red Cedar Book Awards

E-mail: redcedaraward@gmail.com
Website: www.redcedaraward.ca
Deadline: November

Awarded to the author and/or illustrator of the best book of fiction and non-fiction for children. No monetary value, but the prizewinners receive engraved red cedar plaques. These are children's choice awards, voted on by children throughout B.C. during the program year. The authors/illustrators must be Canadian citizens or landed immigrants who have lived in Canada for at least 2 years. The books must have been published by a recognized publisher and be recognized as being of general interest to students in grades 4 to 7. Annual.

Regina Book Award. *See* **Saskatchewan Book Awards.**

David Adams Richards Prize. *See* **Writers' Federation of New Brunswick Literary Competition.**

Evelyn Richardson Non-Fiction Award. *See* **Writers' Federation of Nova Scotia Awards.**

Riddell Award. *See* **Ontario Historical Society Awards for Authors.**

Rocky Mountain Book Award

Michelle Dimnik or Ruth McMahon, co-chairs, P.O. Box 42, Lethbridge, AB T1J 3Y4
Phone: (403) 381-7164 (Michelle Dimnik) or (403) 327-4953 (Ruth McMahon) Fax: (403) 320-9124
E-mail: rockymountainbookaward@shaw.ca
Website: http://rmba.lethsd.ab.ca
Deadline: January 20

Alberta students and educators participate in this readers' choice program, which is designed to stimulate the reading interests of students in grades 4 to 7 by introducing them to exemplary Canadian literature. The winner is chosen from 10 fiction books, including 1 picture book and 10 non-fiction books. Books must be copyrighted in the previous 3 years. The value of the award is a gold medal and an expense-paid trip to Alberta to visit 4 or 5 schools and possibly take part in some other activities such as conferences and writing workshops. Annual.

Rogers Writers' Trust Fiction Prize. *See* **the Writers' Trust of Canada Awards.**

The Royal Society of Canada Awards
170 Waller Street, Ottawa, ON K1N 9B9
Phone: (613) 991-6990 Fax: (613) 991-6996
E-mail: fellowship@rsc.ca
Website: www.rsc.ca

Bancroft Award
Deadline: December 1
    A presentation scroll and a prize of $2,500 is offered every 2 years if there is a suitable candidate. The award is given for publication, instruction, and research in the earth sciences that have conspicuously contributed to public understanding and appreciation of the subject. Nominations must be put forward by 3 persons, 1 of whom must be a fellow of the Royal Society of Canada.

Innis-Gérin Medal
Deadline: December 1
    A bronze medal is awarded every 2 years, if there is a suitable candidate, for a distinguished and sustained contribution to the literature of the social sciences, including human geography and social psychology. Nominations must be put forward by 3 persons, 1 of whom must be a fellow of the Royal Society of Canada.

Lorne Pierce Medal
Deadline: December 1
    A gold plated silver medal is awarded every 2 years, if there is a suitable candidate, for an achievement of special significance and conspicuous merit in imaginative or critical literature written in either English or French. Critical literature dealing with Canadian subjects has priority. Nominations must be put forward by 3 persons, 1 of whom must be a fellow of the Royal Society of Canada.

Sanofi Pasteur Medal for Excellence in Health Research Journalism

Canadians for Health Research, P.O. Box 126, Westmount, QC
  H3Z 2TI
Phone: (514) 398-7478 Fax: (514) 398-8361
E-mail: info@chrcrm.org
Website: www.chrcrm.org
Deadline: April (check website for exact date)

This annual national award recognizes the role of journalists in raising public awareness of the importance of health research in Canada. The award consists of a medal and a $2,500 bursary. The winning article must have been published in a Canadian newspaper or magazine during the previous calendar year.

Saskatchewan Book Awards

Director, Saskatchewan Book Awards, P.O. Box 20025, Regina,
  SK S4P 4J7
Phone: (306) 569-1585 Fax: (306) 949-7263
E-mail: director@bookawards.sk.ca
Deadline: November 1

Aboriginal People's Writing Award

An award of $2,000 is presented to an Aboriginal Saskatchewan author for the best book judged on the quality of writing. Entry fee $50/title. Annual.

Book of the Year Award

An award of $3,000 is presented to a Saskatchewan author for the best book judged on the quality of writing and presentation. Books are considered in the following categories: children's and young adult, drama, fiction (including graphic novels), poetry, and non-fiction (not including cookbooks, how-to books, directories, or bibliographies of minimal critical content).

Children's Literature Award

An award of $2,000 will be given to a Saskatchewan author for the best published book of children's or young adult literature. Annual.

Fiction Award

An award of $2,000 will be given to a Saskatchewan author for the best published work of fiction (novel or short fiction). Entry fee $50/title. Annual.

First Book Award Honouring Brenda MacDonald Riches

An award of $2,000 will be given to a Saskatchewan author for the best published first book in the following categories: children's and young adult, drama (published plays), fiction (including graphic novels), and non-fiction (not including cookbooks, how-to books, directories, or bibliographies of minimal critical content), and poetry. Entry fee $50/title. Annual.

Non-Fiction Award

An award of $2,000 will be given to a Saskatchewan author for the best published work of non-fiction. Entry fee $50/title. Annual.

Poetry Award Honouring Anne Szumigalski

An award of $2,000 will be given to a Saskatchewan author for the best published book of poetry. Entry fee $50/title. Annual.

Regina Book Award

In recognition of the vitality of the literary community of Regina, this $2,000 award is presented to a Regina writer for the best book in the following categories: children's, drama (published plays), fiction, non-fiction (not including cookbooks, how-to books, directories, or bibliographies of minimal critical content), and poetry. Entry fee $50/title. Annual.

Saskatchewan Book of the Year Award

An award of $3,000 will be given to a Saskatchewan author for the best published book in the following categories: children's, drama (published plays), fiction, non-fiction (not including cookbooks, how-to books, directories, or bibliographies of minimal critical content), and poetry. Entry fee $20/title. Annual.

Saskatoon Book Award

In recognition of the vitality of the literary community of Saskatoon, this $2,000 award is presented to a Saskatoon writer for the best book in the following categories: children's, drama (published plays), fiction, non-fiction (not including cookbooks, how-to books, directories, or bibliographies of minimal critical content), and poetry. Entry fee $50/title. Annual.

Scholarly Writing Award

An award of $2,000 will be given to a Saskatchewan author for the published work that is judged to contribute most to scholarship. His or her work must recognize or draw on specific theoretical work within a community of scholars, and participate in the creation and transmission of knowledge. The work must show potential readability by a wider audience and be accessible to those outside an academic milieu. Works in the following categories will be considered: refereed publications, reference works, and/or those published by an academic press. Entry fee $50/title. Annual.

Young Adult Award

An award of $2,000 is presented to a Saskatchewan author for the best book of young adult literature for ages 11–18. Entry fee $50/title.

Saskatoon Book Award. *See* **Saskatchewan Book Awards.**

Margaret and John Savage First Book Award. *See* **Dartmouth Book Awards.**

The Ruth and Sylvia Schwartz Children's Book Award
Ontario Arts Council, 151 Bloor Street W., 5th Floor, Toronto, ON M5S 1T6
Phone: (416) 969-7422 or 1-800-387-0058, ext. 7422 Fax: (416) 961-7796
E-mail: mwarren@arts.on.ca
Website: www.arts.on.ca

A panel of children's booksellers from across Canada selects 2 shortlists of 5 picture books and 5 young adult/middle reader books in February; 2 juries of children then select a winner in each category. There is no application process; all Canadian authored/illustrated children's trade books published in the previous year are eligible. The annual awards are $6,000 for the picture book category, shared between author and illustrator; $6,000 for the YA/middle reader category.

Science in Society Journalism Awards

c/o Canadian Science Writers' Association, P.O. Box 75, Stn. A,
 Toronto, ON M5W IA2
Phone: 1-800-796-8595
E-mail: awards@sciencewriters.ca
Website: www.sciencewriters.ca

Herb Lampert Student Writing Award

Deadline: March 31

An annual cash prize of $1,000 is awarded to the student science writer of the best original material in either print or TV and radio categories. Any student writer who has a science article published in a student or other newspaper or magazine or aired on a radio or TV station in Canada is eligible.

Science and Society Book Awards

Deadline: December 15

Two $1,000 cash prizes are awarded annually to the authors of books that made outstanding contributions to science writing for the general public and for children aged 8–12. Entries may address aspects of basic or applied science or technology, historical or current, in any area including health, science, environmental issues, regulatory trends, etc. Books are judged on literary excellence and scientific content. The writer must be a Canadian citizen or resident.

The Mary Scorer Award for Best Book by a Manitoba Publisher. *See* Manitoba Writing and Publishing Awards.

The Scotiabank Giller Prize

Elana Rabinovitch, 576 Davenport Road, Suite 2, Toronto, ON
 M5R IK9
Phone: (416) 934-0755 Fax: (416) 934-0971
E-mail: elanar@sympatico.ca
Website: www.scotiabankgillerprize.ca
Deadline: staggered throughout March, June, and August, with
 final deadline usually early August

Each year the Scotiabank Giller Prize awards $50,000 to the author of the best Canadian full-length novel or collection of short stories published in English, either originally or in translation, as judged by a jury panel. Each of 4 finalists is awarded $5,000. The author must be a Canadian citizen or permanent resident, and the book must have been published by a Canadian publisher.

Seeds International Poetry Chapbook Anthology Contest. *See* **Hidden Brook Press Poetry Awards.**

The Carol Shields Winnipeg Book Award. *See* **Manitoba Writing and Publishing Awards.**

Dorothy Shoemaker Literary Awards Contest
Sheila Bauman, events planner, Kitchener Public Library, 85
    Queen Street N., Kitchener, ON N2N 2HI
Phone: (519) 743-0271, ext. 254 Fax: (519) 579-2382
E-mail: sheila.bauman@kpl.org
Website: www.kpl.org
Deadline: November
    Named in honour of Dorothy Shoemaker, former chief librarian and ardent supporter of writers, and funded by her generous endowment. $2,400 in prize money is awarded in 2 categories: poetry and prose. Winning entries are published in the anthology *The Changing Image*. Open to residents of Ontario in 2 age categories: youth (17 years and under) and senior (18 years and older). Submissions accepted by e-mail only. Commercially published writers are not eligible. No entry fee, but a limited number of submissions permitted. See website for complete guidelines.

Short Grain Writing Contest
Grain Magazine, P.O. Box 67, Saskatoon, SK S7K 3KI
Phone: (306) 244-2828 Fax: (306) 244-0255
E-mail: grainmag@sasktel.net
Website: www.grainmagazine.ca
Deadline: April 1
    Two categories with 4 prizes in each: poetry in any form including prose poem; short fiction of any style including postcard story. Prizes: 2 first prizes of $1,000; 2 second prizes of $750; 2 runner-up

prizes of $500, plus publication. Entry fee: $35 fee for a maximum of 2 entries in 1 category; U.S. and international entries $40 in U.S. funds. Entrants receive a 1-year subscription to *Grain Magazine*. Guidelines available on website.

Donald Smiley Prize. *See* Canadian Political Science Association Prizes.

Edna Staebler Award for Creative Non-Fiction

Office of the Dean, Faculty of Arts, Wilfrid Laurier University, 75
   University Avenue W., Waterloo, ON N2L 3C5
Phone: (519) 884-0710, ext. 3364
E-mail: staebleraward@wlu.ca
Website: http://libserve.wlu.ca/internet/prizes/staebler.html
Deadline: April 30

A $10,000 prize is awarded annually for an outstanding work of creative non-fiction, which must have been written by a Canadian and have a Canadian location and significance. To be eligible, an entry must be the writer's first or second published book. Established to give recognition and encouragement to new writers.

Stellar Book Awards

E-mail: stellarbookaward@yahoo.ca
Website: www.stellaraward.ca
Deadline: October 15

B.C.'s Teen Readers' Choice Award, voted on by teens, is administered by a steering committee of teens and adults as part of the Young Readers' Choice Awards Society of B.C. Books must be recognized as being of interest to teens, been written by Canadian citizens or landed immigrants who have lived in Canada for at least 2 years, and been published by a recognized publisher in the 2 years prior to the deadline. Prizewinners receive an etched glass plaque. Annual.

Jessamy Stursberg Poetry Contest for Canadian Youth. *See* League of Canadian Poets Awards.

The Summer Dream Poetry Contest. *See* Pandora's Collective Poetry Contests.

The Sunburst Award for Canadian Literature of the Fantastic

The Sunburst Award Society, 2 Farm Greenway, Toronto, ON
   M3A 3M2
E-mail: secretary@sunburstaward.org
Website: www.sunburstaward.org
Deadline: January 31

Presented to a Canadian writer who has published a speculative fiction novel or book-length collection of speculative fiction any time during the previous calendar year. Named after the first novel by Phyllis Gotlieb, one of the first published authors of contemporary Canadian science fiction. The award has 2 categories, Adult Fiction and Young Adult Fiction, and winners in each category receive $1,000 and a medallion with the Sunburst logo. The work may include science fiction, fantasy, horror, magic realism, or surrealism. Annual.

Sunday Star Short Story Contest

Toronto Star, 1 Yonge Street, Toronto, ON M5E 1E6
Phone: (416) 869-4881
Website: www.thestar.com
Deadline: February

A first prize of $5,000 (plus tuition for a 30-week course from the Humber School for Writers Creative Writing Correspondence Program), a second of $2,000, and a third of $1,000 are awarded for the best original, unpublished short stories up to 2,500 words. They will be published in *The Star*. No entry fee, but only hardcopy submissions are accepted.

Eileen McTavish Sykes Award for Best First Book. *See* Manitoba Writing and Publishing Awards.

The Charles Taylor Prize for Literary Non-Fiction

June Dickenson, 18 Blackberry Place, Carlisle, ON LOR 1H2
Phone: (647) 477-6000 Fax: (905) 689-2944
E-mail: info@thecharlestaylorprize.ca
Website: www.thecharlestaylorprize.ca

Commemorates Charles Taylor's pursuit of excellence in the field of literary non-fiction. Awarded to the author whose book best combines a superb command of the English language, elegance of style, and a subtlety of thought and perception. The winner receives $25,000, and the finalists each receive $2,000 as well as promotional support so that all shortlisted books stand out in the national media, bookstores, and libraries. Entries must be submitted by the publisher of the work. Only Canadian authors are considered. Annual.

TD Canadian Children's Literature Award. *See* Canadian Children's Book Centre Awards.

This Magazine Great Canadian Literary Hunt
401 Richmond Street W., Suite 417, Toronto, ON M5V 3A8
Phone: (416) 979-9429 or 1-877-999-8447
E-mail: hunt@thismagazine.ca
Website: www.this.org
Deadline: July 31

"On the trail of Canada's brightest new creative writers." Annual prizes are awarded in 2 categories: poems up to 100 lines and short stories or creative non-fiction stories up to 2,500 words. First prize wins $750 and publication in a *This Magazine* literary supplement; second and third place each win a prize pack plus online publication. All entries must be unpublished. Entry fees are $25 for 1 short story or creative non-fiction story or 2 poems; subsequent submissions are $5 each. Entry fee includes a 1-year subscription to *This Magazine*. See website for more information.

The RBC Bronwen Wallace Award. *See* the Writers' Trust of Canada Awards.

Portia White Prize
Nova Scotia Department of Tourism, Culture and Heritage, 1800 Argyle Street, Suite 601, P.O. Box 456, Halifax, NS B3J 2R5
Phone: (902) 424-6392 Fax: (902) 424-0710
E-mail: kirbypc@gov.ns.ca
Website: www.gov.ns.ca/cch/investing/awards/portia-white/
Deadline: June 15

Awarded annually by the Province of Nova Scotia to recognize artistic excellence and achievement by a Nova Scotia artist. The prize consists of an award of $18,000 to the recipient and $7,000 to

.the recipient's protegé, which may be an individual artist or a Nova Scotia arts organization.

Jon Whyte Memorial Essay Prize. *See* **Writers Guild of Alberta Awards.**

Willow Awards (Saskatchewan Young Readers' Choice Awards)
E-mail: willowawards@willowawards.ca
Website: www.willowawards.ca
Deadline: October 31

A glass sculpture created by Saskatchewan artist Jacqueline Berting is awarded to the winners of the 3 Willow Awards, determined by the voting of students in the province. The Shining Willow Award is for books written for children in kindergarten to grade 3, the Diamond Willow Award is for books written for children in grades 4 to 6, and the Snow Willow Award is for books written for young people in grades 7 to 9.

Books must be written by Canadian citizens or permanent residents, be fiction or non-fiction, be published in Canada, and have been copyrighted in the previous 2 years. Check website for entry forms and guidelines.

The Ethel Wilson Fiction Prize. *See* **B.C. Book Prizes.**

The Kenneth R. Wilson Awards
2 Bloor Street E., Suite 3500, Toronto, ON M4W 1A8
Phone: (416) 939-6200 or (416) 422-1358
E-mail: staff@krwawards.ca
Website: www.krwawards.ca
Deadline: February

Recognizing excellence in writing and graphic design in business-to-business publications and their websites. Open to editorial or design staff, freelancers, and other contributors to such publications. More than 20 categories cover editorial, marketing, retail, technology, industrial, profiles, features, news, graphic design, photography, illustration, web design, and more. See website for entry fee and submission guidelines. Annual.

Winterset Award. *See* **BMO Winterset Award.**

George Woodcock Lifetime Achievement Award

c/o B.C. BookWorld, 3516 W. 13th Avenue (rear), Vancouver, BC
  V6R 2S3
Phone: (604) 736-4011
E-mail: bookworld@telus.net
Website: www.georgewoodcock.com

A $5,000 prize is awarded annually for the exemplary literary career of a British Columbia resident. Administered by *B.C. BookWorld*.

Writers' Alliance of Newfoundland and Labrador Literary Awards

223 Duckworth Street, Suite 202, St. John's, NL AIC 6NI
Phone: (709) 739-5215 or 1-866-739-5215 Fax: (709) 739-5931
E-mail: wanl@nf.aibn.com
Website: www.wanl.ca

Newfoundland and Labrador Book Awards
Deadline: January

Award categories alternate from poetry and non-fiction in 1 year to fiction and children's/young adult literature in the following year. The prize is $1,500 for the winner in each category, and 2 runners-up in each category receive $500. Contests are open to residents of Newfoundland and Labrador only. Books must have been published in the previous 2 years.

Heritage and History Book Award

Awarded annually for a work of fiction, non-fiction, poetry, or young adult/children's literature that exemplifies excellence in the interpretation of the history and heritage of Newfoundland and Labrador. Shortlist is selected from entries to the Newfoundland and Labrador Book Awards.

Newfoundland and Labrador Credit Union Fresh Fish Award for Emerging Writers

Deadline: June

Established by Newfoundland-born author Brian O'Dea and intended to serve as an incentive for emerging writers in Newfoundland and Labrador by providing them with financial support, recognition, and professional editing services for a book-length manuscript in any genre. The winning author will receive $5,000, the editing services of an editor valued at up to $1,000, and a miniature sculpture in the style of *Man Nailed to a Fish* by sculptor Jim Maunder. Two runners-up each receive $1,000. Awarded biennially. Writers must be a member of the Writers' Alliance of Newfoundland and Labrador and be a resident of the province. Writers with a published book in any genre are not eligible.

The Writers' Community of Durham Region Contests

75 Bayley Street W., P.O. Box 14558, Ajax, ON LIS 7K7

Phone: (905) 686-0211

E-mail: querycontest@wcdr.org

Website: www.wcdr.ca

Competitions change from year to year; see website for current guidelines.

Writers' Federation of New Brunswick Literary Competition

Lee Thompson, Writers' Federation of New Brunswick, P.O. Box 306, Moncton, NB EIC 8L4

Phone: (506) 459-7228

E-mail: info@wfnb.ca

Website: www.wfnb.ca

Deadline: February (check website for exact date)

Cash prizes ($200 for first place) are awarded annually in the following categories: poetry, short fiction, creative non-fiction, and writing for children. Manuscripts may be on any subject and should not exceed 4,000 words for prose, 100 lines maximum for poetry, and a maximum of 3,000 words for the children's category. All awards open to Canadian residents.

The Alfred G. Bailey Prize

An annual cash prize of $400 is awarded for an outstanding unpublished poetry manuscript of at least 48 pages. Some individual poems may have been previously published or accepted for publication. Entry fee is $30 for members and $35 for non-members.

The Sheree Fitch Prize for Poetry

A first prize of $100 is offered to youth up to age 18 (as of February 29 in the year of the contest). Maximum length for poetry is 100 lines. Work must be original and unpublished. No entry fee, but limit of 2 entries per person.

The David Adams Richards Prize

An annual award of $400 goes to the author of a collection of short stories, a short novel, or a substantial portion (up to 30,000 words) of a longer novel. Work must be unpublished, although some individual stories may have been published. Entry fee is $30 for members and $35 for non-members.

Writers' Federation of Nova Scotia Awards
Hillary Titley, 1113 Marginal Road, Halifax, NS B3H 4P7
Phone: (902) 423-8116 Fax: (902) 422-0881
E-mail: programs@writers.ns.ca
Website: www.writers.ns.ca

Atlantic Poetry Prize
Deadline: first Friday in December

A $2,000 prize is awarded annually for an outstanding full-length book of poetry by a native or resident of Atlantic Canada. No entry fee.

Atlantic Writing Competition for Unpublished Manuscripts
Deadline: November

There are 7 categories for unpublished manuscripts: novel, short story, poetry, writing for children, juvenile/YA novel, unproduced play, and creative non-fiction. Winners receive prizes of $200 or $300 for first place, depending on the category. All entries receive a brief evaluation. Open to Atlantic Canada residents only. Annual.

Ann Connor Brimer Award for Children's Literature
Heather MacKenzie, Halifax Public Libraries, 60 Alderney Drive,
   Dartmouth, NS B2Y 4P8
Phone: (902) 490-5991 Fax: (902) 490-5889
E-mail: mackenh@halifaxpubliclibraries.ca
Website: www.nsla.ns.ca/index.php/about/awards/ann-connor-
   brimer-award
Deadline: October 30

A framed certificate and $2,000 prize is awarded annually to the
author of a children's book published in the 12 months preceding
the deadline. Books must be intended for youth up to age 15, and
the prize is awarded for text, not illustration. Authors must be resident in Atlantic Canada. Co-sponsored by the Nova Scotia Library
Association and the Writers' Federation of Nova Scotia, the award
is presented in the spring of each year.

Thomas Head Raddall Atlantic Fiction Award
Deadline: first Friday in December

A $20,000 prize is awarded each year for an outstanding novel or
collection of short stories, in English, by a native or resident of
Atlantic Canada. No entry fee.

Evelyn Richardson Non-Fiction Award
Deadline: first Friday in December

A $2,000 prize is awarded annually for an outstanding work of
non-fiction by a native or resident of Nova Scotia. No entry fee.

Writers Guild of Alberta Literary Awards
Percy Page Centre, 11759 Groat Road N.W., Edmonton, AB
   T5M 3K6
Phone: (780) 422-8174 or 1-800-665-5354 Fax: (780) 422-2663
E-mail: mail@writersguild.ab.ca
Website: www.writersguild.ab.ca
Deadline: December 31

A $1,500 prize is awarded annually for excellent achievement
by an Alberta writer in each of the following categories: children's
literature, drama, non-fiction, novel, and poetry. Eligible books
may have been published anywhere in the world. Authors must

have resided in Alberta for at least 12 of the 18 months prior to December 31. Entry fee $25.

The Robert Kroetsch City of Edmonton Book Prize
Deadline: December 31

A $10,000 award to honour the books that contribute to the appreciation and understanding of the City of Edmonton by emphasizing its special character and/or the achievements of its residents. Subjects may include history, geography, current affairs, Edmonton's arts, or its people, or be written by an Edmonton author. Entries may be fiction, non-fiction, poetry, or drama written for adults or children in published form. Entry fee $25.

The City of Calgary W. O. Mitchell Book Prize
Deadline: December 31

Awarded in honour of acclaimed Calgary writer W. O. Mitchell and recognizes achievement by Calgary authors. The $5,000 prize is awarded annually for an outstanding book (fiction, poetry, non-fiction, children's literature, or drama) published in the previous year. The author must be a Calgary resident on December 31 of the event year and for a minimum of 2 years prior. Entry fee $25.

Jon Whyte Memorial Essay Prize
Deadline: December 31

A $700 prize is awarded in recognition of the best essay (no longer than 3,000 words) that "has Alberta at its heart." Open to residents aged 18 years and older who have resided in Alberta for 12 of the past 18 months. Both beginning and established writers may apply. Published and unpublished essays are eligible. Entry fee $15.

Howard O'Hagan Award for Short Story
Deadline: December 31

A $700 award recognizes an outstanding short story (no longer than 5,000 words) written by an Alberta author and published in the previous year. Open to residents aged 18 years and older who have resided in Alberta for 12 of the past 18 months. Entries must have been published within the year in an anthology, magazine, or literary journal. Entry fee $15.

Amber Bowerman Memorial Travel Writing Award
Deadline: December 31

This $700 award recognizes a writer, aged 30 or younger, with an extraordinary non-fiction story to tell about how their life was changed by what they experienced when they travelled outside of North America. Entries must be no longer than 3,000 words and may or may not have been previously published. Entry fee $15.

John H. Gray Award for Short Nonfiction

A $700 award recognizes an outstanding literary short non-fiction piece by an Alberta author on any topic. Entries may be published (within the year) or unpublished, and no longer than 5,000 words. Entry fee $15.

The Writers' Trust of Canada Awards
90 Richmond Street E., Suite 200, Toronto, ON M5C IP1
Phone: (416) 504-8222 or 1-877-906-6548 Fax: (416) 504-9090
E-mail: info@writerstrust.com
Website: www.writerstrust.com

Matt Cohen Award: In Celebration of a Writing Life

An award of $20,000 is conferred on a Canadian writer whose life has been dedicated to writing as a primary pursuit to honour his or her body of distinguished work of poetry or prose in English or in French.

Shaughnessy Cohen Prize for Political Writing

A $25,000 prize is awarded annually to a Canadian author of a work of non-fiction, written in English or translated from French, that enlarges our understanding of contemporary Canadian political and social issues and in the opinion of the judges shows the highest literary merit. Prizes of $2,500 each will be awarded to the other finalists.

Vicky Metcalf Award for Children's Literature

An annual award of $20,000 is conferred on a Canadian writer of children's literature in recognition of his or her body of work that in the opinion of the judges shows the highest literary standards.

Dayne Oglivie Prize

An annual award of $4,000 is presented to an emerging Canadian writer from the LGBT community who demonstrates great promise through a body of exceptional quality work. Developing writers who identify as LGBT are eligible.

Writers' Trust Engel/Findley Award

Created by merging 2 previously existing prizes (the Marian Engel Award and the Timothy Findley Award), this award will be given out once a year to a Canadian writer, not for a single book, but for a body of work and in hope of future contribution. All eligible writers in mid-career are to be considered. The prize is $25,000.

Hilary Weston Writers' Trust Prize for Nonfiction

Deadlines: April, June, or August, depending on publishing date

A $60,000 prize is awarded annually to the Canadian author of the work of non-fiction, written in English, that in the opinion of the judges shows the highest literary merit. $5,000 each will be awarded to the shortlisted authors.

Rogers Writers' Trust Fiction Prize

Deadlines: April, June, or August, depending on publishing date

A $25,000 prize is awarded to the author of the year's outstanding novel or short story collection, written in English, by a Canadian citizen or landed immigrant. Prizes of $3,500 each will be awarded to the shortlisted authors.

The RBC Bronwen Wallace Award

An award of $5,000 is presented, in alternate years, to a Canadian poet or a Canadian short-fiction writer under the age of 35 who is unpublished in book form but whose work has appeared in at least 1 independently edited magazine or anthology. Two finalists each receive $1,000. Applicants should submit 5 to 10 pages of unpublished poetry or up to 2,500 words of unpublished prose fiction.

The Writers' Trust of Canada / McClelland & Stewart Journey Prize

McClelland & Stewart Ltd., 1 Toronto Street, Toronto, ON
M5C 2V6

Phone: (416) 364-4449 Fax: (416) 364-6863
E-mail: journeyprize@mcclelland.com
Website: www.mcclelland.com
Deadline: January 15

The $10,000 Journey Prize is awarded annually to a new and developing writer of distinction for a short story published in a Canadian literary journal. Established in 1988, and made possible by James A. Michener's generous donation of his Canadian royalties earnings from his novel *Journey*, it is the most significant monetary award given in Canada to a writer at the beginning of his or her career for a short story or excerpt from a fiction work in progress. In recognition of the vital role journals play in discovering new writers, an additional $2,000 is awarded to the literary journal that originally published the winning story. The longlisted stories are selected from literary journal submissions and published annually by McClelland & Stewart as *The Journey Prize Stories*. Only submissions from literary journals/magazines are accepted.

The Writers' Union of Canada Awards and Competitions

90 Richmond Street E., Suite 200, Toronto, ON M5C 1P1
Phone: (416) 703-8982, ext. 223 Fax: (416) 504-9090
E-mail: projects@writersunion.ca
Website: www.writersunion.ca

Danuta Gleed Literary Award
Deadline: February 1

Awarded for the best first collection of short stories in the English language, written by a Canadian citizen or landed immigrant and published in the previous calendar year. First prize $10,000; 2 runners-up receive $500 each. Annual.

Short Prose Competition for Developing Writers
Deadline: November 3

An annual award to discover developing writers of fiction and non-fiction. A $2,500 prize is awarded for the best piece of unpublished prose up to 2,500 words by a Canadian citizen or landed immigrant who has not previously been published in book format by a commercial or university press and does not have a contract with a publisher. The winner's and finalists' entries will be submitted to

3 Canadian magazines for consideration. Entry fee $29. Full entry conditions available on the website.

Postcard Story Competition
Deadline: February 14

Open to all writers. A prize of $750 will be given for any text (fiction, non-fiction, prose, poetry, verse, dialogue, etc.) up to 250 words in length. Entry fee $7.50/submission. Annual.

Writing for Children Competition
Deadline: April 24

A prize of $1,500 is awarded annually for the best fiction or non-fiction (up to 1,500 words) written for children. Open to Canadian citizens and landed immigrants whose work has not previously been published in book format by a commercial or university press and who do not have a contract with a publisher. The winner's and finalists' entries will be submitted to 3 publishers of children's literature. Entry fee $15/submission.

8

PROVINCIAL & FEDERAL
WRITER SUPPORT PROGRAMS

Outlined below are the main sources of provincial and federal funding for Canadian writers. Arts council and other government grants are designed to buy the writer time to devote to his or her work for a specified period in order to support a work in progress or the completion of a particular creative project through meeting a varying combination of living, research, travel, or professional-development costs. Such financial support is most often given to the successful published author, but gifted inexperienced writers are sometimes also eligible. Several provincial initiatives are open to new as well as established writers.

All these programs require applicants to develop detailed project proposals and budgets and to provide writing samples and other support materials.

Alberta Foundation for the Arts
10708 – 105 Avenue, Edmonton, AB T5H OAI
Phone: (780) 427-9968 Fax: (780) 422-9132
Website: www.affta.ab.ca
Contact: Arts Branch
The Alberta Foundation for the Arts (AFA) welcomes eligible applications to the Literary Arts Project Grant program. Except for training and/or career development projects, applicants must be professionally published writers who are resident in Alberta. Published writers are those who meet one or any combination of

the publication requirements outlined in the program's guidelines.

The AFA's Literary Arts Project Grant program supports the following projects:

1) Art production: includes the creation of a new manuscript or work in progress that has not been published, produced, or aired. Eligible genres include fiction, drama (for stage, radio, and screen), literary non-fiction, translation, adaptations, and anthologies.

2) Training and/or career development: includes a workshop, master class, retreat, mentorship program, and course of study in creative writing, editing, publishing, or translation. All applicants regardless of experience may apply under this category.

3) Marketing: includes promotional tours, attending a book launch and/or premiere of the artist's work, attending non-academic conferences, literary festivals, or award presentations by invitation.

4) Research: includes activities that support or result in the development of a writing project.

The maximum project grant under this program will not exceed $15,000 and may include up to $3,000/month subsistence allowance. Application deadlines are February 1 and September 1.

The Alberta Foundation for the Arts also offers the Grant MacEwan Literary Arts Scholarship. This scholarship program recognizes two students who demonstrate talent and potential along with clear educational or training goals in the literary arts. Two scholarships are awarded annually to two young Albertans 25 years of age or younger. The value of each scholarship is $5,000 and the annual deadline is May 1.

In addition, the AFA offers the Grant MacEwan Literary Arts Award; for more details, see Chapter 7, Writing Awards & Competitions.

British Columbia Arts Council
Box 9819, Stn. Prov. Govt., Victoria, BC V8W 9W3
Phone: (250) 356-1728 Fax: (250) 387-4099
E-mail: walter.quan@gov.bc.ca
Website: www.bcartscouncil.ca
Contact: Walter K. Quan, coordinator, Arts Awards Programs

Project Assistance for Creative Writers is available to B.C. professional writers with at least the equivalent of 1 book previously published professionally. Awards of up to $5,000 ($10,000 for writers with 3 or more books published professionally) may be used for specific creative projects. Eligible genres include fiction, drama, non-fiction, poetry, and juvenile. One juried competition is held annually. Application deadline September 15.

The Canada Council for the Arts

350 Albert Street, P.O. Box 1047, Ottawa, ON KIP 5V8

Phone: (613) 566-4414, ext. 5537 locally or after hours, or 1-800-263-5588 Fax: (613) 566-4410

E-mail: firstname.lastname@canadacouncil.ca (e.g., Marcel Hull: marcel.hull@canadacouncil.ca)

Website: www.canadacouncil.ca/writing

The Canada Council offers Canadian writers substantial financial support through a variety of programs, most notably Grants for Professional Writers – Creative Writing and Travel Grants, Literary Readings, Literary Festivals, and Author Residencies. It should be noted, however, that these grants are not available to unpublished writers. For fiction, applicants must have had at least 1 literary book published by a professional house or 4 major texts (short stories, excerpts from a novel, etc.) published on 2 separate occasions in recognized literary periodicals or anthologies. (See website for poetry and non-fiction publication requirements.)

Creative Writing Grants help authors working on new projects in fiction, poetry, children's literature, graphic novel, or literary non-fiction. (Literature creation projects based on the spoken word or technology may be submitted to the Spoken Word and Storytelling Program.) Grants range from $3,000 to $25,000. (Contact Marion Vitrac, ext. 5537.)

Travel Grants help writers with career-related travel expenses (e.g., being a keynote speaker at an international conference or festival). Grants are $500, $750, $1,000, $1,500, $2,000, and $2,500. (Contact Marion Vitrac, ext. 5537.)

The Literary Readings program provides opportunities for writers to read from their works and discuss them with the public. (Contact Mona Kiame, ext. 4016.)

Author Residencies provide financial assistance to organizations such as universities, libraries, and writers' associations to retain the services of a writer-in-residence, thus encouraging exchanges between the author and the community as well as enabling the author to work on a writing project. (Contact Mona Kiame, ext. 4016.)

The Literary Performance and Spoken Word and Program supports innovative literary projects not based upon conventional book or printed magazine formats through grants to creation, production, public performance, broadcast, or dissemination. This includes dub and rap poetry, poetry performance, and storytelling. Priority is given to projects that extend the boundaries of literary expression and are not just representing existing literature in a new format. (Contact Mona Kiame, ext. 4016.)

The Grants to Aboriginal Writers, Storytellers, and Publishers Program offers grants to Aboriginal writers and storytellers as well as Aboriginal-controlled publishers, periodicals, and collectives. (Contact ext. 5482.)

Please note that these programs are subject to change. Check website for eligibility conditions and guidelines.

Conseil des arts et des lettres du Québec

Quebec City office: 79 René-Lévesque Boulevard E., 3rd Floor,
    Quebec City, QC GIR 5N5
Phone: (418) 643-1707 or 1-800-897-1707 Fax: (418) 643-4558
Montreal office: 500 Place d'Armes, 15th Floor, Montreal, QC
    H2Y 2W2
Phone: (514) 864-3350 or 1-800-608-3350 Fax: (514) 864-4160
E-mail: info@calq.gouv.qc.ca
Website: www.calq.gouv.qc.ca

Grants are offered for Quebec's professional writers and storytellers (in English or French) in the following categories: grants for up-and-coming writers and storytellers, mid-career grants and development grants, and career grants. Depending on the grant category, a number of activities are eligible for funding: research, creation, and exploration; literary or storytelling shows; development and advanced training; and travel. The program fosters research and creation by making available to professional writers and storytellers the resources necessary for creating works and carrying out activities related to their artistic development throughout their careers. Check website for eligibility criteria and application forms.

Manitoba Arts Council
93 Lombard Avenue, Suite 525, Winnipeg, MB R3B 3B1
Phone: (204) 945-2237 or 1-866-994-2787 (toll-free in MB)
    Fax: (204) 945-5925
E-mail: psanders@artscouncil.mb.ca or info@artscouncil.mb.ca
Website: www.artscouncil.mb.ca
Contact: Patricia Sanders, literary arts program consultant
Offers several potential sources of funding for writers: The
Writers A Grant, worth up to $10,000, is designed to support con-
centrated work on a major writing project by professional Manitoba
writers who have published 2 books and who show a high standard
of work and exceptional promise. The Writers B Grant, for
Manitoba writers with 1 published book, is worth up to $5,000.
The Writers C Grant, worth up to $2,000, for emerging writers
with a modest publication background, is available to support a
variety of developmental writing projects. Writers A, B, and C
Grants have a May 20 deadline.

The Major Arts Grant supports personal creative projects of 6 to
10 months' duration by writers who have made a nationally or
internationally recognized contribution to their discipline. Covering
living and travel expenses and project costs, this grant is worth up
to $25,000. Finally, published Manitoba writers can apply for a
Travel and Professional Development Grant, to a maximum of
$1,200, to support significant career opportunities. Guidelines for
all programs are available on the website. Please note that these
programs are open to Manitoba residents only.

New Brunswick Arts Board
61 Carleton Street, Fredericton, NB E3B 3T2
Phone: (506) 444-4444 or 1-866-460-2787 Fax: (506) 444-5543
E-mail: rbryar@artsnb.ca
Website: www.artsnb.ca
Contact: Robert Bryar, program officer
Several potential sources of funding exist for emerging, mid-
career, and senior writers. Permanent residency in New Brunswick
is required. Deadlines for applications vary by program. Consult
the website for available programs. Application forms can be downloaded from website.

Newfoundland and Labrador Arts Council

1 Springdale Street, P.O. Box 98, St. John's, NL A1C 5H5
Phone: (709) 726-2212 or 1-866-726-2212 Fax: (709) 726-0619
E-mail: krice@nlac.ca
Website: www.nlac.nf.ca
Contact: Katrina Rice, program officer

Newfoundland and Labrador writers can apply to the NLAC for funding support under the Project Grant Program for the March 15 and September 15 annual deadlines. Project grants are intended to help support artists as they carry out work in their discipline. Grants may be used for living expenses and materials, study, and travel costs. They generally range from $1,000 to $7,500. The amount of funding to be awarded changes at each deadline based on the total request for funding in the writing discipline.

Northwest Territories Arts Council

Department of Education, Culture and Employment,
   Government of the N.W.T., P.O. Box 1320, Yellowknife, NT
   X1A 2L9
Phone: 1-877-445-2787, ext. 5 Fax: (867) 873-0205
E-mail: boris_atamanenko@gov.nt.ca
Website: www.pwnhc.ca/artscouncil
Contact: Boris Atamanenko, manager, community programs

The mandate of the N.W.T. Arts Council is to promote the visual, literary, media, and performing arts in the territories. Deadline is February 28 each year. For applications and guidelines, call or write to the community programs manager.

Nova Scotia Department of Tourism, Culture and Heritage

1800 Argyle Street, Suite 601, P.O. Box 456, Halifax, NS B3J 2R5
Phone: (902) 424-3422 Fax: (902) 424-0710
E-mail: kirbypc@gov.ns.ca
Website: www.gov.ns.ca/tch
Contact: Peter Kirby, program officer

The Arts Section of the Culture Division of the Department of Tourism, Culture and Heritage is directed to support the creation of new work by professional artists (both established and emerging) in all disciplines, including literary, media arts (experimental film, video, and electronic art), performing arts (music, theatre, and dance), visual arts and craft, and multidisciplinary work. Applicants must be Canadian citizens or landed immigrants who have lived in Nova Scotia for at least 12 months prior to the application deadline.

Professional Development Grants offer assistance up to $3,000 for formal study programs or to participate in other professional development programs such as mentoring, apprenticeships, conferences, etc.

Creation Grants provide assistance up to $12,000 to assist artists in any art form by contributing toward the artist's subsistence and project costs.

Presentation Grants offer assistance up to $5,000 to help cover direct costs of public presentation of the artist's work.

Application deadlines for programs are May 15 and December 15.

Ontario Arts Council

Literature Programs, 151 Bloor Street W., 5th Floor, Toronto, ON M5S 1T6

Phone: (416) 961-1660 or 1-800-387-0058 Fax: (416) 961-7796

E-mail: info@arts.on.ca

Website: www.arts.on.ca

Contact: John Degen, literature officer

The Writers' Reserve program assists talented, emerging, and established writers in the creation of new work in fiction, poetry, writing for children, literary criticism, arts commentary, history, biography, or politics/social issues. Writers' Reserve grants are awarded through designated book and periodical publishers, who recommend authors for funding support up to a maximum of $5,000.

The Works-in-Progress program offers support ($12,000) in the completion of major book-length works of literary merit in poetry or prose by published writers.

Programs are open to Ontario residents only. Download program guidelines and application forms from the website.

Prince Edward Island Council of the Arts

115 Richmond Street, Charlottetown, PE C1A 1H7

Phone: (902) 620-3417 or 1-888-734-2784 Fax: (902) 368-4418

E-mail: programs@peiartscouncil.com

Website: www.peiartscouncil.com

Contact: Darrin White, executive director

Arts assistance grants are available to support Island writers. Professional development grants are offered from $500 to $1,200; creation/production grants to a maximum of $3,000 are offered for an emerging professional artist, and to a maximum of $5,000 for a senior professional artist; and dissemination/presentation grants to a maximum of $1,000 are offered for an emerging professional artist, to $1,200 for a senior professional artist. Application deadlines are set each spring; see website or contact Council for current dates.

Saskatchewan Arts Board

Regina office: 1355 Broad Street, Regina, SK S4R 7VI
Phone: (306) 787-4056 or 1-800-667-7526 (SK only) Fax: (306) 787-4199
Saskatoon office: 417 – 24th Street E., Saskatoon, SK S7K OK7
Phone: (306) 964-1155 Fax: (306) 964-1167
E-mail: grants@artsboard.sk.ca or saskartsboard@artsboard.sk.ca
Website: www.artsboard.sk.ca
Contact: Deron Staffen, grants coordinator

Creative, professional development, and research grants are offered under the Independent Artists Grant Program. Creative grants assist artists to create, develop, and/or perform new work, and include professional development and research. Maximum grants are $17,000 for established artists and $6,000 for emerging artists. Professional development grants are a maximum of $7,500 for established artists and $4,000 for emerging artists. Research grants are a maximum of $5,000 for established artists and $2,000 for emerging artists. The maximum travel grants are $1,500. Deadlines for all Independent Artists Grants are March 15 and October 1.

Travel grants are offered to assist artists to attend events in which their work will be discussed or presented, or at which they will have an opportunity for career growth or development. Travel grants are a maximum of $750 (individual) or $1,500 (ensemble or collective).

The Indigenous Pathways Initiative offers grants to Indigenous artists to a maximum of $6,000 for the Contemporary Arts Program, which includes the research and/or creation of literary works. Deadlines are April 15 and October 1.

Saskatchewan Arts Board grants are only available to Saskatchewan residents.

Yukon Department of Tourism and Culture

Tourism and Culture Centre, 100 Hanson Street, Whitehorse, YK
   YIA 2C6

Phone: (867) 667-5036 Fax: (867) 393-6456

E-mail: artsfund@gov.yk.ca

Website: www.tc.gov.yk.ca

   Individual Yukon writers may be eligible for an Advanced Artist
Award of up to $5,000 for a specific project. Training support
through the Cultural Industry Training Fund is also available for
writers who meet the eligibility requirements. Artists who present
their work at festivals and other events may apply to the Touring
Artist Fund for assistance. Group projects contributing to development of the arts in the Yukon are supported through the Arts Fund.

9

PROFESSIONAL DEVELOPMENT

Writers at every level of experience can extend their skills and find fresh ideas through all manner of writing courses and workshops. Some believe creative writing is best fostered in the university or college environment by working with a good teacher who understands literary devices and structures and the power of language. Many skills peculiar to non-fiction writing, generally considered more a craft than an art, can be learned through courses or workshops led by experienced writers who have discovered not only how to refine ideas but how to research them, transform them into workable structures, and finally, market them. Some creative writers swear by the hothouse atmosphere, creative exchange of ideas, and collective reinforcement to be found in workshops led by expert facilitators.

Local branches of the Canadian Authors Association, libraries, and adult education classes offered by boards of education are some sources of writing courses and workshops. Regional writers' associations sometimes organize them, too, and are always a good source of information about what's currently available in your area.

This chapter is divided into two parts: first, a review of some of the country's most interesting writing schools, workshops, and retreats; second, a sample of the opportunities for the development of writing skills currently offered by Canadian colleges and universities. Writers' opportunities for professional development are extraordinarily diverse in Canada. Before you commit yourself, define your needs and carefully evaluate each program to see how it might meet them.

The summer courses, generally about a week long and built around small, daily workshop sessions, offer participants the chance to increase their technical skills, to submit their work to group scrutiny and critical feedback, and to enjoy, and learn from, the company of fellow writers as well as editors, agents, and other publishing professionals. Courses are sometimes streamed in order to cater to different levels of experience. Workshop facilitators are often nationally or internationally acclaimed authors, and some course participants enrol simply for the chance to work with them, but the best facilitators aren't necessarily the top literary names.

The workshop experience can be intense and demanding, and the rewards elusive. To get the most from it, bring at least one well-developed piece of writing with you, and be prepared to work hard during and outside the main sessions, but also use the opportunity to rub shoulders with other seekers, to network, and to bask in that all-too-rare sense of being part of a community of writers.

For those writers harried by family and job obligations, frustrated by the distractions of city living, and with a manuscript they simply must finish, writers' retreats and colonies offer peaceful seclusion, a beautiful rural setting, and a "room of one's own" in which to work without interruption, with meals and accommodation taken care of. Note that these are not teaching situations.

The larger section of this chapter, on creative writing and journalism courses offered at universities and colleges, surveys only some of the more significant programs, as well as a number of university-based workshops. The list is far from exhaustive. Many universities, colleges of applied arts, and community colleges offer writing courses at some level, depending on staff availability and student demand. Not all courses are taught every year, and programs can change at short notice. Continuing-education courses are open to all, but entry to credit courses is generally limited to those with specific academic prerequisites, although experienced writers can sometimes win special permission from the course convenor. Find out where you stand before developing your plans.

Creative Writing Schools, Workshops, & Retreats

The Banff Centre Writing Programs
P.O. Box 1020, Stn. 51, Banff, AB TIL 1H5
Phone: (403) 762-6203 Fax: (403) 763-6277
E-mail: arts_info@banffcentre.ca
Website: www.banffcentre.ca

All the following programs provide opportunities for professional writers, who must choose the program that best serves their needs and objectives. Banff staff are happy to discuss this individually with applicants. Also contact the centre to discuss fee schedules and possible funding options.

The Leighton Artists' Colony for Independent Residencies
Application deadline: may apply at any time

This year-round program offers working residencies for independent professional artists engaged in the creation of new work and provides opportunities for concentrated focus in a retreat environment. Writers, screenwriters, playwrights, literary translators, composers, singer-songwriters, curators, art theorists, and professionals working in theatre, dance, and film at the conceptualization or research stage of a project are eligible. The 8 fully equipped studios are situated in a beautiful, quiet, wooded area.

Literary Journalism Program
April–June (off-site); July–August (on-site)
Application deadline: March

The Literary Journalism Program was established in response to an endowment from the Government of Alberta and Maclean Hunter Limited. The program offers 8 established writers of non-fiction an opportunity to develop a major essay, memoir, or feature piece. A month-long residency enables writers to work on their manuscript during individual consultations with faculty and during round-table discussions. Participants are able to advance their professional development through work with both the program chair and experienced editors, and through interaction with each other, invited guest speakers, and artists from other fields.

Applicants are usually accomplished journalists and writers

who have been published in national and/or international magazines, newspapers, anthologies, or literary journals; however, writers with less experience have also been accepted to the program based on merit.

Mountain and Wilderness Writing Program
August–October (off-site); October–November (on-site)
Application deadline: June

In this unique residency program, 6 writers will delve into their own writing projects (essay, memoir, biography, poetry, feature article, or fiction) on a topic in the area of mountain or wilderness culture, including writing with a focus on adventure, history, or the environment. Offers participants the time, privacy, and editorial resources to focus on their proposed piece. Writers work in a diverse and creative environment, interacting with other mountain writers and editors in group discussions and individual consultations, as well as with invited guest speakers and artists from other fields.

Self-Directed Writing Residencies
Application deadline: may apply at any time

Self-directed writing residencies provide time, space, and facilities for individual research, editing, and manuscript development. There are no formal activities organized around a self-directed writing residency; writers structure their own time and are free to maintain privacy or to engage with other artists and activities at the Banff Centre.

Wired Writing Studio
October (on-site); November–March (online)
Application deadline: June

The Wired Writing Studio is a unique opportunity for poets and writers of fiction and other narrative prose to pursue their artistic visions and develop their voices through one-on-one editorial assistance from experienced writers/editors, as well as through involvement in a community of working writers, both on-site at the Banff Centre and online for 5 months following the residency. Intended specifically for those producing work of literary merit who are at an early stage in their careers, this program offers an extended period of writing time: 2 weeks in Banff and the remaining 20 weeks in the writer's own home or work space, working online.

Writing Studio
April–June
Application deadline: December

Offers a unique, supportive context for writers in the early stage of their careers to pursue a writing project. Writers spend 5 weeks at the Banff Centre working on their manuscripts in individual consultation with senior writers/editors. Enrolment is limited to 24 writers.

Writing with Style
September and April
Application deadline: May and February

A 7-day workshop for writers at all levels, led by program director Edna Alford. Resource faculty change from year to year. The program provides writers of all levels with the opportunity to work on a novel, short fiction, memoir, poetry, travel writing, nature writing, creative non-fiction, and writing for children.

Be A Better Writer

190 Scott Point Drive, Salt Spring Island, BC V8K 2P9
E-mail: pearl@pearlluke.com
Website: www.be-a-better-writer.com
Contact: Pearl Luke

Author and Commonwealth Prize–winner Pearl Luke mentors beginning and intermediate writers through any project online with personal feedback, manuscript evaluations, editing, and Q&A. Instruction is flexible and suited to the individual. Hourly and monthly programs starting from $100.

Booming Ground

Creative Writing Program, 1866 Main Mall, Buchanan E462,
    University of B.C., Vancouver, BC V6T 1Z1
Phone: (604) 822-2469 Fax: (604) 822-3616
E-mail: contact@boomingground.com
Website: www.boomingground.com

A non-credit option that offers writing courses as well as an innovative series of writing mentorships in poetry, fiction, non-fiction, and writing for children, as well as manuscript evaluation. Mentorships provide one-on-one feedback by e-mail directly from an instructor as students work on a writing project over 6 months. Manuscript evaluations provide a constructive written report from one of our instructors, giving concrete suggestions for revisions and corrections.

See website for application deadlines and current mentors. Manuscript evaluations may be requested at any time.

The mentorship fee is $500. Manuscript evaluations cost $400 for 30,000 words of fiction or non-fiction, or 60 pages of poetry, with an additional $1/page thereafter.

CANSCAIP's Packaging Your Imagination Workshop
40 Orchard View Boulevard, Suite 104, Lower Level, Toronto, ON
  M4R 1B9
Phone: (416) 515-1559
E-mail: office@canscaip.org
Website: www.canscaip.org/pyi

The Canadian Society of Children's Authors, Illustrators and Performers holds this day-long workshop each November for anyone interested in writing, illustrating, or performing for young people. More than a dozen lectures, talks, and workshops are presented at Victoria College, the University of Toronto, by professionals respected in their fields. Those interested should contact CANSCAIP for a brochure (available in May).

Community of Writers: Tatamagouche Workshops for
  Writers
Tatamagouche Centre, 259 Loop Route 6, R.R. #3,
  Tatamagouche, NS B0K 1V0
Phone: 1-800-218-2220
E-mail: tatacent@tatacentre.ca
Website: www.tatacentre.ca
Contact: Gwen Davies

Week-long writing retreats that combine intensive, small-group workshops that welcome both experienced and serious beginning writers along with an independent retreat program for writers working on a manuscript. Workshops are led by a professional writer and an adult educator. The aim of the week is to discover skills, push the writing, receive support, learn from other writers, and join a community that includes writers at all levels. The schedule includes daily workshop sessions, feedback on your writing, free time to write (and savour the grounds on Nova Scotia's North Shore), readings, and talks by writers. Costs are modest, with largely shared accommodation and wonderful down-home cooking.

Visit the website to check out this year's workshops.

Emma Lake Kenderdine Campus of the Arts and Ecology Creative Residency Program

P.O. Box 429, Christopher Lake, SK S0J 0N0
Phone: (306) 966-2463 Fax: (306) 966-6881
E-mail: emma.lake@usask.ca
Website: www.emmalake.usask.ca
Contact: Paul Trottier, director

Writers, visual artists, performance artists, musicians, composers, critics, curators, arts administrators, and designers are invited to apply for the residency program during June and August. It provides work space, accommodation, and meals in a retreat environment where participants can work independently on their own projects for 1 to 5 weeks, depending on availability. The program also features an invited artist in residence whenever possible, although that artist is not required to provide formal instruction. Cost of the program is $703.55 plus taxes/week. Check website for residency dates.

The Humber School for Writers

School of Creative and Performing Arts, Humber College, 3199
    Lake Shore Boulevard W., Toronto, ON M8V 1K8
Phone: (416) 675-6622, ext. 3448 Fax: (416) 251-7167
E-mail: antanas.sileika@humber.ca or hilary.higgins@humber.ca
Website: www.humber.ca/scapa/programs/school-writers
Contacts: Antanas Sileika, artistic director; Hilary Higgins, secretary

One of Canada's best schools for writers offers a week-long writing workshop in fiction, creative non-fiction, and poetry each July. A residency option is available. The workshop fee (including all lunches) is $949, plus approximately $425 for those who opt to stay in residence. A small number of scholarships may be available for those in need.

Each year the school also offers a unique 30-week certificate program in creative writing by correspondence, beginning in January, May, or September, with application deadlines about 3 months before each start date. This extraordinary program offers promising writers the opportunity to send their work in progress (novel, short stories, or poetry) directly to their instructors, who provide editorial feedback by e-mail or post on a continuing basis for 30 weeks. Over 260 former students have been published, including Vincent Lam, the Giller Prize winner in 2006. Instructors who have taught this program include the distinguished writers Alistair MacLeod, Guy Vanderhaeghe, Edward Albee, Roddy Doyle, Peter Carey, Timothy Findley, Elisabeth Harvor, Isabel Huggan, Paul Quarrington, and D. M. Thomas. The authors' pick for the best fiction manuscripts to emerge from the workshop are submitted to the Humber School for Writers Literary Agency.

This correspondence program in creative writing is offered at the postgraduate level. Applicants must be graduates of a college or university program, or have the equivalent in life experience (Prior Learning Assessment). Applicants must also submit a 15-page writing sample along with a proposal of the work to be completed during the course. The fee is approximately $3,000. A few scholarships are available for those who demonstrate writing promise and financial need, among them the Timothy Findley/William Whitehead scholarship funded by HarperCollins Canada, and the James Appel scholarship. Some scholarships are limited to Ontario residents. Qualified applicants are eligible for Ontario Student Assistance Plan funding.

Maritime Writers' Workshops
College of Extended Learning, University of New Brunswick,
    P.O. Box 4400, Fredericton, NB E3B 5A3
Phone: (506) 453-4646 or 1-866-599-4646
E-mail: ahowells@unb.ca
Website: www.unb.ca/cel/programs/creative/maritime-writers/
    index.html
Contact: Alison Howells, program development officer

"Are you a beginner or a seasoned professional writer? Then the Maritime Writers' Workshop is for you! Spend a day or a week with some of the region's best writers who will lead you through workshop discussions and help you get writing! Go ahead, flex your writing muscles, sharpen your pencil, and dip your quill into the depths of your desire to write!"

Continuing a 30-year tradition of delivering quality literary workshops in a creative, supportive, and affordable environment, the Maritime Writers' Workshop runs the first full week of July in Fredericton. Instructors have included such writers as Governor General Award–winners George Elliott Clarke (fiction) and Anne Compton (poetry), and e-publishing guru Biff Mitchell (mystery and suspense).

Sage Hill Writing Experience

P.O. Box 1731, Saskatoon, SK S7K 3S1
Phone: (306) 652-7395 Fax: (306) 244-0255
E-mail: sage.hill@sasktel.net
Website: www.sagehillwriting.ca

Sage Hill's 10-day summer writing workshops are held annually in rural Saskatchewan at St. Michael's Retreat Centre in Lumsden, in the beautiful Qu'Appelle Valley, north of Regina. The facility has private rooms with bath, meeting rooms, walking woods, and home-style cooking.

The program offers workshops at introductory, intermediate, and advanced levels in fiction, non-fiction, poetry, and playwriting (though not all these courses are available each year). The low writer-to-instructor ratio (usually 6 to 1) and high-quality faculty (all established writers) help make these workshops and colloquiums among the most highly valued in Canada.

Fees per course of $1,195 for the summer program include accommodation, meals, and instruction. Scholarships are available. Enrolment is limited. Applicants should send for guidelines or check them on the website. The summer program registration deadline is in April.

Three annual Teen Writing Experiences, primarily for Saskatchewan writers aged 14 to 18, are held in July. For these free, 5-day creative writing "camps," held in Saskatoon, Moose Jaw, and Regina, out-of-towners may have to arrange their own accommodation and transportation. See website for application deadlines, which vary by location.

A Spring Poetry Colloquium, held in May at St. Michael's Retreat,

Lumsden, is an intensive, 2-week manuscript-development seminar/ retreat, also open to writers from outside Saskatchewan. This program features ample writing time, group discussions, and one-on-one critiques by the instructor, as well as online follow-up with the instructor. The fee of $1,395 includes tuition, accommodation, and meals. Application deadline is in March.

Saskatchewan Writers / Artists Colonies & Retreats

c/o P.O. Box 3986, Regina, SK S4P 3R9
Phone: (306) 757-6310 Fax: (306) 565-8554
E-mail: skretreats@skwriter.com
Website: www.skwriter.com/sk-writers-artists-retreats

The colonies and retreats were established in 1979 to provide an environment where writers and artists (especially but not exclusively from Saskatchewan) can work free from distractions in serene and beautiful locations. They are not teaching situations but retreats, offering uninterrupted work time and opportunities for a stimulating exchange of ideas with fellow writers and artists after hours. All writers and artists may apply for a colony. Costs are subsidized by the Saskatchewan Lotteries, SaskCulture, and the Saskatchewan Arts Board. St. Peter's Abbey is a Benedictine abbey near the city of Humboldt. Spring Valley Guest Ranch is located in southwest Saskatchewan, near Ravenscrag.

A 5-week summer colony (July to August) and a 3-week winter colony (February and March) are held at St. Peter's Abbey. Applicants may request as much time as they need, to a maximum of 3 weeks in winter and 4 weeks in summer, but accommodation in private rooms is limited to 10 people per week in summer, and 18 in winter. A third colony of 2 weeks is held in June at Spring Valley Guest Ranch.

Individual retreats of up to 2 weeks per person annually are offered year round at St. Peter's, with no more than 3 individuals being accommodated at a time. Application procedure is the same as the colony process. Applicants are required to submit a 10-page writing sample of recent work, a résumé, description of the work to be done at the colony, and 2 references.

Consult the website for current fees and complete application information.

University of Toronto School of Continuing Studies Creative Writing Program

University of Toronto School of Continuing Studies, 158
St. George Street, Toronto, ON M5S 2V8
Phone: (416) 978-6714 Fax: (416) 978-6091
E-mail: scs.writing@utoronto.ca
Website: www.learn.utoronto.ca
Contacts: Lee Gowan, program head; Bill Zaget, program
administrator

The School of Continuing Studies at the University of Toronto offers the broadest curriculum of any writing program in Canada. The courses are taught by outstanding writers and publishers, each of whom brings a wealth of experience and accomplishment to the classroom. Enrolment is limited to guarantee that each student receives individual attention. The school offers certificates in creative writing and in freelance writing, and the creative writing certificate can now be taken online.

The annual Random House of Canada Student Award in Writing (a $1,000 prize) is open to writers who are enrolled in the program. The winner of the prize and two runners-up are also published in a chapbook produced by Random House. The Marina Nemat Award ($1,000) is presented to the top certificate student each year.

The wide range of courses includes an introduction to creative writing; writing short fiction; writing the novel; poetry; mystery and suspense writing; graphic novels and comics; popular fiction; screenwriting; dramatic writing; songwriting; creative non-fiction; memoir; freelance and feature writing; meditation and writing; and courses on the business of writing.

Instructors in the program include Michael Winter, Ken McGoogan, Alissa York, Dennis Bock, Ray Robertson, Kim Echlin, David Layton, Dave Bidini, Kelli Deeth, Colleen Murphy, Shaughnessy Bishop-Stall, Kathy Kacer, Ken Babstock, Margaret Christakos, Kelli Deeth, Catherine Graham, and Kathryn Kuitenbrouwer.

Most courses are 20 hours in duration and usually run from October to December, February to April, April to June, and July to August and are priced at $599. Online courses are $625.

There is also the U of T Summer Writing School, a 5-day intensive workshop in mid-July. The program features limited enrolment, daily round-table workshops, a one-on-one tutorial with the instructor, panel discussions, instructor and student readings, and the opportunity to meet and discuss your work with other emerging writers.

The workshops in 2012 featured Joy Fielding on writing a bestseller, poetry with Ken Babstock, memoir writing with Marina Nemat and Dave Bidini, screenwriting with Norman Snider, and songwriting with Justin Rutledge.

For more information, visit the website or contact the SCS by phone or e-mail. A print course calendar is also available.

Vancouver School of Writing
Phone: (778) 300-5152
E-mail: director@vancouverschoolofwriting.com
Website: www.vancouverschoolofwriting.com

Offers online courses and workshops for new writers, aiming to provide "simple, straightforward global learning on how to write a book and get it published successfully, exploring the multiple choices writers have in this electronic age." Core programming is "I Want to Write a Book" program, which is complemented courses on topics such as literary agents, e-book creation, online marketing, and author grants. Also offers 1- and 2-week writing retreats in Mexico each February, manuscript assessments, and occasional free or low-cost in-person events in Vancouver.

The Writing School at Winghill
38 McArthur Avenue, Suite 2951, Ottawa, ON KIL 6R2
Phone: 1-800-267-1829 Fax: (613) 749-9551
E-mail: alex@winghill.com
Website: www.winghill.com
Contact: Alex Myers

For over 25 years, the school has offered creative writing courses by distance. These diploma courses are designed to help the student to publish. They give starting writers a thorough and practical understanding of the needs of the marketplace, and build creative and technical skills. The courses can be completed online.

The student works with his or her tutor on a variety of assignments, each structured to improve specific skills. All tutors at the school are working writers. Assignments are tailored to reflect the individual interests and abilities of each student. Course fees are

$748 in U.S. dollars, which cover all costs, including books, lessons, DVDs, CDs, and tutorial.

The school offers prospective students a free evaluation of their work. Call the toll-free number for a free brochure detailing course contents and methodology, and for more about the evaluation service.

Creative Writing & Journalism at Colleges & Universities

Acadia University

15 University Avenue, Wolfville, NS B4P 2R6
Phone: (902) 585-1502 Fax: (902) 585-1070
E-mail: wanda.campbell@acadiau.ca
Website: http://english.acadiau.ca/creative-writing.html
Contact: Wanda Campbell, creative writing coordinator

The Department of English offers the following credit courses at the undergraduate level: Exploring Creative Writing: An Introduction, Advanced Creative Writing: Poetry, and Advanced Creative Writing: Fiction. There is also the option to write an honours creative writing thesis in poetry, fiction, or drama under the guidance of a published author.

University of Alberta

3 – 5 Humanities Centre, Edmonton, AB T6G 2E5
Phone: (780) 492-3258 Fax: (780) 492-8142
E-mail: efs@ualberta.ca
Website: www.efs.ualberta.ca
Contacts: Thomas Wharton and Christine Stewart, Write Program co-directors

The Department of English and Film Studies offers credit courses in creative writing such as Introductory and Intermediate Poetry, Fiction, and Non-Fiction; Projects in Genre; and Advanced Fiction and Non-Fiction.

In summer, creative writing classes are available through the extension program, and female writers may attend Women's Words: Summer Writing Week. Consult www.extension.ualberta.ca for details.

Algoma University

1520 Queen Street E., Sault Ste. Marie, ON P6A 2G4
Phone: (705) 949-2301 Fax: (705) 949-6583
E-mail: alanna.bondar@algomau.ca or linda.burnett@algomau.ca
Website: www.algomau.ca/departments/english-at-algoma
Contacts: Alanna Bondar and Linda Burnett, associate professors,
   English Department
   The English Department offers the following credit courses:
Creative Writing, Studies in Creative Writing, and Introduction to
Creative Writing.

Algonquin College

1385 Woodroffe Avenue, Ottawa, ON K2G IV8
Phone: (613) 727-4723, ext. 2457 Fax: (613) 727-7707
E-mail: mcinnin@algonquincollege.com
Website: www.algonquincollege.com
Contact: Nadine MacInnes, coordinator/professor
   The School of Media and Design offers 2-year diploma pro-
grams in both print journalism and writing. The Professional
Writing program offers credit courses such as Storytelling Theory,
Writing for the Web, and a Creative Writing Workshop. As well, the
program offers training in writing for corporate, government, and
other professional environments.
   In addition, a 1-year e-publishing graduate certificate teaches
students the technical and business skills necessary to establish and
maintain a web-based publication.
   Publishes *The Algonquin Times* (available online at http://times.
webcitybeat.com/).

Brandon University

270 – 18th Street, Brandon, MB R7A 6A9
Phone: (204) 727-9780 Fax: (204) 726-0473
E-mail: lakevold@brandonu.ca
Website: www.brandonu.ca
Contact: Dale Lakevold, assistant professor, Department of English
   The English Department offers courses in creative writing, cre-
ative non-fiction, ecopoetics, multimedia poetry, playwriting,
poetry, screenwriting, short fiction, and song lyrics, as well as an
advanced thesis-based course leading to a degree in the Creative

Arts. Other courses offered include academic writing (English) and business communications (Business Administration). The BU Publishing Board publishes the students' newspaper *The Quill*.

University of British Columbia

Creative Writing Program, Department of Theatre, Film and
　Creative Writing, Buchanan E462, 1866 Main Mall, Vancouver,
　BC V6T IZI
Phone: (604) 822-0699 Fax: (604) 822-3616
E-mail: patrose@mail.ubc.ca
Website: www.creativewriting.ubc.ca
Contact: Pat Rose, secretary

The Creative Writing Program offers courses of study leading to BFA and MFA degrees. A wide range of creative writing courses are available, including writing for screen and television, the novel and novella, short fiction, stage plays, radio plays and features, non-fiction, applied creative non-fiction, writing for children, lyric and libretto, translation, and poetry. A joint MFA with the theatre program is also possible. Students may choose to take a double major in creative writing and another subject.

The literary journal *PRISM international* is edited by program graduate students.

Brock University

500 Glenridge Avenue, St. Catharines, ON L2S 3AI
Phone: (905) 688-5550, ext. 3469 Fax: (905) 688-4461
E-mail: engl@brocku.ca
Website: www.brocku.ca/humanities
Contacts: Robert Alexander, writing program director; Janet
　Sackfie, administrative assistant

The Department of English Language and Literature offers credit courses in reporting and news writing for mass media and a creative writing course in poetry. A BA with a major in English and professional writing is available, as well as a minor in professional writing and a certificate in professional writing.

University of Calgary

Department of English, Social Sciences Building, Suite 1152,
　2500 University Drive N.W., Calgary, AB T2N IN4

Phone: (403) 220-5470 Fax: (403) 289-1123
E-mail: cbok@ucalgary.ca
Website: http://english.ucalgary.ca/content/creative-writing
Contacts: Christian Bök, coordinator, Creative Writing

The Creative Writing Department offers English degrees with a concentration in creative writing. Courses include Poetry Writing, Fiction, and Prose (in which a book-length manuscript is produced).

The Calgary Distinguished Writers Program ensures an annual writer-in-residence, as well as short-term visits by major writers. The English Literature Student Society publishes *NōD*, a literary journal publishing work by established and emerging writers.

Cambrian College of Applied Arts & Technology
1400 Barrydowne Road, Sudbury, ON P3A 3V8
Phone: (705) 560-0330
E-mail: continuing@cambriancollege.ca
Website: www.cambriancollege.ca
Contacts: Ann Frampton and Marlene McIntosh, program officers

Continuing Education offers several online writing courses, including creative writing, poetry writing, romance writing, short story writing, travel writing, writing for publication, and writing for the web.

Camosun College
3100 Foul Bay Road, Victoria, BC V8P 5J2
Phone: (250) 370-3123
E-mail: niwa@camosun.bc.ca
Website: www.camosun.ca
Contact: Maureen Niwa, English department chair

The English Department offers credit courses in creative writing in fiction, poetry, and scriptwriting.

A variety of Continuing Education courses and programs are available in creative writing, including feature writing, travel writing, romantic writing, and selling freelance writing.

Credit courses in writing for the print and electronic media are offered as components of the 20-month, full-time Applied Communications program. Students write and produce radio and cable television programs.

Capilano University

2055 Purcell Way, North Vancouver, BC V7J 3H5
Phone: (604) 986-1911 Fax: (604) 984-4985
E-mail: humanities@capilanou.ca or ehamilton@capilanou.ca
Website: www.capilanou.ca
Contacts: Reg Johanson, English Department coordinator;
   Edward Hamilton, Communication Studies program convenor
   The English Department offers an Associate of Arts degree in creative writing. The Communications Department offers a degree program in communication studies, and certificate programs in communications and magazine publishing.

Centennial College of Applied Arts & Technology

951 Carlaw Avenue, Toronto, ON M4K 3M2
Phone: (416) 289-5000, ext. 8820Fax: (416) 289-5106
E-mail: bwaite@centennialcollege.ca
Contact: Barry Waite, program coordinator
Website: www.centennialcollege.ca/thecentre
   The Centre for Creative Communications offers a 3-year diploma program in print journalism (or an 18-month "fast track") and online writing. Also a 1-year diploma program in corporate communications and public relations. Programs include courses in reporting, scriptwriting, broadcast journalism, documentary film writing, magazine writing, and feature writing. All programs emphasize practical skills.

Concordia University

1455 de Maisonneuve Boulevard W., Room LB-641, Montreal, QC
   H3G IM8
Phone: (514) 848-2424, ext. 2343 Fax: (514) 848-4501
E-mail: angally@alcor.concordia.ca
Website: http://english.concordia.ca
Contact: Angela Alleyne, assistant to coordinator of Creative
   Writing
   The Creative Writing Program within the English Department offers workshops for credit in writing poetry, prose and drama, and scriptwriting, as well as editing and publishing, and other special-topic courses.

Concordia University College of Alberta

7128 Ada Boulevard, Edmonton, AB T5B 4E4
Phone: (780) 479-9354 Fax: (780) 477-1033
E-mail: ruth.glancy@concordia.ab.ca
Website: http://english.concordia.ab.ca
Contact: Ruth Glancy, professor of English

The English Department offers the following credit courses in
creative writing: Essay Writing, Introduction to Creative Writing –
Non-Fiction, Introduction to Creative Writing – Fiction, and
Introduction to Creative Writing – Poetry. Instructors in the fiction
and poetry courses have graduate degrees in creative writing and
are published authors and poets, respectively.

Conestoga College of Applied Arts and Technology

299 Doon Valley Drive, Kitchener, ON N2G 4M4
Phone: (519) 748-5220, ext. 2377 Fax: (519) 748-3534
E-mail: lcornies@conestogac.on.ca
Contact: Larry Cornies, program coordinator
Website: www.conestogac.on.ca

Offers 2-year diplomas in journalism-print and journalism-
broadcasting, which prepare the graduate for employment in
various fields related to news writing and news production for
Internet publishers and newspapers, magazines, and radio or TV
stations. Students gain practical experience working on the college
newspaper, *Spoke*; the college's FM-radio station at CJIQ; and in
the television studio.

Continuing Education offers a creative writing workshop, and
creative writing classes are also available online through the ontar-
iolearn.com intercollegiate consortium.

Douglas College

P.O. Box 2503, New Westminster, BC V3L 5B2
Website: www.douglas.bc.ca

Creative Writing Department
Phone: (604) 527-5485 Fax: (604) 527-5095
E-mail: whartonc@douglascollege.ca
Contact: Calvin Wharton, chair

College credit and university transfer courses in creative writing are available. Courses include Introduction to Fiction Writing, Introduction to Playwriting, Introduction to Writing Poetry, Introduction to Writing Children's Literature, Writing Short Fiction, Writing Speculative Fiction, Personal Narrative, and Introduction to Historical Fiction Writing.

Publishes the literary journal *EVENT*.

Professional Writing Program
Phone: (604) 527-5292 Fax: (604) 527-5528
E-mail: printfutures@douglascollege.ca
Contact: Maureen Nicholson, program head

The Print Futures professional writing program is a 2-year diploma program preparing students for a professional writing career. It includes courses in writing, research, editorial and design skills, public relations writing, and writing for magazines and trade publications.

Durham College

2000 Simcoe Street N., Oshawa, ON L1H 7K4
Phone: (905) 721-2000 Fax: (905) 721-3195
E-mail: info@durhamcollege.ca
Website: www.durhamcollege.ca

The School of Media, Art and Design offers a 3-year Journalism – Print and Broadcast program and a 2-year Journalism – Print program.

Continuing Education offers non-credit courses in creative writing and getting published.

Publishes *The Chronicle*, a college newspaper that provides students with experience in writing, editing, design, layout, art, photography, and production.

En'owkin International School of Writing and Visual Arts

R.R. #2, Site 50, Comp. 8, Penticton, BC V2A 6J7
Phone: (250) 493-7181 Fax: (250) 493-5302
E-mail: enowkin@vip.net
Website: www.enowkincentre.ca

In cooperation with the University of Victoria's Foundations in Indigenous Fine Arts certificate program, offers the following credit courses: Introduction to Creative Writing; Writing for Children from a First Nations Perspective; Critical Process and World View; and Critical Process, Symbolism and Oral Tradition; First Nations Non-Fiction; Structure in Cinema and Television Drama.

University of Guelph
50 Stone Road E., Guelph, ON NIG 2WI
Phone: (519) 824-4120, ext. 56317 Fax: (519) 766-0844
E-mail: englthea@uoguelph.ca
Website: www.uoguelph.ca

The School of English and Theatre Studies offers the following undergraduate courses in Creative Writing: ENGL2920 Creative Writing: Fiction; ENGL2940 Creative Writing: Poetry; and ENGL4720 Creative Writing Seminar.

The university also offers an MFA program in creative writing, with workshops taught by faculty including Dionne Brand and Judith Thompson.

Humber College of Applied Arts and Technology
P.O. Box 1900, 205 Humber College Boulevard, Toronto, ON
  M9W 5L7
Phone: (416) 675-3111 Fax: (416) 675-2427
E-mail: enquiry@humber.ca
Website: www.humber.ca

Offers a part-time Freelance Writing for All Markets certificate as well as a 3-year diploma program in print and broadcast journalism. Business writing and technical writing courses are offered by Continuing Education. Comedy scriptwriting is available in the program Comedy: Writing and Performance.

See also Humber School for Writers, p. 410–411.

University of King's College
6350 Coburg Road, Halifax, NS B3H 2AI
Phone: (902) 422-1271 Fax: (902) 423-3357
E-mail: admissions@ukings.ns.ca
Contact: Kelly Toughill, director, School of Journalism
Website: www.ukings.ca

The Journalism School offers 1-year and 4-year Bachelor of Journalism programs, and a minor in Journalism Studies. Courses include Feature Writing, Foundations of Journalism, Reporting Techniques, Introduction to Narrative Non-Fiction, Business Reporting for Journalists, Advanced Magazine Workshop, and Investigative Workshop.

Lambton College
1457 London Road, Sarnia, ON N7S 6K4
Phone: (519) 542-7751 Fax: (519) 541-2408
E-mail: info@lambton.on.ca
Website: www.lambton.on.ca

The English and Communications Department offers courses including Creative Writing for Beginners, Essentials in Writing Fiction, Romance Writing, Science Fiction, The Short Story, Writing for Publication, and Writing Mysteries.

Langara College
100 W. 49th Avenue, Vancouver, BC V5Y 2Z6
Phone: (604) 323-5511 Fax: (604) 323-5555
E-mail: geninfo@langara.bc.ca
Website: www.langara.bc.ca

The Department of Journalism offers credit courses in the fundamentals of reporting, daily paper writing, magazine feature writing, advanced reporting, and specialty writing.

A variety of creative writing courses are offered by the English Department, including prose fiction, stageplay, poetry, screenwriting, and non-fiction.

A wide selection of creative writing courses are offered by Continuing Studies, including novel writing, comedy writing, writing a feature film, how to get published, travel writing, and writing for children.

University of Manitoba
Department of English, Film, and Theatre, 625 Fletcher Argue
   Building, 15 Chancellors Circle, Winnipeg, MB R3T 5V5
Phone: (204) 474-9678 Fax: (204) 474-7669
E-mail: english@umanitoba.ca
Contact: Arlene Young, department head
Website: www.umanitoba.ca/faculties/arts/english

The English Department offers an introduction to creative writing and advanced creative writing.

McMaster University

Department of English and Cultural Studies, Chester New Hall
  321, 1280 Main Street W., Hamilton, ON L8S 4L9
Phone: (905) 525-9140, ext. 24491 Fax: (905) 777-8316
E-mail: engdept@mcmaster.ca
Website: www.humanities.mcmaster.ca
  The Department of English and Cultural Studies offers courses in creative writing and also hosts a writer-in-residence.

Mohawk College

P.O. Box 2034, Hamilton, ON L8N 3T2
Phone: (905) 575-2045 Fax: (905) 575-2420
E-mail: ask@mohawkcollege.ca
Website: www.mohawkcollege.ca
  The Communications Media Department offers a Journalism, Print and Broadcast Advanced Diploma Program. Continuing Education offers a Writing for Publication certificate and a wide variety of writing courses, including business writing, technical writing, and creative writing (fiction, non-fiction, science fiction, children's books).

Mount Royal College

4825 Mount Royal Gate S.W., Calgary, AB T3E 6K6
Phone: (403) 440-6901 Fax: (403) 440-6563
E-mail: fcs@mtroyal.ca
Website: www.mtroyal.ca
Contact: Marc Chikinda, dean, Faculty of Communication Studies
  The Faculty of Communication Studies offers a bachelor's degree in Applied Communications with specializations in journalism, information design, and public relations.
  The faculty also offers a diploma in broadcasting and a journalism certificate.

University of New Brunswick

Department of English, P.O. Box 4400, Fredericton, NB E3B 5A3
Phone: (506) 458-7395 Fax: (506) 453-5069
E-mail: leckie@unb.ca
Website: www.unbf.ca/english
Contact: Ross Leckie, director of creative writing

The English Department offers the following undergraduate credit courses: introduction to poetry, drama, fiction, and screenwriting, and advanced courses in poetry, fiction, drama, and screenwriting. Graduate courses include poetry, fiction, drama, and screenwriting.

Continuing Education provides a non-credit course on the fundamentals of writing.

The university has a writer-in-residence and sponsors the Maritime Writers' Workshop in mid-July each year.

Niagara College of Applied Arts and Technology

300 Woodlawn Road, Welland, ON L3C 7L3
Phone: (905) 735 2211, ext. 7725 Fax: (905) 736-6005 Attn: Dayboll
E-mail: pdayboll@niagaracollege.on.ca
Website: www.niagaracollege.ca/jour
Contact: Paul Dayboll, program coordinator, Journalism Program

Offers a 2-year course in journalism with Special Fields of Writing I and II. Continuing Education offers a writing for publication certificate.

University of Prince Edward Island

550 University Avenue, Charlottetown, PE C1A 4P3
Phone: (902) 566-0389 Fax: (902) 566-0363
Website: www.upei.ca/english
Contact: Richard Lemm, professor of English

The English Department offers 3 courses in creative writing as well as an advanced studies workshop It also offers a course on writing memoirs, autobiographies, biographies, and fictive memoirs, called Writing Lives: The Art and Craft of Life-Writing.

College of the Rockies

P.O. Box 8500, Cranbrook, BC V1C 5L7
Phone: 1-877-489-2687 Fax: (250) 489-1790
E-mail: ask@cotr.bc.ca or gwakulich@cotr.bc.ca
Website: www.cotr.bc.ca
Contact: Gail Wakulich, instructor, English and Creative Writing
The University Studies Department offers Creative Writing 1 and 2 and Creative Non-fiction.

Ryerson University

350 Victoria Street, Toronto, ON M5B 2K3
Phone: (416) 979-5000 Fax: (416) 979-5277
Website: www.ryerson.ca
The English Department offers a creative writing course.

The School of Journalism offers a 4-year degree program with courses in reporting, freelance writing, feature writing, online journalism, and magazine writing.

Continuing Education offers a wide range of creative writing courses and workshops, including courses in short fiction and novel writing, poetry writing, playwriting, writing for children, writing romance, writing reviews, writing sitcoms, autobiographical writing, and creative non-fiction.

St. Jerome's University

290 Westmount Road, Waterloo, ON N2L 3G3
Phone: (519) 884-8111, ext. 28238 Fax: (519) 884-5759
E-mail: cgacton@uwaterloo.ca
Website: www.sju.ca
Contact: Carol Acton, chair, Department of English
The English Department offers a creative writing and an arts writing course, both for credit.

University of Saskatchewan

Department of English, 320 Arts Building, 9 Campus Drive,
Saskatoon, SK S7N 5A5
Phone: (306) 966-5486 Fax: (306) 966-5951
E-mail: english@usask.ca
Website: http://artsandscience.usask.ca/english

The Department of English at St. Thomas More College (affiliated) offers courses in advanced creative writing for both fiction and poetry. A creative writing course is also occasionally offered through the Department of English.

Sheridan College

1430 Trafalgar Road, Oakville, ON L6H 2LI
Phone: (905) 845-9430, ext. 2194 Fax: (905) 815-4010
Website: www.sheridancollege.ca

The Journalism Department offers a 2-year diploma in print journalism, as well as a 1-year postgraduate program, Journalism – New Media, which includes training in digital media for broadcast and online journalism. The Journalism Department belongs to the School of Animation, Arts and Design. Two-year-diploma students produce a weekly newspaper, *The Sheridan Sun*. Courses include newswriting for print and online publications.

A 1-year postgraduate program in Canadian journalism for internationally trained writers is also available.

Continuing Education offers various writing courses.

Simon Fraser University

Writing and Communications Program, 515 W. Hastings Street,
   Suite 2300, Vancouver, BC V6B 5K3
Phone: (778) 782-5093 Fax: (778) 782-5098
E-mail: wpp@sfu.ca
Website: www.sfu.ca/wp

A large selection of creative writing classes are available through Simon Fraser's Continuing Studies Department, including Creative Magazine Writing, Writing Stories for Children, Mini-Manuscript Consults, Fiction Writing, and Self-Editing for Fiction Writers. Also offers programming through the Writer's Studio (which offers a certificate in creative writing) and the Southbank Writers' Program in Surrey.

University of Toronto

Department of English, 170 St. George Street, Toronto, ON
   M5R 2M8
Phone: (416) 978-3190 Fax: (416) 978-2836
E-mail: english@chass.utoronto.ca

Website: www.utoronto.ca

Each year the English Department offers 2 creative writing courses, in poetry and prose, to selected students.

The School of Continuing Studies offers certificates in technical writing and creative writing and has courses in writing non-fiction, drama, short fiction, the novel, writing for children, screenwriting, and poetry. Visit http://learn.utoronto.ca/artsci/creative.htm or e-mail scs.writing@utoronto.ca for more details.

Trent University

Depart of English Literature, 315 Dublin Street, Trail College WH
   134, Peterborough, ON K9H 7P4
Phone: (705) 748-1011, ext. 7733 Fax: (705) 748-1823
E-mail: english@trentu.ca
Website: www.trentu.ca/english
Contact: Margaret Steffler, chair

The English Department offers an undergraduate course introducing a range of genres in creative writing and an honours seminar in one of the genres.

Vancouver Island University

900 – 5th Street, Nanaimo, BC V9R 5S5
Phone: (250) 753-3245, ext. 2112 Fax: (250) 740-6459
E-mail: steve.guppy@viu.ca
Website: http://viu.ca/crew
Contact: Steve Guppy

The Department of Creative Writing and Journalism offers a variety of first- through fourth-year courses in poetry, fiction, scriptwriting, journalism, creative non-fiction, and publishing. Several courses are offered online.

The department also publishes the annual literary magazine *Portal* and the electronic journal *Incline*.

University of Victoria

Department of Writing, P.O. Box 1700, Stn. CSC, Victoria, BC
   V8W 2Y2
Phone: (250) 721-7306 Fax: (250) 721-6602
E-mail: writing@finearts.uvic.ca
Website: http://finearts.uvic.ca/writing

Through the Department of Writing, students can major in creative writing, choosing courses (lectures and workshops) in fiction, creative non-fiction, poetry, drama, and aspects of journalism.

Courses in writing for children and young adults, creative non-fiction, travel feature writing, and memoir writing are available through the Division of Continuing Studies.

University of Western Ontario

Graduate Program in Journalism, Faculty of Information and
    Media Studies, North Campus Building, Room 240, London,
    ON N6A 5B7
Phone: (519) 661-4017 Fax: (519) 661-3506
E-mail: journalism@uwo.ca
Website: www.fims.uwo.ca/journalism
Contact: Shelley Long, graduate programs support

Western's 1-year Master of Arts in Journalism is a well-rounded, professional program for candidates with an honours undergraduate degree or equivalent. The program prepares graduates for entry-level positions in newsrooms. The curriculum includes a balance of academic and practical courses, as well as a month-long internship placement, and offers a solid grounding in the basic tools and practices of print and broadcast journalism.

University of Windsor

English Language, Literature and Creative Writing, 2106 Chrysler
    Hall N., Windsor, ON N9B 3P4
Phone: (519) 253-3000, ext. 2288 Fax: (519) 971-3676
E-mail: englishmail@uwindsor.ca
Website: www.uwindsor.ca/english
Contact: Carol Davison, head, Department of English

The Department of English offers many courses in writing, ranging from introductory to advanced seminars/workshops.

University of Winnipeg

515 Portage Avenue, Winnipeg, MB R3B 2E9
Phone: (204) 786-9292 Fax: (204) 774-4134
E-mail: a.turner@uwinnipeg.ca
Website: www.uwinnipeg.ca/index/english-index
Contact: Alden Turner, chair, English Department

Several credit courses are offered by the English Department, including Introduction to Creative Writing, the Creative Process, Writing Poems; Creative Writing; Advanced Creative Writing; and Creative Writing Field Research.

York University
210 Vanier College, 4700 Keele Street, Toronto, ON M3J 1P3
Phone: (416) 736-5910 or (416) 736-5158 Fax: (416) 736-5460
E-mail: crwr@yorku.ca
Website: www.yorku.ca/laps/en/crwr
Contact: Cathie Hueston, program assistant

The Creative Writing Program offers the following credit courses: Introduction to Creative Writing, Mixed Genre Intermediate and Senior, Prose Intermediate and Senior, Poetry Intermediate and Senior, Screenwriting, and Playwriting It is not a direct-entry program; students apply after two years of university-level study.

The Professional Writing Program offers courses in print journalism.

Publishes the literary journal *Existere*.

10

WRITERS' ORGANIZATIONS
AND SUPPORT AGENCIES

Access Copyright (Canadian Copyright Licensing Agency)
1 Yonge Street, Suite 800, Toronto, ON M5E IE5
Phone: (416) 868-1620 or 1-800-893-5777 Fax: (416) 868-1621
E-mail: info@accesscopyright.ca
Website: www.accesscopyright.ca

Alberta Foundation for the Arts
10708 – 105 Avenue, Edmonton, AB T5H OAI
Phone: (780) 427-9968
Website: www.affta.ab.ca

Alberta Playwrights' Network
2633 Hochwald Avenue S.W., Calgary, AB T3E 7K2
Phone: (403) 269-8564 or 1-800-268-8564 Fax: (403) 265-6773
E-mail: admin@albertaplaywrights.com
Website: www.albertaplaywrights.com

Alberta Romance Writers' Association
c/o St. Mark's Manor, 2612 – 14A Street S.W., Calgary, AB
    T2T 3X7
E-mail: membership@albertaromancewriters.com
Website: www.albertaromancewriters.com

Association of Canadian Publishers
174 Spadina Ave, Suite 306, Toronto, ON M5T 2C2
Phone: (416) 487-6116 Fax: (416) 487-8815
E-mail: admin@canbook.org
Website: www.publishers.ca

Association of Canadian University Presses
10 St. Mary Street, Suite 700, Toronto, ON M4Y 2W8
Phone: (416) 978-2239, ext. 237 Fax: (416) 978-4738
E-mail: clarose@utpress.utoronto.ca
Website: www.acup.ca

Book and Periodical Council
192 Spadina Avenue, Suite 107, Toronto, ON M5T 2C2
Phone: (416) 975-9366 Fax: (416) 975-1839
E-mail: info@thebpc.ca
Website: www.thebpc.ca

British Columbia Arts Council
P.O. Box 9819, Stn. Prov. Govt., Victoria, BC V8W 9W3
Phone: (250) 356-1718 Fax: (250) 387-4099
E-mail: bcartscouncil@gov.bc.ca
Website: www.bcartscouncil.ca

Burnaby Writers' Society
6584 Deer Lake Avenue, Burnaby, BC V5G 3T7
E-mail: info@bws.bc.ca
Website: www.bws.bc.ca

The Canadian Conference of the Arts
130 Slater Street, Suite 406, Ottawa, ON K1P 5G4
Phone: (613) 238-3561 Fax: (613) 238-4849
E-mail: info@ccarts.ca
Website: www.ccarts.ca

The Canada Council for the Arts
350 Albert Street, P.O. Box 1047, Ottawa, ON K1P 5V8
Phone: (613) 566-4414 or 1-800-263-5588 Fax: (613) 566-4390
Website: www.canadacouncil.ca

The Canadian Association of Journalists
Box 280, Brantford, ON N3T 5M8
Website: www.caj.ca

Canadian Authors Association (national office)
74 Mississaga Street E., Orillia, ON L3V 6K5
Phone: (705) 653-0323 or 1-866-216-6222
E-mail: admin@canauthors.org
Website: www.canauthors.org

The Canadian Children's Book Centre
40 Orchard View Boulevard, Suite 217, Toronto, ON M4R 1B9
Phone: (416) 975-0010 Fax: (416) 975-8970
E-mail: info@bookcentre.ca
Website: www.bookcentre.ca

Canadian Intellectual Property Office
Place du Portage I, 50 Victoria Street, Room C-229, Gatineau, QC
    KIA OC9
Phone: 1-866-997-1936 Fax: (819) 953-2476 (enquiries only)
E-mail: cipo.contact@ic.gc.ca
Website: www.cipo.ic.gc.ca

Canadian Library Association
1150 Morrison Drive, Suite 400, Ottawa, ON K2H 8S9
Phone: (613) 232-9625 Fax: (613) 563-9895
E-mail: info@cla.ca
Website: www.cla.ca

Canadian Science Writers' Association
P.O. Box 75, Stn. A, Toronto, ON M5W 1A2
Phone: 1-800-796-8595
E-mail: office@sciencewriters.ca
Website: www.sciencewriters.ca

Canadian Society of Children's Authors, Illustrators and Performers (CANSCAIP)
40 Orchard View Boulevard, Suite 104, Toronto, ON M4R 1B9
Phone: (416) 515-1559

E-mail: office@canscaip.org
Website: www.canscaip.org

The Canadian Writers' Foundation
P.O. Box 13281, Kanata Stn., Ottawa, ON K2K IX4
Phone: (613) 256-6937 Fax: (613) 256-5457
E-mail: info@canadianwritersfoundation.org
Website: www.canadianwritersfoundation.org

Conseil des arts et des lettres du Québec
79 René-Lévesque Boulevard E., 3rd Floor, Quebec, QC GIR 5N5
Phone: (418) 643-1707 or 1-800-897-1707 Fax: (418) 643-4558
500 Place d'Armes, 15th Floor, Montreal, QC H2Y 2W2
Phone: (514) 864-3350 or 1-800-608-3350 Fax: (514) 864-4160
E-mail: info@calq.gouv.qc.ca
Website: www.calq.gouv.qc.ca/index_en.htm

Crime Writers of Canada
E-mail: info@crimewriterscanada.com
Website: www.crimewriterscanada.com

Editors' Association of Canada (EAC)
27 Carlton Street, Suite 505, Toronto, ON M5B IL2
Phone: (416) 975-1379 or 1-866-226-3348 Fax: (416) 975-1637
E-mail: info@editors.ca
Website: www.editors.ca

Federation of BC Writers
P.O. Box 3887, Stn. Terminal, Vancouver, BC V6B 3Z3
E-mail: info@bcwriters.ca
Website: www.bcwriters.ca

The League of Canadian Poets
192 Spadina Avenue, Suite 312, Toronto, ON M4W 3C7
Phone: (416) 504-1657 Fax: (416) 504-0096
E-mail: admin@poets.ca
Website: www.poets.ca

Literary Press Group of Canada
192 Spadina Avenue, Suite 501, Toronto, ON M5T 2C2
Phone: (416) 483-1321 Fax: (416) 483-2510
E-mail: info@lpg.ca
Website: www.lpg.ca

Literary Translators' Association of Canada
1455 de Maisonneuve Boulevard W., LB-601, Concordia
   University, Montreal, QC H3G 1M8
Phone: (514) 848-2424, ext. 8702
E-mail: info@attlc-ltac.org
Website: www.attlc-ltac.org

Magazines Canada
425 Adelaide Street W., Suite 700, Toronto, ON M5V 3C1
Phone: (416) 504-0274 Fax: (416) 504-0437
E-mail: info@magazinescanada.ca
Website: magazinescanada.ca

Manitoba Arts Council
93 Lombard Avenue, Suite 525, Winnipeg, MB R3B 3B1
Phone: (204) 945-2237 or 1-866-994-2787 (toll-free in MB)
   Fax: (204) 945-5925
E-mail: info@artscouncil.mb.ca
Website: www.artscouncil.mb.ca

Manitoba Writers' Guild
100 Arthur Street, Suite 218, Winnipeg, MB R3B 1H3
Phone: (204) 944-8013
E-mail: info@mbwriter.mb.ca
Website: www.mbwriter.mb.ca

New Brunswick Arts Board
61 Carleton Street, Fredericton, NB E3B 3T2
Phone: (506) 444-4444 or 1-866-460-2787 Fax: (506) 444-5543
E-mail: chair@artsnb.ca
Website: www.artsnb.ca

Newfoundland and Labrador Arts Council

The Newman Building, 1 Springdale Street, P.O. Box 98, Stn. C, St. John's, NL AIC 5H5

Phone: (709) 726-2212 or 1-866-726-2212 (toll-free in NL) Fax: (709) 726-0619

E-mail: nlacmail@nlac.ca

Website: www.nlac. ca

Northwest Territories Arts Council

Department of Education, Culture and Employment, Government of the N.W.T., P.O. Box 1320, Yellowknife, NT XIA 2L9

Phone: (867) 920-6370 Fax: (867) 873-0205

E-mail: boris_atamanenko@gov.nt.ca

Website: www.pwnhc.ca/artscouncil

Nova Scotia Department of Communities, Culture, and Heritage

World Trade Centre, 6th Floor, 1800 Argyle Street, P.O. Box 456, Halifax, NS B3J 2R5

Phone: (902) 424-5000 Fax: (902) 424-0710

E-mail: cch@gov.ns.ca

Website: www.gov.ns.ca/cch

Ontario Arts Council

Literature Programs, 151 Bloor Street W., 5th Floor, Toronto, ON M5S IT6

Phone: (416) 961-1660 or 1-800-387-0058 (toll-free in ON) Fax: (416) 961-7796

E-mail: info@arts.on.ca

Website: www.arts.on.ca

Ontario Ministry of Tourism, Culture, and Sport

900 Bay Street, 9th Floor, Toronto, ON M7A IL2

Phone: (416) 326-9326 or 1-866-997-9015 Fax: (416) 314-7854

E-mail: general_info@mtc.gov.on.ca

Website: www.culture.gov.on.ca

Outdoor Writers of Canada

T.J. Schwanky, Executive Director, P.O. Box 934, Cochrane, AB
 T4C 1B1
Tel: (403) 932-3585 Fax: (403) 851-0618
E-mail: outdoorwritersofcanada@shaw.ca
Website: www.outdoorwritersofcanada.com

P.E.I. Writers' Guild

c/o Volunteer Resource Centre, 81 Prince Street, Charlottetown,
 PE C1A 4R3
E-mail: peiwritersguild@gmail.com
Website: peiwritersguild.wordpress.com

PEN Canada

24 Ryerson Avenue, Suite 301, Toronto, ON M5T 2P3
Phone: (416) 703-8448 Fax: (416) 703-3870
E-mail: queries@pencanada.ca
Website: www.pencanada.ca

Playwrights Guild of Canada

215 Spadina Avenue, Suite 210, Toronto, ON M5T 2C7
Phone: (416) 703-0201 Fax: (416) 703-0059
E-mail: info@playwrightsguild.ca
Website: www.playwrightsguild.ca

Playwrights Theatre Centre

1398 Cartwright Street, Suite 201, Vancouver, BC V6H 3R8
Phone: (604) 685-6228 Fax: (604) 685-7451
E-mail: plays@playwrightstheatre.com
Website: www.playwrightstheatre.com

Praxis Centre for Screenwriters

149 W. Hastings Street, Suite 3305, Vancouver, BC V6B 1H4
Phone: (778) 782-7880 Fax: (778) 782-7882
E-mail: praxis@sfu.ca
Website: www.praxisfilm.com

The Prince Edward Island Council of the Arts
115 Richmond Street, Charlottetown, PE CIA IH7
Phone: (902) 368-4410 or 1-888-734-2784 Fax: (902) 368-4418
E-mail: info@peica.ca
Website: www.peica.ca

Professional Writers Association of Canada
215 Spadina Avenue, Suite 123, Toronto, ON M5T 2C7
Phone: (416) 504-1645
E-mail: info@pwac.ca
Website: www.pwac.ca

Public Lending Right Commission
P.O. Box 1047, 350 Albert Street, Ottawa, ON KIP 5V8
Phone: (613) 566-4378 or 1-800-521-5721 Fax: (613) 566-4418
E-mail: plr@canadacouncil.ca
Website: www.plr-dpp.ca

Quebec Writers' Federation
1200 Atwater Avenue, Suite 3, Westmount, QC H3Z IX4
Phone: (514) 933-0878
E-mail: admin@qwf.org
Website: www.qwf.org

Saskatchewan Arts Board
Regina office: 1355 Broad Street, Regina, SK S4R 7VI
Phone: (306) 787-4056 or 1-800-667-7526 (SK) Fax: (306)
  787-4199
Saskatoon office: 417 – 24th Street E., Saskatoon, SK S7K OK7
Phone: (306) 964-1155 or 1-800-667-7526 (SK) Fax: (306)
  964-1167
E-mail: info@artsboard.sk.ca
Website: www.artsboard.sk.ca

Saskatchewan Writers Guild
P.O. Box 3986, Regina, SK S4P 3R9
Phone: (306) 757-6310 or 1-800-667-6788 Fax: (306) 565-8554
E-mail: info@skwriter.com
Website: www.skwriter.com

Scarborough Arts Council
1859 Kingston Road, Toronto, ON M4K 3E3
Phone: (416) 698-7322 Fax: (416) 698-7972
E-mail: info@scarborougharts.com
Website: www.scarborougharts.com

SF Canada (speculative fiction)
7433 E. River Road, Washago, ON L0K 2B0
Website: www.sfcanada.org

Storytellers of Canada / Conteurs du Canada
192 Spadina Avenue, Suite 201, Toronto, ON M5T 2C2
E-mail: admin@storytellers-conteurs.ca
Website: www.storytellers-conteurs.ca

Toronto Arts Council
141 Bathurst Street, Toronto, ON M5V 2R2
Phone: (416) 392-6800 Fax: (416) 392-6920
E-mail: claire@torontoartscouncil.org
Website: www.torontoartscouncil.org

Vancouver Children's Literature Roundtable
Contact using website form
Website: www.vclr.ca

Vancouver Cultural Services
453 W. 12th Avenue, Vancouver, BC V5Y 1V4
Phone: (604) 871-6434 Fax: (604) 871-6005
E-mail: culture@vancouver.ca
Website: vancouver.ca/commsvcs/cultural

The Word Guild
P.O. Box 1243, Trenton, ON K8V 5R9
E-mail: info@thewordguild.com
Website: www.thewordguild.com

Writers' Alliance of Newfoundland and Labrador
223 Duckworth Street, Suite 202, St. John's, NL A1C 6N1
Phone: (709) 739-5215 or 1-866-739-5215 Fax: (709) 739-5931

E-mail: wanl@nf.aibn.com
Website: www.wanl.ca

The Writers' Circle of Durham Region
P.O. Box 14558, 75 Bayly Street W., Ajax, ON LIS 7K7
Phone: (905) 686-0211
E-mail: info@wcdr.org
Website: www.wcdr.org

Writers' Federation of New Brunswick
P.O. Box 306, Moncton, NB EIC 8L4
Phone: (506) 459-7228 Fax: (506) 459-7228
E-mail: info@wfnb.ca
Website: www.wfnb.ca

Writers' Federation of Nova Scotia
1113 Marginal Road, Halifax, NS B3H 4P7
Phone: (902) 423-8116 Fax: (902) 422-0881
E-mail: programs@writers.ns.ca
Website: www.writers.ns.ca

Writers Guild of Alberta
11759 Groat Road, Edmonton, AB T5M 3K6
Phone: (780) 422-8174 or 1-800-665-5354 Fax: (780) 422-2663
E-mail: mail@writersguild.ab.ca
Website: www.writersguild.ab.ca

Writers Guild of Canada
366 Adelaide Street W., Suite 401, Toronto, ON M5V IR9
Phone: (416) 979-7907 or 1-800-567-9974 Fax: (416) 979-9273
E-mail: info@wgc.ca
Website: www.wgc.ca

Writers in Electronic Residence
Ontario Institute for Studies in Education of the University of
   Toronto, 252 Bloor Street W., Toronto, ON M5S IV6
Phone: (416) 978-0024 Fax: (416) 926-4737
E-mail: wier@wier.ca
Website: www.wier.ca

The Writers' Trust of Canada
90 Richmond Street E., Suite 200, Toronto, ON M5C IPI
Phone: (416) 504-8222 Fax: (416) 504-9090
E-mail: info@writerstrust.com
Website: www.writerstrust.com

The Writers' Union of Canada
90 Richmond Street E., Suite 200, Toronto, ON M5C IPI
Phone: (416) 703-8982 Fax: (416) 504-9090
E-mail: info@writersunion.ca
Website: www.writersunion.ca

Young Alberta Book Society
11759 Groat Road, Edmonton, AB T5M 3K6
Phone: (780) 422-8232 Fax: (780) 422-8239
E-mail: info@yabs.ab.ca
Website: www.yabs.ab.ca

Yukon Department of Tourism and Culture
Tourism and Culture Centre, 100 Hanson Street, Whitehorse, YT
    YIA 2C6
Phone: (867) 667-3535 Fax: (867) 393-6456
E-mail: artsfund@gov.yk.ca
Website: www.tc.gov.yk.ca

11

RESOURCES

For those seeking practical advice and inspiration about their craft, there is a cornucopia of writers' resource books on the market: style guides, practical handbooks, personal meditations, marketing primers, as well as more advanced "workshops" on the narrative and descriptive arts. In addition, there are numerous writers' websites that offer everything from dictionaries to articles on how to deal with rejection.

With a growing industry in writing about writing, it is possible to offer only a short selection of resources here. As you'll see, the following listing includes books from the United States and Britain, as well as from Canada. Most are available here in good bookstores or through the Internet; a few are out of print but may still be held in libraries.

Stylebooks, Handbooks, & Guides

Armstrong, David. *How Not to Write a Novel: Confessions of a Midlist Author*, Allison & Busby Limited, London, 2003.

Ballon, Rachel Friedman. *Breathing Life into Your Characters*, Writer's Digest Books, Cincinnati, 2003.

Bates, Jefferson D. *Writing with Precision: How to Write So That You Cannot Possibly Be Misunderstood*, Penguin Books, New York, 2000.

Bell, Julia, and Paul Magrs (eds.). *The Creative Writing Coursebook: Forty Authors Share Advice and Exercises for Fiction and Poetry*, Macmillan, London, 2001.

Bernstein, Theodore M. *Miss Thistlebottom's Hobgoblins: The Careful Writer's Guide to the Taboos, Bugbears and Outmoded Rules of English Usage*, Centro Books, New York, 2006.

Berton, Pierre. *The Joy of Writing: A Guide for Writers Disguised as a Literary Memoir*, Anchor Canada, Toronto, 2003.

Blamires, Harry. *The Penguin Guide to Plain English*, Penguin Books, London, 2000.

Bly, Carol. *Beyond the Writers' Workshop: New Ways to Write Creative Nonfiction*, Anchor Books, New York, 2001.

Bly, Robert W. *Secrets of a Freelance Writer: How to Make $100,000 a Year or More* (3rd rev. ed.), Henry Holt, New York, 2006.

Brown, Judy, and Ramona Montagnes. *The Canadian Writer's Handbook* (5th ed.), Oxford University Press, Toronto, 2007.

Bruce, Harry. *Page Fright: Foibles and Fetishes of Famous Writers*, McClelland & Stewart, Toronto, 2009.

Bulman, Colin. *Creative Writing: A Guide and Glossary to Fiction Writing*, Polity, Cambridge, U.K., 2006.

The Canadian Writer's Guide: Official Handbook of the Canadian Authors Association (13th ed.). Fitzhenry & Whiteside, Toronto, 2003.

Cheney, Theodore A. Rees. *Getting the Words Right* (2nd ed.), Writer's Digest Books, Cincinnati, 2005.

The Chicago Manual of Style (16th ed.). University of Chicago Press, Chicago, 2010.

Clark, Eliza. *Writer's Gym: Exercises and Training Tips for Writers*, Penguin Books, Toronto, 2007.

Editors of Writer's Digest Books. *The Complete Handbook of Novel Writing: Everything You Need to Know About Creating & Selling Your Work* (2nd ed.). Writer's Digest Books, Cincinnati, 2010.

Dial, Cynthia. *Get Your Travel Writing Published: A Teach Yourself Guide*, McGraw-Hill, New York, 2010.

Driscoll, Susan, and Diane Gedymin. *Get Published! Professionally, Affordably, Fast* (revised ed.), iUniverse, Inc., Bloomington, IN, 2010.

Dufresne, John. *The Lie That Tells a Truth*, W. W. Norton & Co., New York, 2004.

Editing Canadian English (2nd ed.), Editors' Association of Canada, Macfarlane Walter & Ross, Toronto, 2000.

Ellis, Sherry (ed.). *Now Write! Fiction Writing from Today's Best Writers and Teachers*, Jeremy P. Tarcher/Penguin, New York, 2006.

Embree, Mary. *The Author's Toolkit: A Step-by-Step Guide to Writing and Publishing Your Book* (3rd ed.), Allworth Press, New York, 2010.

Evanovich, Janet. *How I Write: Secrets of a Bestselling Author*, St. Martin's Press, New York, 2006.

Fee, Margery, and Janice McAlpine. *Guide to Canadian English Usage* (2nd ed.), Oxford University Press, Toronto, 2011.

Fish, Stanley. *How to Write a Sentence: And How to Read One*, HarperCollins, New York, 2011.

Formichelli, Linda, and Diana Burrell. *The Renegade Writer: A Totally Unconventional Guide to Freelance Writing Success* (2nd ed.), Marion Street Press, Oak Park, IL, 2005.

Frank, Steven. *The Pen Commandments*, Anchor Books, New York, 2004.

Frank, Thaisa, and Dorothy Wall. *Finding Your Writer's Voice: A Guide to Creative Fiction*, St. Martin's Press, New York, 1996.

Frey, James N. *How to Write a Damn Good Mystery: A Practical Step-by-Step Guide from Inspiration to Finished Manuscript*, St. Martin's Press, New York, 2004.

Gardner, John. *The Art of Fiction: Notes on Craft for Young Writers*, Vintage, New York, 1983.

Goldberg, Natalie. *Writing Down the Bones: Freeing the Writer Within*, Shambhala, New York, 2001.

Grobel, Lawrence. *Endangered Species: Writers Talk About Their Craft*, Their Visions, Their Lives, Da Capo Press, Cambridge, MA, 2001.

Harper, Timothy (ed.). *The ASJA Guide to Freelance Writing*, St. Martin's Press, New York, 2003.

Hart, Jack. *A Writer's Coach*, Pantheon Books, New York, 2006.

Heffron, Jack. *The Writer's Idea Workshop*, Writer's Digest Books, Cincinnati, 2003.

Hemley, Robin. *Turning Life into Fiction*, Gray Wolf Press, Saint Paul, MN, 2006.

Herman, Jeff, and Deborah Levine Herman. *Write the Perfect Book Proposal*, John Wiley & Sons, New York, 2001.

Hicks, Wynford. *English for Journalists* (3rd ed.), Taylor & Francis, London, 2006.

Hodgins, Jack. *A Passion for Narrative: A Guide for Writing Fiction* (revised ed.), McClelland & Stewart, Toronto, 2001.

Jenkins, Jerry B. *Writing for the Soul*, Writer's Digest Books, Cincinnati, 2006.

Kane, Thomas S., and Karen C. Ogden. *The Canadian Oxford Guide to Writing*, Oxford University Press, Toronto, 1993.

Kelton, Nancy Davidoff. *Writing From Personal Experience: How to Turn Your Life into Salable Prose*, Writer's Digest Books, Cincinnati, 2000.

Kercheval, Jesse Lee. *Building Fiction: How to Develop Plot and Structure*, University of Wisconsin Press, Madison, WI, 2003.

King, Stephen. *On Writing: A Memoir of the Craft* (10th anniversary ed.), Scribner, New York, 2010.

Kiteley, Brian. *The 3 A.M. Epiphany: Uncommon Writing Exercises That Transform Your Fiction*, Writer's Digest Books, Cincinnati, 2005.

Konner, Linda. *How to Be Successfully Published in Magazines*, St. Martin's Press, New York, 1990.

Kress, Nancy. *Characters, Emotion & Viewpoint*, Writer's Digest Books, Cincinnati, 2005.

LaRocque, Paula. *The Book on Writing*, Marion Street Press, Oak Park, IL, 2003.

Lamott, Anne. *Bird by Bird: Some Instructions on Writing and Life*, Anchor Canada, Toronto, 1995.

Landenheim-Gil, Randy. *The Everything Get Published Book* (3rd ed.), Adams Media Corp., Avon, MA, 2012.

Larsen, Michael. *How to Write a Book Proposal* (3rd ed.), Writer's Digest Books, Cincinnati, 2003.

Lerner, Betsy. *The Forest for the Trees: An Editor's Advice to Writers* (revised ed.), Riverhead Books, New York, 2010.

Levin, Donna. *Get That Novel Written: From Initial Idea to Final Edit*, Writer's Digest Books, Cincinnati, 1996.

Levin, Martin P. *Be Your Own Literary Agent: The Ultimate Insider's Guide to Getting Published*, Ten Speed Press, Berkeley, CA, 2002.

Levinson, Jay Conrad, Rick Frishman, Michael Larsen, and David L. Hancock. *Guerrilla Marketing for Writers: 100 No-Cost, Low-Cost Weapons for Selling Your Work* (2nd ed.), Writer's Digest Books, Cincinnati, 2010.

Lukeman, Noah. *The First Five Pages: A Writer's Guide to Staying Out of the Rejection Pile*, Fireside, New York, 2000.

Lyon, Elizabeth. *A Writer's Guide to Fiction*, Berkley Publishing Group, New York, 2004.

Maisel, Eric. *The Art of the Book Proposal*, Jeremy P. Tarcher/Penguin, New York, 2004.

Masello, Robert. *Robert's Rules of Writing*, Writer's Digest Books, Cincinnati, 2005.

McFarlane, J. A., and Warren Clements. *The Globe and Mail Style Book* (9th ed.), McClelland & Stewart, Toronto, 2003.

McKercher, Catherine, and Carman Cumming. *The Canadian Reporter: News Writing and Reporting* (3rd ed.), Harcourt Brace Canada, Toronto, 2010.

Mencher, Melvin. *Melvin Mencher's News Reporting and Writing* (12th ed.), McGraw-Hill, New York, 2010.

Mettee, Stephen Blake. *The Fast-Track Course on How to Write a Nonfiction Book Proposal* (2nd ed.), Linden, Fresno, CA, 2012.

The Modern Language Association of America. *MLA Style Manual and Guide to Scholarly Publishing* (3rd ed.), The Modern Language Association of America, New York, 2008.

Neubauer, Bonnie. *The Write-Brain Workbook: 366 Exercises to Liberate Your Writing*, Writer's Digest Books, Cincinnati, 2006.

Oxford Style Manual (2nd ed.), Oxford University Press, Oxford, 2012.

Perkins, Lori. *The Insider's Guide to Getting an Agent*, Writer's Digest Books, Cincinnati, 1999.

Pfeiffer, William S., and Kaye E. Adkins. *Technical Writing: A Practical Approach* (8th edition), Prentice-Hall Canada, Toronto, 2012.

Roth, Martin. *The Writer's Partner: 1001 Breakthrough Ideas to Stimulate Your Imagination*, Michael Wiese Productions, Studio City, CA, 2001.

Rubens, Philip (ed.). *Science and Technical Writing: A Manual of Style*, Routledge, New York, 2001.

Seidman, Michael. *The Complete Guide to Editing Your Fiction*, Writer's Digest Books, Cincinnati, 2000.

Staw, Jane Anne. *Unstuck: A Supportive and Practical Guide to Working through Writer's Block*, St. Martin's Press, New York, 2003.

Stone, Todd A. *Novelist's Boot Camp: 101 Ways to Take Your Book from Boring to Bestseller,* Writer's Digest Books, Cincinnati, 2006.

Strunk, William, Jr., and E. B. White. *The Elements of Style* (4th ed.), Allyn and Bacon, Boston, 2000.

Tasko, Patti (ed.). *The Canadian Press Stylebook* (16th ed.), The Canadian Press, Toronto, 2010.

Truss, Lynne. *Eats, Shoots & Leaves: The Zero Tolerance Approach to Punctuation,* Gotham Books, New York, 2003.

Watson, Don. *Death Sentences,* Viking Canada, Toronto, 2003.

Williams, Malcolm (ed.). *The Canadian Style: A Guide to Writing and Editing,* Dundurn Press, Toronto, 1997.

Words into Type (3rd ed. rev.), Prentice-Hall, Englewood Cliffs, NJ, 1974.

Zinsser, William. *On Writing Well: The Classic Guide to Writing Non-fiction* (30th anniversary ed.), HarperCollins, New York, 2006.

Dictionaries & Thesauruses

The Canadian Oxford Dictionary (2nd ed.), ed. Katherine Barber, Oxford University Press, Toronto, 2006.

Canadian Thesaurus (2nd ed.), ed. Richard Dionne, Fitzhenry & Whiteside, Markham, ON, 2009.

Collins English Dictionary (Canadian ed.), HarperCollins, Glasgow, 2005.

Collins Gage Canadian Paperback Dictionary, HarperCollins Canada, Toronto, 2006.

The Concise English Dictionary (8th ed.), HarperCollins, Glasgow, 2006.

Gage Canadian Thesaurus, ed. T. K. Pratt, Gage Learning Corp., Toronto, 1998.

Merriam-Webster's Collegiate Dictionary (11th ed.), ed. Frederick C. Mish, Merriam-Webster, Springfield, MA, 2003.

The New Fowler's Modern English Usage (3rd ed. rev.), ed. R. W. Birchfield, Oxford University Press, Oxford, 2004.

Oxford Canadian Thesaurus of Current English, eds. Katherine Barber, Robert Pontisso, Heather Fitzgerald, Oxford University Press, Toronto, 2006.

Oxford Compact Thesaurus (2nd ed.), ed. Maurice Waite, Oxford
   University Press, Oxford, 2001.

*New Oxford Dictionary for Writers and Editors: The Essential A–Z
   Guide to the Written Word,* Oxford University Press, Oxford,
   2005.

The Penguin English Dictionary (3rd ed), ed. Robert Allen, Penguin
   Books, London, 2007.

Random House Webster's Unabridged Dictionary (revised ed.), ed.
   Wendalyn R. Nichols, Random House, New York, 2005.

Roget's International Thesaurus (7th ed.), ed. Barbara Ann Kipfer,
   HarperCollins, New York, 2010.

Yearbooks and Other Regularly Published Reference Sources

The Book Trade in Canada (annual), *Quill & Quire,* Toronto.

Canadian Almanac & Directory (annual), Grey House Publishing,
   Toronto.

The Canadian Global Almanac, John Wiley & Sons, Toronto, 2005.

Canadian Who's Who (annual), Third Sector, Orillia, ON.

CARD (Canadian Advertising Rates & Data) (biannually), Rogers
   Media, Toronto.

Canadian Publishers Digest (biannual), digital supplement to *Quill
   & Quire* magazine, Toronto.

Guide to Literary Agents (annual), Writer's Digest Books,
   Cincinnati.

Literary Market Place (annual), Information Today, New York.

Novel and Short Story Writer's Market (annual), Writer's Digest
   Books, Cincinnati.

Poet's Market (annual), Writer's Digest Books, Cincinnati.

Publication Profiles (annual), Rogers Media, Toronto.

Writers' & Artists' Yearbook (annual), Bloomsbury, London.

Writer's Market and Writer's Market Online (annual), Writer's
   Digest Books, Cincinnati.

Some Major Canadian Magazine Publishers

Annex Business Media, P.O. Box 530, 105 Donly Drive S., Simcoe, ON N3Y 4N5 Phone: (519) 429-3966 or 1-800-265-2827 Fax: (519) 429-3094 Website: www.annexweb.com (trade)

Baum Publications Ltd., 2323 Boundary Road, Suite 124, Vancouver, BC V5M 4V8 Phone: (604) 291-9900 Fax: (604) 291-1906 Website: www.baumpub.com (trade)

Business Information Group, 80 Valleybrook Drive, Toronto, ON M3B 2S9 Phone: (416) 442-5600 or 1-800-668-2374 Fax: (416) 442-2191 Website: www.businessinformationgroup.ca (business)

Canada Wide Magazines Ltd., 4180 Lougheed Highway, 4th Floor, Burnaby, BC V5C 6A7 Phone: (604) 299-7311 Fax: (604) 299-9188 E-mail: cwm@canadawide.com Website: www.canadawide.com (business, consumer, trade)

Craig Kelman & Associates Ltd., 2020 Portage Avenue, Suite 3C, Winnipeg, MB R3J 0K4 Phone: 1-866-985-9780 Fax: 1-866-985-9799 E-mail: info@kelman.ca Website: www.kelman.ca (trade)

Family Communications Inc., 65 The East Mall, Toronto, ON M8Z 5W3 Phone: (416) 537-2604 Fax: (416) 538-1794 E-mail: admin@parentscanada.com Website: www.parentscanada.com (consumer)

Glacier Media Group, 1970 Alberta Street, Vancouver, BC V5Y 3X4 Phone: (604) 872-8565 Fax: (604) 879-1483 E-mail: info@glaciermedia.ca Website: www.glaciermedia.ca (business, trade)

Koocanusa Publications Inc., 100 – 7th Avenue S., Suite 100, Cranbrook, BC V1C 2J4 Phone: (250) 426-7253 or 1-800-663-8555 Fax: (250) 426-4125 E-mail: info@kpimedia.com Website: www.koocanusapublications.com (business, consumer)

Metroland Media Group Ltd., 3125 Wolfedale Road, Mississauga, ON L4C 1W1 Phone: (905) 279-0440 Fax: (905) 279-5103 Website: www.metroland.com (business, consumer)

Naylor (Canada) Inc., 1630 Ness Avenue, Suite 300, Winnipeg, MB R3J 3X1 Phone: 1-800-665-2456 Fax: (204) 947-2047 Website: www.naylor.com (trade)

OP Publishing Ltd., 200 W. Esplanade, Suite 500, North Vancouver, BC V7M 1A4 Phone: (604) 998-3310 Fax: (604) 998-3320 Website: www.oppublishing.com (consumer)

Quebecor, 612 Saint-Jacques Street, Montreal, QC H3C 4M8 Website: www.quebecor.com (consumer)

Rogers Publishing Limited, 1 Mount Pleasant Road, Toronto, ON M4Y 2Y5 Phone: (416) 764-2000 Fax: (416) 764-1802 Website: www.rogerspublishing.ca (business, consumer, trade)

St. Joseph Communications, 50 MacIntosh Boulevard, Concord, ON L4K 4P3 Phone: (905) 660-3111 Fax: (905) 669-1972 E-mail: communications@stjoseph.com Website: www.stjosephmedia.com (consumer)

Trajan Publishing, P.O. Box 28103, Lakeport P.O., St. Catharines, ON L2N 7P8 Phone: (905) 646-7744 Fax: (905) 646-0995 Website: www.trajan.ca (consumer)

TC Transcontinental, 1 Place Ville Marie, Suite 3315, Montreal, QC H3B 3N2 Phone: (514) 954-4000 Fax: (514) 954-4016 Website: www.tctranscontinental.com (consumer)

Tribute Publishing Inc., 71 Barber Greene Road, Toronto, ON M3C 2A2 Phone: (416) 445-0544 Fax: (416) 445-2894 Website: www.tribute.ca (consumer)

Online Resources

The following list of online resources is by no means exhaustive. Rather, it is intended to give the writer a starting-point from which to begin his or her investigation into what sites are available on the Internet.

About: Freelance Writing
www.freelancewrite.about.com
Includes job postings, articles, newsletters, and forums.

Authorlink
www.authorlink.com
An American site that offers writers education, information, guidance, services for writers, a writers' registry, a critique service, publication guidelines, and the opportunity to get a literary agent

and sell their work to publishers throughout the English-speaking world. Fees apply to some sections of the site.

The Bible Gateway
www.biblegateway.com
Allows you to look up any verse or phrase in many versions of the Bible.

BookNet Canada
www.booknetcanada.ca
Gathers information about the Canadian book market and publishes consumer research. Also hosts Canadian book publishers' interactive catalogues through its CataList service (www.bnccatalist.ca).

CanadaInfo
www.craigmarlatt.com/canada
A source of facts about Canada and its people.

Canadian Authors Association
www.canauthors.org
News about the organization and literary awards, and extensive links of interest to writers.

The Canadian Encyclopedia
http://thecanadianencyclopedia.com
A convenient site on which to research Canadian topics, including a selection of articles from *Maclean's* magazine since 1995.

Canadian Studies: A Guide to the Sources
http://people.stfx.ca/jblackwe/canada3.html
Provides links to many Canadian sites of interest to researchers.

Canadian Studies Research Guide
www.library.yale.edu/humanities/canada
Includes bibliography of reference sources useful to researchers.

CARDonline
www.cardonline.ca

Database of Canadian media, including newspapers and magazines. Some information requires a subscription.

Chicago Manual of Style
www.chicagomanualofstyle.org

Answers queries about the 16th edition of *The Chicago Manual of Style*, and includes a guide for citing sources and tools to help authors prepare their manuscripts for publication. Subscribers have access to an online *Chicago Manual of Style*.

CopyrightLaws.com
http://copyrightlaws.com

Canadian media and copyright lawyer Lesley Ellen Harris provides information on Canadian, U.S., and international copyright law and web-related legal issues.

Dictionary.com
www.dictionary.com

Features English dictionary, thesaurus, quotation database, and translator.

The Elements of Style
www.bartleby.com/141/index.html

Contains rules of usage, principles of composition, and commonly misused and misspelled words.

Encyclopedia of Canada's Peoples
www.multiculturalcanada.ca/ecp

Provides an overview of people within Canadian geographic and social framework, including arrival and settlement, economic life, culture, religion, and politics.

Encyclopedia.com
www.encyclopedia.com

Contains information from more than 100 encyclopedias, dictionaries, and thesauruses (including those from Oxford University

Press and Columbia University Press). Subscribers have access to the HighBeam Research database with 35 million documents.

Encyclopedia Britannica Online
http://eb.com

Subscribers have access to the *Encyclopedia Britannica*, plus headlines from publications from around the world, graphics, maps, and related Internet links.

Familiar Quotations
www.bartleby.com/100

Database of many famous quotations, including *Bartlett's Familiar Quotations*. Allows users to search for quotations by subject, author, or title.

Fiction Factor
www.fictionfactor.com

Features articles on writing, getting published, how to promote and market a book, and more. Also hosts a discussion forum.

Freelance Writing.com
http://freelancewriting.com

Includes a reading room, articles, author interviews, news, a career centre, a freelance job bank, and databases for magazines, freelance recruiters, and book publishers.

Grammar Girl
http://grammar.quickanddirtytips.com

Tips and grammar exercises on punctuation, word choice, and more.

Indie Go-Go
www.indiegogo.com

Online platform for crowd-funding creative projects; a number of authors have successfully used the site to finance the self-publication of their books.

Kickstarter

www.kickstarter.com

Another popular crowd-funding platform on through which authors have successfully financed their books. (Note: Canadians currently need a proxy to accept payments through the U.S.-based Amazon Payments service.)

Literary Market Place

http://literarymarketplace.com

Subscribers have access to databases of Canadian, U.S., and other international publishers, as well as literary agents.

MediaFinder

http://mediafinder.com

Subscribers can access detailed information on 70,000 U.S. and Canadian magazines.

Merriam-Webster Online

www.m-w.com

May use the dictionary, thesaurus, and Spanish-English dictionary for no charge. Subscribers have access to the Merriam-Webster dictionaries, a thesaurus, Spanish-English and French-English dictionaries, an atlas, style guide, word games, and more.

National Writers Union

www.nwu.org

This American site provides writer alerts for book publishers, organizations, and magazines, as well as copyright information.

Oxford Dictionaries Online

http://oxforddictionaries.com

Free site offering current English dictionary, grammar guidance, and bilingual dictionaries in French, German, Italian, and Spanish. Linked to subscription-only *Oxford English Dictionary Online*, which includes etymology and historical context.

PoeWar

www.poewar.com

Contains articles and exercises about all aspects of writing.

Publishers' Catalogues
www.lights.ca/publisher
Provides access to information on publishers around the world.

Purple Crayon
http://underdown.org/articles.htm
Articles on writing and illustrating children's books and getting them published.

Rosedog Books
www.rosedog.com/default.asp
Subscribers can post their manuscripts for viewing by agents and publishers.

Shaw Guides: The Guide to Writers Conferences and Workshops
http://writing.shawguides.com
Provides information about writers' conferences and workshops worldwide.

The Vocabula Review
http://vocabula.com
A monthly e-zine that seeks to promote the richness and correct use of the English language.

Writer Beware
http://sfwa.org/for-authors/writer-beware
Lists agents and publishers that writers should be wary of, provides sample contracts, and has articles on all aspects of writing. Maintained by the Science Fiction and Fantasy Writers of America, Inc.

Writers Guild of Canada
www.writersguildofcanada.com
Provides lists of literary agents, lawyers, available funding, employment opportunities, workshops, and seminars, as well as links of interest to writers and screenwriters.

WritersMarket.com
www.writersmarket.com

Subscribers have access to listings of agents and publishers, plus advice and daily industry updates.

Writers Write
www.writerswrite.com

Provides a long list of general topics with the publications that publish writing on those topics, both paying and non-paying. Includes *The Internet Writing Journal* with articles about writing and writers.

Writing for Dollars
http://writingfordollars.com

Provides a database of markets and a newsletter covering the business side of writing.

Writing-World.com
http://writing-world.com

Offers more than 600 articles on all aspects of writing, lists of classes and contests, and job listings.

YourDictionary.com
http://yourdictionary.com

A free online dictionary, a thesaurus, dictionaries in many languages, and specialty dictionaries.

INDEX OF CONSUMER, LITERARY, & SCHOLARLY MAGAZINES

PROFESSIONAL DEVELOPMENT

Writers at every level of experience can extend their skills and find fresh ideas through all manner of writing courses and workshops. Some believe creative writing is best fostered in the university or college environment by working with a good teacher who understands literary devices and structures and the power of language. Many skills peculiar to non-fiction writing, generally considered more a craft than an art, can be learned through courses or workshops led by experienced writers who have discovered not only how to refine ideas but how to research them, transform them into workable structures, and finally, market them. Some creative writers swear by the hothouse atmosphere, creative exchange of ideas, and collective reinforcement to be found in workshops led by expert facilitators.

Local branches of the Canadian Authors Association, libraries, and adult education classes offered by boards of education are some sources of writing courses and workshops. Regional writers' associations sometimes organize them, too, and are always a good source of information about what's currently available in your area.

This chapter is divided into two parts: first, a review of some of the country's most interesting writing schools, workshops, and retreats; second, a sample of the opportunities for the development of writing skills currently offered by Canadian colleges and universities. Writers' opportunities for professional development are

Yukon Department of Tourism and Culture

Tourism and Culture Centre, 100 Hanson Street, Whitehorse, YK
   YIA 2C6
Phone: (867) 667-5036 Fax: (867) 393-6456
E-mail: artsfund@gov.yk.ca
Website: www.tc.gov.yk.ca

Individual Yukon writers may be eligible for an Advanced Artist Award of up to $5,000 for a specific project. Training support through the Cultural Industry Training Fund is also available for writers who meet the eligibility requirements. Artists who present their work at festivals and other events may apply to the Touring Artist Fund for assistance. Group projects contributing to development of the arts in the Yukon are supported through the Arts Fund.